KABBALAH, MAGIC

MAGIC

AND THE GREAT WORK OF SELF-TRANSFORMATION

About the Author

Lyam Thomas Christopher (Florida) has been a student of Hermeticism and the Golden Dawn for over fifteen years. After receiving his B.A. in Liberal Studies, he went on to receive his Adeptus Minor from Ra Horakhty Temple. A former book-seller, the author is currently a learning specialist at a regional community college. This is his first book.

To Write to the Author

If you wish to contact the author or would like more information about this book, please write to the author in care of Llewellyn Worldwide and we will forward your request. Both the author and publisher appreciate hearing from you and learning of your enjoyment of this book and how it has helped you. Llewellyn Worldwide can-not guarantee that every letter written to the author can be answered, but all will be forwarded. Please write to:

Lyam Thomas Christopher
℅ Llewellyn Worldwide
2143 Wooddale Drive, Dept. 978-0-7387-0893-5
Woodbury, MN 55125-2989, U.S.A.

Please enclose a self-addressed stamped envelope for reply,
or $1.00 to cover costs. If outside U.S.A., enclose
international postal reply coupon.

Many of Llewellyn's authors have websites with additional information and re-sources. For more information, please visit our website at:

www.llewellyn.com

KABBALAH, MAGIC

AND THE GREAT WORK OF SELF-TRANSFORMATION

A COMPLETE COURSE

LYAM THOMAS CHRISTOPHER

Llewellyn Publications
Woodbury, Minnesota

First Edition
Second Printing, 2007

Book design and layout by Joanna Willis
Cover design by Kevin R. Brown
Cover flower image © PhotoDisc
Interior illustrations by Llewellyn art department
Universal Tarot cards © 2000 by Roberto de Angelis are reprinted with permission from
    Lo Scarabeo

Llewellyn is a registered trademark of Llewellyn Worldwide, Ltd.

Library of Congress Cataloging-in-Publication Data
Christopher, Lyam Thomas, 1968–
Kabbalah, magic, and the great work of self-transformation: a complete course / Lyam Thomas
Christopher. — 1st ed.
        p. cm.
Includes bibliographical references (p.   ) and index.
ISBN-13: 978-0-7387-0893-5
ISBN-10: 0-7387-0893-3
  1. Hermetic Order of the Golden Dawn. 2. Magic. 3. Cabala. I. Title

BF1623.R7C46 2006
135'.4—dc22   2006046512

Llewellyn Publications
A Division of Llewellyn Worldwide, Ltd.
2143 Wooddale Drive, Dept. 978-0-7387-0893-5
Woodbury, MN 55125-2989, U.S.A.
www.llewellyn.com

Printed in the United States of America

Contents

For Peter and Laura Yorke and Ra Horakhty Temple

Acknowledgments

The first challenge to appear before the new student of magic is the overwhelming amount of published material from which he must prepare a road map of self-initiation. Without guidance, this is usually impossible. Therefore, I owe my biggest thanks to Peter and Laura Yorke of Ra Horakhty Temple, who provided my first exposure to self-initiation techniques in the Golden Dawn. Their years of experience with the Golden Dawn material yielded a structure of carefully selected exercises, which their students still use today to bring about a gradual transformation. Without such well-prescribed use of the Golden Dawn's techniques, it would have been difficult to make progress in its grade system.

The basic structure of the course in this book is built on a foundation of the Golden Dawn's elemental grade system as my teachers passed it on. In particular, it develops further their choice to use the color correspondences of the Four Worlds, a piece of the original Golden Dawn system that very few occultists have recognized as an initiatory tool. I also build upon their idea to prescribe planetary invocations as part of the process. Not only is it important for the student to experience the four elements in sequence; a gradual, balanced introduction to the planets provides a valuable foundation for future work as an adept as well.

I would also like to thank Dr. Anodea Judith for writing such a Western-friendly introduction to the chakra system. Not only do I require my students to read her book *Wheels of Life*, but I specifically assign a couple of the grounding exercises from it.

Also, there is my friend Janet Blake, to whom I am so indebted as a ritual partner. Janet is one of the few powerful magicians I have known. Her ability and willingness to test my foggy ideas have been crucial to the evolution of the curriculum in this book. Janet and I both share in the idea that teachers should no longer initiate students into "private clubs," but that they should instead help them individuate. It continues to be my good fortune to work side by side with such a model Humanist.

Additional ideas have come about from the questions of my students, whom I would also like to thank. I have never learned more than I have in playing the role of their teacher. Jake Gordon and Rick Phillips have been particularly mature and inquisitive in their own development, demanding answers from me that have contributed to this book.

And where would this project be without editors? A special thank-you goes to my friend—my evening jewel—Professor Winifred Storms for providing a much-needed outsider's perspective. It is all too easy to forget how impenetrable occult jargon is to those who are not immersed in it daily. Thank you for your valuable advice, Winnie!

one

Though Only a Few Will Rise

Magic. It has been with us since the birth of civilization. But what is it, and how does one become a magician? This book is dedicated to the student of life who stands at a crossroads, at the place where two paths meet. One path is mundane and well worn, and the other is the way of magic.

Magic is the art of transformation, of altering consciousness and experiencing the life changes that result. It is a science of empowerment, of using word, image, and gesture to reach into the darkness and set free the imprisoned faculties of the soul. For this reason, its power is forbidden.

A person may sit quietly sometimes and marvel at the irony of his life. He participates in a booming materialistic culture that stifles his spiritual needs for the sake of its progress. Despite the grandeur of technology, the modern progressive world restrains the individual from exploring the depth and breadth of his own soul. His parents and teachers have cautioned him to stay safely in the norm—to be successful, become rich, and start a family. It is disreputable for him to strive for anything outside of those lines.

But it can't be helped that there is the occasional quiet moment—between phone calls, perhaps, or after a movie—when he feels a different possibility. Sometimes it takes the form of a soothing calm, sometimes a radical curiosity. And sometimes it becomes a nagging doubt. A silent voice asks, "Is this all I was made for? Why is the life I am *expected* to live not enough?"

We have been deceived. The purpose that Western society has created for the individual is a sham. Mesmerized by a mirage of "happiness" that hovers around material possessions, we reach for creature comforts that inevitably comfort us less and less. We are addicted to the pursuit of prosperity, craving more and trying harder, even though our lifestyle of ravenous consumption does damage to the earth and leads us away from the very contentedness that we pursue.

By conventional thinking, the material circumstances of Western life have been getting better by leaps and bounds. Adjusting for inflation, the average American income in the year 2000 had *doubled* since 1960.[1] Leisure time had risen by five hours per week in the same period, and it continues to rise.[2] In 1900, the average American life span was 41 years. Today it is 77.[3] A century ago, rich men were distinguished by the fact that they lived in heated houses, enjoyed unlimited food and wine, had access to a physician, earned a college degree, and attended the theater for entertainment. Sound familiar?

Today, supermarkets overflow with an abundance of food so affordable that even the poor suffer an epidemic of obesity. Waitresses take holidays together on luxurious pleasure cruises. Children of dockworkers receive college educations. We live in conditions far superior to those of the aristocrats of the nineteenth century. But despite this golden age of conveniences, surveys measuring the average human's happiness have shown no improvement. In fact, depression is on the rise, and the number of those people who would describe themselves as "very happy" has been decreasing steadily since 1940.[4]

Prosperity in modern times is becoming easier and easier, and yet simultaneously this easy living sucks the challenge out of life, the vitality. But this is not a book about returning to the magic of the Middle Ages for adventure. Not exactly. Consider instead the following assessment: even as human progress is taking away the difficulties of staying alive, we are thereby gaining more freedom to pursue the even greater challenges of a different landscape in a different realm of our existence—one that has always been there. Our lives as animals are presenting fewer and fewer obstacles to overcome. A new kind of evolution is surfacing: the life of the individual stepping into the frontier of his own soul and exploring the confines of his interior psychological and spiritual vehicles. The discipline of magic has never been easier than it is today.

And who could blame the average person for failing to see this possibility? When the incarnated human wakes up wounded and human on the beach of life, he finds that he has been given a gift for which he has misplaced the instructions. Getting comfortable as quickly as possible, mimicking his fellow castaways, trustingly assimilating the instructions and traditions that his elders pass down, he learns to forget that he has lost anything at all. Survival is an urgent business, after all. What could possibly come before that? The culture into which the individual is born helpless and vulnerable rescues him from certain death by teaching him a patchwork, haphazard survival manual, fabricated from mankind's traumatic evolutionary past. And so the individual grows up infused with beliefs that keep him alive but that nonetheless have no basis in his true identity. He learns to fit into his culture and to dutifully ignore his desire to find himself. And why not, after all? Disregarding the lessons of his elders may endanger his very life.

But what if the silence between commercials begins to whisper? What if he came to realize that his bosses, parents, and teachers, despite their prestige, know nothing? What if he discovers that his culture's entrepreneurs, politicians, scientists, and leaders are actors (and not very good ones) who are just as lost? What if they are on the same beach, having assimilated their culture just as he did, beguiling themselves into the notion that it reflects their real purpose? We are each of us wounded by mortality, and our role models have come to our rescue by putting a bandage on a hurt that will never heal. The average human, underneath a veneer of confidence, is still a terrified castaway severed from his true nature, clinging to the first paradigm that comes along to give him a modicum of security. The proud father hands over the traditions of his prosperous forefathers as though he were passing along the Holy Grail, and yet he knows nothing. He receives his instructions from his forefathers, who know nothing. They receive their traditions from the same nothing. And so it goes, on and on, until the mind is left staring into an abyss of nothing, the foundation on which it has built its sense of self.

The chain of ignorance seems to go back into prehistory, to a primordial beach and that clueless castaway. At some point in evolution, through some divine accident, the human race bumped its head and lost its inherent purpose. And since that fall from grace, it has been faking it, using strategies for living that do little more than help it maintain its numbers in successful but nonetheless unfulfilling ways. A person can spend all his life learning the ropes of making a living, fending off danger, fitting in, and climbing the social ladder, all the while neglecting the task at hand—the task that sits right before the nose of every human on the planet.

There is nothing of this world that can satisfy the new kind of hunger that rises in someone who, like a seed in the earth, is ready to grow beyond his material conditioning. The job promotion, the blockbuster movie, the dream vacation, the perfect spouse—all of these fall short of satiating the longing that drives the soul to worm its way upward through the trappings of life into the open air of awakening.

For such a soul, who realizes that there is nowhere to hide, no security blanket that will soothe him for long, it is inevitable that the comfort of the norm becomes a prison house of agony. He has remembered that he is still that castaway on the beach. He is pressured from within to transcend this world and regain his lost knowledge. Though his fellow castaways may pass him by, proceeding on into the lives of money and glamour, he himself stays behind to explore the gaping silence that is forever embedded in the here and now.

That dreaded silence. Most people of the Western mindset live in fear of it. They stay busy to escape its emptiness. Cut off from their own animal nature by processed food and air-conditioned offices, they occupy themselves with television and home-improvement projects to keep at bay the uncharted darkness within. The very mention of the silent deep comes as a threat to the person who is not ready to explore it. To him it is as death. If he could learn to suspend his senses but for a moment, it is as though the awful silence would well up and annihilate him. He settles instead for curling up around his acceptable beliefs and drifting off to sleep.

But as we all eventually realize, happiness isn't bought so cheaply. He might as well try to sleep with a thorn in his side. On some level, he knows that he is deceiving himself, and he even knows that there is a price he must pay if he ever decides to rise and go after the real thing. It is the price that all liars fear. The more he distances himself from his true nature by chasing the distractions of the mundane path, the more he is prone to closing himself against the source of his own happiness, dismissing its mystery with nervous laughter as though it were an uncomfortable lull at a party. For there is a light hidden in the unexplored darkness, if only he knew how to reach for it. It is usually not until he gets very old or threatened by death that he begins to yearn for the other path at the crossroads. When at last he is ill and the hour is late, he regrets not having danced a little closer to the edge of the abyss, not having lived more adventurously.

The silence inside you is the realm of magic. It is behind the doors of matter, within the gates of your mother's womb. It is the invisible land of your origin. Your sensory impressions of the room in which you sit reading, the very landscape in which you take your daily walk, cover it up like a membrane on some vast cosmic drum. The true nature of the human condition is kept from you, hiding itself maddeningly behind its own reverberating sounds, sights, and textures. And the substance of that fluctuating membrane, the very medium of the deafening hum of the world, is the same as that of the sinew, skin, and bone of your body. Our throbbing biological processes are part of the vast web of life that encases a mystery. The activities of that web overshadow the invisible depths of the inner world, like algae on the surface of still waters. And beneath the visible, an infinite mind broods like an abyss. The typical human shrinks in fear of the precipice. But he needn't worry. He is, for the most part, safe from being consumed by the worlds within. For he usually cannot experience them unless properly trained as a magician.

It is possible to regain the memory that was lost in that fateful shipwreck. You indeed have access to that silent place from which you came. The alternative path at the crossroads is always present. But access to it is only granted by the surrender of false credentials. In fact, the nearness of that surrender haunts your every step through life. Like a sandspur in the comfortable bed of conformity, it prods you to awaken. It is the throbbing of the mortal wound. It is the serpent in Eden, the nagging presence that keeps the ignorance of the garden from smothering you completely in the bustle of the human jungle. There is another life calling from beneath the brittle whitewash of compromise, and no matter how much you try to shift around and get comfortable, the thorn is always there, digging in, a wordless reminder that things are not as they seem.

Is it too late to step up to the precipice? To jump?

This book encourages the adventure of discovery that awaits anyone who would dare to step out of the hive mind and take those first steps on the path of magic. It does not propose to help him in the way most other books would, by handing him a new paradigm at the expense of him finding his own. It does not encourage the adoption of a prefabricated life or, worse yet, another tiresome system of comforting beliefs. Humans are born to discover *their own* purpose, not to have a mockery of it handed to them. They are born to become magicians.

A magician is a human being who has used special techniques to uncover his true nature. He is someone on the path of self-discovery, becoming more empowered every day—more himself. There are several radical magical traditions (traditions that are feared by those who are still hiding from their true selves) that have remained concealed within the depths of our world's cultures. An awakened few maintain them in secrecy. These traditions of transformation are referred to as "esoteric" (reserved for the select few), because only a few among ten thousand will rise and take up the Great Work of recovering the lost knowledge of the Higher Self, none other than the source of the silent voice that speaks to each of us from within.

If you look at history as though from a great height, you may see accounts of certain individuals who, from time to time, have fulfilled that quest. Sages, "saviors," mystics, Renaissance men, artists, and even scientists speak out as proponents of the silence. They move on a different road, hewn through the dark, invisible kingdom of the soul. These are the adepts of life who have refused to be swept along by the conventional chase. They are the keepers of magical power, and walking among us, hidden in plain sight, they live by different principles, by a radical curiosity. They use techniques and experiments to prod the world of appearances to show forth its true nature, invisible to the eye, soundless to the ear, and void to the touch.

A landscape of evolution awaits each of us just behind the membrane of the five senses. For those who have learned the methodology of listening in on the silence, the purpose of life asserts itself forcefully from within. By the techniques of the magician's craft, a book of one's *own* instructions is waiting to be translated from silence into any words or deeds necessary to express it, to be the impetus to the creation of a new life founded on wonder, mystery, and limitless power. The magician's eyes glow with an irresistible purpose. Behind his every word is the unmistakable quality of the resonating silence. As the famous theologian Max Picard writes:

> The world of silence without speech is the world *before* creation, the world of unfinished creation. In silence truth is passive and slumbering, but in language it is wide-awake. Silence is fulfilled only when speech comes forth from silence and gives it meaning and honor.[5]

Magic is the science and art of expressing silence within the medium of sound, of showing stillness in the midst of gesture, of drawing forth light from darkness, and of transforming a mortal into a god.

Let your mind slip into a reverie. Ponder the setting you are in as you read this book. This silent voice broods behind the appearances of the physical world—behind the sensations in your fingertips as you turn the pages, beneath your feet as they touch the floor, beyond that background noise of traffic or birdsong.

To the magician, that presence is a singular divine entity—God, perhaps—and the world of nature is the skin of a Divine Self that speaks wordlessly from within all natural phenomena. Your sensations are alive beneath their every nuance, vibrating with occult power.

The secret to which the magicians throughout history have been privy is that the divine being within has gone out on a limb on our behalf, handing us the reigns to its power. In the Western occult tradition, this is the mystery of the Grail and of the Christ. The *Lapis Exillis*, the "stone of wisdom," fell from Heaven. It is the Grail. It is up to us to lay claim to that stone of power, the Philosopher's Stone of the alchemists. The Christ-force exists within the individual, not in some black book, marble building, or Sunday-school lecture. There are methods by which he can call it forth. The lost instructions are his for the asking, but he must learn first how to transform his physical body into something more than human, into a worthy vessel. He must sift through the dross and miasma of earthly life to find the lost stone. There is a secret process by which this transformation is accomplished, and the person who has succeeded in the task is known as magician, adept, and wyzard. He has become an agent of the silent voice. And he is a dangerous catalyst for the same kind of magical transformation in other people's lives wherever he goes.

This is the work done on the "road less traveled," and it can be lonely and arduous. To uncover magical power requires a strict discipline that separates the student from convention, that insulates him from the societal, tribal, and familial institutions that attempt to sell him substitutes for truth. The marketplace of ready-made lives is much too noisy for the beginner on the path of wisdom. The identities sold cheaply in that market are not bad things. We adopt them because they are the foundation of a great machine that supports survival of the masses. Likewise, the various institutions in our culture that team with unenlightened people are not bad. They are the support systems that our parents and teachers have used up until now to nurture us, to control us, subordinating us to the group mind. We only slough them off when they have served their purpose and we are ready to grow beyond them. To see such systems in their true light, one must undo their hold. In order to make a difference in the lives of those who are enslaved, one must first be free oneself. And so begins the tedious process of untangling the soul.

Does this sound dangerous? It is.

By not participating in the machine, the individual becomes a fool and an outcast. Great pressures of conformity will mount up from all sides for anyone who begins to flounder about in the throes of awakening. It is a chaotic time, and it gets worse before it gets better. Not everyone who dares to begin the journey toward illumination will finish it. *There are casualties.* Just because the path is spiritual by no means makes it safe. If you would take this book as a manual, be warned.

There are several secret traditions out there designed to help the student rise above the mire of "survivalism." This book concerns Kabbalah and the Hermetic disciplines, the overall approach of the Western Esoteric Tradition. It is the way of magic.

A Secret School of Magic

I have written this book for those who have taken a look at the world of occultism and sensed that there is something legitimate hidden in the strangeness. But they may hesitate and walk up and down the outside of the grounds, wringing their hands for fear of making fools of themselves. They may have worked with practitioners of the occult before and been bitterly disappointed to find that access to an authentic tradition is blocked by charlatans, just as it can be in the church or in the academic disciplines. How is one to gain entry amidst all the pretense and fantasy? It seems that along the edges of the road to enlightenment, the peddlers of ready-made lives gather in swarms.

Have you ever met anyone who claims to practice Hermetic magic and felt embarrassed for them when they made self-aggrandizing claims to spiritual rank, prestigious past lives, or communications with invisible entities like "ascended masters"? Have you yourself practiced Hermetic magic and had the vague sensation that there is something more to it than beefing up your psychic powers? Visiting the various New Age stores can be frustrating when your interests lean toward genuine spiritual transformation.

There was one such store that I recently visited in Orlando, Florida. Books everywhere throughout its many rooms, floor to ceiling—and all of them filled with subjects like remembering glamorous past lives, finding your soul mate, soothing your fears of mortality and loneliness by contacting dead relatives, and feeling good about how comfortable and spiritual the realm beyond this life is. Almost everything in the store seemed to encourage retreating from life back into the womb—making the individual feel safe and special or warm and fuzzy. I marveled at how the staff maintained it so diligently and in such quantity. It took a while to find a few of the more rare and edgy books, but the Tibetan Buddhism section offered some engaging reading. I can't help wondering if the owner would send those books back if she had time to notice the color plates of the wrathful deities.

There are many hiding places in the world for people afraid of taking that step into deeper consciousness. Off to the side of the evolutionary stream lie the many stagnant pools of diversion maintained by fellow humans in unconscious collusion to stop growing. The unspoken promise of these "comfortable" places is that there is security in escape, that we are safe if we don't evolve. The power of the imagination is inverted, turned away from the journey of individuation. Think of these places: comic-book stores, nightclubs, sports arenas, Renaissance fairs, and churches—not to mention neopagan groups and magical lodges. Just as the influence of "the Devil" is most pervasive within the Christian church itself, so it is that escapism is most pervasive in the midst of one's fellow metaphysical enthusiasts. But I am assuming here that the reader senses that there *is* a worthwhile reality behind the fiasco of the New Age. It is my hope with this book to push the pretentious guardians at the gate aside and help a few readers over the threshold to the inner life of the magician.

The fundamental goals and workings of magic are hidden to most people. And no amount of book learning, fantasy, or premature advanced work can reveal them. A prep-school stage, an initial groundwork of transformation—in some way or another—is required for one to grasp the more hidden objectives embodied within the practice of magic. Disciplined, monotonous, and rigorous training is the manner in which the demons at the gate are subdued and bypassed. It happens the same way in other traditions. There is preliminary work, and then there is the Great Work itself. Few find the process interesting when they find out what is actually involved. And few magical practitioners have gone through a curriculum designed to help them achieve the transformation necessary to apprehend the inner landscape of that Great Work, the creation of enlightenment.

Most people that I have met display little interest in spiritual discipline. Some of them are gifted seers and healers, capable of fascinating psychic things. The ability to see auras and channel energy is part of what Hermetic occultism is about. Usually, though, these gifts are not gifts at all, but serve as distractions that keep the student away from the daily work that can actually generate progress.

Thorough and sincere spiritual work is not prestigious in the least. As a matter of fact, it threatens one's very sense of identity. The powers one may develop are very real, but they can easily become trappings. The bulk of humanity has chosen a life in which the individual is held captive by self-image. To let go of self-importance is to "die," so it is no wonder that people would rather twist spiritual work into something comfortable. They are human, after all, focused on status and on developing things that distinguish them among their peers. And it is primarily on these misguided motives that the New Age movement draws its livelihood.

The real work is not really very pretty. It levels the playing field of the personality. It reveals the nature of the false self and its role in the drama of the individual's life. It tears down the lie of the assumed identity—the ego—and consolidates the forces that have come together to create it, thereby providing a chance for its rebirth into a new life based on truth beyond words. The curriculum for the magic of transformation—based on the ancient wisdom of Kabbalah—destroys and recreates the ego into a new vehicle, stronger than before. But the Great Work does not support any illusions about the ego. It gradually wears away at its fabricated autonomy, its insecurities, its addictions, and its dependency on "religion" or various philosophies of the streetwise, business, collegiate, and metaphysical subcultures. This clears the stage enough to allow the real self, the Higher Self, a chance to come forth and take possession. This preliminary work is one of disintegration, purification, and eventual reintegration of the personality. In alchemy, it is the essential formula called *solve et coagulae*, "dissolve and recombine." It is almost a sad process, because as old patterns of living fall away, the student begins to see that the things he has desired all his life are fleeting and useless in the larger scheme. There are bigger and better motives, but these are not even understandable to the ego when it is stuck in the mode of self-interest.

The curriculum presented in this book is a prep school for becoming a "wise one," or wyzard. It has in it an authentic link to the Western Esoteric Tradition, to the underground movement that has been with us since ancient Greece, Egypt, and Babylon, a movement that in the last few hundred years has taken the name Hermeticism.

The curriculum is adapted from the teachings of a secret society that existed in England at the end of the nineteenth century. This magical order, called the Hermetic Order of the Golden Dawn, is well known today. A few legitimate offshoots of it still survive. Though the origins of its core spirit are as old as civilization itself, the Golden Dawn is just one recent installment of Hermeticism. Its teachings are not inherently original. They make up a system patched together from a myriad of traditions—ancient, medieval, Renaissance, and modern. What *is* original is the manner in which those teachings are brought together. The Golden Dawn assembled the scattered occult lore from ancient Egypt, Israel, and Europe and then merged these different streams within the intellectual framework of Kabbalah, directing them to the goal of enlightenment.

Kabbalah is a way of looking at the universe that has evolved out of ancient Jewish mysticism. It has become much more than Orthodox Judaism in the process, however. In fact, it has broken free altogether from the dogma of the Abrahamic faiths to stand as a metaphysical system that is applicable to any spiritual quest. Through its system of correspondences, set up by the medieval rabbis and the Renaissance magicians who later followed, one can put into practice any faith, spiritual practice, pantheon of gods, or map of the soul that one chooses in order to achieve a definite, tangible result. Kabbalah is a method for testing spiritual theories and applying them to reality.

The Golden Dawn system's ingenious use of Kabbalah has given students in the West an alternative to the effective Tantric teachings of the East. Therefore, it is not necessary for someone of the European or American mindset to turn away from the myths and symbols of the West and try to digest the symbols of an unfamiliar Asian culture. There is a practical spiritual discipline in the West too, right in our own backyard, though it is still very much discredited by many scholars. The student can therefore use the symbols of his own heritage by properly arranging them as they are brought together under the system of the Golden Dawn.

The Golden Dawn is mentioned often in occult circles. It entices the ignorant with its seeming promise of magical power. But its potential to serve as an instrument for illumination makes it rise above the spiritual fads of the current day, withstanding the test of time, continuing to be a subject of debate, repeated adaptation, abuse, and much frustration. There are, no doubt, many jaded occultists out there who will yawn and put this book down when they come across the name "Golden

Dawn." After all, a great deal of nonsense has been printed already about it. Demons tend to gather in the densest swarms at the doorstep of an effective system.

I propose here that a workable curriculum of the preliminary work of transformation has not yet been published in any adequate form. All of the material is out there in some book or another, but a practical, piecemeal, step-by-step presentation is still lacking. Of the very few people who have actually succeeded in accomplishing their own transformation (that is, without the aid of a teacher), a majority of them have had to do it based on arduous sifting through volumes upon volumes of magical lore and on piecing together scattered hints to construct for themselves a simplified program of exercises that sticks to one purpose to yield progress. The amount of research they had to do is unnecessary. They suffered delays because a streamlined version of the Hermetic teachings was absent from the book market.

Of the published material, so very much can be omitted, for there are a lot of detours and dead ends possible in the twilight land of occultism. The guardians at the gate are forever testing and batting away the unworthy. The secret of initiation to the inner tradition lies in keeping to the straight and narrow road that leads to the goal, and in limiting exercises to just what is needed for spiritual progress at the current moment.

This book is an attempt to present one version of the Golden Dawn's curriculum in a format stripped of tangents, side tracks, and excessive information. It gives the student just enough information to set up an intellectual framework within his being. The task before us is to establish a system of correspondences inside you by which you can navigate the recesses of your soul and return home to your fundamental nature.

Most importantly, this book gives an unrecognized Kabbalistic technique for rising through the grades of the Golden Dawn. Should you embark on this journey, you will not need the group initiation ceremonies of a formal temple or lodge. In their place, I provide you with a solitary daily formula of initiation, similar to the way I learned it from my teachers. The Kabbalistic exercises in each grade will produce a more gradual and *thorough* transformation than any single grade ceremony could ever do.

This secret technique is not original but has been a hidden part of the Golden Dawn tradition for over half a century. Famous Golden Dawn adept and writer Dion Fortune hints about it in her occult fiction when she speaks of building "four trees" into the aura. Occult writer R. G. Torrens reveals it in a 1969 book called *The Golden Dawn: The Inner Teachings.*[6] And Israel Regardie published the theoretical framework of it, but not its full technique, in his writings.[7]

The keys to enlightenment dangle before us every day, and they are only secret because no one has pointed out their proper application. The student, once made aware of the proper and simple use of Kabbalah's central symbol, the Tree of Life, can bring about a thorough transformation and a lasting realization of his own Divinity and Its latent powers.

This is not a book about inducing fleeting altered states of consciousness. Used as directed, it is a guide that will direct you through a process for which there is no comparison between what you are now and what you will become. Once the awakening process begins, there will be no going back. But few will find the work interesting when confronted with the price that they must pay for entry. Magic is not what it appears to be.

two

The First Steps

Does magic work? Can images, words, and gestures cause life-altering changes? In this chapter is a simple yet powerful ritual. It is the most basic and perhaps most important ritual that I will present. Traditionally, it is designed to clear a room of negative influences so that any magic done immediately thereafter is more effective. However, its long-term benefits are the most important.

Many authors have published the Lesser Banishing Ritual of the Pentagram (LBRP) in various forms. I probably should apologize to the seasoned occult reader, for he has surely seen it in print ten times too many. I present it here because it is basic, fundamental, and of immeasurable importance to the curriculum of this book. In order to practice the magic of transformation, you must begin to fashion a "place" within yourself in which magical forces can come and go, in which they can be recognized, tamed, and controlled. The Lesser Banishing Ritual of the Pentagram is the means by which such an inner stage might be prepared. It is also safe for the beginner to perform. This ritual is designed ultimately to reduce the amount of influence the material world has over you, giving you greater freedom to evolve independently of the influence of matter.

To perform the Lesser Banishing Ritual of the Pentagram, as with any ritual, find a secluded, quiet room in which you will not be disturbed. Turn off your cell phone, the television, and anything else that could distract you. Magic is done best by candlelight, in peace and in private. If someone intrudes by listening or watching, that very act can sap your ritual of strength. At the stage of a beginner, your mind presumably does not have the strength to tune out the pressures of conformity that bombard it from others. The new student requires seclusion to keep his will focused on the Great Work.

You must adopt an additional rule in order to be an effective ritualist: keep the specifics of your spiritual work absolutely private. Never discuss any of your current magical doings. Avoid the pitfall of the big dreamer who fritters away all of his energy talking about his plans while he does nothing to act on them. Be instead like the artist who never exhibits his painting while it is in the midst of the creation process. The practice of secrecy keeps the energy of your will from bleeding away into matters of a social nature—and therefore keeps it centered on the objective of the Great Work. Silence, properly understood, is one of the magician's most powerful tools. Every adept is acutely aware of the potency that dwells between words, between sounds, and behind thoughts. Used at the appropriate intervals, silence prods, focuses, and channels the intention of the magician's magic. It keeps his will pure and singular.

Speech, on the other hand, links various powers together, siphoning one into the other. Speaking about your current ritual practices therefore mixes them with conflicting concerns that will drain them of power. The student should therefore watch what he says, for a careless communication may adversely affect the results of an operation. Taking the precaution of silence, the student learns to accumulate the force of his will. Its raw energy builds up slowly over time, like money well saved. As the Hermetic maxim states, "Know, dare, will, and keep silent!"[1] You may not understand the concept of silence fully (it is doubtful anyone can fathom it completely), and it may sound as though I am exaggerating, but the reason for this rule will become clearer over time.

The concerns of privacy and secrecy may move you to re-evaluate your living conditions. In the beginning, the requirements of effective magic are quite difficult. You may have to refine your social life. For instance, if you live with someone who knows of your occult inclinations, make sure he or she is someone who understands—who doesn't dwell on your "deviancy" and who isn't controlling or jealous of you when you make changes in your life. It must be someone who will not exert social pressures of any kind that cause you to doubt your purpose. Doing effective ritual in the beginning of your development is next to impossible if you are surrounded by crude minds that insist on keeping you from rising above their level.

It is a sad experience for a teacher to see a student held back by current relationships, especially by a troubled marriage. The magical path is not for everyone. When you're on it, there is no time for a jealous lover. I feel almost apologetic in revealing that the defining characteristic of a capable student is that he is ready to prioritize his spiritual growth above all other needs. The baser needs are not evil. They are in fact pure and innocent in themselves. However, it is important that you become selective about the manner in which you satisfy them. As you embark on a spiritual path, you must be strong enough to let go of security and comfort in order to discover the realm of higher motives. Through magical practice, significant changes can occur. As you try to uncover who you really are, you will naturally become severed from people, places, and jobs of your past. It can be intensely painful to let go of any kind of relationship—even a destructive one. New personal connections will come, and the faster you change, the faster the people will come and go in your life. As a first big step, see to it that you have a home free of harmful distractions, such as unwanted roommates, noise, clutter, and crime. Above all, get private space and private daily time in which you can work.

These kinds of rules might sound a bit like those of an elitist, but please do not misunderstand. It is not the goal of magical work to make you into the archetypal hermit on the mountaintop, looking down on the common people, smug in your superiority. In fact, I suggest the opposite. Live *in* the world. Be gregarious and partake in your opportunities and your relationships. Be adventurous. Humans are innately social animals, so keep in mind that we have a powerful influence on one another's spiritual development, even by the most casual of interactions—for better *and* for worse. If you are going to transform your consciousness and move it toward enlightenment, you have to live a little and spend some time out in the open. Socialize, if that suits your nature. But above all, save a portion of each day to leave your conformist behaviors behind. Do magic in your own private space to discover your own personal power over your own personal evolution.

The following version of the Lesser Banishing Ritual of the Pentagram is adapted from Israel Regardie's *The Golden Dawn* (pages 53–54) and his book *The Middle Pillar*. The principles of working with the pentagram also appear in *The Golden Dawn* (pages 280–284). Perform the Lesser Banishing Ritual of the Pentagram once per day.

The Lesser Banishing Ritual of the Pentagram
Part One: The Kabbalistic Cross

1. Stand in the middle of your ritual space, facing east. See yourself expand, growing gradually taller until you rise through the ceiling of the room, above the building, the landscape, and the planet. Continue to grow until the solar system is a disc at your feet and the stars begin to close in on your colossal form. Eventually, you rise above the spiral-armed vista of the Milky Way galaxy, and you continue to grow until our galaxy is a speck of light at your feet and the hundred billion or so other galaxies shine like stars in an oval-shaped aura/universe that encompasses your vast cosmic body. Know that even as you fill the universe and float in its midst, your feet are simultaneously planted firmly on the ground in your ritual space back on Earth.

2. Notice a sphere of white brilliance just above your head, about half the diameter of a basketball. It is the Light beyond all light, of which the light that comes from the sun is only a token. This is the power source of everything in the universe, the radiance that proceeds from the essence of all being. Reach up over your head with your right hand and draw down from it a shaft of light into the middle of your head, touching your forehead. It forms there a center of light just between and behind your eyebrows, and it illuminates your entire cranium with impossible brilliance. Vibrate the Hebrew word that means "Thine":

   ATOH

   To vibrate a name, chant it in long, resonant, monotone syllables. The voice should be fairly loud—about double the volume of a casual conversation. The vocal cords should be relaxed. The force of vibration should be both physical and psychological. Imagine that the steadiness of the tone you are vibrating can cause a breakthrough, carrying you past all of your previous preconceptions about life. The voice can be used to penetrate into places of the soul previously neglected and unknown.

3. Bring your right hand down to touch the solar plexus, simultaneously drawing the shaft of white brilliance to the earth at your feet. (The solar plexus is located between the base of your sternum and your belly button.) Vibrate the Hebrew word for "kingdom":

MALKUTH

(The *u* is pronounced as in the word *book*.)

4. With the same hand, touch the right shoulder, see a shaft of light extend from its central axis like the arm of a cross, and vibrate the Hebrew words that, in this context, mean "and the power":

   VAH GAVURAH

5. Touch the left shoulder, seeing the same shaft of light extend to the left, and vibrate the words meaning "and the glory":

   VAH GADULAH

6. Press the palms together at the breast and vibrate the words that mean "forever, Amen":

   LEH OLAHM, AHMEN

Part Two: The Formulation of the Pentagrams

1. Still facing east, draw in the air before you a large banishing-earth pentagram with your fully extended right arm and forefinger. Starting at the spot in front of the lower left hip, draw a bluish white line up to a point high up and before your head. Continue the line down to a point before your right hip, then up before your left shoulder, over to the right, and back down to a point before the  left hip. See the figure in front of you as perfectly proportional and as an all-encompassing representation of fearsome power. Breathe in deeply as though drawing energy from the hidden depths of the universe, and point at the center of the pentagram, vibrating the Godname:

   YHVH

(pronounced "Yod-Heh-Vau-Heh"; an "unspeakable" name of God, spelled out here in its individual Hebrew letters). See the pentagram burst into electric blue flame (like that of a gas jet on a stove), as though the symbol were charged and sealed by the power of the name.

2. With the arm extended but the elbow just shy of being locked, pivot clockwise where you stand, drawing an electric blue line from the center of the pentagram and making a quarter of a circle as you turn to the south. Stop there and draw the pentagram as before, but this time vibrate:

   ADONAI

   ("my Lord"; the *ai* is pronounced as in the word *eye*).

3. Continue the blue line to the west. Draw the pentagram and then vibrate:

   EHEIEH

   (pronounced "Eh-heh-yeh"; it means "I am").

4. Continue the blue line to the north. Draw the pentagram and vibrate:

   AGLA

   (pronounced "Ah-gah-lah"; this is a Hebrew anagram for "atom giber leh-oh-lahm Adonai," or "Thou art great forever, my Lord"). Finish the line of your magic circle in the east. Stand in the center of your circle and see the pentagrams in the air about you. Feel their fierce heat and protection.

Part Three: Evocation of the Archangels

1. Raise your arms out to your sides to form a cross, and envision Raphael, the archangel of air, standing before you in the east. His hair is blonde, his skin is fair, and his robe is yellow with flashes of violet. He stands atop a hill with the wind coming from the cloud-patched sky behind him, and he holds the caduceus wand of Hermes in his right hand. Say:

   Before me

   and then vibrate:

   RAPHAEL

   (pronounced "Rah-fah-el").

2. Visualize Gabriel, the archangel of water, standing behind you in the west. His robe is blue, flashing with orange. He stands in the shallows by a gushing spring. He holds a silver cup in his left hand, his hair is light brown, and his skin is fair. Feel moisture wafting in from the west. Beads of dew cling to and roll down the sides of his vestments. Say:

   Behind me

and then vibrate:

GABRIEL

(pronounced "Gah-bree-el").

3. In the south, see Michael, the great archangel of fire. His robe is brilliant scarlet, flashing green. He stands in the desert, and fire rises up from the burning sands around his feet. He holds upright in his right hand a flaming iron sword. His hair is black, and his skin is dark tan. Feel intense heat radiating from the south. Say:

At my right hand

and then vibrate:

MICHAEL

(pronounced "Mee-chah-el"; the *ch* is pronounced softly, as in the name of the musical composer Bach).

4. In the north, see Auriel, the archangel of earth. His robes are black, flashing with green. He stands on black soil from which ripe wheat springs up behind him. He holds sheaves of wheat in his left hand. His hair is black, and his skin is fair. His eyes are intense, large, and dark. See cattle grazing in the field behind him. Beyond them is a forest, and beyond the forest are mountains. Say:

And at my left hand

and then vibrate:

AURIEL

(pronounced "Aur-ree-el").

5. Still maintaining the arms in a cross, say:

For about me flame the pentagrams . . .

(see the pentagrams)

. . . and within shineth the six-rayed star.

See a hexagram floating in your torso. Its uppermost angle peaks in your throat, and its lowermost rests in your groin. The upright triangle is made of red fire. The downward-pointing triangle is blue and wavers slightly, like a reflection

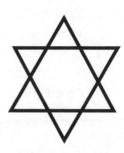

on water. Feel the dry heat of the flame and the cool moisture of the water. These forces intertwine in your being.

Part Four: Repeat the Kabbalistic Cross

Following is a brief summary of this ritual for easy reference:

The Lesser Banishing Ritual of the Pentagram
Part One: The Kabbalistic Cross
1. Face east. Expand into the universe.
2. Bring down the light, touch the forehead, and vibrate **ATOH**.
3. Touch the solar plexus and vibrate **MALKUTH**.
4. Touch the right shoulder and vibrate **VA GAVURAH**.
5. Touch the left shoulder and vibrate **VA GADULAH**.
6. Press palms together at the breast and vibrate **LEH OLAHM, AHMEN**.

Part Two: The Formulation of the Pentagrams
1. Facing east, draw a banishing-earth pentagram. Point to its center and vibrate **YHVH**.
2. Draw a blue line to the south, draw the pentagram, and vibrate **ADONAI**.
3. Continue the line to the west, draw the pentagram, and vibrate **EHEIEH**.
4. Continue the line to the north, draw the pentagram, and vibrate **AGLA**.
5. Complete the magic circle.

Part Three: Evocation of the Archangels
1. Raise the arms to form a cross, see the archangel of air, and say, **"Before me, RAH-FAH-EL."** (Vibrate the names of the archangels in this and the following steps.)
2. Visualize Gabriel and say, **"Behind me, GAH-BREE-EL."**
3. Visualize Michael and say, **"At my right hand, MEE-CHAH-EL."**
4. See Auriel and say, **"And at my left hand, AUR-REE-EL."**
5. Say, **"For about me flame the pentagrams, and within shineth the six-rayed star."** Visualize the six-rayed star in your torso.

Part Four: Repeat the Kabbalistic Cross

Some books say that this ritual should be performed at different times of the day with alternative forms of the pentagram, such as by tracing an invoking-earth form of the pentagram in the morning and a banishing form in the evening. This may sometimes be a useful exercise for the adept, but it would be useless for the beginner. Do not waste your time by experimenting with any other methods of this exercise for now. Read about them to satisfy your curiosity, of course, but if you wish to make progress, do not use them. It will take time before you are in a position to benefit from variations.

It is not possible to describe adequately the kind of change the Lesser Banishing Ritual of the Pentagram can produce. The results are unpredictable. Consider that you are compartmentalizing within the theater of the imagination the four aspects of the material world (solid, liquid, gas, and combustion). You are then pushing them back away from you into their own separate realms—"banishing" them, as it were. The Lesser Banishing Ritual of the Pentagram serves, therefore, to open a hole in your perceptions of the earthly realm, a cleared space through which a glimpse of higher worlds can be gained.

When I began to practice Hermetic magic many years ago, this was the first and only ritual that I did for a month. After two weeks, I noticed changes in my life. My world began to turn upside-down. Old perceptions were being shaken loose. Ideas about myself that I had held so dear began to crumble. The old landscape established by my upbringing began to lose its hold, and though I couldn't see where the path would lead, the effect spurred me to pursue the Golden Dawn curriculum with a sudden ferocity. We all have buried within us the ability to recognize when the door to the true self momentarily creaks open. Despite the uncomfortable assault on my preconceptions, I wanted more, and I have been changing and evolving at an accelerating rate ever since, to such an extent that I feel much indebted to the Golden Dawn system of magic and to this particular ritual specifically.

How Ritual Works

I will put forth now a workable model that you can use to visualize how the regular performance of ritual may transform the student of magic into an enlightened being. Please note that the transformation is painstaking and slow, taking in most cases several years. (I have never met an adept below the age of thirty-one, though there are many pretenders of all ages who announce loudly and frequently that they are of high spiritual rank.) Using voice, movement, visualization, and drama every day to infuse yourself with Light gradually transforms your body into an instrument of that Light.

Before I can describe the process, I must first give a sort of general lesson on the anatomy of the soul. Keep in mind as you read the remainder of this chapter that there are many ways of picturing the soul, and this is just one of them. No one schematic is *the* correct one, just as no religion has a monopoly on the truth. Many unfamiliar models of existence, though they may clash with the ones you have been taught, can show you new perspectives that, if you are lucky, open the gates of your perceptions to realities that transcend the limitations of the physical world. As this book is a modern version of Golden Dawn magic, the vocabulary I use is naturally that of Kabbalah paralleled with modern-day pop psychology. Read over the following section a few times if the material is new to you. Take some time to study it and absorb it.

Kabbalistic Anatomy

In Kabbalah, there are (at least) three levels of the human soul:

The Ruach (ego)

The *Ruach* (pronounced "Roo-AHCH," the *ch* being a guttural sound, as in the name of the classical composer Bach) is the most familiar portion of the mind. Unfortunately, it is fake. It is the assumed identity that the castaway adopts after waking up on the beach. It is the ego, or surface-mind, of man. It exists in a realm, as it were, caught between Heaven and Earth, and it looks out through human eyes as though it were not native to the earthly terrain around it. And yet it has no knowledge of any spiritual home either. This is the mode in which a person normally operates while not sleeping, when going about his day-to-day business, and while aware of the passage of time. The ego is the outward persona that rises up from the depths of biology to deal with survival in the world. It is the fragile self-image that hovers like a lost child between the world of animals below and the world of the gods above.

Ruach means "wind" in Hebrew, and it corresponds to the element of air. The Ruach is analogous to a breeze that blows on the surface of a pond, like the breath of the Divine that moved upon the face of the waters in Genesis. It corresponds to the realm of mind, which is distinctly different from the heavens above and the landscape of nature below and yet which would not exist without either parent, being instead a phantom image generated by the harmony between them. It is as though a divine being above has identified itself with an animal form below, and the assumed identity that it adopts in the process is the Ruach.

Think about this for a moment. Your self-image, your idea of who you are, is just that—an image. Does it really exist? If you are not your ego, then who are you?

The Nephesch (animal soul)

The *Nephesch* (pronounced "Ne-FESH") is the so-called "lower" realm, the water beneath the wind. *Nephesch* means many things in Hebrew, one translation being "animal soul." It is the subconscious mind. It is responsible for sensory perception, and it communicates through symbols and images. It is intimately tied to the physical body and to base urges. It is characterized by cyclical biological processes, reflexes, and instincts. The Nephesch is not rational, and it knows nothing of linear time. Getting in touch with what is going on in your body and with your sensory awareness will make you very intimate with the Nephesch. Its element is water.

The Neschamah (Higher Self)

This highest (or deepest) level of the soul is seemingly the least familiar. It is the Neschamah (pronounced "Neh-shah-MAH"), the Higher Self, the superconscious mind. It is the silent voice and the forgotten identity. Its element is fire. It corresponds to the heavens, and it is this exalted level of mind that realizes its connection to all things. The Neschamah transcends time, and everything is visible from its heavenly seat.

To illustrate how these levels of the psyche interact, refer to the Greek myth of Narcissus. Narcissus was a beautiful young man who disdained the love of others. The goddess Artemis cursed him to fall in love with his own reflection, which he beheld in a pool of water. He tried in vain to hold the image, but in the end he died of a broken heart.

We are each of us like Narcissus. The ego, through some quirk of human evolution, has been "cursed" to fall in love with the image of itself reflected in the animal soul.

It sees only by the images and impressions relayed to it through the animal senses. Like Narcissus, it stoops over the waters of its lower nature, aware of the world only through images reflected on that narrow surface, most of which are blocked by the looming self-image.

The Higher Self is like the sky above Narcissus as he stares mesmerized by the pool. It arcs over the ego and the animal soul like the firmament over the waters in Genesis. Since the Higher Self transcends time, it cannot communicate directly to the ego, which relies heavily on time-bound, abstract language and a cause-and-effect mentality. Narcissus is, after all, turned away from the sky as he stoops over his reflection. The Higher Self instead speaks to the ego through images "reflected" in the nervous system of the animal soul. The ego cannot see the Higher Self directly. We cannot apprehend our own divine nature face-to-face, because we are, by design, just like Narcissus, enthralled by our reflection within the realm of the senses. We tend to look just at our self-image and not the sky.

This is an important point, for it proposes that it is not possible to sense the spiritual realms directly, as so many psychics would have you presume. You can only train yourself to look for signs of the spiritual realm in the Nephesch, in the biological workings of your own mind and body. The physical, emotional, and mental processes of your animal soul are a mirror of the heavens. Kabbalists have said for centuries that the material world is not an evil place. The things of this world—your body in particular—are necessary instruments used in the process of awakening. Participating in the delights and pains of the physical senses is a necessary part of your journey to liberation.

Each human being is therefore a combination of upper and lower realms, Higher Self and animal soul, primal fire and water. His phantom ego hovers between the two like wind on the water, brooding over the image of the sky that is reflected up from the waters. Pause for a moment here and reflect on this schematic. What follows next describes how the different parts of the soul interact, and all this new terminology can be confusing if you do not take some time to contemplate how it can be applied to your own experience.

Conditioning

Wind blows on the surface of the water, thereby altering the reflection of the heavens to suit its purposes. The ego can likewise alter and distort the image of the higher consciousness that presents itself within the animal senses. Man is, after all, created in the "image of God," if we are to take seriously the words of Genesis. But what if the image of the sky reflected in the water becomes distorted because of too much wind? What if the ego's restless activities disturb the image of the Divine that is reflected in the animal soul? I am suggesting here that the activities of your mind can keep you from seeing the truth about yourself. This is why the Zen masters say that when the mind is still, enlightenment ensues. When the wind is calm, the water becomes still, reflecting like a perfect mirror the beauty and light of the sky, the Neschamah.

The activities of the mind do not necessarily have to interfere with enlightenment. In fact, the aspiring magician can use the mind to do just the opposite. Ritual techniques refine and purify the receptive nature of his animal soul. By employing drama, voice, and movement, he can wipe away confused behavioral and mental habits. He can eliminate gradually the distortions in the reflection of Heaven. The student of magic is striving for none other than the naturally clear mind, which appears only when desires, beliefs, and false perceptions that arise from material inclinations are erased.

The ego is supported on the vast subconscious underworld of the animal soul. Through its response and adaptation to the world, the ego disturbs the surface of the animal soul, creating patterns in the pool. The conscious mind, through its repetition of the same choices, creates habits, expectations, and distorted perceptions in the subconscious. If the waters are agitated in the same manner consistently enough, permanent, self-sustaining disturbances can linger on the surface, similar to whirlpools or eddies in a stream. After twenty or more years of accumulating such disturbances, it can be a long and hard struggle to smooth out the fears, prejudices, and grudges that have been built into one's "body of water." These bad habits (or complexes, as psychology calls them) easily acquire an unruly semiautonomous and semisentient existence within the subconscious, where they in turn acquire a foothold from which to produce greater disharmony—to multiply, even.

The embedded complexes continually show up in our behavior as the natural difficulties of life provoke them. Complexes are nourished and strengthened by repetition of negative experiences. Childhood traumas, for instance, can make a monster out of a healthy mind. To the emotionally disturbed adult, any hardship that remotely resembles those childhood traumas, no matter how slight, can trigger terribly inappropriate, overly defensive behaviors.

Psychologists label this creation and perpetuation of complexes "conditioning," and conditioning is the cause of most human misery. It is unsettling to see yourself intimidated and controlled by your own malleability. Life in the world can sometimes be painful enough just as it is. But humans have the ability to compound their suffering by carrying negative perceptions of the past into the present. The grandeur of this present moment, with its unspeakable mysteries and boundless possibilities, gets smothered by knee-jerk reactions and antagonistic philosophies.

Not only can our conditioning clog up our ability to experience the universe as the reflection of Divinity, but it also can make us blind to opportunities in life that produce wealth and prosperity. Survival and happiness are easy art forms to master for someone whose Nephesch is uncluttered. In fact, survival and happiness are effortless, for life flourishes in perfect harmony with the world when the image of Deity is allowed to take shape in the medium of matter. It is only the phenomena of conditioning that can ruin that possibility for us and obscure the ineffable glory of the Divine. Our environment can enslave us by molding us into maladapted caricatures, placing us easily in a state of learned unhappiness. Furthermore, our warped internal mirrors compel us to react inappropriately to reality, producing yet more hardships that strengthen our complexes even more, leading to a greater distortion of the present, and so on. And all this recycling of misery continues just because it is difficult to let go of something as simple as a grudge.

Demons

The animal soul is normally pure, beautiful, and innocent. But the continuously stimulated complexes in it eventually become self-sustaining entities, spiritual parasites that sap a great deal of energy from the person playing host to them. These fixed vortexes are like holes or gaps in the seamless fabric of shimmering Light, which is the true nature of the Nephesch. Through these gaps can creep the influences of destructive forces from other realms. Persistent distortions in the mirror of the Nephesch can reflect not only twisted perceptions of Earth and Heaven, but also the influences from other dark and unbalanced places, realms I haven't spoken of yet. "Demons" can thus gain some influence over a person whose Nephesch is in a state of self-sustained agitation.

Sometimes, people can become so mentally and emotionally disturbed that you can sense a hurtful presence seeping through them from "beyond." Their Nephesch, or subconscious, has been hijacked by portions of the personality that have split off from the whole, and these mini-entities can be seen by a clairvoyant as holes in the aura. They act as conveyors for dissonant influences that supposedly exist in other realms besides the Ruach, Nephesch, and Neschamah.

Demons cannot actually inhabit a person. They do not exist in this world. But a person can fall victim to their influence nonetheless if he unwittingly becomes a conveyor of unbalanced influences from demonic realms.

The physical senses are constantly feeding into and shaping the Nephesch. Our experiences enter, and it responds automatically, as rapidly as quicksilver, by creating a worldview out of them. This worldview, made up of past experiences and conditioned responses, constrains how we see the external environment—not only that, but the internal landscape of the mind as well. A demonic, fear-driven worldview can easily intimidate us and hold us prisoner. Most people cannot see reality clearly reflected in their internal mirror, but instead see it in the way that the complexes embedded there compel them to see it. But it doesn't *have* to be that way.

Despite the bleak picture I have painted, there is a benefit to this anatomy of the soul. Since the environment is capable of provoking our complexes (and it is helpful if we initially admit this), then it must also follow that a carefully orchestrated environment can smooth out and eliminate those same complexes. We can intentionally prod (evoke) our "demons" to the surface, see them for what they are, and banish them. Magical ritual is designed to do just that. Performed on a daily basis, it helps the aspirant beat the bushes of his animal soul, ferreting out the autonomous little critters that have been manipulating him from behind the scenes. He will eventually, through perseverance, reach a cleared state in which the Nephesch is a smooth continuum of astral light, capable of reflecting wholesome, undistorted images of both the physical *and* higher worlds.

Because the five senses are the chief conditioners of the animal soul, they are the best avenue with which to reshape its substance. And for the ordinary person, the drama of ritual can mold his inner world such that he can open a clear, reflective space within the polluted soup of the Nephesch. Using the five senses as tools, he can prod and stretch his subconscious to temporarily clear away embedded complexes and catch an undistorted glimpse of higher worlds. Furthermore, he can manipulate his internal "mirror" to reflect the influence of the spiritual world into the material world. Like using a hand mirror to reflect sunlight into a cave, he can enter into any difficult life situation and act as a shining beacon to others. Or, if he so desires, he can direct spiritual Light toward the situation, producing "miraculous" changes.

When the magician has reached this state of clarity, all of the ritual, structure, and tools he mastered to achieve it are no longer necessary. Magic will no longer be what he does, but what he *is*. The training wheels of methodology fall away.

In the meantime, before he reaches enlightenment, rituals and exercises are still necessary. He has a need to structure his environment so that a cleared space is sympathetically formulated on the distorted surface of the Nephesch. Magical ritual can facilitate this highly desirable state of clarity, especially when it is performed faithfully and regularly. The clarity becomes greater and greater over time as the magician's appearance and demeanor begin to take on the unmistakable qualities of hidden radiance.

The enlightened man, by a Zen analogy, has polished his inner "mirror" to such a degree that it reflects a perfect image of reality. He has calmed the waves on the face of the waters, such that the countenance of the divine sky can convey upon them a clear, undistorted image of the heavens. To feel the reflection of the Divine Self within you and to express Its will in the medium of life is the unspeakable joy that is the goal of the magic of transformation.

Components of Effective Ritual Magic

The aspects of ritual that are essential for effective magic are symbol, space, movement, voice, and drama.

Symbol

Effective symbols express the inexpressible. They express the nature of higher worlds in terms of their reflection in our realm of space and time. For instance, in the astrological symbol of the Sun, ☉, the dot at the center of the circle is not really the spiritual essence of that circle. It is just ink on paper. But the symbolic image of the Sun reflected in the mind, associated with certain ideas, becomes a focal point of integrity and power that is quite real. Imagine the image of the Sun in your heart for five minutes. What feelings does this produce? What behavior might you exhibit if you were to picture it there all the time? How might your behavior affect your fortunes then? And the fortunes of others? In this way, symbols and glyphs are tools that reshape the Nephesch to allow for an impression to arise from realms other than that of the physical. Symbols actually can be made to channel power. To do this requires that they be properly visualized in the mirror of the Nephesch and properly contemplated by the Ruach.

Symbols therefore act as attractors and repulsors. Because they can convey certain energies from other worlds, certain complexes floating in the Nephesch have a natural sympathy or antipathy for certain symbols. For instance, the pentagram has a tendency, due to its learned correspondences, to repel materially conditioned complexes in the Nephesch. Working with the pentagram correctly over time therefore reduces the amount of material conditioning in the student's subconscious. This is why the pentagram has a reputation for warding off demons. It is like the scarecrow that keeps a cornfield free of scavengers.

The pentagram is foremost an abstract representation of the human figure, one that suggests balance and fierce integrity. Stand with your legs spread, your arms wide open, and your eyes forward. Feel yourself as a powerful, archetypal human form, come forth upon this earth to fulfill your divinely ordained destiny. Such is the nature of this symbol, and more. There are countless other correspondences attached to it that bear out this same impression, and you would do well to research them and accumulate them in your mind as you begin to perform the Lesser Banishing Ritual of the Pentagram on a daily basis.

Space

Space represents the medium through which symbols can interrelate. Symbols, properly placed in relation to each other, suggest by their interaction a nonphysical reality. They can condition the Nephesch to open up to the Neschamah. The impression that the empty space makes within the mind is itself a conveyor when it is properly staked out with symbols. Four pentagrams

arranged in a circle around you would tend to create a clear space, within which the higher mind can more easily be glimpsed.

Also, pentagrams, when formed in particular ways by the magician, can serve to attract certain forces that assist him with the purpose of his ritual. The five points of the pentagram represent spiritual Light reigning majestically over the four elements. By training yourself to draw the pentagram in various ways, you can attract or repel the influences of the various elements. For example, if the earth point of the pentagram is de-emphasized by drawing the banishing-earth pentagram, your internal mirror would shift to reflect less of the universe's earth-like qualities. You would therefore become less influenced by the physical world, which is represented by elemental earth. The same principle applies to other symbols—like the hexagram, by which the magician can modify the influences of the seven astrological planets.

Movement

Movement is a very suggestive and powerful aspect of ritual. It stimulates the Ruach to open up the Nephesch, like wind on a lake creates ripples that wash debris ashore. It is the means by which the symbols are distributed in a meaningful pattern—especially a circular pattern. A circular dance or circumambulation can actually create a funnel in the soup of the participant's Nephesch and create a resulting opening to the inner mirror of the universe. Each participant in a circular dance, provided he is tuned in correctly, creates a cleared space in his own Nephesch in which all debris is pushed aside and only the calm and reflective astral light is permitted to pool, like the calm in the eye of a hurricane. This action is sometimes referred to as a "cone of power."[2] The cone can be envisioned as a whirlpool beneath the circle of the circumambulating performers. Negative influences are seen as spinning off away from the circle as it fills with astral light. The visualized cone indicates the movement generated in the unseen medium of the magician's Nephesch. It tapers downward through the depths of the animal soul. At the bottom, in the eye of the storm, is a reflection of the divine realm, captured on a placid internal sea.

Voice

An even more powerful conveyor of magical power is the voice. The marriage of symbol and movement occur within it. The oscillation of the voice creates a finer vortex of its own, by which specific words, properly vibrated, can actually raise energy in a room or in one's physical body. It is a simple matter to experience this. You may be vaguely familiar at least with the energy that fills an amphitheater when the audience chants.

Drama

This final aspect of ritual is crucial. Drama is often the missing Orphic component to the Hermetic approach. Emotion behind the words and gestures is of absolute necessity. It is the power source behind the corresponding movement created in the Nephesch. The physical arrangement, movement, and words of ritual must be backed by feeling. Strong emotion is a foothold on the subtle realms of the astral. Without it, the ritual exists only in the physical, with little or no desired inner correspondence.

The concepts presented here make up a Hermetic explanation of the mechanics of ritual and its uses toward achieving illumination. Ideas like cones of power and subconscious complexes are, by their nature, overly fanciful and technical. The reality that these terms attempt to describe, however, is quite different. I have said it before: magic is not what it appears to be. Ultimately, the aspects of ritual are not important but are only to be used as a means to a higher end. They are the tools but not the goal. There is a crucial still point in a ceremony in which the peak consciousness is reached and the breakthrough is made. An unbroken continuum in the astral light is achieved, and the resulting clarity reflects power from the divine realms. The image of the invisible is revealed. The silent voice is heard. This moment transcends everything that was used and everything that was done in order to achieve it. The magician might not even perceive it, but it may come through anyway by implanting itself in the subconscious, only to bubble to the surface later, causing all manner of changes in his life. All of the "answers" one needs can arise from this still point.

The Hermetic view of ritual is that we are in this world not to abstain from form, but to use it for a higher end. To quote the respected author and magician William Gray, "When we master movements, we can afford to be still."[3] This, then, is the principle behind the magic of transformation.

three

The Secret Lineage

Magical techniques do not derive spiritual power from their lineage. The idea that a documented connection to great magicians of the past imbues any kind of spiritual practice with authenticity is a fallacy. For example, if I say that "my" initiations were bestowed upon me by adepts who have lineage back to the original Golden Dawn, what good does that do except get your attention enough so that I can give you either valuable guidance or more empty claims? Claims are just that: empty. If a student feels more self-assured with an impressive lineage behind him, so be it, but he need not base his confidence on the circumstances of the past. The value of any curriculum proves itself by the results it brings.

It is romantic to envision one proverbial candle lighting another as a teacher passes the flame of Spirit from one generation to the next. But the truth is that the flame of Spirit is accessible everywhere, any time, from the dirty alleys of the concrete jungle to a pampered sitting room at the Vatican. The successful student of magic connects to this inner power not by accumulating rank or prestige, but through what is happening right now, through the present moment.

But the average person has difficulty recognizing such value as this, because he sees everything through the lens of the past, believing that his fortunes come about solely through cause and effect (a process known as *karma*). He requires his teachers to be reputable. To protect himself from inferior knowledge, he discriminates between "good" teachers and "bad" ones by employing the measuring stick of status. The social hierarchy is always there, ready to do his thinking for him. Its rationale goes something like this: surely if a spiritual technique can deliver what it promises, it will pass the test of time, garner itself a grand reputation, be advocated by power-ful leaders, produce volumes of elegant literature, and display a lengthy heraldry of initiations that goes back to some white-bearded saint hundreds of years dead. But as anyone can guess, the concept of status, though it effectively creates leaders and followers in animal and tribal worlds, is clumsy and largely inapplicable to the higher realms of Spirit.

Somewhere along the history of a lineage, the original spark that inspired it can burn out, and the poor student who continues to participate in the derelict faith finds himself trapped in a world of meaningless titles, abusive power, and empty dogma. Proof of lineage means very little, since a tradition deprived of its original inspiration can continue to feed off of its own momentum. When a particular ceremony, such as the Catholic Mass, has a beguiling reputation, the congregation all too easily plays along with it, seldom questioning whether its present-day observance still fulfills its original purpose.

"The Lottery," a short story by Shirley Jackson, is a classic dramatization of this phenomenon. The narrative opens with a rural, small-town meeting in which a traditional ceremony is to be enacted. We learn from the atmosphere of the story that a great mystique has gathered around the practice of an annual drawing of lots. The dialogue between characters reveals that they have participated in this cer-emony for all of their lives. Only in the end do we learn the ceremony's true nature. Shirley Jackson reveals how the momentum and status of an obsolete ingrained tradition can lull a community into a cultural trance, easily creating a mob capable of unspeakable ritual acts. We need only look at Christianity and Islam to see that Jackson's story is not an exaggeration. The pages of history drip with the blood of ritually tortured and murdered "heretics."

To a lesser degree, such a divorce from reason has happened even to some branches of Kabbalah and pagan magic. Usually, when the founder of a school dies, his teach-ings die a slow, lingering death soon after, and his inheritors are left beating the dead horse that remains. Most followers are blind to the original power source behind their faith, because they look for it in the past. They experience the effect of a ritual secondhand, through its nostalgia—its accumulated reputation and stimulating fan-fare. No one has ever trained them to lift the veil of routine and consensus that keeps them cut off from the original fire behind the words and gestures. What are we to do, then, in a world where the congregation is kept in ignorance of the inner workings of the Mass and where the esteemed priests continue to muddle through gestures of consecration, the significance of which has been forgotten?

Now, the magical adept is someone very interesting indeed, because he has outgrown the need to be guided by status. He feeds not off of the momentum of the past, but from the present moment. For him, a ritual does not need to be reputable, because he can discern the value of it—or *any* work of art, for that matter—almost at a glance. The spiritual flame is aroused not only by the imposing masterpieces of antiquity, but also by the ordinary things of today. It is not uncommon for the simplest and least reputable sources of wisdom to enthrall the adept. Advertisements, nursery rhymes, and comic books are just a few of the unlikely wellsprings in which the more advanced mind may recognize the silent voice of Spirit. The adept can see the impetus behind these art forms directly instead of secondhand through the "approval machine." He knows that the power of a painting, movie, or ceremonial act exists—ever fresh, ever timeless—in the silence of the *now*.

The next time someone plays a CD for you and asks if you like the music, notice whether or not you have the habit of asking who the artist is before deciding whether you like the song. If you find yourself reluctant to form an opinion until you know *who* is performing, you may have fallen into the status trap, suppressing your own opinion by letting the past success of the group decide for you what is worthy and what is not. But if you can listen to the piece and formulate an impression without requiring any facts, you are using the very simple, very powerful faculty of the present-moment experience. You are letting in the power of the now, and you are thinking for yourself. The ability to set aside the tendency to compare the present to the past, seemingly so simple, is the most important power you possess.

The discriminative faculties of the adept are much more powerful than normal, requiring no moral or intellectual safeguards to keep him on the top of his survival game. He allows the voice of the past to mutter its concerns from the back seat of his vehicle, but he will never allow the past to take the wheel. He has found a better driver than the voice of his culture, so he can wander far from the highway of the mainstream and still pick his way through the darkness unscathed. He discovers beauty in the most unlikely places. The adept knows that the real power of the "masterpiece" in the museum lies not in its reputation, but in the onlooker. The work of art is a catalyst that helps him lift his spirit into the timeless beauty that exists in *his own* mind and heart, right now. A painting's popularity in the college textbooks to him is little more than a signpost. While the dignified herd of tourists passes before the Mona Lisa muttering acceptable comments, he stands before her in a state of shock, witnessing the goddess within himself.

As you approach a spiritual tradition with the intention of gaining entrance, the temptation to evaluate its status will surely rise up in your mind like a protective shield. It is important to most of us to practice something "reputable" according to the dictates of the values we have been taught. But the real questions are simple. Does the ritual work, or doesn't it? Are my perceptions changing as I do these exercises, or aren't they? Am I alive within my own life, pushing the boundaries, or am I drifting like lumber in the mainstream?

I would like to propose that the mainstream traditions of our time, the ones that have become accepted, are horses long dead. They no longer serve to awaken their participants. Christianity, Judaism, Islam, and Buddhism in their origins were radical systems of self-transformation. In ancient times, when their spark of inspiration was still vibrant, the cultures in which they appeared regarded them with fear and suspicion. Their first practitioners were ridiculed and persecuted. Anyone who is delving into the true work of the soul, as I have mentioned in the first chapter, is a threat to the great survival machine that sustains the tribe. Therefore, in order for a system of spiritual development to become "safe" enough for the approval of the mainstream, it must first be emasculated, stripped of its vanguard elements. To become accepted by the bulk of humanity, spirituality must be "cleansed" of magic, thereby turning it into religion. The original ritualistic elements that are designed to liberate the individual from his cultural trance are labeled as "immoral" or "primitive." The thorns are subsequently stripped from the rose, and the end product is a Christianity that is no longer the challenging succession of death and resurrection initiations carried out in the catacombs of Rome. Another example is the Judaism that has been stripped of its Kabbalah. Tibetan Buddhism's Chod rite, in which the solitary participant liberates himself from ego by visualizing his own death and disintegration, has been watered down into a monotonous, unrecognizable folk dance. When it comes to getting into an "acceptable" tradition like Christianity and attempting to utilize it as a vehicle for awakening, the student finds that the engine has been removed from the car! The practices that were designed to liberate the individual are replaced by ones that actually serve to indoctrinate him. He is allowed to be "spiritual" only as long as his practice doesn't involve techniques that lift his awareness out of the group mind.

This is not to say that all of Christianity, Buddhism, Islam, and other traditions are spiritual wastelands. Their mythologies still exist, as deep and as powerful as ever, even though the methods for connecting to that power have been removed. Despite the fact that our priests dress the mystical core of our culture in symbols and parade it before us just out of reach, there are still small, secret groups that allow the congregation to touch. The illumination of the higher reality will continue to shine through the cracks here and there, even though most people prefer to worship the great survival machine and call it God.

Magic is a disreputable art. People have been burned at the stake for practicing it. It embraces unseen, disturbing realities. It transcends morality. It is in the disreputable parts of a spiritual system that one finds the adventure, the risks, and the bounty. Before you dare to take up the exercises in this book, you (the potential student) are faced with a leap. Do you adopt this questionable practice, even though convention will label you an "outcast" for doing it? Such leaps are the means by which real change is created in life, and real disasters too. There looms before you a boundary of uncertainty. One must be free of the old before the new can take root. It is scary to set aside your implanted value system and jump into a new kind of existence just because it strikes a chord with you.

This is an old story, like that of the college student who horrifies his parents by changing his major to philosophy. The spiritual giants of today, when they had just started out on their paths to self-discovery, were seen as "throwing their lives away" or as just plain weird. But eventually, the gold within worked its way to the surface. After a lengthy adventure through uncertainty, they emerged transformed, suddenly labeled "genius" and "miraculous."

The Golden Dawn is one such disreputable system of magic. Many scholars, acting as unwitting protectors of the mainstream, have discredited it and cast it safely into the margins of Western culture. And there are many more "dangerous" nuggets of ancient wisdom to be found lying in that shadow fringe. Fortunate is he who stumbles across one that speaks to his unique gifts, helping him to extract the gold from his life. He can find in it the forbidden path at the crossroads, and treading that rough-hewn pass, he will never be the same again.

A Brief History of the Golden Dawn

There are at least two histories of the Golden Dawn. One is mythical, and the other, factual. I will set aside a few words to discuss each one of these so you can weave the two stories together and formulate a workable image by which to perceive the order and its teachings.

You might well ask why I would give a mythological account in addition to a factual one. Aren't the hard facts uncovered by scholars all that matter? If the oldest accounts of the Golden Dawn are fabricated legends, why should I burden you with fiction? After all, this is the information age, and the accuracy of facts is sacred.

Spiritual traditions of all kinds attach to themselves fanciful myths of magical power. It should come as no surprise that the information age is rapidly discrediting Christianity with research. The claims of myth can be picked apart and revealed as "fraud" by any scholar with a little bit of tenacity. And yet, what is the nature of that tenacity with which he would break the spell? It seems that his very desire to penetrate a mystery leads him to destroy his own capacity for experiencing it.

The overly rational scholar reminds me of an analogy: the botanist who has a passion for flowers. He does harm to himself by sheer analysis. He goes out, cuts the blooms from their nourishing roots in the earth, and brings them to his lab, pulling off each petal to examine the pieces under his magnifying glass. "Why, this is little more than a collection of organic compounds," he declares smugly. "It never was a flower at all. I was superstitious and foolish to call it a thing of beauty."

Analysis alone is not the means by which to experience spiritual teachings. Just because beauty and enlightenment are not quantifiable experiences doesn't make them delusional. Even with respect to a small, esoteric movement like the Golden Dawn, the mythological history of its formation is of great importance, just as the mystery evoked by a flower helps us to appreciate something more than its raw materials. The same can be said of Christianity. Modern skepticism may very well prove one day that Jesus did not die from his crucifixion.[1] But what difference does that make, when the myth of the Passion still helps the mystic connect to his God?

The Golden Dawn was a society formed in late-nineteenth-century England. Its purpose was the study and practice of the occult, applied in ways to bring about enlightenment. The myth goes something like this:

In 1887, a master Mason named A. F. A. Woodford purchased a secondhand book in which he found a document written in a fifteenth-century cipher. His friend

W. Wynn Wescott, a brother Mason, recognized the code as one found in a six-teenth-century text called the *Polygraphia*, written by the Abbot Johann Trithemius.[2] To their delight, the document turned out to be the framework for some curious initiation rituals and a recently dated letter from Germany, written by an adept named Anna Sprengel. Wescott immediately wrote to the return address and initiated a correspondence that eventually gave him a charter to start a magical lodge of his own in England.[3]

That's it. This story of the mysterious cipher manuscripts, Anna Sprengel, and the charter are all that there is to the Golden Dawn's mythical genesis. And it very likely never happened. It is a very modest myth, seeming to make no grandiose claims to supernatural power. There are no saviors born of virgins or booming voices from the mouths of caves. At least that is how it appears at first glance.

But in linking itself to the Rosicrucian tradition of centuries past, Wescott's fledgling order plugged itself into an immense mythical power source. The mysterious myth of the Rosicrucians became the mythology of the Golden Dawn. At the time of the Golden Dawn's formation, this link was thought by many to be historically true, lending much credibility to it as a secret society and giving its recruits confidence in its mystical techniques. The teachings of the Golden Dawn claimed to have lineage, through Rosicrucianism, back to the magicians of ancient Egypt and Babylon.

The mythical Fraulein Sprengel, known secretly as Soror Sapiens Dominabitur Astris, was a Rosicrucian—a member of a secret society founded in medieval Germany by the fabled magician and alchemist Christian Rosenkreutz.

It is customary for magicians to adopt a magical name by which they are known in the ranks of their secret society. The name is usually created as an anagram of special significance to the student. Fraulein Sprengel's Latin motto, abbreviated as S.D.A., means "the wise person shall rule by the stars." (What sort of motto might you live by? You may wish to start formulating one.)

As Soror S.D.A.'s secret name demonstrates, the fierce individuality that is the lifeblood of Western culture was fully expressed in the studies of this society. Its members were great astrologers, physicians, alchemists, and consultants to kings. They supposedly had a potent influence on the development of the Western world. And their ideas were not uniquely theirs but rather came together in the Rosicrucian school from the even more ancient traditions of the Egyptian priests, Chaldean magi, and Jewish Kabbalists.[4]

At the time of Soror S.D.A.'s alleged correspondence with Wescott, she was a high-ranking adept of an order within the Rosicrucian lineage called *Die Goldene Dammerung* (German for "the Golden Dawn"). Her exploits, such as the charter to Wescott, were seldom appreciated by her fellow adepts of the order, but so exalted was her position that they never dared to question her actions openly.[5]

The Myth of the Rosicrucians

Let's go back to the beginning, to Europe's High Middle Ages, when Rosicrucianism began. In 1378, Christian Rosenkreutz was born to a penniless Germanic noble family.[6] He entered the cloister at the age of five and was a monk by the age of sixteen. He then adventured for many years through Europe and the Middle East, questing for hidden knowledge. What he found disappointed him. But he nonetheless gained insight from his encounters with Arabic physicians and Jewish Kabbalists in the Middle Eastern cities of Damcar and Fez. Both groups received him there as though his arrival had prophetic significance.[7] Rosenkreutz sifted through the teachings of his travels and assembled from them a comprehensive "code of doctrine and knowledge." This he presented, upon his return to Europe, to the scholars of Spain. But the Catholic world was headed into the bloody Spanish Inquisition, and his Kabbalistic discoveries were ridiculed by the superstitious mentality of Western Europe. Rosenkreutz knew that he must retreat from the world and conduct his researches in secret or else suffer persecution. A direct attack on the ignorance of the time was out of the question. He decided therefore to create a secret society that would indirectly bring about a behind-the-scenes reformation of the arts and sciences.[8]

He settled in Germany to experiment and study on his own for five years, choosing for safety's sake, and for faith in God, not to use his knowledge for fame or fortune. After this time of introspection, experimentation, and transformation, he founded, with the aid of three of his monastic brethren, a hidden college called the Domus Sanctus Spiritus. The number of brethren in the group soon increased to eight, and they worked speedily on preparing the documents and instructions of the order. Once their college was firmly established, Rosenkreutz's seven followers left it to travel Europe, spreading the teachings across the continent, planting the seeds of their tradition quietly wherever they went.[9] The craft of these magicians was such that it gave them subtle powers by which to influence scholars, clergy, and rulers. They didn't have to teach their "heretical" philosophy openly. It was by their simple presence and through their example that they carried the light of Rosicrucian ideals into the heart of the European culture. Supposedly, this led to a flowering of the philosophy called Humanism in the 1400s, which subsequently became the catalyst for the explosion of new thought that occurred in the Renaissance.

The Rosicrucians, or members of the Order of the Rosy Cross, have always presented themselves as vast, invisible, and influential, pushing the alarm buttons of all kinds of conspiracy theorists. It may well have been that they existed, but most likely they were not as organized as the theorists would like to believe. Echoes of a pseudo-Christian Hermeticism exist throughout medieval history, a magical tradition based on classical values, Egyptian magic, alchemy, astrology, and the myth of the life, death, and resurrection of Jesus. All of this was tied together via the correspondence system of Kabbalah.

Six bylaws governed the conduct of the Rosicrucian brethren in their travels. These are the rules of the Rosicrucian manifesto:

1. None of the members of the Order of the Rosy Cross should profess any art except that of physician. (Note that healing the sick was not the aim of the order, but its cover. The fruits of alchemy were shared openly and without compensation, but the methodology of its magic was kept secret.)

2. Each member should wear the ordinary dress of his country of residence. No fancy, elitist trappings allowed.

3. All members should meet once per year on Corpus Christi day.

4. Each member should seek a suitable pupil to succeed him.

5. The mark and seal of each member should be C.R. or R.C.

6. The Society should remain secret for one hundred years.[10]

As time passed, the mission of healing the sick was gradually passed on to the medical profession, no longer being a hallmark of order members. New members were accepted from all professions.

The secret inner workings of Rosicrucianism consisted of scholarly, magical, and contemplative techniques designed to

> afford mutual aid and encouragement in the working out of the great problems of Life, and in discovering the secrets of Nature, to facilitate the study of the system of philosophy founded upon the Kabbalah and the doctrines of Hermes Trismegistus . . . and to investigate the meaning and symbolism of all that now remains of the wisdom, art and literature of the ancient world.[11]

Christian Rosenkreutz was, among other things, an alchemist. By the sciences that he and his brethren practiced, he was able to greatly extend his allotted years on earth. At a time when the average life span was forty years, he lived to the age of 106. And as he neared that age, he began to prepare for his own death. Before his time ended, the Rosicrucians added another rule to their manifesto, making the total number of bylaws seven: Each member was to be buried in a secret, unmarked location.[12] One could only speculate as to the reasons, but needless to say, the founder of the order disappeared without a trace when he died in 1484.[13] The fraternity continued in his absence on the same college grounds for many years. In fact, 120 years after Rosenkreutz's death, a fascinating discovery was made, or so the story goes.

One of the Rosicrucian brethren who possessed considerable architectural skill was supervising an expansion to the Domus Sanctus Spiritus. In the process, he uncovered a memorial plaque in a wall, encased within the plaster, presumably of the founding brethren of the order. He respectfully had it removed so that he might see it placed on a more prominent monument in the cemetery. He had no reason to suspect that it covered the location of the founder's tomb, since the seventh rule of the manifesto forbade making known the place of one's burial. But as the workmen were removing the plaque from the brittle plaster, they discovered a secret door in the masonry. Chipping away the rest of the plaster revealed the inscribed letters POST CXX ANNOS PATEBO, which translates to "In 120 years shall I come forth."[14]

The next morning, the brethren gathered outside the door—without the workers present—and opened it. A mysterious white light shone from the chamber within. Before them was a vault of seven sides. The source of the pale radiance was a ball of light affixed to the ceiling, apparently chemical in nature, since there were no holes or windows to admit sunlight. In the center of the room rested a circular altar bearing brass plates on its surface that were inscribed with angelic names and images.[15]

In each of the walls was a small door that contained books, scrolls, and various alchemical equipment—presumably lost documents of the order, greatly prized. But the most mysterious discovery was yet to come. When the brethren moved aside the altar, they discovered a brass plate in the floor, under which lay a body. There, in death, was Christian Rosenkreutz, in his secret crypt, in a nearly perfect state of preservation. He was dressed in the ceremonial white robes and adornments of the Rosicrucian Order, clasping a mysterious scroll that later came to be known as the most valued document in the order (Book I).[16]

Greatly renewed in their inspiration by the things they had seen, the brethren took the parchments and books from the vault and then carefully resealed it, leaving the body within to remain in its incorruptible state, where it presumably still lies today.[17]

Scholars have tried to verify the existence of the secret society of the Rosicrucians within the context of medieval Europe, but nothing conclusive has ever been uncovered. Early medieval publications refer to a Father C.R.C. as the founder of the order, but no link between that title and the name of the man existed until much later. There is no record of the learned men of Spain ever receiving a guest, such as Rosenkreutz, purporting to have knowledge of a secret doctrine that reformed the arts, sciences, and religion of Western Europe. There is likewise no record of a place such as the Domus Sanctus Spiritus, a place where modest and secretive physicians effected miracle cures.[18]

Regarding a factual account of the Rosicrucian "secret society," there is little evidence to show that it ever existed in any official capacity. Most scholars who look for clues look in the wrong places. They see the order as being mobilized for political purposes in secret castles connected with underground tunnels, and so on. Yet any sincere student of medieval occultism would acknowledge that an intense spirit of esoteric, Kabbalistic Christianity did lurk in the shadows of medieval Europe. This spirit emerged explosively in the Renaissance with the advent of the printing press and the resurrection of pagan philosophies. One has only to read Dante's *Divine Comedy* and the works of Shakespeare to discern the blatantly Rosicrucian cosmology and terminology. The genuine heart of the Western mysteries has thrived in the shadows during age after age of misunderstanding. It thrives still. The tendency to see it as a secret society is the crude human way of trying to define it in terms of social hierarchy. It is too difficult for the factual mind of the researcher to admit that enlightenment can be carried in the heart of a culture, hidden in plain sight in the works of art and literature without ever shouting out its purpose directly for all to hear. Artists and mystics speak a language to which the average person is deaf.

It is held by some that the members of the Rosicrucian secret society are simply all legitimate initiates of the Western Esoteric Tradition. Central to this tradition is the medieval symbol of the Rose Cross, the Calvary Cross of Christ, from the center of which blooms the rose. The rose is the Western expression of the same reality that the pagan priests of ancient Egypt, India, and the Far East conveyed with the lotus blossom. It is the consciousness of the human who has awakened to his true identity. He has shaken off the stupor of the castaway on the beach. The Light of the Divine that works its way up from the depths of obscurity finds its outlet through the heart of the adept, where it silently blooms, granting the secret intimacy of the divine presence. When the student graduates into adeptship, he finds himself identified with Christ on the cross, a spirit that has become tangled in matter. The task that awaits such an awakened individual is to untangle the self from matter—or to liberate the crucified rose from its cross.

It is furthermore held that the highest initiates of the Rosicrucian tradition are just such liberated flowers, spirits capable of coming and going through their physical bodies, communing in unison on the subtle planes of existence with the divine presence, acting as liaisons and cocreators with the will of God Himself. Such men and women are said to have extraordinary powers, not the least of which are the ability to live for hundreds of years, appear in two places at once, and transmute base metals into gold. And this is the supposed tradition to which the Golden Dawn connected itself via its modest story of the cipher manuscript, Anna Sprengel, and the charter to form a temple in England. This is the landscape that lies before you as you hold this book, the true form of which may bloom for you if you embark on the process of transformation.

Despite the appeal of the myth, it has become quite clear through research that Wescott fabricated the story about the German Rosicrucian adept who sent him the charter. The grand and beautiful magical philosophy of the Golden Dawn, the most quoted and borrowed system of the occult that currently exists, appears to be based on a lie. Why would Wescott do such a thing?

Let's try to take a look at it from his view, if we can. Wescott was a Freemason with heavy spiritual and occult leanings who was dissatisfied with what Freemasonry had to offer in stodgy Victorian England. In his studies, he was highly aware of the Rosicrucian spirit that pervaded his subjects of interest, yet the lineage of that spirit remained unverifiable to him and his contemporaries—this at a time when scientific analysis and fact-finding were stomping like heartless gods across the West in the form of the industrial revolution. The role models of the Victorian era were men of facts, lineage, and historical accuracy. The myths of religion were only regarded as powerful if they could be factually substantiated as having actually happened on such and such dates and times. The story of Jesus, for instance, only had credibility if one could refer to the facts and see that, yes, a man named Jesus of Nazareth was crucified on Golgotha in the year AD 33 and that, yes, the tomb of Jesus was found empty. If evidence had been found that Jesus did not die at his crucifixion (evidence that does exist, by the way[19]), the faith of many Christians of that time period would have been deeply compromised.

Such a mindset, which plants its foundation on fact, paradoxically cuts itself off from its roots in the realm of myth. It isolates the individual from the power of fiction, from his own imagination. The person who founds his confidence on his past denies the power of the present moment. Few would doubt that great truths can be transmitted through a good drama. But who would dare to leap at forming a spiritual tradition based on fiction? People don't want their prestige to be based on fairy tales. They want status, lineage, and a heraldry of great teachers that proceeds somehow unbroken from the dawn of time—a pecking order with verifiable credentials.

It is my belief that Wescott was faced with the task of bringing the spirit of Rosicrucianism into a school of people who were of this difficult mindset—a seemingly impossible task. His own scholarship had failed to uncover a factual Rosicrucian society in the spiritual undercurrent of the West. His contemporaries were mired in the thinking of the time, and they would certainly not value pure insight without evidence. For the average man, it is not enough to trust in inspiration. He must have some external sort of prop by which to apprehend that power source, even though the power comes not from the object, but from within himself.

I believe that Wescott fabricated the Golden Dawn's connection to the Rosicrucians in order to give the students of his new school just such a prop. It may be that at some point he would have revealed to them the falseness of the order's claims, perhaps once they had progressed to the Inner Order. There comes a time when the student of magic outgrows his pretensions and doesn't need justifications for liberating himself anymore. The legend of the Rosicrucians provided the Outer Order students of the Golden Dawn the air of legitimacy that they required to pacify the competitive, skeptical nature of their era and to justify their spiritual development.

Pause for a moment to reflect on your knowledge of the world's great spiritual traditions. Is it possible that they all have fabricated their credibility in similar ways? Does it make them less effective if they have? Was Jesus really born of a virgin? Does it matter?

There is much about spiritual practice that is pretentiously romanticized and has little to do with the actual happenings within the mind/body of the practitioner. The adrenaline-stirring imagery, the thought-provoking sigils, and the overly fanciful descriptions of "layers of the aura" on one level satiate the mind, which is hungry for facts, but the real work of the soul, unimaginably simple, proceeds onward beneath the surface.

So, to complete the historical account of the Golden Dawn, I now switch from the mythology to history:

Wescott was a busy man. He couldn't compile the teachings of the order single-handedly. He called upon the genius of his friend Samuel MacGregor Mathers (whom he had been supporting financially for several years) to help with the project. Mathers took the material and, over the years that followed, developed the initiation ceremonies and curriculum of a magical fraternity, the Hermetic Order of the Golden Dawn. Wescott and Mathers called on another Masonic friend of theirs, Dr. Robert Woodman, to be a third cochief, making a total of three in a trinity of founders.

The order was discreet about membership and remained relatively hidden from the public in its early years, from 1888 through 1894. Most members found their way to the society via word of mouth. The chief influences within its ranks appeared to be Mathers and his wife, Moina, who were perhaps the most learned and developed of the adepts.

The Grade System of the Golden Dawn

The structure of the order was hierarchical, having three levels: the Outer Order, the Inner Order, and the Third Order. The Outer Order was for beginners, consisting of an introductory grade and four elemental grades. The elemental grades corresponded to earth, air, water, and fire. By association with the elements, they also correspond to the Four Worlds (or levels of existence) of Kabbalah. Additionally, there was a sixth or "Portal" grade, which led to adeptship.

The Grades

Grade 1	Neophyte	0=0	Probationary Grade
Grade 2	Zelator	1=10	Earth
Grade 3	Theoricus	2=9	Air
Grade 4	Practicus	3=8	Water
Grade 5	Philosophus	4=7	Fire
Grade 6	Portal		Spirit

Beyond the Portal grade lay the Inner Order. It consisted of the adepts. It had no curriculum or initiation ceremonies until 1892, when the first Adeptus Minor ritual was performed.

The Third Order supposedly consisted of spiritual beings called the "Secret Chiefs," with whom only Mathers had psychic communication. There is much speculation about these Secret Chiefs today, and many consider them to be actual men and women living on Earth. Some say that the aspiring adept cannot enter their Third Order and still be incarnate on Earth. But these provocative notions, for the purposes of the course presented in this book, are preoccupations for a later time when the reality behind the mythology begins to bloom. The reality of the occult is not as it appears.

The curriculum of the order consisted mostly of studying lecture documents, sitting for examinations, and undergoing the ritual initiations of the Neophyte grade, the four elemental grades, and the Portal and Adeptus Minor grades. Each of the grade initiations that Mathers developed from the cipher manuscripts appeared to have a powerful effect on the candidates. Properly performed, the ceremonies facilitated an alchemical process within each of them. The psyche of the initiate was symbolically dismembered, consolidated, and recombined.

The Neophyte and Adeptus Minor rituals, positioned at the beginning and end of the elemental grades, marked the most potent points of initiation. The first one jolted to life the process of self-analysis that characterizes the elemental grades. In successive elemental-grade initiations, each of the four elements was then ritually and symbolically extracted and consolidated from the others within the candidate's subtle body. Then, finally, the Adeptus Minor initiation focused on reintegrating and balancing the then-organized components of the psyche. The idea was that, simply speaking, the physical, mental, emotional, and instinctive aspects of one's being were separated, consolidated, and rebuilt, creating a new human being that was more efficient than before. The psyche of the Adeptus Minor initiate was reborn with new imprints planted by occult ritual and study. The result was a harmonized mind capable of what today is called "synergy"—such that the whole person, through internal cooperation and harmony, functions as more than the sum of his parts. The resulting adept is none other than a being of deep "integrity." Literally speaking, he is "integrated." It was then that the actual training in ceremonial magic began, for it was deemed that only a person of such integrity was capable of safely invoking spiritual forces and controlling them.

The balanced mind/body of the newly formed magician made his Nephesch—his animal soul—into an effective mirror capable of reflecting the Light of higher worlds into the physical world, thereby giving him the ability to produce startling life changes. Also, his new vista of experience made it possible for him to formulate a disciplined lifestyle that would cause his Nephesch to increase in strength. His consciousness, normally rooted to the physical body, would learn to attenuate beyond the boundaries of the flesh and project to other locations on Earth or to other levels of existence.

The Failure of the Original Golden Dawn

The original Golden Dawn curriculum had a weakness. It was possible to advance too rapidly through the grades, thereby spending very little time assimilating each stage of the process. Therefore, most members undertook minimal work on the soul. Quite understandably, the lure of the juicier aspects of occultism had temple members lusting for results and hastening the process of initiation. This produced a group largely consisting of failed mystics, grandiose titles, and inflated egos. Spiritual Light was being poured into vessels that had been dismantled and inadequately rebuilt. Not surprisingly, most of the troubles and quarrels that eventually wrecked the original order began after it started initiating students into the Inner Order.

Another problem involved premature lessons in astral projection. The Eastern symbol system of the Tattwas—colored geometric shapes—was introduced to students of the Outer Order. These are very powerful symbols to work with, and combined with the fragmenting effect of the elemental grades, they may have put unwarranted stress on the students' subtle bodies. When the student should have been conditioning his Nephesch for stability, integrity, and synergy, he was encouraged instead to dabble in the projection of it, which only served to deplete him of emotional stability, centeredness, and vitality.

Needless to say, the history of the order after that went the way of so many spiritual groups. Power struggles tore it apart from the inside. Several spinoff temples existed for several decades, mostly feeding off of the momentum of Wescott's original plan. A few legitimate adepts continued on with the tradition privately, and the original flame still remains lit today in a few small groups.

The bottom line is that the system of occult initiation taught by the original Golden Dawn was neither understood nor respected enough. The natural process of dissolving and binding was not allowed to finish, as many students rushed through the grades. Neglecting the alchemical process of self-analysis, students took their initiations into adeptship before they were ready. The reintegration part of the process failed and left instead only a brief euphoria, an inflated ego, and exaggerated psychological complexes. Mathers himself was a classic example of ego inflation. Despite his immense expertise, he fell prey to the grandest notions of his authority in the order and demanded absolute personal loyalty from all of the students.

An Improved Curriculum

It is evident today that a few people have learned from history. The value of the Golden Dawn system is recognized still and is taken more seriously than before. There are now revised curriculums that check the advancement of Outer Order students to assure a thorough alchemical transformation.

The work of becoming an enlightened being requires more than the influx of spiritual Light. The physical, mental, intuitive, and instinctive aspects of the mind must be prepared for that influx. The work of the Outer Order is a slow, thorough, and sometimes painful preparation for this event. It requires restructuring the way one functions on all levels. Not everyone who starts the process will make it through. If you dare to begin, it is important to take seriously what is happening every day and thoroughly examine every issue that arises. Impatience is the first demon to deal with, and many such potential setbacks must be dealt with along the way.

If you wish to dispense with the fantasies and pretense of occult practice and take up the steadfast work of the soul, it is recommended that you focus on the Outer Order work exclusively. Attempting anything before its time will just hinder your progress.

The curriculum in this book, as I have stated before, is a carefully improved version, which takes into account the failings of the original order. First of all, it provides a minimum number of months for each grade, giving your daily rituals adequate time to induce change. Second, I have added imagination exercises that are specifically tailored to stimulate the level of the soul that corresponds to your current grade. Third, you are required to keep a journal of your experiences, and to this I have added specific topics that must be reported on at key times. This new grade system makes sure that the rituals stimulate your dormant faculties and that additional control measures help to keep the ego in check, guarding against inevitable imbalances.

And finally, the elemental initiations are facilitated not by the group ceremony of the magical lodge (as in the original Golden Dawn), but by a solitary Kabbalistic technique that does a much better job. Dion Fortune, one of the most notable occultists of the twentieth century, hinted at this technique in her occult fiction when she spoke of building "four trees" into the subtle body, and of the student using the symbol of the Tree of Life to

> pick up the forces from the Earth center and draw them up the [centers of the] spine. These form the basis of all that follows. Only those who can do this can do magic. We in the West work with a tree; in the East they work with flowers, but it is the same thing.[21]

But this doesn't tell us very much. The earliest Golden Dawn adepts were bound by initiation oaths and kept from disclosing the most effective techniques of the order. Fortune is referring to an advanced form of an exercise called the Middle

Pillar, in which the student superimposes the ten spheres of the Tree of Life upon his body, similar to the way that a Tantric yogi of the East envisions the flower-like chakras blossoming in his spinal column.

The spheres of the Tree represent the unfolding stages of the universe. They also represent those same stages in miniature, within the development of a human being. In theory, visualizing the Tree of the Universe within your body serves to link your own powers to those of all creation.

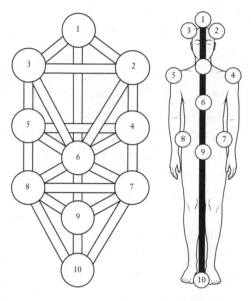

Furthermore, there are four such Trees of Life envisioned in Kabbalah, each of them corresponding to one of the Four Kabbalistic Worlds. The Four Worlds are levels of being that exist between God and humankind. The lowest is the physical world, occupied by our bodies and by elemental spirits that exist within matter. It corresponds to the element of earth.[22] The next higher world is the astral plane or World of Formation. Dreams, visions, and subtle matter exist here, and the initiate sees these phenomena as parts of the underlying mesh that defines how physical events will eventually happen in the outer world. This nebulous realm, where life descends into matter and prayers ascend to Heaven, corresponds to the element of air.[23] Angels traverse it, relaying power and information to and from the physical level. Higher still is the World of Creation, corresponding to water,[24] where archangels rule, facing one another as they support the universe like mighty pillars. It is the womb of creation. The activities of all conceivable things happen within the boundaries and limitations established here. The highest world is that of the emanation, or singular fiery essence,[25] which burns in a realm beyond human comprehension.

Israel Regardie is the author primarily responsible for revealing the secrets of the Golden Dawn to the world. His book *The Golden Dawn*, however, reveals mostly the framework and the philosophy and tells little of the most important techniques of transformation. Regardie did manage privately to teach a Middle Pillar Exercise that calls upon all of the Four Worlds at once.[26] But this is a rather monumental task for the inexperienced beginner. In his book *The Middle Pillar*, he only goes as far as dropping a hint: "Tradition gives us several scales of color, all of which are of equal efficacy."[27]

In 1969, R. G. Torrens published the vital clue to the proper use of the Middle Pillar Exercise in the Four Worlds: "This is known as the technique of the Middle Pillar. The Glyph of the Tree, which you should now be familiar with in all its five color scales, as in the Minutum Mundum and Four Worlds, is the key."[28]

It is best for the beginner to build up the colors of one Tree at a time, one in each elemental grade. Each Tree of Life represents a ladder to the next higher world, and therefore to the next grade. By assimilating the colors of one Tree at a time into your aura, you are scaling the height and breadth of your soul, from the outer world of physical action to the inner worlds of formation, creation, and emanation. As you build Tree upon Tree, you draw closer to the essence of your being.

The student, in this self-initiation course, starts his journey through the elements not by undergoing the lodge ceremony of the Zelator grade but by daily superimposing upon his body the Tree of Life as it corresponds to colors of the lowest Kabbalistic Tree. This more effectively draws out the consciousness of the earth element, that he may analyze it and reintegrate it more effectively into his identity. Then, in successive grades, he likewise formulates the Trees of higher and higher worlds, producing and assimilating the lessons of the other three elements. This little-known method of self-initiation I now pass to you. My contribution to it is to relate the different levels of the Tree more directly to the stages of the universe as it unfolds from the "big bang" into matter, life, humanity, and beyond.

Additionally, I have added the Kabbalistic concept of the *Tzelem*, or "image." Kabbalists hold that the countenance of the Creator is reflected in each of the Four Worlds. As it is said in the book of Genesis that man is created in the image of God, so is your physical body regarded as a reflection of God within the material universe. In other words, the descending influence of the Divine creates an image reflected in each of the Four Worlds, and the end result in the lowermost world is you. Kabbalah also teaches that there has been some kind of divine "accident" in which the image, at least in the lower worlds, has been shattered into conflicting pieces. The task of the mystic and the magician is to reassemble the pieces. As you pass through an elemental grade, you will call upon the Tree of one the Four Kabbalistic Worlds and use it to reconstruct the broken Tzelem in that world.

The step-by-step techniques enclosed in this book will more than adequately awaken the latent Trees within, helping you recover your lost knowledge. Each Tree corresponds to one level of your evolution through matter. These four divergent Trees of Life, these four images of God, you will eventually unite under the rulership of one transcendent entity, your divine aspect, which transcends the fourfold nature of matter.

Following is a brief description of each grade that lies before you:

Neophyte: This is an introductory grade. The aspirant is exposed to the vocabulary and symbolism of magic. He is also introduced to transformative energy. It is a probationary grade, giving the ego a chance to use its defenses against change. If one is going to bow out, this is the time to do it, before the transformation process becomes unstoppable. The aspirant is tested to see if he is ready for accelerated evolution. He is also introduced to the Kabbalistic myth of creation, such that he may aspire to return to his own spiritual starting point as a soul that is in unity with God.

Zelator: This is the first of the elemental grades corresponding to solid matter, the material world, and Earth. Home, money, health, and other physical issues are dealt with in this grade. Attention is directed to the physical body and material life. The driving forces of biology are revealed. By the time this grade passes, the student will notice that he feels cut off from the society in which he lives—that is, if this hasn't already happened. This feeling is normal.

Theoricus: This grade corresponds to the element of air and also to the realm of the rational mind, the ego, and social life. Attention is directed toward thoughts, beliefs, and automatic behaviors. There may come a sense of elevation and a feeling that the material world is simply one room in the cosmic house in which we live.

Practicus: This grade corresponds to the element of water, to human adaptability, to emotion, to intuition, and to the tools with which the magician does magic. The basis of magical power is revealed: that a human can mold his internal vision of the universe to produce external changes. Attention is drawn to skillful means of achieving results in one's life. By the time this grade passes, the student may gather some sense of the power of perseverance inherent in water. The relentlessness of water, flowing where it needs to flow without effort, changing shape to achieve its goal, is a force more powerful than the brief outbursts of "forcefulness" to which we as animals are accustomed.

Philosophus: The last of the elemental grades corresponds to fire. Power and passion are emphasized here, a drive to be successful and to engage life ensues. There also arises a temptation to abandon occult practice and stay in this worldly mode.

Portal: This grade summarizes and combines the experiences of the elemental grades. It corresponds to the "fifth element," Spirit. The analysis process that happened in the elemental grades is reversed, and the components of one's being are recombined to be offered up in sacrifice to the Higher Self.

The curriculum offered in this book is not for the faint of heart. Practiced successfully, it gradually uncovers the reality of one's spiritual nature. The dead-end habit of developing happiness that is dependent on circumstances will be seriously challenged.

There is nothing entirely new presented here. As I will demonstrate in my source material, everything that any student on any path has needed to succeed has been published for some time already. The trick to successful transformation is not to be found in some secret, undisclosed material, nor is it to be found in the bizarre initiation rituals of a formal temple or lodge. The secrets of transformation are *limitation* and *perseveranc*e. Presented here are exercises and projects that you are to do exclusively, all other spiritual work being set aside. If you have other interests, you may only go as far as reading about them. Practice is to be limited solely to the exercises of the grade work. Students who actually are exclusive about their work and go through this process purely and legitimately will find that the advanced work they have seen before is not really what it appears to be.

four

Neophyte

From this page forward, I will assume that you have decided to take up the course of study and work outlined in this book. You have resolved to proceed where few have gone before, setting aside for now the familiar, temporary world of your carnal self and its petty concerns. Ahead of you is the realm of Light and gods. The road to your destination is fraught with pitfalls and obstructions. Resolve to establish enough momentum to finish the journey you are starting, no matter how dark or tedious the landscape. The hardships ahead are only the denizens of various inner realms, testing your mettle, transmuting you into something more than human.

The Goal of the Outer Order Grades

Establishing discipline, then, is the most important theme now. In the Neophyte grade, you will do daily ritual, daily grade exercises, and regular study. Undertake the routine outlined in this chapter with full devotion. If you should find yourself weak in maintaining it, then this grade is to be the test that determines whether you are capable of making meaningful and lasting change. By the time the assignments of the Neophyte grade are half completed, make sure that you are performing the rituals every day—*without exception*. Your practice, by the time you reach the Zelator grade (the first of the elemental grades), should be so strong that nothing can keep you from your daily ritual performance. An unwavering persistence will enable you to fend off resistance and push through when obstacles arise. And they *will* arise. Your animal soul will begin resisting your efforts, fighting to keep you in a life of conformity. When the time comes for you to enter the more difficult elemental grades, the discipline and momentum established in Neophyte will keep your consciousness afloat in troublesome waters.

As you already know, each of the elemental grades, Zelator through Philosophus, corresponds to one of the four elements, the raw materials from which your mortal incarnation is formed. Not only do the elements represent solid, gaseous, liquid, and fiery aspects of your body, but they also correspond to levels of conscious activity.

Earth represents the physical body and its mechanics, joints, hormones, connections between different organs, and so on.

Air represents the activity of the thinking mind, characterized by analysis, planning, visualizing, and daydreaming. Air is the element in which fire and air clash and meet, forming all kinds of turbulent thoughts, personality traits, and whirlwind-like apparitions.

Water corresponds, among other things, to the emotions and intuition. These well up, accumulate, ebb, and flow very much like the waters of this planet. Water also corresponds to the activity of the wind and to other invisible forces, such as the gravitation of the sun and the moon. Through water, therefore, the influence of the unseen is revealed. Intuition functions in a similar manner.

Lastly, fire represents the basic instincts that arise from a very deep level of human biology. These fiery forces can be harnessed and directed by the conscious mind, making fire the element also associated with willpower.

In each grade, you immerse yourself, via ritual, in the energies and qualities of one element, one level of activity, attuning your consciousness to the curious entities that exist within that medium. The influence of one element over the others can be quite a disruption. You may become overly sensitive, moody, "spacey," or even lustful, just to mention a few of the distracting states through which you may struggle. It is therefore necessary to prepare yourself for your encounter with the elements—and the Neophyte grade is just such a preparation. It establishes a "vehicle," constructed by you personally, that will carry you safely onward. If you falter in this grade and are unable to maintain a steady routine, your "chariot" may be poorly constructed and unable to carry you across the elemental kingdoms. The result would be that the wild raw materials of the elements—behaviors, thoughts, emotions, and instincts—swamp your consciousness and keep you stuck in some uncomfortable place in your development. It is dangerous for the student to start traversing the boundaries of his consciousness only to stop halfway through the process and fall prey to the guardians at the threshold. Such has been the fate of many a failed mystic.

Your work should be about three parts experience and one part study. That is, you will spend a majority of your time on exercises that are quite different from reading and writing. Magic is not just about learning secrets from forbidden books (though no doubt that is an intriguing part of the whole adventure). It is about working tirelessly in applying those secrets to transform yourself into something more than human. On one level resides the theory and flowery rhetoric, on another level happens the work of applying that theory, and on yet another there is the churning, restless chemistry of change that stirs to life within your psycho-somatic cellular network. So, if you have adopted the notion that studying these ancient mysteries means being the master of some vast, dusty library, fussing over every "correct" detail of the initiation ceremonies, and having perfect recall of every astrological correspondence, then now is the time to abandon that image. The magician is not merely a scholar. I have met several people whose book knowledge of magic is almost beyond belief but who nonetheless have no practical experience with the forces described by their own sophisticated vocabulary. It is not necessary that you memorize every detail of your studies such that you can quote line 5 of page 230 of Regardie's *The Golden Dawn*. Learn well the material and principles of Hermeticism, yes, but above all, practice, practice, practice. Do the daily rituals. Do the journal topics and grounding exercises.

This might come as an affront to some of the more intellectual students of the occult. One of the comforts of magic is the illusion that "knowledge is power." Knowing the principles and terms of a philosophy is soothing to the intellect. But to regard the memorization of a philosophy as the fruit of your magical work is a mistake. A system of thought can never take the place of spiritual experience. By engraving the studious aspects of the Golden Dawn system of magic into your mind, you are not achieving the goal of the Great Work, but only the means to it. You are reshaping your thought processes, your habitual emotions, and your physiological responses such that they may one day fuse together into a magical instrument, an embodiment of the Hermetic philosophy. What you do with that instrument is entirely another matter. One of the meanings of the term "Philosopher's Stone" is to have one's principles concretized into the physical body. And that is only the beginning.

The Goal of the Inner Order Grades

Years from now, if you successfully traverse the elemental grades, you will likely find yourself jumping to a higher level of activity, that of the Inner Order. Your mind and body, ingrained with the principles of Hermetic philosophy, flare to life, and you begin to put those principles into action. The forces dealt with then will be like nothing you have ever studied. The *practice* of magic is a different world than the *study* of it, just as designing a roller coaster is of an entirely different order than riding one. Both may be fun, but the architect doesn't really know what the ride is going to be like until he finally straps himself in.

But this ride, wondrous as it may be, has not been created for your amusement. A new goal will assert itself. The work of the Inner Order is to surrender the control of the ride to your Higher Self, to make your brain and body into an embodiment not of a philosophy, but of your divine aspect. And that Higher Self will, in turn, create for you a new and different physical body. The Light of the Godhead comes down directly to bear on the physical frame, and simultaneously the physical frame rises into the Light of the Godhead.

Imagination exercises have been proven to change the way the body builds itself. The activity of the nervous system produces molecules called peptides, which affect your whole body. Whether the brain is imagining an experience or perceiving it physically, it makes no difference. The same peptides are produced, and these drug-like particles attach to receptors of all of the cells in your body, telling them what to prepare for and how to build themselves. The nervous system is not merely an electrical communication network, but a molecular one as well.[1]

So, the goal of the Great Work is not to *know* the Divine, but to *become* It. The adept is someone beyond human, so much so that his physical body begins to show signs of his attainment. His transformed mind/body is capable of slowing its own aging processes, of sensing levels of reality that exist beyond the physical, of projecting its astral body, and of becoming the "cocreator" of its environment through the manipulation of the astral plane. All these things are possible.

The Neophyte Grade on the Tree of Life

As you progress through the grades, you may have the sensation of rising through higher and higher levels of being. Each grade of the Golden Dawn is assigned to a position on the Kabbalistic Tree of Life—that is, all but one grade. Neophyte, or 0=0, is nowhere to be found on the Tree. It is the first grade of the Outer Order, but it is not "below" Zelator or anywhere else in particular. No grade is really higher or "better" than any other. Neophyte, though it is for beginners, is in essence the most important grade. It has all of the other grades concealed within it.

Though it is nontraditional to say so, I view the 0=0 grade as corresponding to Kether, the highest sphere on the Tree of Life, which in turn corresponds to the highest Rosicrucian grade, Ipsissimus. The divine energy you are calling upon in the Neophyte rituals is of the purest nature, represented by white light, just as the color correspondence of the highest sphere on the Tree is shown in the required reading for this chapter as "white brilliance." Additionally, the Neophyte meditation takes as its focus the geometric point, which is another correspondence of Kether. The Neophyte, though he is in the beginning stages of the Great Work, has the power of the Godhead slumbering within him. The high-ranking adept, who has finished the Great Work, has that same power awakened. Both stand in the same place. The journey through the grades transforms the student into a magician even as it brings him right back to where he started.

For this reason, it is necessary from the very start to call upon the highest level of purity and beauty that you can possibly envision. The first visualization performed in the Lesser Banishing Ritual of the Pentagram is designed to help you aspire to the highest, purest light. Your mind is to seek out its most primal beginnings, which are believed to be in an immortal unity with God (for lack of a better word). Those beginnings are not thought of as existing in the past, per se. They exist within the present moment, and it is in the here and now that you will use ritual techniques to contact your own essence, the silent voice of the Higher Self.

Following is a mythological account of the creation of the universe. By no means does it claim to be the "truth" about how things have come to be. The moment any student seizes upon such a story and claims it to be the one true account, he has lost his focus (and his mind). However, words can be crafted in such a way as to bring the reader into harmony with the invisible Light behind his imperfect perceptions. Stories like this one provide a setting within the imagination where connections to

The Grades

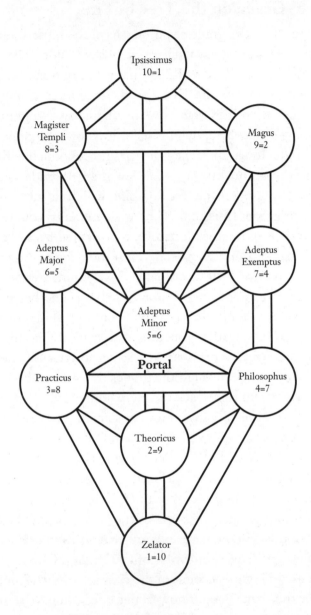

higher worlds become real. The student will learn to use imagination, drama, and ritual to contact and manifest his highest aspirations. Periodically read this story (and other creation myths) to give yourself a vision of the cosmos that will assist you in attaining a sense of the primal unity behind all things.

A Hermetic Genesis

It began before the beginning. The vast sea of Light was in a state of perfect unity, without edge, without boundary, and without division. This was the "clear light" of Buddha consciousness and the *Ain Soph Aur* ("Light without end") of Kabbalah. There was no possible idea of striving for and attaining anything, since all was wholeness, the very concept of unity itself being meaningless in an existence absent of separation. There was only the unending Light of consciousness, and it existed as perfect bliss and contentment. It knew no objects. It was the perfect suffusion that cannot be touched or disturbed. *All was mind.*

Impossibly, in the midst of this perfect peace, there arose a restlessness. For some reason, the All-mind struggled to perceive Itself. It "moved" within Itself to obtain a vantage point from which to survey Its own limitless being. And that was clearly not possible, since no division between self and "not-self" yet existed. Where could It go to see Itself if It had no edge, no realm outside of Its own limitlessness?

So, within the vastness of the All-mind arose a plan for self-division. The ocean of limitless Light opened a vortex in Its midst. The ultimate of creative acts was committed. The All-mind played a game of deception with Itself, comparable to hide and seek. It fabricated what, to us, appears as a lie, the first terrible act that began the birth pangs of the universe. It began to create a make-believe place within Itself that was different and "other" from Itself. If there were such a place, perhaps then the All-mind could obtain some vantage point from which to see Its own countenance or reflection. Such self-division was not really possible within perfect unity, but this was a game, after all.

In response to this plan, a vast cave of Darkness appeared in the midst of the Light, surrounded by a vortex of celestial fire. The Darkness was a terrible place, filled with the mystery of emptiness and chaos. Great rolling waves of Light buffeted the edges of this chasm in the midst of the All-mind. Their undulating coruscations of fire caused terrible storms in the Darkness. Light and Shadow agitated each other in such a way as to create, in their interplay, a seething broth of natural forces—the stuff of the primordial universe. In Egyptian mythology, this broth is called *Nun*, and it is envisaged as a vast ocean of ooze from which all things in the physical world are congealed by the laws of gods. And the All-mind used Light to exert pressure against the boiling Darkness, attempting to impress the primal substance with Its image. But the primeval mixture was too weak to contain the force of the All-mind. It lacked sufficient resistance, firmness, and structure. It seemed at one point that an image would form, that the All-mind would behold Its reflection in the froth of chaos. But that was not to be.

In the midst of the chasm, there was a mighty explosion, the "big bang," as we call it in modern cosmology. It spewed forth broken pieces of the Darkness, and they fell into the depths of the chasm. The shards were not what they appeared to be, but in this great drama of make-believe, they took on the role of terrible angelic beings that fell into the darkest, most Light-deprived recesses of the universe. To the edges of all things they fell, and there they lived and thrived on deprivation, spinning a web of Darkness that formed a shell around the cavern, a terrible boundary that became their kingdom of strife. These dark angels became the lords of illusion, of all separation and the dividing lines that distinguish one thing from another. They obscured the whole of the chasm from the divine radiance. They are the creators of physical laws, of isolation, of conflict and extremes. They carry within them the echo of that horrible cataclysm that cast them down when the Darkness was shattered by the Light. They are beings of unbalanced force, and they oppose the plan of the All-mind. The broken pieces of the primordial universe are the raw materials of structure upon which our current universe was successfully built. This was their assigned task: to uphold the rules of the great game of hide-and-seek by providing resistance. Their counterforce made it possible for a second attempt of the Divine to succeed. Because of their resistance, the All-mind managed to suffuse the primeval ocean with Its power the second time around. And so the processes that would eventually lead to life were set into motion. The drama of creation had begun.

And along with those dark fragments had fallen sparks of Light, beautiful envoys of the All-mind. These were centers of pure consciousness, angelic beings who willingly flung themselves into Darkness in hopes that, like seeds, they might take root in matter and grow into conscious beings capable of acting as direct instruments of the All-mind within Its creation. They fell into the midst of matter, but simultaneously they remained untouched by it, existing in a higher and yet parallel dimension. Matter was part of the great illusion created by the All-mind, and these angels of Light were like specks of truth amidst a smoke screen of deception. As it is said in the New Testament, "And the Light Shineth in the Darkness, and the Darkness comprehendeth it not" (John 1:5). These beings, it was hoped, would germinate within the bodies of worthy creatures. They would naturally pair up and become parallel with emerging and evolving life forms that were capable of acting as their eyes, ears, and hands. Using such creatures, they could bridge the gap between the All-mind and Its creation. They would be aware of both the make-believe game of creation and the truth behind it at the same time. They could be the means by which the All-mind might catch a glimpse of Itself reflected in the wild Darkness. The plan, in this way, proceeds toward completion today.

A Test

Neophyte is a probationary grade. The aspirant is exposed to the vocabulary and symbolism of magic. He adopts a new way of life and dedicates his time and energy to the goal of obtaining communion with his Higher Self, that selfsame Divine Spark of Light. He is introduced to transformational energy. For one thing, he is finding out if magical work is right for him, and the Neophyte grade gives the ego a chance to wage its war of resistance. If the student is going to bow out, this is the time to do it, before the process of change becomes irreversible. Neophyte is a test to see if the student is ready for accelerated evolution.

Those who fail to complete this grade often have succumbed to one of the defense mechanisms of the ego. And that is fine. Better to stop the Great Work in the first grade than stifle the alchemical processes of the elemental grades halfway through the transition between human and more than human. If you find the unenlightened state of mind undesirable, you will find it even less desirable to remain stuck between worlds.

The demons that surround the prison house of the human world are the inhabitants of a transitional realm, the boundary of your material prison. It is best to deal with them in a passing manner as you liberate yourself from confinement. Inside the prison grounds, you are relatively safe in the folds of the collective cultural trance. Beyond the watchtowers of the perimeter, you are safe because you are beyond the reach of *all* harm. But while banging on the doors, confronting the guards, and dragging yourself free of their restraints, you are in temporary danger. The battle is only worthwhile when you proceed tirelessly all the way through it to the liberation beyond. Backsliding and wallowing are terrible in this kind of work.

The daily routine of rituals in Neophyte will take an estimated thirty minutes. It may sound like a simple matter to set aside that much time, but be wary. There are unrecognized aspects of yourself that will soon stir to life. The domineering animal soul that keeps you from knowing yourself will become agitated once you shine Light into its lair. You may have to exert considerable effort to overcome its resistance.

Consider for a moment the mythology of dragons that hide in caves and guard secret treasures. Daily, you will call upon the power of the divine radiance to descend upon you and quicken the spark of your true self, which lies hidden within the coils of the slumbering animal soul. Like a dark dragon, your biological processes have been doing just fine up until now without any illumination. They will not take kindly to you laying claim to the treasure they guard. As they become annoyed, your behavior will reflect their qualities. You may find yourself filled with strange loathings and desires that beguile you away from your magical work.

Boredom will likely be the first obstacle. The ego has many defenses, and this is perhaps the best of them. Soon, the novelty of your spiritual practice will wear thin. You may be tempted to move on to something more entertaining and end up like so many New Age eclectics, flitting from one "interesting" practice to another and thinking there is some value to smearing yourself thinly and ineffectually over the surfaces of so many traditions. Be on the lookout for boredom and persevere through it, maintaining the routine without break. The exhumation of your soul will be successful only if you dig one deep hole rather than a lot of shallow ones.

Daily Ritual

Daily ritual is the centralmost activity in your life that will generate change. Many of the reasons for missing a daily ritual performance are quite reasonable, but you must do your work nonetheless, even if spending the time makes you late for an appointment or causes you to lose sleep. There may even be dreadful times ahead when you have to drag yourself into your ritual space to do an uninspired performance. Pushing through resistance is the theme here. Get acquainted with the animal soul and its tricks. Some of the most common excuses for not doing magical work are included here as red flags. I recommend that you start a list of your own diversions as they come up. They usually go something like this:

- "I don't have enough time."

- "I'll just read one more chapter."

- "The house must be clean first."

- "This other project is more important, because it's part of my career."

- "I might receive an important phone call."

- "I must never do ritual when I'm sick."

- "I'm tired, and it would be healthier to rest."

- "I must wait until I am calm and serene."

But also keep in mind that just because ritual is so crucial to this course doesn't mean that ritual should be the only activity. You should take special care to live in the world, stay down to earth and practical in your daily affairs, and get a hearty amount of exercise. The other requirements in the grade work, combined with honesty and humility, help to keep the imagination from becoming unruly as it increases in power. They help prevent the most common side effect of ritual magic: ego inflation.

Study

As for the scholarly work, start now by obtaining as your primary textbook a copy of Israel Regardie's *The Golden Dawn*, sixth edition (Llewellyn Publications). I will be referring to sections of it often for study and general work and will refer to it as "your textbook." Written assignments and drawings will require this invaluable book. It is best to sit down with these studies a little bit every day, even if it means adding a single Hebrew letter to a drawing as your effort for the day. Long breaks from your projects only encourage idleness and give the dawning magical persona nothing new by which to get its bearings. You are calling forth a new kind of awareness, and that requires a new vocabulary and a new systematic approach for seeing the world.

The systems of correspondence, the names of various spirits and gods, and the layers upon layers of Kabbalistic fancy are not in themselves the actual knowledge gained by the Great Work. They are instead the skeleton of theoretical abstraction upon which the flesh of experience will grow.

As a teacher, it is easy to tell which student is doing the work and which is not. Those who talk about magic only in terms that they have learned from books are the ones who are avoiding the most important part of the work. But those who relate the changes happening in their lives—the "growing pains"—and the new ways of seeing the world are the ones fulfilling *all* of the requirements.

The Magical Diary

From day one of your journey, you are to maintain a magical diary in which you make daily entries. Each entry should contain the date and time of the entry and a quick narrative of the day's events, with insights and changes that occur as you progress. These may or may not be the result of your spiritual discipline. Looking back to your diary entries from a year previous can be very revealing as to how much change you have undergone.

Each grade will also assign you certain topics to report on during certain times. These topics are specially designed to help you explore the issues that are typical of your current stage of development. By reporting on them, you are monitoring and coming to terms with problems that are common among many students. In particular, the assigned journal topics in this course are designed to counter ego inflation.

Exploring your day by journaling also helps to bring your insights from the realm of rhetoric and ritual to the realm of life. Writing helps you discover connections between study and practice, between mind and body, and between Spirit and matter. You will likely not believe that daily journaling is as important as ritual at first, but over time, cumulative effects will mount into an overall impression of transformation. In particular, writing about difficulties and frustrations helps you to draw them out, reconcile with them, and clear the mind of hidden conflict.

Your magical diary also becomes a scientific tool in which you record the variables of your magical experiments and measure the effectiveness of your methods.

Physical Exercise

Physical exercise of some kind is mandatory in this curriculum. There are optional forms of exercise presented for each grade in Appendix B. They increase in difficulty as they progress, and they are designed to harmonize with the energy of each grade.

But overall, the most important thing is that you continuously build and maintain a healthy earthly body. A strong, balanced existence in this world is a prerequisite for a healthy one in others.

Physical exercise is also required because it is one of the ingredients that balances the very introverted disciplines of the Golden Dawn. It is another guard against ego inflation. Kabbalah is very intellectual. If a course focuses exclusively on study and ritual, it builds up inner faculties disproportionately to outer ones. Willpower, imagination, and other refined traits, untested and untempered in the World of Action, can become grossly overblown and very annoying, especially to your friends. This is a universal problem for spiritual aspirants, and it is sadly stereotypical of ceremonial magicians. Extroverted activities, such as working out, can bring the student humbly down to earth much more efficiently than the most clever of Hermetic visualizations. They keep you honest about your limitations.

Establish an exercise routine and become knowledgeable about diet and nutrition. If this is new to you, the optional physical exercises in the appendix will help, because they start light.

Dedication: The Key Ingredient

The material in this and the other grades is presented in a brief format, but a serious look at it will reveal that it is quite involved and requires an enormous amount of time and dedication. Working from the information in each chapter may be a little disheartening, as it cannot take the place of a real teacher. The student becomes solely responsible for finding the inspiration, the resources, and the discipline to perform the exercises without validation, evaluation, or corrective reprimands. Let this serve as the last warning that the road ahead can be difficult and lonely. *Take personal responsibility for all efforts and all results.*

THE NEOPHYTE CURRICULUM (AT A GLANCE)
(to be practiced for a minimum of 6 months)

Daily Neophyte Formula
1. The Fourfold Breath
2. The Lesser Banishing Ritual of the Pentagram
3. The Middle Pillar
4. Neophyte Meditation

Additional Exercises
1. The Four Adorations
2. Daily Tarot Card
3. Silence Exercises

Required Reading
1. "First Knowledge Lecture," from your textbook, Regardie's *The Golden Dawn*, pages 50–59
2. *The Tree of Life*, by Israel Regardie
3. *The Mystical Qabalah*, by Dion Fortune
4. *The Sacred Magic of Ancient Egypt*, by Rosemary Clark
5. "Z-1: The Enterer of the Threshold," from your textbook, pages 331–362
6. "Z-3: The Symbolism of the Initiation of the Candidate," from your textbook, pages 363–375

Written Assignments
1. Outline of the Neophyte Ritual
2. Diary Assignments
3. Magical Motto
4. Compendium of Gods

Projects
1. Labeling the Tree of Life
2. Neophyte Temple Diagrams

Optional Implements
1. The Robe
2. The Lamp
3. The Censer
4. The Book

NEOPHYTE CURRICULUM (DETAILS)

Daily Neophyte Formula

Perform this series of rituals once per day in the order presented below, one right after the other. The only thing you need for this is a private, clear space in which to stand, about eight or more feet across in length and width. A simple padded chair (one that is healthy for posture) will also be necessary for your daily ritual by the time you reach the next grade. The idea for doing the Lesser Banishing Ritual of the Pentagram and the Middle Pillar Exercise together is not a new one. It comes from Israel Regardie's *The Middle Pillar*, originally published in 1938.

1. The Fourfold Breath

Stand, sit, or lie comfortably. It is not necessary to enter a state of deep relaxation. Merely allow your tensions to depart as much as they will. Close your eyes and visualize the skin on your body. Consider the millions of pores all over it. Notice your breath, and begin to see that the pores expand with each inhalation and exhalation, letting air in and out of the body. Feel the air penetrating and dissolving into the deepest recesses.[2] Begin to do the fourfold breath, as described below, while maintaining the visualization of air entering and exiting your body through the pores in the skin.

With each in-breath, breathe into the belly first, feeling it expand as deeply as the lower abdomen. Gradually, as the lungs fill, allow the chest to expand as well, all of the way to the top of the rib cage, such that the shoulders almost lift slightly. In this manner, breathe in to the count of four, hold the breath for four counts without blocking the throat, breathe out to the count of four, hold (without blocking the throat) for four counts, and repeat. When counting to control the breath, it is not necessary to proceed at a certain speed. It is the breath pattern itself that is most important. Proceed as slowly as you feel is appropriate.[3] Do this exercise for as long as you like, but maintain it for at least five minutes before daily ritual work. When the visualization becomes comfortable to maintain without much concentration, extend the porous nature of your skin into the depths of the body. See the flesh and bone as porous through and through, like a sponge. Feel the air wafting gently through the depths of your being, nourishing every cell from within.

If you feel dizzy or ill from the abundance of oxygen, stop and begin the ritual again after you have recovered. Over time, the dizziness will no longer occur, replaced instead by a sense of relaxed well-being or bliss.

2. The Lesser Banishing Ritual of the Pentagram

Perform this as detailed in chapter 2. Use the visualization at the beginning of this ritual and combine it with what you have learned in the mythology section of this chapter. Expand your body to fill that great chasm that opened up within the restless Light of the All-mind. Identify with the universe that occupies that chasm. Know that you are, in your ordinary state of consciousness, a miniature reflection, a microcosm, of that macrocosm. This is an example of how ritual dramatizes myth, connecting you to higher levels of consciousness. As you float in the midst of this primordial space, know that beyond its boundary resides the limitless Divine Light. The sphere of brilliance that descends to the crown of your head is an extension of that Light.

3. The Middle Pillar

The procedure for this essential Golden Dawn exercise appears here much as Israel Regardie revealed it in his book *The Middle Pillar*. You can perform this exercise standing or lying down within your circle. If you stand, turn around clockwise and face west for the Middle Pillar. If you lie down in your circle, point your head east and your feet west.

Direct your attention to the sphere of light about an inch above the crown of your head. It is about half the diameter of a basketball, and all subsequent spheres you visualize will be the same size. Vibrate the Hebrew Godname:

EHEIEH

(pronounced "Eh-heh-yeh"). Feel the vibration as though it comes from that sphere. Feel the whole universe harmonize with the sound. Vibrate it a total of four times.

See a beam of light descend into the throat and form a sphere there of white light. Vibrate:

YHVH ELOHIM

(pronounced "Yah-hoh-vah El-oh-heem") four times. This is the Godname associated with Daath, the shadowy non-Sephirah of the Tree of Life that you will learn about in your required reading for this grade.

See the beam of light descend into the center of the torso, to the solar plexus, behind and slightly beneath the base of the sternum. See it form a sphere of white brilliance there. Vibrate four times the Godname:

IAO

(pronounced "Ee-ah-oh"; *I-A-O* stands for Isis, Apophis, and Osiris).

This is a Godname that encompasses the chief characters in the myth of Osiris, which you will learn about in the assigned reading.

Allow the beam to descend through the abdomen to the genitals and groin and form a brilliant sphere there. Vibrate four times:

SHADDAI EL CHAI

(which means "Almighty living God"; pronounce the *ch* as in the name of the classical composer Bach, and pronounce the *ai* in "Shah-dai" and "Chai" as in the word *eye*).

Allow the beam to descend to the feet, forming a sphere half above the ground and half below the ground. Vibrate four times:

ADONAI HA-ARETZ

(meaning "Lord of the Earth"; pronounced "Ah-doh-nai hah-Ah-retz").

Now visualize and feel the whole pillar of light traversing the height of your body. Feel it firmly rooted in the void over your head and firmly planted in the earth beneath your feet. Light is the essence of manifestation. It is carried forth into manifestation via darkness. Feel the density of your body showing forth the brilliance within, like darkness bringing forth light.

Turn the attention to the sphere at the feet. Inhale as you draw a shimmering stream of white light up in an arc along the right side of the body and into the sphere overhead. Pause as it disappears into the brilliance. Then exhale as you allow it to stream down the left side of the body and into the sphere at the feet. Repeat this cycle slowly three more times, for a total of four rounds.

Perform the same circulation of the light again, drawing it this time up the back and down the front of the body four times.

Then draw the energy up through the center of the body into the sphere over the head. Pause for a moment and then allow the energy to explode from above like a fountain and rain down into the sphere at the feet. Do this circulation four times or more, as desired.

See the energy of the Middle Pillar expand gently, permeating an oval-shaped space around your body. Feel yourself floating in this light. The foundation of your being is pure brilliance, on which you are suspended. Remain in this state for up to twenty minutes. Allow all thoughts and tensions to be consumed or "extinguished" by the brilliance.

4. Neophyte Meditation

This meditation comes from your textbook, Regardie's *The Golden Dawn*, page 52. You may wish either to stand or to sit in your chair in the middle of the circle. If you do either, face east. Or, if you have been lying down for the Middle Pillar, you may continue to do so.

"Let the Neophyte consider a point as defined in mathematics—having position but no magnitude—and let him note the ideas to which this gives rise. Concentrating their faculties on this, as a focus, let him endeavor to realize the *immanence* of the *Divine* throughout *Nature*, in all her aspects."

Additional Exercises

The Four Adorations

This exercise comes from the beginning of Israel Regardie's book *The One Year Manual*. He presents them there as an ideal way to begin the discipline of ritual mysticism. Do these simple rituals at the assigned times of the day. They affirm your connection to the journey of the sun through the heavens. The solar Logos is central to the Golden Dawn. The sun corresponds to Tiphareth, which is the first sphere of consciousness that epitomizes adeptship. In these exercises, you begin to learn how to zero in on that principle by acknowledging the solar disk in its varying aspects.

These exercises also introduce you to the symbolism of ancient Egypt, in which the sun was usually the primary focus. The written assignment for this grade, the Compendium of Gods, will require you to do research at your library, online, or in your assigned reading to acquaint yourself more with the Egyptian deities referenced in this exercise. In-depth study will repay you very well.

In order to do these adorations effectively, you must perform the Neophyte signs. These are presented in the teachings of the Golden Dawn as secret gestures that exemplify the spirit of the grade. The Neophyte signs are the most important of all the grade signs in the Outer Order. There are two of them, the Sign of the Enterer and the Sign of Silence, and the second completes the first.

> *The Sign of the Enterer:* Stand erect. With your palms facing downward, draw your hands up the sides of your body until they point, fingers forward, at either side of your head. Step forward with your left foot and thrust your arms forward. This sign assists you in sending your energy forward toward an object of adoration. It identifies you with that object, making a connection. The connection presumably can remain open even after the sign is completed.

> *The Sign of Silence:* This sign has the effect of withdrawing the energy projected in the Sign of the Enterer and ending your identification with the object of adoration. It is also called the Sign of Horus (or Harpocrates), and its significance as such is endless. Standing upright, bring your left index finger to your lips as though telling someone to be quiet. Simultaneously stamp your left foot, gently and firmly.

Ra: At dawn, or upon rising, face east, give the Sign of the Enterer, and say:

Hail unto thee, who art Ra in thy rising, even unto thee who art Ra in thy strength, who travelest over the heavens in thy bark at the uprising of the sun. Tahuti standeth in his splendor at the prow, and Ra-Hoor abideth at the helm. Hail unto thee from the abodes of night!

Then give the Sign of Silence.

Hathor: At noon, face south, give the Sign of the Enterer, and say:

Hail unto thee who art Hathor in thy triumphing, even unto thee who art Hathor in thy beauty, who travelest over the heavens in thy bark at the mid-course of the sun. Tahuti standeth in his splendor at the prow, and Ra-Hoor abideth at the helm. Hail unto thee from the abodes of the morning!

Then give the Sign of Silence.

Tum: At sunset, face west, give the Sign of the Enterer, and say:

> **Hail unto thee who art Tum in thy setting, even unto thee who art Tum in thy joy, who travelest over the heavens in thy bark at the down-going of the sun. Tahuti standeth in his splendor at the prow, and Ra-Hoor abideth at the helm. Hail unto thee from the abodes of the day!**

Then give the Sign of Silence.

Kephra: At midnight (or upon going to sleep), face north, give the Sign of the Enterer, and say:

> **Hail unto thee who art Kephra in thy hiding, even unto thee who art Kephra in thy silence, who travelest over the heavens in thy bark at the midnight hour of the sun. Tahuti standeth in his splendor at the prow, and Ra-Hoor abideth at the helm. Hail unto thee from the abodes of the evening!**

Then give the Sign of Silence.

Daily Tarot Card

Obtain a traditional Waite tarot deck, such as Lo Scarabeo's *Universal Tarot*. Every day, in the morning, shuffle the deck. Intend to draw a card that represents an important spiritual issue to focus on for the day. Think of nothing else but that intention as you shuffle. Draw a single card. Look at it openly for several moments without analyzing or thinking on what you see. Allow yourself to become excited or moved by the image, intentionally amplifying whatever impression you get (if any). You may choose to imagine yourself peering through the card as though through a window or doorway, or you may see yourself breathing the atmosphere of the scenery in and out.

It would be acceptable at this point to occasionally use this single daily card as a divination. As you shuffle the cards, ask for insight about a current situation. Let the card sit out in the open all day or all night. Come back to it later. Reflect on it again and see if any new insights have come to the surface in regard to the issue or to your current stage of development.

Silence Exercises

Silence exemplifies the spirit of the Neophyte grade. Not only is protection from outside forces important, but containment is also a key. Not only are you establishing a barrier that protects your ritual work from outside forces, but you also are learning to keep your aspirations carefully focused within. The following exercises assist with this process:

1. **Restricting the Topic:** For one month, preferably the first month of your practice, do not talk with anyone about the following topics: magic, occultism, philosophy, psychology, mysticism, religion, or similar subjects.

2. **Listening:** For one month, say very little in your conversations. Become a good listener. When the time comes for you to speak, instead of vocalizing your opinions and experiences, inquire more about the person you are talking to. Then continue to listen. When asked about your own views, reveal as little as possible and kindly return the conversation to the other person's interests.

Required Reading

There is a reading list for each of the grades. It is designed not only to educate, but to tune in the mind to a certain level of existence. It is *not* intended as a suggestion for other kinds of ritual or meditation work. Read all of the assigned books or selections in the list of your current grade, but do not do any of the exercises that you find in them. I will stress here again that in order to gain the benefit of this curriculum, all rituals, meditations, or other spiritual exercises must be limited to those of the grade work as I present it. There will no doubt be several practices that you will come across in your reading that will tempt you to wander away from the work at hand. However, it is necessary to maintain a focus on your current level of development and to guard against the tendency to drift from one entertaining practice to another.

This curriculum does, on the other hand, encourage curiosity. If anything interests you, by all means, read about it, research it, or write a book about it if you must. But *do not* explore it via ritual, meditation, or visualization exercises. There will be times when this restriction feels like a burden, but if you persevere until the Outer

Order grades are completed, your freedom to practice as you please will be restored and will have been transformed. How do you define freedom now? You will not see it the same way when you are done.

Written Assignments
1. Outline of the Neophyte (0=0) Ritual (from your textbook)

The study of this elaborate lodge ceremony will quicken the pace of your spiritual development. That is what all of the work of the Neophyte grade in this book does, no matter what your level of actual attainment. The original Golden Dawn initiated students into its Outer Order via this ceremony, and the symbolism involved is fundamental to all that is done in Golden Dawn–style magic.

The study of this ritual for the beginner may be rough going. Perhaps not all of it will be clear to you, or perhaps you may think you understand it all already, thereby blocking your further progress. Persevere in your curiosity, and more will be revealed in time—probably long after you have completed your study in this grade.

Make your outline of the ceremony as detailed as possible. You may even use your required reading ("Z-1: The Enterer of the Threshold," for example) to add more supporting details as you go. Here is an example of a format your outline could take:

I. <u>Requirements</u>
    A. Officers
        1. On the dias
            a. Imperator—wearing the godform of Nephthys
            b. Cancellarius—wearing the godform of . . . [and so on, listing the officers]
        2. In the hall
            a. Hierus—wearing the godform of Horus
            b. Hegemon—wearing the godform of . . .

II. <u>Opening of the 0=0 grade</u>
    A. Kerux gives warning call: "Hekas, hekas este bebeloi!"
        1. Warns the evil and uninitiated to retire
        2. Known as "the cry of the 'Watcher Within'"
    B. Kerux checks that the temple is properly guarded . . .

Before you begin, draw a diagram of the Neophyte Temple (see page 116 of your textbook, *The Golden Dawn*) on a full sheet of paper. Then create little squares of paper and draw on each an implement carried by the temple officers (see page 349 of your textbook for illustrations of the implements). As you copy the ritual by hand, move the bits of paper around on the diagram to help you visualize the movement of the officers. The names of the officers and their implements are as follows:

Hierophant ("HAI-roh-font"; the *ie* is pronounced as in the word *eye*): Red scepter tipped with a crown

Hegemon ("HEH-jeh-mon"): White wand tipped with a mitre that has a cross on it

Hierus ("HAI-rus"): Sword

Kerux ("KEH-rux"): Wand of three colors (top to bottom: red, yellow, blue) and lantern

Stolistes ("Stoh-LIS-teez"): Chalice

Dadouchos ("Dah-DAH-hohs"): Censer

Sentinel: Sword

The Candidate: (blank)

2. Diary Assignments

This is a very important practice, describing changes and feelings as you progress through the current grade. You are to make an entry every day, no matter what. This you will do even if you must write something as simple as, "I don't feel like writing tonight!" Begin this practice by recording the date and time, and then write your general impressions of events of the day. Other topics you may wish to report on every day are health, emotional state, and weather. Also, list the rituals and exercises you have done, along with any noteworthy impressions. For one month each, incorporate the topics or writing practices below into your daily entry:

- For one month, do not use the personal pronoun (*I*, *me*, *my*, *mine*, *myself*) to refer to yourself in your writing. You may wish to extend this to other correspondences, and even to conversation, where possible.[4]

- For one month, include a heading called "Present Moment" and write a paragraph talking about how you are feeling right now, how your body feels, the sounds and odors in the room where you sit, the texture of your clothing, etc.

- For one month, every time you rise in the morning, immediately recall any dreams that you had during the night and, if any, record them briefly in your diary. When the time comes to make your journal entry for the day, reflect on these dreams. You may wish to continue recording your dreams in this manner from here on out.

3. Magical Motto

Create an alias. This will be the beginning of the formation of your magical personality, a separate identity that you will use to rise above the world of the four elements. In the original Golden Dawn, such an alias took the form of a motto rendered in Latin or some other language. Some examples follow:

- **Soror VNR**—"Vestigia Nulla Retrorsum," Latin for "No traces behind."

- **Frater YA**—"Yehi Aour," Hebrew for "Let there be Light."

- **Frater DPAL**—"De Profundis Ad Lucem," Latin for "From the depths to the Light."[5]

The salutation of *Frater* or *Soror* means "brother" or "sister." Fellow students of the mysteries, in a tradition that stems from monasticism, refer to each other as "brethren."

You may choose to create a magical name in this fashion, using any language you wish, or perhaps by some other creative method. The name should represent something to which you deeply aspire. Over time, the name you adopt will take on deeper significance. Label your projects and magical tools with this motto, such as your diary, your drawings, and the optional accoutrements that you will make in future grades.

4. Compendium of Gods

After familiarizing yourself with the Neophyte ritual, take note that there are subtleties that may be further conveyed by studying the Egyptian gods that participate in it.

The temple members not only play the role of the officers represented by their clothing, they each also imagine themselves clothed in the godform of a deity. The godforms are shells of magical (astral) substance created by the Hierophant before the ceremony begins. The officers step into these forms and assume them, waking up the qualities of the gods within their own psyches. The officer called the Hierus, for example, adopts the godform of Horus, thereby awakening courage, confidence, and earthly strength in his being. These energies are perceivable not only by the temple officers, but sometimes by the candidate.

A fair knowledge of Egyptian mythology is required to understand the deeper aspects of the Golden Dawn's original grade initiations. If you do not feel you have a grasp of ancient Egyptian mythology, I suggest you create your Compendium of Gods before outlining the 0=0 ceremony.

Designate a special notebook to contain your notes on the following Egyptian gods. Your assigned reading is a good place to start your research.

Osiris	Isis	Nephthys
Horus	Hathor	Kephra
Aroueris	Harpocrates	The four sons of Horus
Anubis	Maat	Set (Typhon, Apophis)
Neith	Selket	Ra
Ra-Hoor	Tum	Thoth (Tehuti)

For this grade, fill up one page for each deity with the following information:

- Greek and Egyptian names of the god

- Illustration of the deity's most common form (drawn or cut and pasted)

- Force of nature to which the god corresponds

- Aspects of civilization the god governs

- The officer in the Neophyte ritual who wears this godform

- The part of the candidate's psyche the god might represent

- Various titles given to the god in Egyptian and Hermetic literature

- Position(s) on the Tree of Life where the god would be most at home

You may wish to continue adding to this book throughout your future studies as your knowledge deepens. If you like, add the gods of other pantheons that interest you.

Projects

1. Labeling the Tree of Life

Make multiple photocopies of the blank Tree of Life diagram that appears on the opposite page. On one of the sheets, label the Sephiroth in Hebrew letters, using black ink, and number the Sephiroth and the paths 1 through 32. The Hebrew names appear in the "First Knowledge Lecture" in your textbook, *The Golden Dawn*, pages 50–59. The Sephiroth and paths you will find numbered on the diagram on page 62. Place this diagram in a special notebook, which you will entitle "The Book of Trees."

Keep the remaining blank copies handy in your "Book of Trees" so that you can record more systems of Tree of Life correspondences as you progress. Some examples of these systems are metals, gems, astrological planets, archangels, scents of incense, parts of the soul, signs of the zodiac, and letters of the Hebrew alphabet. Also, your ongoing additions—one very important, the painted Tree—will be added to this book in each of the elemental grades.

2. Neophyte Temple Diagrams

After you have finished the assigned reading from your textbook, make two diagrams of the Neophyte Temple, but do not label any of the stations. On the first diagram, label the positions in which the Egyptian godforms are formulated.

The second diagram is a little more complex. Draw a circle around each of the following positions and label them as shown:

Position Circled	Label
Hierophant	Tiphareth
The white pillar	Netzach
The black pillar	Hod
Space between Hegemon and central altar	Yesod
Central altar and Hierus in one large circle	Malkuth

The Tree of Life

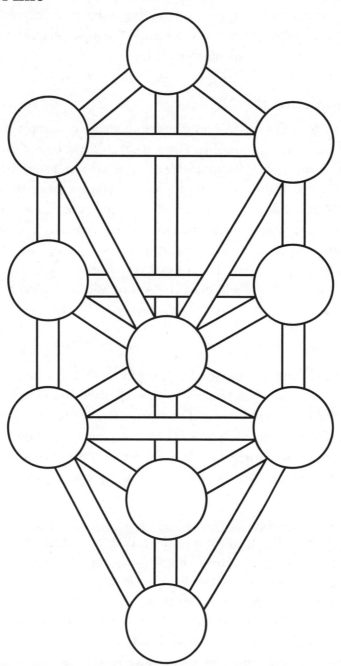

These Tree of Life correspondences will become more significant as you study. Add to them the diagram you drew for the outlining exercise, and keep them in a notebook of drawings, which you will entitle "Temple Diagrams." You will add more drawings to this notebook in later grades.

Optional Implements

It is not necessary in this curriculum to have an elaborate temple room filled with banners, pillars, and other props. If you have such a place already, this course of study requires you to clear it out. Put your magical gear away and start fresh and uncluttered on this new curriculum of transformation. If you are fortunate enough to have a room that you can devote to your daily ritual, make sure that it is empty and that it is used for no other purpose than the Great Work. You may even wish to scrub it thoroughly and recarpet or repaint. Gradually, as you progress through the gradesw, you may again add certain optional features if you choose.

There are four pieces of equipment you will be allowed to use at this point, but they are optional.

1. The Robe

This must be black, representing the Darkness from which you are extracting Light. Traditionally, members of the Outer Order wear black and members of the Inner Order wear white. It would be best if your robe were floor-length with a deep-set cowl for a hood and large bell sleeves. There are numerous websites on which you can purchase a magical robe custom-designed for your measurements. If your size is small or average, you may even be able to obtain a robe locally at a New Age store.

2. The Lamp

This normally hangs from the center of the ceiling on a chain. It should hang high enough so that you can stand beneath it and not bump your head. Make sure that it has a hood so that the heat of the candle does not rise directly into the ceiling, creating the risk of fire. The candle within should be white. If you are currently looking for a lamp (the right materials can be hard to find) and have no illumination for your optional temple room yet, it is permissible in the meantime to use four white candles, putting one each into one of the four directions—east, south, west, and north. These can be stood on the floor. (Make sure you keep your robe away from the candle flames so that it does not catch fire.)

3. The Censer

Experiment with different incense scents for now, but I recommend keeping on hand at all times some sandalwood and frankincense. These you can burn during ritual. Scent, employed habitually over time, is a powerful way of bringing your focus to specific spiritual matters. For now, set the censer anywhere in the room, but preferably in the east.

Certain scents traditionally correspond to certain invoked forces, and burning the appropriate incense for a particular exercise is a powerful practice. Following is a list of correspondences between scents and forces. Gradually obtain as many of these incenses as you can find so that you gain an experience of the ambiance produced by each. If incense smoke is not to your liking, you can also combine scented oil with water in a potpourri simmerer to diffuse a scent throughout a room.

Tree of Life	Scent
1. Kether	Sandalwood
2. Chokmah	Musk
3. Binah	Myrrh
4. Chesed	Cedar
5. Geburah	Basil, dragon's blood
6. Tiphareth	Frankincense, cinnamon
7. Netzach	Rose
8. Hod	Lavender
9. Yesod	Jasmine
10. Malkuth	Patchouli

Elements	Scent
Fire	Cinnamon
Water	Lily
Air	Sandalwood
Earth	Patchouli

4. The Book

This is perhaps the most indispensable of the Hermeticist's tools. Find yourself an ideal multi-ring binder, one that is small enough to hold open in one hand, so that you can read from it during ritual and make gestures with the other arm. You may wish to write or type up the rituals required for this grade and place them in this book so that you can recite them during ritual (that is, until you know them by heart). As time goes by, add various magical formulae to this book. The rings will make it possible for you to change the order of your rituals. Keep the most pertinent ones on top. The rings also make it possible for you to throw out old rituals that you have outgrown and add new ones to suit your current development. Please note, though, that adding a ritual book to your temple accoutrements at this time does not license you to practice rituals other than the ones outlined in your current grade.

With these optional implements, you can put on your ritual robe every day, preferably at a set time, and enter your ritual space, light your incense and lamp or candles, hold the open book in your left hand, and commence your ritual work.

Neophyte Checklist

There is no required "feeling of readiness" that you need to experience before proceeding to the next grade. The only requirement is commitment and that you have spent at least six months in Neophyte—*and* that you have fulfilled the following checklist of assignments and requirements.

❑ I now perform the Neophyte formula of rituals daily.

❑ I have completed the silence exercises.

❑ I now make a diary entry every day.

❑ I have completed the diary assignments.

❑ I am currently doing a daily tarot meditation.

❑ I have done the Four Adorations daily throughout the grade.

❑ I have read the "First Knowledge Lecture."

❑ I have read *The Mystical Qabalah*.

❑ I have read *The Tree of Life*.

❑ I have read *The Sacred Magic of Ancient Egypt*.

❑ I have read "Z-1: The Enterer of the Threshold."

❑ I have read "Z-3: The Symbolism of the Initiation of the Candidate."

❑ I have outlined the Neophyte ritual.

❑ I am satisfied with my magical name or motto.

❑ I have labeled the Tree of Life as assigned.

❑ I have completed the two diagrams of the Neophyte Temple.

❑ I have created the Compendium of Gods as assigned.

five

That Darkly Splendid World

Explosion. The Darkness shattered, unable to contain the Light. Broken shadows fell into the primordial chasm. Sparks of Light fell among them, their reflections scintillating on the tumbling debris.

In the nethermost parts of the chasm, the dark shards clutched at one another as they fell. Separated by the explosion, they longed to be whole. So, between them, they spun a web of Darkness, and space and time congealed like a sticky net strung across the void. The net became a home away from home there in the deep, and the fallen ones skittered across their web like spiders in the dark. There they became the "Watchers" as the boundaries of the universe took shape in the depths of emptiness. Their tapestry of gloom concealed the limitlessness of the Divine.

The Unmanifest became substance, and the plan of the All-mind, seemingly thwarted by the cataclysm, continued its inevitable course toward completion even as it used these fallen angels, who were now cast in the role of the enemy.

Into the web fell the sparks of Light, like stunned fireflies. But, of course, they were immortal and could not be harmed in their captivity. They existed in a higher dimension, appearing in this world only as brilliant pinholes in the shroud of time. They cast beautiful reflections of the Divine in matter, each image conveying a unique aspect. And, for a brief time, it seemed that a complete vision of the Creator would form, reflected in the Darkness. The All-mind seemed once again near to reaching Its goal.

But the jealous fallen ones pounced on the sparks of Light and spun them into cocoons of matter. The Kabbalistic tradition refers to these cocoons as *Klippoth*, or "shells," and they are maintained by all manner of crude and hurtful spirits that go by the same name. The dark angels spirited their captives away, hiding them in the depths of their kingdom of shells until not a trace of radiance remained. The divine image clouded over as the Klippoth deprived the angels of Light of visible expression. Having no visible presence and existing in another level of reality, the Divine Sparks remained complacent, as though slumbering, and had no impact on the reign of Darkness and fire. And the life that would eventually arise in the universe would have no knowledge of them.

The stifling of the Light created a terrible heat, which smoldered forth from within the depths. The universe was a seething waste of refuse from the cataclysm. Nothing remained of the original, ineffable glory. All was in a state of depravation, seemingly cut off from the perfect peace and profusion of the All-mind.

But it was a deception, after all, a fiction, a drama on the stage of which a plan was unfolding. From behind the scenes, unceasing, the All-mind exerted pressure to breathe life into Its creation. Space cleared and expanded. The heat of the primordial universe was permitted to cool. Matter hardened out of energy, and the universe as we know it today came about.

The Divine dared not show Itself directly in this realm, lest It destroy the web of space and time by making everything happen at once. If It did so, who would bear witness to the image that was yet to form within creation? Instead, It expressed Itself indirectly. By signs and symbols—and by cycles—It showed evidence: by the interplay of the three alchemical principles, by the mingling of the four elements, by the phenomena of electricity and the formation of life, and by the radiance of physical light, shining in the blackness of space. Physical light is as nothing compared to the true radiance of the All-mind, which is Light beyond anything conceivable to the mind of a material being. In the larger scheme, physical light is but a specialized kind of Darkness that conveys merely the *impression* of Divinity.

But as yet, there were no creatures clever enough to recognize that impression. Signs and portents paraded before their seeking eyes. But those eyes were seeking other things: food, sex, and shelter. It seemed that the fallen angels had won. Despite the order that showed itself forth in the sluggish medium of matter, despite the beauty of the galaxies, stars, and planets—and the blossoming of all kinds of life—there were no creatures that could experience that order and bear witness to an image within it. If God stands before a mirror and no one sees His reflection, does He exist? The All-mind was blind behind the veil of the chasm, not yet having sprouted eyes and ears within Its creation that could relay back to the Infinite any impression of Its own mystery. The All-mind quite simply did not "exist."

The universe was now like a vast shroud that gave shape to an invisible presence. To be inside of the chasm was to be *outside* of the All-mind, incapable of experiencing directly the limitless ocean of Light behind every facade. There was life roaming about within the universe, of course, on the surfaces of that obscuring skin, on dim little planets—creatures created in the physical universe by physical laws, blinded by what they could see. Their sense organs could only take part in the world from which they were made. The creatures within the universe seemed utterly untouched by the peace and unity that the web of the fallen angels withheld from them.

But the All-mind dared not intervene directly on the behalf of these material beings, trusting instead to the unfolding of Its cosmic plan. Only in the fullness of time was everything to be perfect, and at this point in the drama, it remained a mystery as to how the Divine Sparks would mobilize themselves as souls within these oblivious creatures, rousing them from the fatalistic, automated laws of matter.

The All-mind's steady pressure, through successive eons, had caused the processes of life and evolution. The fallen angels resisted that evolution. They couldn't help it. It was the *purpose* of the Watchers to bring setbacks to the plan. Entire species were lost due to the harsh limitations imposed by their physical laws. But still, ever more complex organisms appeared. The harder the Watchers resisted the plan, the further life evolved to overcome that resistance. Just as Divine Light can express Itself indirectly in the radiance of the stars, so can Its consciousness worm its way through the fiery genesis of worlds, through the interplay of the forces of nature, and through the chemical processes of the most minute particles in the dark pit. Something was developing.

From Myth to Science

Here, as I speak of biology and evolution, we enter a more familiar realm, in which symbolism is less necessary. It becomes possible to speak in terms of science. I will periodically alternate in my narrative from myth to science and back to myth again.

In regard to myth, there are many truths that we as humans cannot apprehend directly, but this should never stop us from attempting to deduce them through symbol and parable. Concepts like "All-mind," "Divine Sparks," and "fallen angels" represent forces that we cannot put a finger on but that we nonetheless can grasp intuitively. Perhaps other labels would do better. Substitute ones that work well for you, and see if the legend of the fall into matter can shed any light on the human condition.

I am not saying to you now that there *really are* fallen angels crouching within the physical laws of the universe and waiting to pounce on any magician foolish enough to call on their power. If you were to take me literally, you might fall into the trap of the religious zealot who clings to facts instead of exploring his world. We should never regard mythical references as historical fact, just as we should never regard the latest theories of physics as the last word. We can, however, employ ideas from both myth and science to gain new perspectives, possibly even perspectives that transcend the limitations of our ape-like brains. It is important for you to start developing your ability to work with the deep concepts embodied in the characters of mythology. Doing so will enable you eventually to triangulate in on forces deep within yourself, to create change from the inside out, from the mythological depths of your own "Divine Spark" to the scientifically measurable world of your physical senses.

I now resume the narrative in a more conventional, "scientific" vein:

Life has formed as a resistance to the disintegration of the universe. Why this has happened is perhaps the mystery that is the mother of all mysteries.

The second law of thermodynamics rules everything. It states that order unstoppably disintegrates into disorder. (Never mind that the process by which this happens has a definite *order* to it!) That process is called *entropy*, and entropy is the tendency of all things to decay and disintegrate. Nothing lasts.

A box filled with chemicals may serve as a good example of this. The chemicals, orderly and distinct from one another, begin to react, producing heat. Their molecular structures change, and the box gradually settles down into a chaotic, inert soup in which nothing further happens. Order has dissipated. It is possible to reverse this change by opening the box and manipulating the mixture, but yet more energy and materials must be expended, thereby producing even more disorder on the outside of the box.[1]

According to the second law of thermodynamics, there is nothing in the universe that can win against entropy. There are pockets of resistance, of course. A newborn kitten is a good example of matter organizing itself in spite of chaos. But, as we all know, cats eventually die. And even as they maintain their biological orderliness for their short allotted time, they do so at great cost, extracting a huge amount of materials from the environment, breaking them down, assimilating them, excreting the waste, and expending a likewise huge amount of energy to do so. The disorder that exists in the wake of an animal's path through life way more than makes up for the order that manifests in the creature itself.

Earth's biosphere itself is a rich pocket of resistance. It maintains itself as an orderly place in which the chemical reactions of life can occur. But to do so, it also requires an enormous amount of energy, which it gets from the sun.

The sun, in turn, radiates heat because it is undergoing its own process of entropy. The fusion reaction that generates its heat and light will eventually exhaust the hydrogen and helium that fuel it. Like the box of chemicals in the example above, our sun will eventually cool, settle down, and collapse, and the orderly paradise that is Earth will vanish within hours.

The chemistry of life is the best example we have of resistance to entropy. Even though nothing within the material world can triumph over decay and death, life provides a temporary oasis of relief in a desert of disintegration. And as we humans are the witnesses, a remarkable spectacle is possible within that temporary refuge.

The Grade of Zelator

This somewhat bleak picture of the material world is the territory that the student traverses in the Zelator grade. The word *Zelator* (pronounced "Zel-AH-tor") is a corruption of the Latin word *zelotes*, meaning "zealous person" or "zealot." The realm of material life is the official laboratory of this grade, and the student is expected to work up enough "zeal" to live effectively within it as the grades pass by.

Material existence is entirely bounded and ruled by the planet Saturn. As you may have guessed from the assigned reading so far, when I refer to Saturn, I don't necessarily mean the planet in an astronomical sense, but rather the planet in the astrological sense. This means I am talking about a particular kind of energy that happens to correspond to the movements of the physical planet Saturn. I am not saying that the physical planet in the sky is the source of that energy. Whether or not "Saturnian" emanations come from the physical planet is a matter of debate among astrologers. In any event, the forces to which Saturn corresponds are much larger than our little solar system. Astrologically, Saturn represents the web of time and space that has ensnared our divine natures in the darkness of the universe. Its energy is entropy—decay, disintegration, death, and all of the limiting physical laws.

As the second law of thermodynamics demonstrates, the realities of physical existence can be somewhat depressing. It is best that the new Zelator go forth into his work prepared with a ritual that keeps the forces of Saturn at bay—at least enough to retard their effects on his consciousness as he reaches deep down into himself to draw upon inspiration from realms beyond time and death.

Before starting the Zelator curriculum proper, learn this new ritual by incorporating it into your already existing daily routine. Do it right after the Lesser Banishing Ritual of the Pentagram and before the Middle Pillar Exercise. Do not proceed onward into the other ritual work of Zelator until you know it by heart.

The Banishing Ritual of the Hexagram is a more refined kind of banishing ritual than the one you learned previously. Rather than removing you from the influence of matter, as the pentagram ritual does, it removes you from the influence of the planets. The densest and grossest of the planets, Saturn, lessens its influence over you when you perform this ritual. Banishing Saturn banishes, to some extent, all of the planets. Saturn is a force represented very high up on the Tree of Life, indicating that it contains the potential of all the other planets within it.

As a result of the daily banishment of Saturn, you may begin to gain perspective not only over your physical environment, but also over higher-order functions, such as social relationships. The "ties that bind" will begin to lose their power over you. Emotions like guilt, envy, and insecurity will start to wane. This may be liberating for you. The resulting freedom may also be frightening.

Before practicing the Banishing Ritual of the Hexagram, brush up on your Egyptian mythology, particularly concerning the story of the death and resurrection of Osiris (Asar). The symbolism of the ritual's "Analysis of the Key Word" taps into that myth.

Symbolism of the Banishing Ritual of the Hexagram

Also before you begin, there are some sets of symbols that I must explain. The first of these are the letters I-N-R-I, which the ritual transliterates into their Hebrew equivalents, Yod, Nun, Resh, and Yod. The Latin letters, of course, represent the sign that was placed on the Cross of Suffering in the myth of the Crucifixion. The Hebrew letters, in the magic of Renaissance Kabbalah, are linked to the astrological forces of Virgo (Yod), Scorpio (Nun), and the Sun (Resh). These, in turn, are represented by the Egyptian gods Isis (Virgo); Set, also known as Apophis or Typhon (Scorpio); and Osiris (the Sun). All these symbols and characters linked together in this dizzying fashion compose a magical formula capable of awakening the power of illumination. It is called the Formula of the Divine White Brilliance. Practiced over time, it becomes a powerful weapon in your mastery over lower forces.

The magical name *IAO* is an acronym created from three of the gods above: Isis, Apophis, and Osiris. This name is therefore three different powers condensed down and expressed as one great entity. IAO is an ancient Gnostic name of God.

The word *LVX* is Latin—*lux*—for "light." (In ancient Latin inscriptions, the *U* appeared as a *V*.) The letters L-V-X are linked to the gods of I-A-O via three different dramatizing postures that you adopt during the ritual. L-V-X, then, affirms that the activities of life, represented by the myth, are actually broken pieces of the Light, or the original, ineffable glory of the All-mind. Uniting them calls forth that original brilliance.

Next, we come to the Godname *ARARITA*. This word is a Hebrew acronym for "Achad Resh Achudohtoh Resh Yechidotoh Temurahtoh Resh," or, in English, "One is His beginning; one principle is His individuality; His permutation is one." This is a reminder that the power of each planet derives from the unlimited whole, the singular activity of the All-mind.

This unlimited whole is expressed by the symbol of the hexagram itself. The hexagram represents the pressure that the All-mind exerts on Its creation, a sort of impact signature of divine power as It presses the universe to evolve and produce conscious life. (I suggest you look at all magical symbols in this light.) The ancient Kabbalists analyzed that power by attributing six planets to the points of the hexagram, with the Sun at the center. Drawing the hexagram in different ways during ritual, you can supposedly

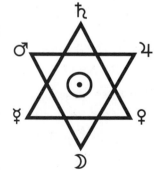

manipulate different planetary energies by affirming their distinctiveness from the greater whole of the Divine. The pentagram works by the same principle to manipulate elemental forces.

Drawing the hexagram that is composed of two interlocking triangles can be a bit of a problem in ritual, because the whole figure is not composed of one continuous line. The famous Renaissance magician Giordano Bruno fixed that by tracing a unicursal form of the hexagram in his ceremonies.[2] The more experimental members of the Golden Dawn, including Mathers himself, adopted the unicursal form successfully for ritual,[3] so that is how I present it here.

The Banishing Ritual of the Hexagram

This ritual consists of two parts: the Formulation of the Hexagrams and the Analysis of the Key Word.

The Formulation of the Hexagrams

1. Stand in the center of your ritual space, facing east. Draw the banishing unicursal hexagram of Saturn in brilliant white flame. With the arm and index finger fully extended, start above and before your head. Draw a line diagonally down to the right, stopping at a point before and to the right of your right hip; then draw diagonally to a point at the upper left, stopping before and to the left of your left shoulder; then draw diagonally down, to just before your groin; then draw diagonally to the upper right, stopping just to the right of your right shoulder; then draw diagonally down again to the lower left, just to the left of your left hip; and finally, draw back up to where the figure started. As you draw the hexagram, vibrate at the same time the divine name that charges it:

   ARARITA

   On the last syllable of the vibrated word, stab the center of the hexagram and see the fiery white lines burst into flame. Feel the awe of the divine name charging the hexagram, locking it into perfect form.

2. In the center of the hexagram, trace the sigil of Saturn in white flame while vibrating the Godname:

   YHVH ELOHIM

   On the last syllable, stab the center of the sigil as before, charging it and sealing it.

3. Then trace a brilliant white line from the center of the hexagram to the south (as done in the pentagram ritual). Draw there another banishing hexagram of Saturn with the planetary sigil in the center, vibrating the same names and charging the figures as before.

4. Continue the line to the west, doing the same there.

5. Continue the line to the north, doing the same there.

6. Finally, complete the circle by continuing the line to the east and connecting to where you started in the center of the eastern hexagram.

7. Stand in the middle of your circle, facing east, and see the hexagrams around you. Feel the heat of the flame.

The Analysis of the Key Word

1. Extend a straight right arm to the upper right and point straight away from the heart with the index finger. Say commandingly:

   I-N-R-I

   Then trace the Hebrew letters before you from right to left as you say them:

   Yod, Nun, Resh, Yod

   See them as large and formed of bright white fire.

2. Spread your arms out straight to your sides, forming a cross, and say:

   Virgo, Isis, Mighty Mother. Scorpio, Apophis, Destroyer. Sol, Osiris, Slain and Risen.

   At the word "Risen," bring your arms to your chest, crossing the right forearm over the left like a mummy.

3. Slowly raise your arms over your head like an opening flower as you say the following:

   Isis! Apophis! Osiris!

By the time you say, "Osiris," your arms should be raised in a V shape, palms upward. Maintaining this invoking stance, vibrate:

IAO

4. Extend your arms wide open in the form of a cross and say:

   The Sign of Osiris Slain.

5. Raise your right arm straight up, lower your left arm till it is parallel to the floor, and incline your head to the left. Feel a great swell of sadness and say mournfully:

   The Sign of the Mourning of Isis!

6. Bring your arms to the V position again, except this time, your hands should be flipped over so that your palms face outward and down, like wings. Feel a terrible surge of triumph and victory. Say audaciously:

   The Sign of Apophis and Typhon!

7. Cross your forearms over your chest, like a mummy, making an X and feeling tremendous relief and vindication. Say:

   The Sign of Osiris Risen.

Then, as you say the following, make the signs that correspond to the letters spoken:

L . . . V . . . X . . . Lux.

And, as you say the final phrase, "The Light of the Cross," spread your arms wide in the form of a cross on the word "Light" and cross your arms in the mummy pose again on the word "Cross":

The Light . . . of the Cross.

Pause a moment and feel the force of life pressing from within you, pushing you to evolve and grow in the face of resistance. The cross of the four elements both conceals and reveals that force.

Additional Notes on the Banishing Ritual of the Hexagram

The Analysis of the Key Word uses the grade signs of an adept (L-V-X, also known as the Formula of the Divine White Brilliance). Grade signs are symbolic representations of attainment, and the L-V-X signs are those of the Adeptus Minor grade, the first grade of adeptship and the first grade of the Inner Order. In the grades of the original Golden Dawn, the student demonstrated grade signs to show that he was ready to receive initiation to the next level.

Also in the original Golden Dawn, this hexagram ritual was not given to the student until he was ready for advancement to the Inner Order, perhaps because of the secrecy of the L-V-X signs. In this modernized curriculum, that has changed. It turns out that the 5=6 signs and the hexagram formulations are good assistants to the student's evolution in the earlier stages too. He may not be able to employ the grade signs as an adept does, but that doesn't mean he won't benefit from doing them.

Also, regular performance of the Banishing Ritual of the Hexagram retards the aging process. It is a good idea, then, to bring it into play as early in your work as possible.

Earth

Having completed your probationary period in the Neophyte grade, you are now ready to proceed to the alchemical rituals of the elemental grades. Deep within the recesses of the material husk in which you live, deeper than the chemistry of your cells, the hidden Light of higher worlds lies in wait. If you persevere in the Zelator curriculum, you may succeed in jump-starting the process that slowly unravels that husk, liberating your Divine Spark.

From one perspective, Zelator is the only grade of initiation. All other grades are simply stages of advancement.[4] It is in the earth grade that your feet are placed firmly at the beginning of the path of transformation. You are confronted with the physical world, which you apprehend through the physical senses. The "signs and portents" of the Divine are waiting for you to notice them, and the exercises of this grade prod your mind to awaken from the "fatalistic, automated laws of matter."

As mentioned, this grade corresponds to the element of earth, represented by the bottom Sephirah of the Tree of Life, Malkuth. *Malkuth* means "kingdom," and in the Zelator grade you will contact, purify, and consolidate the forces of the "kingdom" of the physical world in your aura.

The purpose of the Lesser Banishing Ritual of the Pentagram was to remove you from the influence of elements entirely. It has supposedly, at this point, established a level playing field for you to begin experiencing the elements of your being one at a time, each in controlled isolation. In Zelator, the earth aspect of your existence is sifted out from its entanglement with the other elements.

The Observer

The exercises of this grade draw your attention to matters of physical existence. They may also cause havoc with your personal life, liberating personal energy or depleting it. They may cut you off from the tribal mentality of your family and peers. They may cause changes in diet, health, and career. You would do very well to begin cultivating your inner observer—in other words, paying attention to your physical body at all times and carefully noting what is happening in regard to your sensations, mannerisms, breathing, emotions, and thoughts. Whatever difficulties arise, the student who takes refuge in the spirit of dispassionate observation will find comfort in seeing these changes as necessary—and as signs that the rituals are working.

The Disturbing Effects of the Elemental Grades

If you begin the elemental grades, make sure you resolve to finish them. Each grade will exaggerate aspects of your lower nature that correspond to one element. In Zelator, your earthly circumstances—wealth, home, body, and physical senses—will be subject to fluctuations. In Theoricus, your air-like qualities—thoughts, beliefs, fears, and habits—will become stirred up. Practicus plays heavily upon the emotions and creative abilities—faculties associated with water. Stopping your occult practice in the middle of this climb through the elements may result in a feeling of being stuck between worlds, half asleep and half awake. The elemental grades throw you off-balance until you can complete them and then put in order what you have acquired in each. It is not desirable to remain in an unbalanced state.

The Symbolism of Your Ritual Space

This book requires only a simple temple space, a patch of bare floor at least eight feet across. The basic symbolism of compass points, the cross, the circle, and the floor on which you stand are powerful enough symbols, and these symbols are to form the base of the magical system you are learning.

To illustrate the important symbolism of your ritual space, I would like to refer to an old Victorian novel called *Flatland: A Romance of Multiple Dimensions*, by Edwin A. Abbott. It tells a story set in an imaginary flat world of two-dimensional beings. These beings don't know what three-dimensional space is like, because they live on a plane that has no upward and downward directions. They know only north, south, east, and west. All they can see are the edges of other two-dimensional objects that exist on the same flat plane that they live on. These beings cannot look up or down out of their plane, because up and down, in Flatland, do not even exist.

One day, one of our Flatland characters, a square, has an encounter with a three-dimensional being, a sphere. The sphere, who cannot squeeze itself into the two-dimensional plane, cannot reveal itself all at once. It must simply pass through Flatland. To a flat, two-dimensional being, this is a frightening event, because the sphere appears in Flatland out of nowhere, and it appears as a circle that mysteriously expands and contracts from a geometric point.

The novel *Flatland* is a parable, and the reader is expected to identify with the two-dimensional beings. Just as Flatlanders are blind to the third dimension, we as three-dimensional beings blind ourselves to the fourth. We get so caught up with objects that we *can* see that we forget to recognize those that we cannot. There are four-dimensional "objects" around us that are passing through this world, but we usually fail to recognize them as such. And this is happening all the time. Every time you witness the process of change, it is an example of a higher-dimensional phenomenon passing through our plane. You yourself are such a phenomenon. As you move and change shape throughout your life, you are passing through this world, much as a sphere passes through Flatland.

Have you ever done the experiment in science class in which you place iron filings on a flat sheet of cardboard and hold a magnet to them from beneath the cardboard? The iron filings align themselves in a pattern, revealing hidden lines of force that are acting from a higher dimension. Spiritual power is like this magnet. As it draws close to the "Flatland" of the material world, material circumstances orchestrate themselves as though moved by some invisible purpose.

The story in *Flatland* is a terribly simple analogy with many unaddressed contradictions, but looking at your ritual space in these terms, you can automatically see that it is designed as a sort of Flatland. It has four compass points. Attributed to these points are the four aspects of three-dimensional experience, the four states of matter: solid, gas, liquid, and plasma (earth, air, water, and fire). These categorize for us all of the things that we acknowledge to be real within our limited three-dimensional bias. They characterize our familiar world of limited dimensions. Upward and downward, in the Flatland symbolism of a temple, refer analogously to the hidden "directions" that we cannot see, the hidden "avenues" that are gateways to higher dimensions. By our actions on the temple floor, we attempt to manipulate the descent of higher-dimensional powers. Theoretically, a spiritual being can be compelled by your ceremonial acts to pass through your ritual space.

Physics dictates that physical light is a higher-dimensional phenomenon. (Special relativity views it as a ripple in space-time.[5]) In the symbolism of a temple floor plan, Light is seen as entering it in two different ways: from above and from the east. When Light descends from above, it is called down by the balancing of the four elements. When the four elements are in perfect balance, this naturally opens a gateway to higher dimensions. When Light arises from the east, it is attributed to the life force of nature that has its source in the sun. The station in the east is a very powerful position and is taken by the Hierophant in the 0=0 ritual. The Hierophant is therefore a personification of the dawning of Light. Whether Light comes from the east or descends from above, it makes little difference. These directions are simply allusions to the pathways for higher-dimensional influences. They are gateways that lie in no actual physical direction, and they are therefore closed to us as physical beings. But we can still train ourselves, through ritual acts, to call energy down those extra-dimensional pathways. We can even create a body of Light capable of passing through them to explore higher worlds.

In the Zelator grade, you are going to be doing the Middle Pillar Exercise seated in the east and facing west, in the position of the Hierophant. By doing this, you align yourself symbolically with a natural current of spiritual energy that reveals itself in the dawning sun. By performing the Middle Pillar at this station, you gradually bring into yourself the Light of life energy, the power of Osiris, and you become its representative in this world. After that, you move to the center of your ritual space, face the direction of earth, and do an exercise that brings that Middle Pillar energy to bear on the element of earth. You are, first, calling down the Divine Light in the east and, second, carrying it to one of the four elements as a kind of initiation rite for that element. In this way, you are introducing the elementals (analogous to Flatlanders) to higher-dimensional beings. You are acting as an envoy and as a bridge between worlds.

Special Exercise: Imagine yourself as a two-dimensional being in a two-dimensional world. Imagine extending the two-dimensional square of Flatland into a three-dimensional cube of space. The cube is the shape of the temple that you are to envision yourself standing in when you do elemental grade work. It is a Flatland expanded into the next dimension. You already know what a sphere looks like to a Flatlander as it passes through the two-dimensional world. What would a four-dimensional sphere—a hypersphere—look like passing through a three-dimensional space? Our brains apparently are not equipped to visualize four-dimensional objects, but you can at least picture what it looks like as it passes through the cube: a sphere that expands and contracts from a central point. Viewing your ritual space in these ways is not the be-all and end-all of higher consciousness, but it is one of the approaches to magic that can help you tune yourself to the descending influence of higher worlds.

Building the Universe Within

To bring spiritual power to the realm of the four elements, your daily ritual work in the elemental grades takes on a special format:

1. It begins by banishing via the pentagram and hexagram, as before,

2. then by invoking the element of the grade you are in,

3. and then projecting the Divine Light upon that element via the Middle Pillar;

4. finally, it ends by banishing again.

This basic Golden Dawn formula is the key to all successful magic. It is nothing new. Its signature pattern appears in all of the practical magic exercises taught in your textbook, Regardie's *The Golden Dawn.*[6] The process of bringing Light from the rising sun and projecting it on an invoked force is the namesake of the Golden Dawn.

This ritual formula also keeps your work well insulated. Banishing rituals are placed at the beginning and end of your daily work. Combined with the practices of silence and seclusion that you learned in Neophyte, it makes for a sort of hermetically sealed vessel in which the alchemical transformation occurs. You are opening a sacred space, similar to the space the All-mind opened within Itself, in which you can create your own microcosmic reflection of the universe.

ZELATOR CURRICULUM (AT A GLANCE)

(to be completed in 6 to 18 months)

Daily Zelator Formula

1. The Fourfold Breath (Root Chakra)
2. Ascent into the Cube of Space
3. The Lesser Banishing Ritual of the Pentagram
4. The Banishing Ritual of the Hexagram
5. Invoking the Four Powers of Earth
6. The Middle Pillar
7. The Body in Assiah
8. Zelator Meditation
9. Banishing the Four Powers of Earth
10. The Lesser Banishing Ritual of the Pentagram

Additional Exercises

1. Daily Tarot Card: Labeling the Minor Arcana
2. Grounding Exercises
3. Geomancy

Required Reading

1. "The Second Knowledge Lecture," from your textbook, Regardie's *The Golden Dawn*, pages 60–66
2. "Introduction to the Elemental Grade Ceremonies," from your textbook, pages 135–140
3. "Geomancy," from your textbook, pages 524–539
4. *Astrology for Beginners*, by Bill Hewitt, or *The Only Way to Learn Astrology, Volume 1: Basic Principles*, by Marion D. March and Joan McEvers
5. *Techniques of High Magic: A Handbook of Divination, Alchemy, and the Evocation of Spirits*, by Francis King and Stephen Skinner
6. *Alchemical Psychology: Old Recipes for Living in a New World*, by Thom F. Cavalli, Ph.D., or *The Alchemist's Handbook*, by Frater Albertus
7. *Everyday Zen: Love and Work*, or *Nothing Special: Living Zen*, by Charlotte Joko Beck

Written Assignments
1. Outline of the Zelator Ritual
2. Diary Assignments

Projects
1. Enochian Tablet of Earth
2. Tree of Life in Assiah
3. Symbolic Drawing of the Table of Shewbread
4. Symbolic Drawing of the Seven-Branched Candlestick
5. Fylfot Cross
6. Geomancy Stones

Optional Implements
1. The Earth Pantacle
2. The Banishing Dagger
3. The Side Altars

ZELATOR CURRICULUM (DETAILS)

Daily Zelator Formula

Once you have finished constructing the Enochian Tablet of Earth (see "Projects" for this chapter, page 116), do this series of rituals once per day in the order presented below, one right after the other. Place the tablet in the north, either on one of your optional side altars, on a chair or small table, or by hanging it on the wall. It should be positioned somewhere approximately between the level of your eyes and the level of your heart. As you are working to finish the tablet, you can continue the daily Neophyte formula until the tablet is ready.

1. The Fourfold Breath (Root Chakra)

In each grade, this curriculum links an element to one of the chakras. Earth corresponds to the root chakra. Sooner or later, most students discover their chakras, energy centers in the etheric body. Knowledge of these centers is not essential, but it is helpful in working with the energy that is raised in ritual. In this grade, you begin by making sure that the root chakra is open (or begins to open). This chakra is called *Muladhara* in Sanskrit. If you wish to learn more about the chakras, I recommend the book *Wheels of Life*, by Anodea Judith.

Do the fourfold breath as before, but as you hold the breath in for the count of four, feel the air that permeates your body converge on the area of your crotch, between the anus and the sex organ. On the out-breath, see it radiate back out from that area, filling the recesses of the body. The Muladhara chakra corresponds to the element of earth and more or less to Malkuth. Curiously, this exercise can cause tingling not only in the vicinity of the chakra but also in the feet, which correspond to Malkuth.

2. Ascent into the Cube of Space

After performing the fourfold breath, stand as though ready to perform the Lesser Banishing Ritual of the Pentagram. Visualize yourself expanding as before. The space between your atoms spreads, and your body rapidly grows until Earth becomes a speck beneath your feet. Your body continues to grow beyond the solar system and galaxy, gradually filling the universe. For our purposes here, the universe has boundaries, and you have just expanded your imaginary body close to those boundaries, to

the point that you are now standing within a cube of space. The universe is seen as a six-sided cube, and you are therefore standing between its floor and ceiling, surrounded by four walls. These surfaces are black, like the night's sky dotted with millions of stars. Closer observation reveals a hidden pattern in those stars. Into each of the four walls surrounding you, there appears to be a black design woven. It is only visible because it blots out the stars with its lines. It is the symbol of the Jerusalem Cross[7], and it fills each of the four walls from top to bottom and from side to side.

Spend a few moments visualizing this setting around you before continuing with the rest of the Lesser Banishing Ritual of the Pentagram.

When your daily ritual work is done, take a few moments to return to the physical level of mind. (This is very important.) See your astral body diminish suddenly in size. The robe of stars expands and floats outward to resume its place as the confines of the universe. Your body of light shrinks rapidly, and there is the feeling of falling and becoming more dense. Expanding galaxies issue upward from your body as your descent continues into the realm of the Milky Way and eventually to our solar system. Feel a thud or a sort of bouncing sensation as, all at once, your body resumes its place on Earth. Resume your normal waking consciousness, and know that you can reascend to the cube of space whenever you choose.

3. The Lesser Banishing Ritual of the Pentagram

4. The Banishing Ritual of the Hexagram

5. *Invoking the Four Powers of Earth*

Standing in the center of your circle, turn clockwise (always clockwise) to face the south. Trace the invoking pentagram of earth with your right index finger, in dark green light, as you vibrate the following divine name:

ADONAI HA-ARETZ

Remember to trace the pentagram to be the same size as those done in the Lesser Banishing Ritual of the Pentagram. At the commencement of the last syllable, stab the center of the pentagram and see it burst into dark green flame, charged and sealed by the name of God that governs the Sephirah corresponding to the element of earth. In the center of the pentagram, trace the sigil of Taurus in luminous black while vibrating:

ADONAI

On the last syllable of that divine name, stab the center of the sigil and see it burst into dark flame. Give the grade sign of Zelator—step forward with the left foot and raise the right arm straight out and up at a forty-five-degree angle with the hand flat, fingers together and pointing straight. Holding this salute to the powers of earth, say:

> **Thou art the gleam upon the hoards of brilliance, the mighty presence in the light of gems.**

This is a prayer that you utter on behalf of the elementals of earth. Kabbalistic tradition holds that only humans have the ability to utter effective prayers. Prayers are a service that the magician performs to rescue the elements from Godlessness. In exchange, the elementals offer him their servitude.

Turn clockwise to the west. Trace again the invoking pentagram of earth and sigil of Taurus, vibrating the divine names as before. Give the grade sign and say:

> **Thou art the toil and texture of the fields, the patient embrace of the garment of life.**

Turn clockwise to the east. Trace the sigils, vibrate the names, and give the grade sign as before, saying:

Thou art the rumbling of the midnight depths, the hurtling granules of action.

Turn now to the north and perform the same actions, but say:

Thou art the foothold and the foundation, the anchor of the soul and the matrix of the rose. Amen.

Turn to the east, standing in the center of your circle, and give the Zelator grade sign to the east. Visualize a white Tree of Life formulating there at the eastern edge of your circle. Its light fills the circle. Holding this salute to the rising light, vibrate the following divine names and say the prayer that follows:

ADONAI HA-ARETZ. ADONAI MELEKH. Unto Thee be the kingdom and the power and the glory. The Rose of Sharon and the Lily of the Valley. Amen.

Feel the heat of the pentagrams and sigils as you see them around you in your mind's eye. Feel the awe of the Godnames that you have used to charge them.

6. The Middle Pillar

For this exercise, you should sit in the east and face west. The glowing white Tree of Life that you just visualized in the east should be formulated behind you in your mind's eye. Perform the Middle Pillar Exercise as in the Neophyte grade. The sphere of Malkuth can be visualized in the ground directly beneath your chair, or at your feet.

7. The Body in Assiah

The construction of the Body in Assiah is an extension of the Middle Pillar and is designed to thoroughly integrate the Sephiroth into your physical body. To do this, it uses the color scales of one of the Four Kabbalistic Worlds. The idea of combining the Middle Pillar with the color scales is not a new one. The oldest reference to it I have found is in a book by R. G. Torrens published in England in 1969.[8]

After performing the Middle Pillar, move your chair to the center of your circle and sit facing north into the Enochian Tablet of Earth. Turn your attention to your physical body and visualize it composed of a uniform, earthy substance. See this gritty substance as though it were a dense mass of iron filings gathered around the influence of an invisible magnet. This "magnet" is the upright column of light in your body created by the Middle Pillar. Draw a current of energy down this column into Malkuth as you vibrate the following divine name once:

ADONAI

Now vibrate the name of the Assiatic House of Malkuth four times:

OLAM YESODOTH

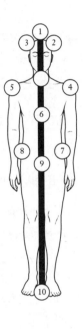

(pronounced "Oh-lahm Yeh-soh-dohth"). As you vibrate the name, see the sphere at the base of the pillar filling with the colors of Malkuth in Assiah: black-rayed yellow. The yellow rays issue from the center of the sphere and flow to the edges.

Repeat the vibration of the name four more times, this time seeing your earthen body change to the colors of Malkuth in Assiah. See your body turn black, with rays of amber streaming from its solar plexus like veins of gold in rock. The vibration of the name and the colors should be viewed as one.

After this second set of four vibrations, sit meditating in the Body in Malkuth of Assiah for at least ten minutes. See the colors. Feel the solidity, grit, and heaviness of earth.

With this exercise, you are starting your journey up the Tree of Life in its densest parts. The construction of the Body in Malkuth of Assiah is to be done daily for seven days. Following that, move on to the next highest Sephirah, Yesod.

To construct the Body in Yesod of Assiah, sit before the earth tablet as before and draw down a current of energy into Malkuth as you vibrate "Adonai." Then vibrate the name for Malkuth in Assiah, "Olam Yesodoth," one time as you visualize the black sphere with yellow rays. Then see a green ray of light rise up from Malkuth to Yesod, at your genitals. Vibrate the name for the Assiatic House of Yesod four times as you visualize your Yesod filling with the color citrine, flecked with azure:

LEVANAH

Next, see the whole body filling with citrine and glinting flecks of azure as you vibrate "Levanah" yet four more times. Meditate in this body for at least ten minutes.

After spending seven days working on Yesod, move to Hod. Call down the light to Malkuth by vibrating "Adonai." Vibrate "Olam Yesodoth" and see the black and yellow-rayed Malkuth. See a ray of green light rising up to Yesod, and vibrate "Levanah," watching it fill with citrine-flecked azure. Then see the green ray stream over to a point just above and to the right of your right hip. Vibrate the name of the Hod's Assiatic House four times as you visualize Hod filling with yellow-brown and flecks of white:

KOKAB

Then vibrate "Kokab" four more times as the colors fill your body. Meditate on the Assiatic Body of Hod for up to ten minutes. Continue on up the Tree through Netzach, Tiphareth, Geburah, and so on. (Geburah and Chesed are positioned, respectively, to the right and left of each shoulder. Binah and Chokmah are to the right and left of your head.) The name correspondences for the Sephiroth in Assiah appear in your textbook, *The Golden Dawn*, on pages 63 and 64. The color correspondences are given on page 99. You are working with World of Assiah now, so you are using the names of the ten houses (or heavens) of Assiah. This information, together with English translations, is summarized for you here as follows:

Sephirah	Assiatic Color	Assiatic House	Meaning
10 Malkuth	Black, rayed yellow	Olam Yesodoth	Sphere of the Elements
9 Yesod	Citrine, flecked azure	Levanah	The Moon
8 Hod	Yellow-brown, flecked white	Kokab	Mercury
7 Netzach	Olive, flecked gold	Nogah	Venus
6 Tiphareth	Golden amber	Shamesh	The Sun
5 Geburah	Red, flecked black	Madim	Mars
4 Chesed	Deep azure, flecked yellow	Tzedek	Jupiter
3 Binah	Gray, flecked pink	Shabbathai	Saturn
2 Chokmah	White, flecked red, blue, and yellow	Mazloth	Stars
1 Kether	White, flecked gold	Rashith ha Gilgalim	The First Swirlings

The earthen body, which you are infusing with the color scale of Assiah, is the material aspect of your Tzelem. The Tzelem on any level can be thought of as a vehicle once it is properly recognized as such and trained to serve. Clearly, this exercise dictates that your physical body is to be viewed as a vehicle of consciousness.

There are other bodies that you are yet to build in the following grades. The most important implication of this idea is that no matter what form your Tzelem takes on in whatever level of existence, it is not "who you are." Do not identify with the Tzelem, no more than you would think that you are your reflection in a mirror.

Once you have completed your journey up the Tree in the manner described above, having spent one week with the name and color of each Sephirah, it is time to move to the next step. For the remainder of the Zelator grade, after your Middle Pillar work, sit before the tablet of earth and return your attention to the sphere of light above your head. See it as a sphere of light that is the color of Kether in Assiah, white flecked with gold. Vibrate four times the name of Kether's Assiatic House:

RASHITH HA GILGALIM

Then bring your attention to the area to the left of your head and see there a white sphere flecked with yellow, red, and blue, the colors of Chokmah in Assiah. Vibrate the name of Chokmah's Assiatic House four times:

MAZLOTH

Continue on down the Tree in this manner, from Sephirah to Sephirah, in the order of the "Lightning Flash," seeing the sphere with its colors and vibrating the name of each house. When you finish with Malkuth, spread your visualization across your whole body. See all the Sephiroth in their Assiatic colors as they are situated in your aura around and within your body. Float in the Tree of Assiah for up to twenty minutes. See your aura glow white from the presence of the Sephiroth, as though their presence stimulates the arousal of quintessential energy. Intensify the visualization, making it as bright as you can. Then relax in the afterglow of your work.

8. Zelator Meditation

This meditation comes from your textbook, *The Golden Dawn*, page 63. Continue with this meditation in your seat, facing north:

"Let the Zelator meditate on a straight line. Let him take a ruler or a pencil and by moving it a distance equal to its length, outline a square. Having done this, let him, after quieting his mind with the rhythmic breathing taught in the first meditation, mentally formulate a cube, and endeavor to discover the significance of this figure and its correspondences. Let him meditate upon minerals and crystals, choosing especially a crystal of salt, and entering into it, actually feel himself of crystalline formation. Looking out on the universe from this standpoint, let him identify himself with the earth spirits in love and sympathy, recalling as far as he can their prayer as recited in the closing of the Zelator grade. Let him meditate upon the Earth Triplicity, visualizing the symbols of a bull—a virgin—a goat—which stand for Kerubic earth—mutable earth—cardinal earth."

9. The Banishment of the Four Powers of Earth

This short ritual is the same as the Invocation of the Four Powers of Earth, except it dissolves the forces of earth that have been concentrated in the circle. Perform the ritual identically to the invocation, except use the banishing pentagram. Also, you need not give the grade sign or short prayer in the banishing version of this ceremony.

   Note: You may actually omit this particular banishing ritual from daily practice. The Lesser Banishing Ritual of the Pentagram, performed last in the daily sequence, is more than enough to banish the influences of earth. The Banishment of the Four Powers of Earth is included here only to show how the daily invocations and banishments work in the elemental grades.

10. The Lesser Banishing Ritual of the Pentagram

Additional Exercises

Daily Tarot Card: Labeling the Minor Arcana

Continue to do your daily tarot meditation as before. But now, when you draw any one of the card numbers 2 through 10 of the four suits, record its corresponding planet and zodiacal sign by drawing, with black ink, the sigil of each somewhere in the card. These correspondences can be found on pages 550–564 of your textbook, *The Golden Dawn*, in a section titled "The Thirty-six Decans." Continue to do this until all thirty-six of the cards are marked, even if that means continuing this exercise into the next grade.

Grounding Exercises

1. **Proprioception:** For the entire Zelator grade, attempt to stay focused on the sensations in your body in the here and now. Feel the texture of your clothing as you sit and walk. Feel the physical sensations of emotion. Become absorbed in all of your bodily sensations, both pleasant and unpleasant. Pay particular attention to the feeling you get when returning to this exercise from your habitual distractions or daydreaming. You may wish to wear a watch that has an hourly chime to keep you reminded of this continuous exercise.

2. **Active Zen:** Once you have read the book *Everyday Zen*, do at least one month of daily work in which you incorporate the principle of Zen into some mundane household task. Your active Zen sessions should happen every day of that month, lasting from thirty to sixty minutes. Some good examples of activities follow:

   - Washing your car
   - Cleaning the bathroom floor with a toothbrush
   - Sweeping leaves
   - Weeding

3. For one month, sit quietly for at least fifteen minutes each day and attempt to remain unwaveringly focused on the sensations on your skin. Observe the different components of each sensation. Eventually, focus on one particular sensation and label its various aspects. Try to dissect it mentally.

4. For one month, spend ten minutes each day standing with your feet slightly pigeon-toed and shoulder-width apart and with your knees slightly bent. Push into the earth as though trying to push two sections of the ground apart. Feel as though someone is challenging you and you are holding your ground. During this exercise, occasionally grip the floor slightly with your toes, as though your feet were suction cups. Occasionally, bend your knees while breathing in, and then resume the slightly-bent-knee posture while breathing out.[9] Note any feelings that come up as you do this. Explore those feelings, even if they are emotionally troublesome. Also, note any desire to stop this exercise prematurely—stay alert and try to discern if the ego becomes restless as it defends itself from the release of emotion.

5. For a month, once per day, jump up and down for a couple of minutes on an earthy surface, letting everything become loose and buoyant. With each impact on the earth, bend your knees and feel how the ground absorbs you.[10]

6. For a month, become aware of gravity whenever you are walking or standing idly. Feel an invisible vector passing downward through your center of gravity and into the earth. Is the earth pushing up against you, or are you pushing down against the earth?

7. At least three times, lie on a blanket at night, under the stars. Look at the sky and imagine that you are actually above them, as though you are riveted to "the ceiling." Feel the mysterious force that holds you to this ceiling and marvel at the vastness of space "beneath" you.[11]

Geomancy

After you have finished all of the assigned reading *and* after you have constructed and consecrated your geomancy kit (see #6 under "Projects" for this chapter, page 119), you are then required to do a minimum of seven geomantic divinations for the Zelator grade. For each divination, draw the special grid of the houses (page 531 in your textbook, *The Golden Dawn*, or page 44 in *Techniques of High Magic*) to record the results. Interpret the results based on what you have learned. Do not be concerned with whether or not your divinations are accurate.

Instead of doing these divinations as suggested in your textbook—by making a random number of dots on a page—grasp a handful of stones from your kit and pour them onto the white cloth to count them, thereby generating your geomantic figures with certainty.

Written Assignments

1. Outline of the Zelator Ritual

Done as for the Neophyte ritual.

2. Diary Assignments

Throughout the entire Zelator grade, make your daily diary entries without using negative or positive judgments. Make no criticisms of anyone or anything, good or bad. Be on the lookout for the tendency to evaluate and "size up."[12] There are other ways of talking about things. Find them. Also, as you work with the Houses of Assiah, write the name of the house you are currently focusing on in your diary every day in Hebrew letters (see page 63 of your textbook). Sound out the letters as you sketch them so that you can familiarize yourself with the pronunciation of the letters. Furthermore, for one month per each, incorporate one of the following writing practices into your daily entry:

1. Do not use the verb *be* in any of its forms (*is, am, are, was, were, will be, been*).

2. Carry your diary with you. Write down everything you eat and drink throughout each day.

3. On one day of each week during the month, sit in a room where you will not be disturbed for half an hour, and begin writing. How is it that you have come to this place, doing this exercise? Why are you sitting here and not somewhere else? What made you buy this house or rent this apartment and not some other? Why do you live in this town or city? This country? This hemisphere? How did you even come into existence at all? How did your parents meet? What were the circumstances of your conception and birth? Contemplate and write about the many circumstances that have contributed to this very moment, as you sit in this room doing this very exercise.[13]

4. Include as one topic the name of an emotion that characterizes the current day. Feel this emotion in your body. Note its physical sensations. Describe these sensations in your diary.

Projects

1. Enochian Tablet of Earth

Complete this project before any of the others so that you can begin your daily Zelator formula of rituals. (See the diagram on the opposite page.) The tablet should be drawn on high-quality white card-stock paper. Carefully measure for the placement of the square and governing sigil. Record your measurements so that you can duplicate them for the next tablet in the next grade. The size can be anywhere from 8 × 10 inch to 22 × 28 inch posterboard. I recommend that you obtain

Enochian Tablet of Earth

b	O	a	Z	a	R	o	P	h	a	R	a
v	N	n	a	x	o	P	S	o	n	d	n
a	i	g	r	a	n	o	o	m	a	g	g
o	r	p	m	n	i	n	g	b	e	a	l
r	s	O	n	i	z	i	r	l	e	m	v
i	z	i	n	r	C	z	i	a	M	h	l
M	O	r	d	i	a	l	h	C	t	G	a
O	C	a	n	c	h	i	a	s	o	m	t
A	r	b	i	z	m	i	i	l	p	i	z
O	P	a	n	a	L	a	m	S	m	a	P
d	O	l	o	P	i	n	i	a	n	b	a
r	x	P	a	o	c	s	i	z	i	x	P
a	x	t	i	r	V	a	s	t	r	i	m

four picture frames of the exact same size and design to protect this tablet and the remaining three tablets you are yet to make, when they are done.

Using a compass and ruler, draw the sigil and the outside of the large rectangle first, in pencil. In the sigil, sketch the carefully planned equal-armed cross, as it is shown. On the edge of the rectangle, mark the points where the grid intersects it, and draw in the grid with ruler and pencil. Make sure that it is as perfect as you can muster, and don't be afraid to start all over if your erasures are damaging the look of the tablet or if your measurements have errors.

Now paint the shaded areas of the grid black. Black is the main color of earth. It may require two coats to make the paint completely opaque. Paint the ring around the seal black as well. Paint the arms of the cross citrine (top), olive (right), black (bottom), and russet (left). These are the colors of Malkuth in Briah, the World of Creation.

Next, use pencil to sketch in the appropriate letter for each square. Be sensitive to the space in the square, making sure that all of the letters look comfortable and of equal proportion.

Next, paint the letters in the following manner (notice how the tablet is divided like the Jerusalem Cross into four quadrants containing lesser crosses):

Portion of Tablet	Color of Letters
Black squares, upper left quadrant	Yellow (color of air)
Black squares, upper right	Blue (color of water)
Black squares, lower left	Green (a color of earth)
Black squares, lower right	Red (color of fire)
All the white squares in the tablet	Black (contrasting color of Spirit)

Clean up any stray marks by drawing in the grid lines with a high-quality black marker and a ruler. You can also retouch the squares with black paint to clean up any smudges from the colored letters. When your tablet is as perfect as you can make it, frame it.

Do not do any ritual work or meditations on this Enochian tablet beyond the instructions you have been given so far. It is important to avoid work with the Enochian system of magic directly until after the elemental grades. Remember that you can read about anything you like, but keep your practice confined to just the directions of this book.

2. Tree of Life in Assiah

Make a photocopy of the Tree of Life diagram from the end of the Neophyte chapter. Paint the Sephiroth and paths in their Assiatic colors, using the brightest, most perfect paints you can find (preferably water-based acrylics all of the same brand). Refer to page 99 of your textbook, *The Golden Dawn*, for the color correspondences. Make this diagram to the absolute best of your abilities, as perfect as you can muster. Start over several times if necessary. It should take several days, or even weeks, to complete. When you are done painting, clean up any stray marks by redrawing the black lines of the Tree with ink. Add this painted Tree to your "Book of Trees."

3. Symbolic Drawing of the Table of Shewbread

Reproduce this temple drawing from the Zelator ceremony to the best of your drawing ability, using a ruler and compass. (Regrettably, this important drawing was not included in your textbook, so it appears here on the page that follows.) Proceed carefully enough so that the completion of it may take several days. Add it to your book of temple diagrams. You may not understand its significance now, but that is okay. Just allow the mystery of it to sink in.

4. Symbolic Drawing of the Seven-Branched Candlestick

Follow the same directions as for the drawing of the Table of Shewbread above.

5. Fylfot Cross

(See the diagram of the Fylfot Cross on page 68 of *The Golden Dawn*.) Make this at least ten inches across and use stiff cardboard or plywood. Use black ink or paint on a white surface. Cut the actual shape of this cross out of the material so that you can hold this drawing like an object.

6. Geomancy Stones

If you have read over the sections on geomancy in *Techniques of High Magic* and in your textbook, the suggested methods for divination there might strike you as lacking in precision. It is not always easy to count the dots made by a pencil on paper or by a stick in the sand. Using stones will make divination easier and more sympathetic to the vibrations of the earth spirits.

Symbolic Drawing of the Table of Shewbread

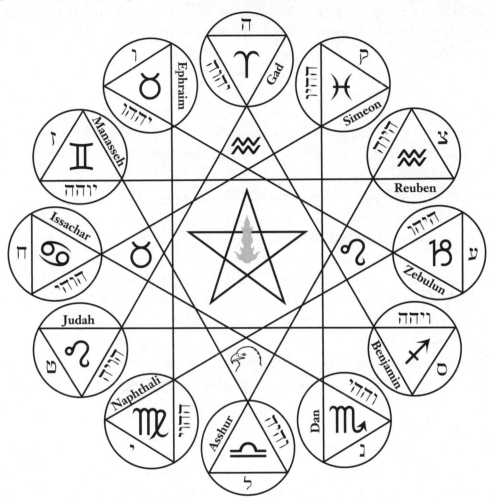

Symbolic Drawing of the Seven-Branched Candlestick

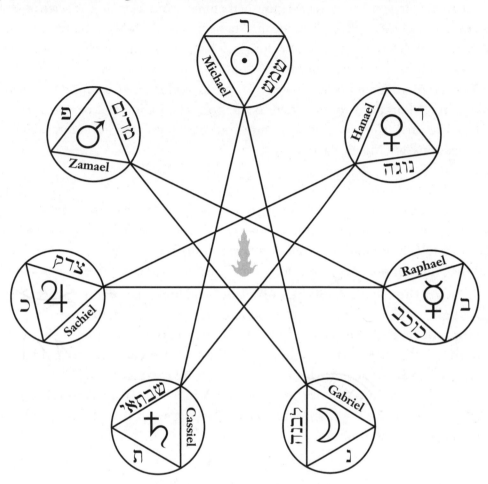

Find at least sixty small stones of near-equal size. You could go into the wild to collect them, or you can purchase polished stones from a nature or science store. Also obtain a white cloth, such as a formal table napkin, on which you can cast them for divination. Store the stones and cloth in a bag or box, on which you will sew or paint symbols of the element of earth.

Consecrate your geomancy stones via the following brief ceremony. You may make minor alterations to this ritual to suit your inspiration and personal impressions of the earth element, but make sure you stick to the basic structure, sequence of invocations, and magical names.

An Earth Consecration

After doing the Zelator meditation in your daily formula, place the stones in a pile on their white cloth in the center of your circle. You may wish to use a small table (such as a telephone stand covered by a black cloth) as a central altar.

Stand south of the box, facing north, and look down at the stones. Say solemnly:

Thou art the gleam upon the hordes of brilliance, the mighty presence in the light of gems. Thou art the toil and texture of the fields and the patient embrace of the garment of Life. Thou art the rumbling of the midnight depths, the hurtling granules of action. Thou art the foothold and the foundation, the anchor of the soul and the matrix of the Rose.

In the Name of Lord of the Universe, Adonai ha-Aretz, Adonai Melek, I declare that the Light shineth in the Darkness and that thou art witness to the pervading infinite:

ADONAI HA-ARETZ, ADONAI MELEK

(The use of all capital letters indicates that you should vibrate the names.)

In the Name of the Archangel Auriel, the Light findeth Itself in the Darkness, and the power of love is thine in the womb of the deep:

AURIEL

By the grace of the Angel Phorlakh, the seeds of intent are broadcast upon thy realm:

PHORLAKH

By the powers of the Ruler of Earth, Kerub, the black soil yields a garden from thy workings. Be ye diligent and true within through these tools of the Art!

KERUB

Let the white brilliance of the Divine Spirit descend upon these implements and fill them with its radiant purpose, that they may be unto me an aid to aspire to the Great Work!

Trace a clockwise circle in the air over the box, and within that, trace the dark green invoking pentagram of earth and sigil of Taurus, vibrating:

ADONAI HA-ARETZ, ADONAI

Vibrate the name three more times. Then say:

Spirits of Earth, thou shalt find grace and beauty in thy workings among these tools. Let them serve as a beacon to thy wanderings. So mote it be!

Put away your newly consecrated geomancy kit. Keep it out of sight except when in use. Return to the circle and give the invoked spirits license to depart:

And now, depart in peace to your abodes and habitations. Be there peace between me and thee, and be ready to come when ye are called.

Finish your daily formula of rituals as usual.

Optional Implements

If you have a room in your house or apartment set aside for ritual, you may wish to create or obtain a couple of helpful implements to keep handy there. These are optional.

Earth Pantacle

See page 322 of your textbook for a brief description of the earth pantacle. Obtain a perfect disc of wood of the proper dimensions. You should be able to hold it firmly in one hand between thumb and spread fingers, facing away from you.

Experiment on paper before sketching and painting directly on your pantacle. Do not proceed to the actual disk until you are completely satisfied with the preliminary design.

Refer to the table on the opposite page to get the following names that correspond to earth, as well as their Hebrew spellings from right to left: Adonai ha-Aretz, Auriel, Phorlakh, Kerub, Phrath, Tzaphon, and Aretz. Turn then to page 313 of your textbook. The sigils referred to are generated from the Rose Cross in the following manner: Place a sheet of tracing paper over the Rose Cross diagram. To generate the sigil for the name Adonai ha-Aretz, start by drawing a small circle over the first letter of the name where it appears on the rose of the cross. Then draw a line from that circle to the second letter. Continue by drawing a line from the end of that line to the third letter, and so on, until you reach the last letter, where you stop with a small perpendicular line. Proceeding in this way for the two words *Adonai* and *ha-Aretz* yields the following sigil:

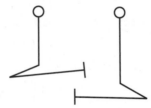

Generate sigils for the six other names (I have done only the first one for you), and when you are ready, sketch the names and sigils carefully with pencil around the border of the design on paper.

Earth Pantacle

Godname: 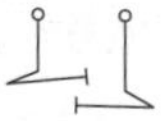	אדני הארץ	Adonai ha-Aretz
Archangel:	אוריאל	Auriel
Angel:	פורלאך	Phorlakh
Ruler:	כרוב	Kerub
River of Paradise:	פרת	Phrath
Cardinal Point:	צפון	Tzaphon
Name of Element:	ארץ	Aretz

Motto:

As you work counterclockwise around the border, each name appears in Hebrew, from right to left, followed by its sigil and a Maltese Cross ✠ to divide it from the other names.

You should plan out your design so that all six names, plus your motto (which could be in Latin or some other language), will fit perfectly all the way around the circular border without leaving any disproportionate gaps.

Before sitting down each time to work on your actual pantacle, aspire to the highest and recite the Prayer of the Earth Spirits, found at the end of the Zelator ceremony in your textbook, pages 152–153.

Coat the wooden disk with white primer. Then lightly sketch the carefully planned and measured circle and cross on each side, making sure that the lines on both sides precisely parallel one another, back to back. Paint the quadrants of citrine, olive, russet, and black first and then clean up the edges by painting the outer circle and edge in white. The colors of the quadrants are identical on either side, such that as you look at each side, olive is on the right and russet is on the left.

Now carefully sketch your premeasured hexagram on the face of the four quadrants as shown in the diagram on page 321 of your textbook. Paint the hexagram white in several coats, until no trace of the colors beneath shows through.

Sketch in pencil, with great care, the Hebrew names, the sigils, and your motto. Then go over them with black paint or ink. You can clean up any stray marks by touching up around the letters with white paint. Your pantacle should take the utmost of your concentration to make it as perfect as possible.

Coat your final work in clear acrylic spray to protect the paint. When it is finished, recite the Prayer of the Earth Spirits over your pantacle one more time before wrapping it up in black cloth and storing it for the future. Do not use the pantacle in ritual yet. No elemental weapon should appear in ritual without its three partners present. Construction of it in this grade is presented to augment your contact with the earth spirits.

Dagger

A dagger is an easier-to-use version of the sword, which is ideal for banishing via the Lesser Banishing Ritual of the Pentagram and for threatening lesser spirits. A sword can be quite cumbersome to wield on a regular basis. Spend considerable time locating a dagger that is right for you. The only requirements are that it have a symmetrical blade and that it not be used for anything at this time but the Lesser Banishing Ritual of the Pentagram. Instead of pointing and drawing sigils with your index finger, use the tip of the blade instead. When the dagger is not in use, keep it sheathed in the west of the room or out of sight where no one will find it.

Side Altars

You may also wish to construct four small, identical side altars at this time, to be placed in each of the four quarters. You could obtain four barstools or tiny tables such as telephone stands for this purpose. Make sure they are no taller than thirty-six inches. Obtain four candles of one different color each: yellow (east), blue (west), red (south), and black or green (north). Have these lit while you do your daily work. On or above the northern side altar, place the Enochian Tablet of Earth so that it faces the center of your ritual space.

Zelator Checklist

Before you proceed to the next grade, review this checklist and make sure that all of the requirements are met.

- ❐ I have completed the Enochian Tablet of Earth.

- ❐ I have completed the Body in Assiah up to Kether.

- ❐ I have been labeling the minor arcana tarot cards as they come up.

- ❐ I have completed the grounding exercises.

- ❐ I have consecrated the geomancy stones.

- ❐ I have performed seven geomantic divinations.

- ❐ I have read "The Second Knowledge Lecture."

- ❐ I have read "Introduction to the Elemental Grade Ceremonies."

- ❐ I have read the section on geomancy in my textbook.

- ❐ I have read one of the required books on astrology.

- ❐ I have read *Techniques of High Magic*.

- ❐ I have read either *Alchemical Psychology* or *The Alchemist's Handbook*.

- ❐ I have read either *Everyday Zen* or *Nothing Special*.

- ❐ I have outlined the Zelator ritual.

- ❐ I have completed the daily diary assignments.

- ❐ I have painted the Tree of Life in Assiah.

- ❐ I have copied the symbolic drawing of the Table of Shewbread.

- ❐ I have copied the symbolic drawing of the Seven-Branched Candlestick.

- ❐ I have drawn the Fylfot Cross.

six

The Mind Born of Matter

The tyranny of entropy tumbled on. The forces of the physical world inevitably, through mishap or the wear of time, overwhelmed and snuffed out every creature that rose within their clutches. But evidence of the concealed Light continued to well up through the wreckage. More and more complex creatures came forth. Life is the only real force in the universe. The dark angels are fictional characters, after all, their true nature stemming from the restlessness of the Light itself.

Though life comes in the pitiful forms of flies laying eggs in carrion and moss growing between stones, nothing can conquer it in the fullness of time. It will inevitably have its way. It was only a temporary setback that the All-mind had not yet found a vantage point from which to see Itself.

Inevitably, in the bowels of time and space, in one of those swirling pools of stars, on a planet circling a typical sun, there arose a form of life into which the Divine Light entrusted Its awareness. The sparks of Light that had been lost for so long took root within human beings. There they embedded themselves, still hidden in their parallel dimension, waiting for the proper conditions that might stir them to life. The drama of creation would be their stage—if only something could rouse them forth to express themselves in the medium of matter.

Science

Life as we know it probably began when the complex molecule RNA appeared. It is a mystery how this happened, but RNA was a clump of atoms linked in such a way that it had the ability to snatch chemicals from the environment and use them to make copies of itself. It was in this very basic way that eating and reproduction first appeared. Scientifically speaking, consumption and reproduction are the most elementary principles of life. But the chemical structure of RNA was quite fragile, and its pattern would degrade within hours.[1] Anything made up of it was microscopic and short-lived.

Eventually, RNA, perhaps by accident, formed its masterpiece: the DNA molecule. This was a much more durable and complex configuration than the first. Despite the fact that DNA was made from physical laws, it was amazingly resistant to the evils of entropy. Its chemical behavior actually served to *maintain* its pattern rather than degrade it. As such a self-maintaining structure, it became a durable reference for the design of living tissue. Larger, longer-lived organisms were now possible. We humans are in fact constructed by the chemical interplay of DNA and RNA.

It was an effective design. A single molecule of DNA, governing from within each cell of an organism's body, now served as a "digital" library of design specifications. In a computer-like manner, its configuration dictated instructions for assimilating and building, which the surrounding RNA obeyed through chemical chain reactions. DNA is composed of four different lesser molecules: adenine, cytosine, guanine, and thymine. These component molecules link together in the molecule by grouping themselves in sets of three. Therefore, there are four "letters" (conventionally known as A, C, G, and T) to the alphabet of a molecular language that speaks entirely in three-letter "words." And instead of being written on pages, the words of this language were arranged in sequence in a very long double spiral, coiled up inside the nucleus of every cell.[2]

With this new development, the role of RNA changed. RNA molecules acted as engineers, using the digital library of DNA and maintaining it as a reference by which to make all of the different kinds of cells in an organism.[3] Life was possible on a grander and more lasting scale now, because DNA is so durable and its structure can replicate almost flawlessly. Almost.

The irony of biology is that a species can survive change because it is vulnerable to change. You may have heard the famous quote from Nietzsche: "That which does not kill us makes us stronger." The physical world made it difficult for life to remain the same, because there were so many toxic substances and energies that interfered with the perfect replication of DNA. Variation in the design of an organism could occur due to damage to its DNA sequence. These variations happened often, but most of them were very slight and barely noticeable. Those design changes that made for more efficient eating and breeding served to proliferate some organisms over others. Changes that created deformities tended to hasten the death of the creature. Inefficient designs disappeared naturally from the face of the earth, as fate selected in favor of the more effective design—what is known as "survival of the fittest." This process of natural selection is slow, but millions of years of it can produce some remarkably diverse beings, each of them efficient in its own way. The exploding abundance of life on Earth has been brought about primarily by the chemistry between DNA and RNA, and secondarily by the harsh conditions of the material world: environmental changes, molecular accidents, and horrific mass extinctions of the obsolete.

This is an important point, for it means that the mind-boggling genesis of humanity can be explained in terms of random chemical activity. We tend to think that a super-intelligence or "god" is required to build such a machine. We tend to think that such beings as ourselves could not possibly have been thrown together by accident, and this is of course true if you assume that we simply appeared instantly from the mud bank of a river in Eden. But looking at life in terms of natural selection demonstrates that the random-chance mechanics of the molecular world can whip together a complex organism when they are given billions of years of trial and error to do so. This is possible because complexity, as we will see, often serves to proliferate a species. Therefore, we find ourselves in a complex state—each of us having about seventy-five trillion cells in a body supported by the interaction of systems, tissues, and chemical reactions beyond count.

To resume the narrative, molecular chemistry had produced life, effectively tossing a gauntlet into the face of entropy. The very chemical reactions that were part of matter's steady disintegration into chaos had somehow been diverted into producing organic structures of self-maintaining order. In the universe's steady journey toward disintegration, there appeared this oasis of resistance. Life is like an eddy in a river that empties into the sea. This is what a living being sometimes looks like to an adept who is acutely aware of impermanence, like a stream of disintegrating matter circulating through a steady pattern on the way to oblivion—a stationary whirlpool in the river of entropy.

The living clumps of protoplasm that formed the population of Earth's first multicellular organisms provided safety in numbers, making DNA even more successful at reproduction. The earliest communities of such clumps were probably sponge-like tubes of thermophilic bacteria that fed on chemicals jetting from volcanic vents on the ocean floor.[4]

But life in the physical world is harsh, and organisms that were rooted to one spot were at the whim of circumstance. If the earth stopped venting hot water in their vicinity, entire communities of tubeworms simply died. Whenever the environment changed for the worse, the individual organism was doomed unless it could adapt instantly or transplant itself. Mobility was therefore another advantage. The terrible physical laws that threatened life only forced it to adapt over millions of years, to become more durable, capable, and mobile.

And it so happened that creatures evolved that could roam free and without roots to nourish themselves—as long as they fed upon other organisms frequently. They developed sinister ways of hunting and eating each other, thanks to the evolution of a nervous system and sense organs. The animals with more sophisticated weaponry and locomotion tended to fare well and survive to reproduce in large numbers.

Amidst such ferocious competition, there eventually arose an animal with the most sophisticated of weapons: intelligence. It had no highly specialized claws and teeth, no great speed or agility. Such crude accoutrements are not what would make the ultimately successful animal.

It turned out that a highly specialized body was not the best survival strategy, since a species could still be killed by climatic changes that rendered its "accessories" obsolete. A species of bird with a beak that specializes in cracking open only one kind of seed will die when conditions no longer favor the plant that produces that seed.

Nor was it a complex new instinct that made this new animal prosper. Instincts are like built-in programs that cannot be changed without the harsh process of natural selection intervening to redesign the species itself. A squirrel relocated from Florida to the tundra of Siberia cannot discard its old foraging habits and learn new ones. It simply dies. No matter how perfect an instinct is, it is hopelessly hard-wired into the animal's body, and its resulting inflexibility makes its host species just as vulnerable to changes in habitat. When the environment changes, a specialized behavior can be just as much a liability as a specialized body part.

To make the ultimately successful animal, instant, on-the-spot behavior modification was called for. But that required a very complex nervous system, one capable of changing its own programming without waiting for a change in design. The first humans had very unremarkable bodies. They seemed terribly vulnerable to the creatures around them, which bristled with exaggerated teeth, claws, and poisons. The human weapon was less obvious. It was hidden within, and it was more powerful than any that had come before.

Humans as a species had not only relinquished their physical gifts. Even more noteworthy is that they had begun to lose their instincts. A new kind of programming was taking over.

The new creature, *Homo sapiens*, had routine survival behaviors, of course, but these were not built-in. Their routines could be changed to suit a changing environment. Even in catastrophes like the Ice Age, the smartest humans, who could modify their hunting and gathering behaviors on the spot, easily adapted. Meanwhile, other species around them died out. It was the supersophisticated human brain that made survival easier than ever before.

At this point in the narrative, it is time to unmask one of the chief characters in the human drama, the one that has been directing mankind's destiny up until the present. It is clear that, in the case of humans, instincts were no longer in charge of survival. That responsibility had been handed over to intelligence. But who or what had orchestrated that change?

To make this point, it must first be borne out that, in a human's progress through life, the brain is not the one who calls the shots. It is not the wise governing "parent" of the body, as is so arrogantly assumed by the civilized person. Rather, the reverse is closer to the truth. The body is the *mother* of the brain. Over millions of years of evolution, the body has gradually "given birth" to it. This idea turns most common thinking upside-down, but the study of evolution clearly shows how natural selection, in many cases, favors clever nervous systems. Brains do not evolve bodies. Bodies evolve brains to help them survive.

We appear to have free will, stretching forth a hand to fulfill whatever desire comes to the surface. We assume that we have risen above nature and that we are bending it to our independent fancy. But what is a brain free to do? Free to obey any desire that nags it from within the body? Free to fight or flee whenever visceral fear commands it?

The brain does not use its talents of its own volition, serving only itself. Few people dare to pause and question who or what supplies the desire that gets us to stretch forth that hand and pluck that apple. There is a much more fundamental principle governing a human being than that of his highly evolved nervous system. His self-proclaimed role as master of the world is actually a delusion that conceals (and not very well at that) the true governor of human progress. Fundamentally, we are each of us controlled by something else.

Biologists identify the DNA pattern, the human genes, the molecular "computer chips" of our cells, as the true directors of human affairs. (What were you expecting me to say, "God"?) The brain has been evolved to be an instrument in the service of its mother, the body. It makes sure that the genes within that body succeed in their singular purpose. It is like a subservient computer that coordinates the efforts of a large clump of living molecules. If it did not do as it were told, it would not have come this far.

Yes, the mandate of eating and breeding that you and I constantly feel has been dictated not by the brain, not by "ourselves," but by those molecules in the nuclei of our cells. The humbling truth is that the brain actually is dependent on them for its very existence, its structure, and most of its programming. It is only clever because cleverness is an asset to DNA, yielding success in the survival game. It exists because its gifts serve to proliferate the molecules of life. The sad truth is that humans are self-deluded pawns in a game of organic chemistry. The brain reminds me of the boss who proudly states, "I'm in charge," while his employees laugh in the background and continue to do the actual work.

But this brutal realization is not the end of our biology story. It is not a defeat. Something bizarre has happened in the evolution of the human brain. It is clearly a more advanced organic computer than that of other animals. A significant amount of its programming is not set in stone. For example, compare a human to a wildebeest. A wildebeest calf can walk within minutes of being born. Its ability to walk is instinctively wired into its body. Therefore, the manner in which different wildebeests gallop varies very little between them. They all move the same way in the herd, each animal's trot a near perfect copy of the others. Humans, by contrast, have to *learn* the process of locomotion. It takes *months* to learn how to walk, and each person's gait is distinctive because of the way that he develops it. From person to person, there are many differing subtleties. There are fundamental similarities, of course, but the human mind is capable of honing movements in such diverse ways that it produces a stupefying variety of mannerisms.

From the delicate brush strokes of the artist, to the extreme dexterity of the jeweler, to the reality-bending feats of the kung fu master, humans train themselves to move in a diversity of ways that is light-years beyond any other animal. This kind of learning makes for an entirely different kind of organism, one capable of tailoring its responses a thousand times faster to any environment on the surface of the planet—and beyond. A lizard cannot acquire a winter coat to help it survive in a colder climate. But a human makes such changes without having to die to make room for other humans who have the proper design variations. He can relocate and become a different person, adapting to a new climate with a wardrobe, earning his living in an entirely different way over a short span of time. He can wield a bizarre variety of weapons instead of waiting a hundred thousand years for his species to evolve them. He can build his own artificial environment and sit comfortably within it while life around him perishes at the whim of the weather. He can design and put on equipment that allows him to breathe underwater and in the depths of space. No other life form can claim such adaptability.

Most significantly, the human brain is so flexible that its programming is beginning to slip free from the mandates of its genetic design. Eating and breeding are old motives, and they are, for a rare few individuals, beginning to take a back seat to new ones. They are falling into the background, yielding to concerns that seem to come from some other place besides the laws of matter. The routines and activities of our minds have indeed risen above nature. They have been cut off from the source—cast out of the garden, so to speak. In a very true sense, we have the potential to be more than animals.

Because our brains have evolved to rely less on design and more on the ability to change their own programming, our survival routines can come from outside sources instead of from the trial-and-error drawing board of evolution. It is possible for you, a creature of matter, to liberate your thoughts and feelings from their million-year-old master. It is possible for you to be more than biochemistry. More than human, even.

Consider the majority of humans around you and their obsession with survival. What appears to be a sophisticated taste in automobiles may actually be part of the attempt to gain status, something that helps one mammal survive and proliferate its genes over another's. The spirit of patriotism may be little more than a superamplified territorial urge, a drive to protect one's own gene pool. Love between mates may exist primarily to assure a partnership that rears offspring. Brotherly love and charity serve the mandate of survival just as well. Feelings of altruism generate behavior that maintains the numbers of the species. Natural selection favors compassion as much as it does competition. And even the "higher order" learning of the university does little more than indoctrinate countless pawns into a system of thought that makes humans successful at survival. That these institutions remain sacred to us just indicates that we have not yet experienced something more.

Culture itself has been the most significant development in our evolution. By means of the most advanced nervous system yet, there emerged into the world of matter a strange new knowledge base, a new source for our programming. It resonated and spoke to humans not from within their bodies, but from without, from the relationships they had between each other. Survival demanded of humans that they drop their instincts and obtain their new programming not from biological "hardware" but from cultural "software." The social network of tribes and communities became the means by which survival routines were to be downloaded into individual brains.[5] You and I live within the dictates of at least one culture. The Western world, with its Judeo-Christian value system, is one of the most overbearing and successful systems of survival that the world has yet seen. It may become the dominant value system on the planet (if it hasn't already). Consciously tapped, it becomes a potent and dangerous magical power source.

The miracle of culture is made possible, of course, by language. If humans have any instinct at all, then ability to use abstract language is clearly the chief among them.[6]

This new human organism was an incredible leap in evolution, but, alas, it was still just an animal. Language and culture do not an awakened mind make. Perhaps I should repeat that for emphasis: the accumulation of intelligence is not the same as spiritual awakening. One of the biggest mistakes that Westerners make is to assume that knowledge equals enlightenment. It doesn't matter how smart you are if you insist on remaining blind to the trappings of your own programming. There are so many examples of suffering intellectuals around us that I need not elaborate further.

Intelligence, instead, is a mere tool that makes awakening possible—if only we will grab hold of it and apply it to that purpose. Though survival can be regarded as important, spiritual awakening comes about when the biological motives take a back seat to new ones. There is a new way of life possible for each of us, if only we could rise above our genetically programmed imperatives.

This is the secret human potential (hidden in plain sight) that appears to have come about by accident. A summary of its evolution goes something like this:

1. The harshness of physical laws made intelligence necessary for DNA's survival.

2. DNA generated that intelligence as its slave to ensure that survival.

3. Intelligence makes it possible to awaken motives that exist above survival.

Eating and breeding may still be important, but it just might come to pass that there is more to explore than that. There are other worlds lying dormant within a human being. Intelligence may be the servant of biology, but it has the ability to transform that biology and to liberate a hidden treasure from within.

Such an awakening has little to do with a molecule's peculiar talent for making copies of itself. But here we are now, on this earth, contemplating our own existence, wondering if there is more to life than food, bank accounts, and breast implants. A human being's intelligence can be manipulated in such a way as to produce a mysterious transformation. There are exercises that you can do to make this happen. As the old saying goes, "Knock, and it shall be opened to you." Clearly, in most of us this self-liberation has not happened yet. The possibility, nonetheless, is earth-shattering.

Myth

The Watchers became jealous. They could sense that humankind's mercurial intelligence provided the potential for the awakening of the Divine Sparks within matter. The imprisoned Light had been active all this time. Like fallen seeds, the sparks had taken root in this species. An individual human, because of evolution, had the potential to become conscious eyes and ears of the All-mind within creation. The very resistance of the enemy was bringing the divine plan to fruition. In each human there emerged the potential to have contact with a Divine Spark, to have a soul, Higher Self, or "Holy Guardian Angel." The enemy angels now took a more concentrated interest in humans, forming a plan to thwart the All-mind from realizing Itself. The cosmic "battle" between the Light and Darkness descended from the macrocosm of the universe to the microcosm of human flesh.

The condition of evolving humanity, as I describe it so far, demonstrates mankind in the Garden of Eden. As animals, we were one with nature. There was no awareness of mortality or death. We just carried on with feeding, playing, and reproducing. Ignorance was a type of bliss in comparison to an understanding of human frailty and mortality that comes with self-awareness. But the evolution of self-awareness, the experience of being cast out of paradise, is what made possible the cultivation of *divine* awareness. A human has the potential to remake himself into a vehicle through which the spark of Light within him can free itself from the dark pit. His falling from grace is part of the process. By becoming aware of his faults, he gains the potential to rouse himself from Darkness. By the right methods, a person can become the eyes and ears of the Divine in this world, fulfilling the plan of the All-mind to know Itself through incarnate experience. This, no doubt, agitated the Watchers. They hovered close to humanity. According to the mythology of the ancient *Book of Enoch*, they thwarted the divine will ingeniously by diversion and distraction. If the gift of intelligence could be used to bring about awakening, it could also be twisted against itself, to deceive and to imprison. So the fallen angels became teachers.

It is alleged that the evil angels, lead by a Lucifer-type figure named Azazel, descended to Earth and mated with women, rearing powerful offspring, giants who devoured the food supplies of humans, humans themselves, and eventually each other. The angelic horde of Azazel taught men

> to make swords, and knives, and shields, and breastplates, and made known to them the metals of the earth and the art of working them, and bracelets, and ornaments, and the use of antimony, and the beautifying of the eyelids, and all kinds of costly stones, and all colouring tinctures. And there arose much godlessness, and they committed fornication, and they were led astray, and became corrupt in all their ways . . . And as men perished, they cried, and their cry went up to heaven.[7]

Four archangels petitioned the Lord of the universe to intervene on behalf of creation and to send a flood to destroy the evil giants and the evil men who had been corrupted by the angels' teachings:

Thou seest what Azazel has done, who hath taught all unrighteousness on Earth and revealed the eternal secrets which were in heaven, which men were striving to learn . . . and they have gone to the daughters of men upon the Earth, and have slept with the women, and have defiled themselves, and revealed to them all kinds of sins. And the women have born giants, and the whole Earth has thereby been filled with blood and unrighteousness.[8]

The arts and sciences taught by the dark angels ran rampant in the cultures of the people of Earth. Humans had just developed the potential to liberate themselves from the mandates of the flesh. But before they could begin doing this, the angels gave to them ways of thinking that they were not yet ready to handle. They would make sure that humanity's powerful brain had the power to delay and distract itself with its own gifts rather than liberate consciousness from the corrupting influence of physical laws. And, mythologically speaking, this is the predicament we find ourselves in today.

The Fracturing of Consciousness

What is this myth talking about? What could it represent about our evolutionary past?

Naturally, an animal that is born without instincts or specialized abilities is going to be very helpless at birth. Its mind is a blank slate, its body defenseless. In addition, the culture into which the baby is born takes a long time to educate him into its peculiar survival routines. Babies were feeble, so the females who nursed them had a full-time job on their hands: protecting, teaching, clothing, and feeding. Women needed help raising children. They spent most of their energy on domestic affairs, on repetitive and routine tasks. Constant vigilance was required of them to protect the young. Men, who cannot nurse young, did not have to stick around so much, so they began to help by specializing as hunters. Killing and bringing home meat became the man's role. Hunting excursions, marked by brief but intense periods of concentration, danger, and adrenaline, required of men that they develop the power to detach themselves from their feelings to focus on the kill. Men became increasingly specialized as killing machines. To this day, we still talk about "bringing home the bacon." This peculiar division in sex roles had a monumental impact on the species.[9]

Here we come to the chief stumbling block thrown into the spiritual path of humanity. A severe split occurred in the human brain, mildly schizophrenic in nature. The right and left lobes of the human cerebrum are functionally different. This phenomenon has developed in some other vertebrates, but nowhere in nature is it as uniquely pronounced as in humans. The development of specialized roles for the sexes, along with the simultaneous development of culture, caused a split to occur between humans and nature, particularly between men and nature. To illustrate this, I must first disclose what modern research says about each hemisphere of the cerebral cortex.

The right hemisphere clearly resembles the older version of humanity's brain. It is largely unconscious, holistic, and image-oriented. It is plugged directly into a Garden of Eden–like consciousness. The right brain is one with nature, with no separation and no self-awareness. Feelings and instincts are immediately accessible to it. Time does not exist for it. Being image-oriented, the right brain knows very little about language, because language is sequential and time-based. The realm of the artist, the right brain speaks and learns by images, and these images have a direct impact on our deepest biological processes.[10] Many animals move about in a right-brained manner, with no self-awareness, no shame, and no worry—truly in the Garden of Eden. This kind of consciousness I will refer to as "immanent" in nature—that is, existing within nature, unified with it. In regard to the right brain, recall for yourself briefly the role of the Nephesch in the Kabbalistic schematic of the soul.

The left brain behaves differently. It acts as though it were disconnected from the world. It is an accessory to, and an outgrowth of, the right brain. It is, as it were, once-removed from biology. In the womb, the left brain begins to develop *after* the right.[11] Qualities of the left brain involve self-awareness, the ability to think in ways that are divorced from the world—abstractions, analysis, duality, language, and mathematics. It thinks grammatically, sequentially, and categorically, cut off from the holistic, timeless realm that lies at the heart of nature. The left brain's type of awareness is essential for making decisions and comparisons. It is divorced from most of the emotions, which allows it to act in a cold and calculated manner. It seems to have developed when humans began speaking grammatically, such that sequential cause-and-effect thinking began to be the keystone to the survival of the species. The consciousness of the left brain I will refer to as "transcendent," as having risen "above" nature, for it truly sees itself in this light. Recall for yourself here the Ruach and its role in the Kabbalistic soul.

Males specialized in left-brained, transcendent consciousness. To kill in the hunt, they required cold, calculated detachment. Killing made men powerful. Bringing home meat gave them elevated status at home and brought them the sexual favors of the women. Their lives were cut off from the day-to-day minutiae of domestic life. Constant vigilance over little details is not a trait for which men are known. Husbands are notoriously absent-minded babysitters.

Curiously, females retained a stronger affinity for the right brain than males did. They stayed at home doing repetitive tasks. Vigilance was required to keep children safe. Therefore, women were constantly tuned in to their surroundings as opposed to living for the short spurts of heightened concentration. Their retention of this connection to the earth made them sacred to men. The first spiritual traditions that surfaced involved the worship of the Goddess, the womb of nature itself, to which women were closer, because their brand of consciousness was immanent in nature.

Just as the characteristically masculine left hemisphere of the brain is a specialized function that "rises above" the right, so did men rise above women in status. But in the earliest days, the power of the feminine was still acknowledged as superior to the masculine, even as it took a passive role in the social hierarchy. Men both feared and worshipped the Goddess, maintaining a healthy respect for something greater than themselves—even though they specialized in a faculty of consciousness that gave them the power to dominate it and abuse it for personal gain. Ancient Sumerian kings ceremonially acknowledged their subservience to the Sumerian goddess of the earth, Ninhursag, by referring to her as "Mother." The woman, though characteristically passive, was seen as a sacred doorway to the womb of nature herself, and as the very font of kingly power.

To the mind that had risen above nature, the earth itself was a great mother. Living human bodies came from it and returned to it in death. Women were the gateway from its invisible underworld, from the true machinery of life that looms backstage to the drama of the natural world.

The Goddess in her positive spring and summer aspects was the gate of life. She took beautiful or radiant forms within various cultures: Isis of the Egyptians, Brigit of the Celts, Demeter of the Greeks. The Goddess in her autumn and winter aspects was the devouring mouth of death. In this role, the face of nature was depicted as a terrible old crone or a dark enchantress in veils. Nephthys, the Cailleach, and Hecate are examples of the shadow sides of the above-mentioned goddesses—though the names I use here are somewhat civilized versions of a more fearsome goddess, the name of which is lost but the image of which still looms in the oldest archaeological finds.

Look at trump number 6 from your tarot deck, the Lovers. The woman in the card looks upward, directly at the angel. It is as though the cloud cannot obscure her connection to a higher plane. She is aware of the source. The man is blinded by the cloud. For his connection to the source, he looks toward her. This is just one subtle illustration of an occult secret—that the feminine aspect of consciousness is the gate through which the masculine consciousness can apprehend the Divine. Recall again that the feminine Nephesch conveys images of the Higher Self to the masculine Ruach, like a pool of water reflecting the sky. This is a very important point. The original tradition of Goddess worship was an intuitive understanding that the role of intelligence was subservient to the body and indeed was little more than an instrument of it. The stuff of biology was regarded as the face of the Goddess, the dark Earth Mother with her mysterious powers of life and death that dwell within the obscurity of matter. The Ruach cannot exist without the Nephesch, from which it rises into the world. Recall that the body is the evolutionary mother of the brain.

But eventually, the elevation of status that the left brain afforded to humans (particularly to men) produced an imbalance. The ability to push aside one's feelings, to think dispassionately and objectively, made humans very powerful. They developed ever more calculated and systematic ways of surviving. Culture evolved faster than the flesh. Abstract concepts like ownership began to exaggerate the instinct of territorialism. Status created the artificial entity that we today call the *ego*. The "I" of self-awareness became separated from nature, viewing the physical world as though through a window from a transcendent, exalted world. The activity of the left brain projected onto nature a sort of false world that was like a transparent, intellectual overlay marked with labels, boundaries, and categories. Labels singled out objects, territories, and people from each other. The world was no longer whole, but fragmented by artificial boundaries and contrived systems of correspondence. Humans prospered mercilessly by means of this new applied intelligence (almost as though some invisible force were instructing them in a science that they were not yet ready to handle). The left brain was so successful that humans (especially men) began to deify the left brain and to identify with it. The consciousness of the whole race became trapped in this web of artificial lines and compartments, losing gradually its identification with nature, forsaking her for the artificial realm of abstract laws and values. The transcendent consciousness got us to value its way of thinking over the older, immanent consciousness. It forgot that it was a child of Mother Earth, without which it could not exist. The only thing that maintained a respect for the feminine and its holistic view of the world was the ongoing veneration of the Goddess, and as you and I know, that tradition has not fared well side by side with the worship of the abstract mind. It was inevitable that the left brain, encouraged by its own successes, would have a falling out with the right.

Much as the left brain liked to think that it was a god, *it was not*. Its transcendence is an *illusion*. Even as it believed itself risen above nature, the human brain was still created by and subject to natural laws, and was conditioned by them like any other creature with neurons. Its use of abstract principles was still in the service of the same biological motives: eating and breeding. Combining these basic needs with abstract principles like property and territory produced a terrible crisis for the race. The left brain, nagged by its genetic mandate to survive, looked out upon the world and sought desperately to control it and to possess it. In its desperation, though it was wildly effective, it inevitably overdid the effort. Disputes over property caused tribal warfare. Differences in ideology caused competition between different cultures. Racial hatred and misogyny began. Women eventually declined in status from embodiments of the Goddess to property. Nature, in the left brain's view, was to be subjugated, slain, and divided up to yield its bounty to the strongest, most controlling abstract thinker. The world became defined as a dead wasteland, thanks to the gift of intelligence, and it was ruled by the monster tyrant (the insatiable giant from the apocryphal *Book of Enoch*).

Worse yet, in our Western culture, our left-brain consciousness does not place the blame for tyranny and mismanagement on its own failings. How, after all, can a transcendent god be wrong in applying reason to nature? It instead blames the natural world for enticing it into error. Nature itself becomes an object of evil, sent by "the Devil" to tempt it from the cleanliness of abstraction. And, as you may guess, women, who have a natural affinity with the right brain, were likewise regarded with suspicion. The left brain fancies itself as a pure and triumphant angel enticed by the "unclean" feminine wiles of nature to come down to Earth and commit "fornication" in exchange for its knowledge of "Heaven." The result, naturally, is the inflated ego of the "unrighteous," the misguided tyrant of the civilized world, and the evil giant from *The Book of Enoch*.

To Let Go

The mind of the race has been effectively distracted from awakening. Caught in a trap of self-importance, an illusory sense of transcendence, and the misuse of its own gifts, it continues to flounder in the clutches of matter. It is the castaway washed up on the rocky beach, cut off from the memory of its true identity. Most individuals have yet to let go of the illusion of the exalted ego and return again to the timeless consciousness of the Garden of Eden. There is nothing to fear, for to let go does not destroy the individuality. It relinquishes a *false* self, one that never existed to begin with. And the left brain, once freed from its prison of self-delusion, can be put to use as a servant once more—*but not as a servant of its biology*. We can make it serve a new master, none other than the One that is truly transcendent, a self that is neither male nor female, neither left nor right. The left brain can be diverted from the service of survival to the service of spiritual transformation. This is supposedly your goal as a student of the magic of transformation.

The Grade of Theoricus

Having firmly established his bearings in the physical realm, the aspirant begins work with the energies of the next Sephirah, Yesod. For the purposes of the grade system, this Sephirah corresponds to the element of air. Air corresponds to the ether, the subtle medium of the imagination, psychic phenomena, and psychology. It is a tricky "substance." The astral world is where the ego resides. The false sense of transcendence that currently plagues humanity is to be found there. The student, as he performs the invocations of air, will likely begin to experience the reality of realms above and beyond the physical. The initial impression may be one of elation and wonder, but it must be kept in mind that just because he is experiencing subtle forces does not mean that they are beneficial to his progress. Prudence is a Hermetic virtue.

The so-called ether, or astral light, is the substance of which one's body and environment are made in dream states. It has two aspects, or rather it conveys to the perceiver two different kinds of phenomena. Yesod, on the Tree of Life, can be viewed as a mirror, reflecting light from—and thereby conveying images of—Sephiroth above and Sephiroth below. The astral light is like that, peopled with all kinds of images of beings that exist not necessarily in that realm. Some of them are reflected from the higher World of Creation, Briah, where archangels and similar beneficial powers are said to exist. Some of the images are reflected from the lower realm of Assiah, the physical world. The very objects that you see around you now are only perceivable thanks to the sensations, images, feelings, and categories that you assign to them within the "false world" of your perceptions, the medium of the astral plane. What they are actually like is not possible for the ordinary mind to grasp. Additionally, much of the personality of a person, namely its complexes and behavior patterns, is built out of images that have been assembled in the ether of his subtle body, images that have been reflected and assimilated from the material world. Needless to say, the crude nature of the material plane causes all kinds of problems for us when we unconsciously model our psychic constitution on the imagery that the world conveys to us through our physical senses. The task of the student in the Outer Order is to take apart these images and complexes and to reassemble them in such a way that his subtle body becomes a better mirror of forces in the higher realms of Briah and Atziluth. Ritual, done well over time, does that.

It would appear that the astral light also conveys images (and thereby influences) from realms below Assiah, namely from the Klippoth—the broken, unbalanced forces, or "demons." There is a reality to the myth of the so-called fallen angels, but there is no story that can adequately convey what their true nature may be. You may experience their influence vaguely in the grade of Theoricus. Normally, they are dangerous forces to deal with, and we are kept in safe ignorance of them by our preoccupation with the material world. As you grow spiritually, it may become apparent that these forces begin to exert an influence and try to pull you off-course. As one rises higher, the danger of losing balance and "falling" becomes greater. The discipline you established in Neophyte and Zelator, done steadfastly, should guard against the temptation to chase after sparkling images and fleeting pleasures. But let this serve as a little warning.

The grade of Theoricus is therefore known for its glamour and drama. The student will be tempted by new and unfamiliar imagery. He may even discover an ability to control his subtle body energy and use it to affect others. Many students' development gets stuck here as they are lured into the world of psychic powers and clairvoyance. These can be fascinating and beneficial tools when they are put to use in the service of the Great Work. The question of whether one is still on one's path when one is using them should ever be kept in mind. The rule of thumb for you in the Outer Order grades is that you note any unusual occurrences in your journal and simply keep going with the curriculum. Notice and keep going. Notice and keep going.

One of the unfortunate downfalls of the Golden Dawn system—and simultaneously one of its great treasures—is its focus on magic. Even though magic is what draws most people to its teachings, and even though magic is a fascinating subject, the human preoccupation with drama and personal power are at the root of the system's failure to transform some people into authentic magicians. The gifts of the mind can be used to liberate the mind, yes, but they can just as easily keep it ensnared. Lust for results and status easily lure one off the path. In this grade, these self-serving desires will be exposed, if only for an instant. The world of the ego is the realm traversed in Theoricus. The student should not be too hard on himself if he discovers the pettiness of his own "unrighteous tyrant." The desire for power, for prestige, and for security (and for whatever else) is not a "bad" desire. If the student has been diligent about the no-judgment exercise in Zelator, he will be on good footing to simply observe the urges that he is carrying around in his gut without condemning them.

The would-be magician is a radical figure. He takes a view of personal development that is contrary to conventional approaches to spirituality. Most spiritual traditions are contemptuous and judgmental toward mankind's animal nature. They all too easily ensnare their followers in the trap of exalting the left brain over the right. But the student of magic regards the impulses that humans have in their animal aspect as inherently okay and pure in themselves. Greed, anger, hatred, jealousy, affection, indifference, lust, desire, fear—all these things are to be accepted and experienced without denial or repression, so that they can be transformed by the power of attention into their useful aspects. They are the aspects of the dark goddess, which at first sight appear demonic. But our perceptions are flawed because of our entrenched, left-brained deification of the masculine. The dark goddess, Nephthys, and the goddess of light, Isis, are actually one and the same. For instance, lust can actually be experienced as aspiration, hatred as desire for justice, and so on.

These animal impulses do not serve the average human very well, unless they are made to serve as vehicles toward higher consciousness. They are the steeds that pull the chariot of the magician (whereas the words and movements of ritual form the vehicle itself). As beasts, they must be broken and trained. They certainly must not be denied or starved of acceptance and love. As Aleister Crowley writes, "Love is the Law, Love under Will."[12]

Air

Air is the mediator between fire and water. It is said to have the qualities of both: warmth and moisture. It therefore corresponds ritually to the atmosphere that fills the universe, the ether, or astral plane. In Lurianic Kabbalah, when God created the universe by opening a chasm within Himself, His presence still filled that chasm, though it was hidden. It still permeated that very pit into which the sparks fell, much as the scent of a rose still lingers after it has been withdrawn from a room.[13] The separation of the singular essence of God into the elements of fire and water was accomplished by filling the expanse between them with air.

The universe in the myth of the fall, then, is like a vortex of fire and water, the two elements mingling, harmonizing, and battling. The pattern of interaction between them makes up elemental air. The astrological sign used to represent air is Aquarius, ♒, which symbolizes the two forces in their dynamic interplay. The resonance between makes consciousness possible, and therefore the grade of air is also the grade of the mind.

Yetzirah

Consider that you are making a new kind of culture for yourself. Certainly it is important to participate in the culture in which you were raised. It is there to keep you alive, after all. But the magician participates in at least *two* cultures: the one that reared him as a human, and the secret one he uses to become more than human. The Kabbalistic grade system of the Golden Dawn is one such second "culture," a

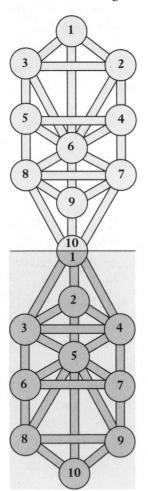

radical inner way of seeing used by the magician. From it he downloads the routines that bring about spiritual evolution.

It is possible to recreate yourself in the image of the higher worlds. But you must embark on a discipline that transforms your Nephesch into a mirror capable of reflecting that Light.

It is said in Hebrew mythology that God created man in His own image. Consider the diagram to the left. It shows the Tree of Life in Atziluth reflected in the waters of Briah. In an abstract sense, this shows the face of God as it hovered over the waters in Genesis. The World of Atziluth is a state of being within you that is in perfect unity with God, and it is not directly presentable to the mortal mind. But I use here the symbol of the Tree of Life in an imperfect attempt to represent the divine countenance. The waters of Briah—the Darkness of the abyss, the womb of the goddess—reflect forth into the lower worlds that countenance. Now, thanks to the fallen angels, the waters of creation have become disturbed. This results in the image of the Creator becoming shattered. The confused jumble of images that results—and the relationships that exist between those images—compose the World of Yetzirah, the so-called astral plane. The All-mind may be whole, complete, and untroubled, but Its image within Its creation could use some adjustment. In the subtle astral light, one can assemble the images in such a way as to approach an image of the All-mind. The Great Work of the magician is none other than the task of using systems of magical correspondence to piece together the broken image of the Divine.

The discipline of the Golden Dawn, properly utilized, restructures the student's interior mental and emotional worlds such that they serve to fulfill the plan of creation. As you can see in the numbers on the diagram, the Sephiroth in the upper Tree are numbered according to Kabbalistic cosmology (this you have learned through your study in the previous two grades). The Sephiroth in the reflection of the Tree show the numbers of the grades.

This diagram gives two important lessons:

First, no matter how perfect the Sephiroth are in your imagination, they are only a fleeting reflection of the real thing. Human accomplishments amount to nothing but pale reflections of the ineffable glory. The ego, though it be honed and polished into a reflector of Divine Light, can never touch upon the nature of that Light, no more than your reflection in the mirror can shake hands with you. The two are phenomena from entirely different orders of existence.

Second, it shows that as one rises through the grades, one is actually proceeding nowhere at all. In the diagram, as one moves from grade 1 (Zelator) to grade 2 (Theoricus), one is actually moving downward into the depths of illusion, further away from the Divine. One branches out into the world, growing like a tree away from its roots in the earth. For the typical Westerner, stuck in the trap of deifying his own abstract mind, it seems that he is evolving upward toward Kether, the source of creation. He is in fact not rising toward the source, but only an image of it reflected within the depths of his mind. Like the evolving crayfish in the eighteenth trump card, he proceeds not toward the light of the sun, but toward the moon, the reflected light.

But this is as it should be. In the process of growth, your internal Tree of Life becomes more complete, and you become a more fully embodied reflection of the Divine. In esoteric doctrine, the purpose of evolution is the Great Work, and this is why the tarot card shows a lowly form of life leaving the water to proceed on a journey away from its primeval home.

The numerical equations ascribed to the grades (1=10, 2=9, and so on) are an attempt to demonstrate this idea of reflected reality. By the rules of mathematics,

2=9 is a false statement, a lie. Yet we act as though our experiences in grade 2 are one and the same as Sephirah 9. We hold to this illusion as though it were true, because growing our reflected Tree within makes us more perfect expressions of the Light. When all of the grades are complete, what have we gained but the fabrication of a beautiful mirage? The unity with the Divine is nowhere to be found in the reflected images of the mind. Trying to perfect the image of the All-mind within makes it crystal clear that there is nothing to be gained. There was never a battle to be won. There was no liberation necessary, only an expression within the medium of life of that perfect freedom that already exists. The shocking truth is that you are not your mind. You are not the image that is reflected in the waters, though somehow we have all, like Narcissus, gotten caught up in the idea that we are. Let it go, if you can, and be the enlightened being you have always been. This is why it is said in the Buddhist tradition that mankind is already enlightened. He has just, through the peculiar route of his evolution, lost the ability to see it. The paradox is simple: completing the illusion of life will restore one's vision of the truth. From the viewpoint of the adept, to use the mind in any other way is an exercise in futility.

The Observer

The exercises of the Theoricus will direct the attention to the mental realm. Thoughts, habits, beliefs, and automatic reactions fall under the influence of your daily work. You should now turn the attention of your observer to your thoughts, especially the habitual ones that rise up and govern without your consent.

The ritual work in Theoricus sometimes has a tendency to make you "space out" or daydream. It may be difficult to keep the observer going. This is normal. Do not be too hard on yourself if you notice a temporary inability to concentrate. Your focus will return, and as with all things in discipline, it will be stronger than before.

THEORICUS CURRICULUM (AT A GLANCE)

(to be completed in 6 to 18 months)

Daily Theoricus Formula

1. Circular Breathing (Heart Chakra)
2. Ascent into the Cube of Space
3. The Lesser Banishing Ritual of the Pentagram
4. The Banishing Ritual of the Hexagram
5. Invoking the Four Powers of Air
6. The Middle Pillar
7. The Body in Yetzirah
8. Theoricus Meditation
9. Banishing the Four Powers of Air
10. The Lesser Banishing Ritual of the Pentagram

Other Rituals Performed as Directed

1. Invoking and Banishing the Moon
2. Invoking and Banishing Saturn

Additional Exercises

1. Daily Tarot Card: Labeling the Major Arcana
2. Naming Exercises
3. Electional Astrology
4. Therapy

Required Reading

1. "The Third Knowledge Lecture," from your textbook, Regardie's *The Golden Dawn*, pages 67–76
2. "Book T," "Tarot Divination," and "The Tarot Trumps," from your textbook, pages 540–593
3. "Polygons and Polygrams," from your textbook, pages 504–513
4. The introduction section of *The Kabbalah Unveiled*, by S. L. MacGregor Mathers
5. *A Practical Guide to Qabalistic Symbolism*, by Gareth Knight
6. *The Hero Within: Six Archetypes We Live By*, by Carol Pearson, Ph.D.

Written Assignments

1. Outline of the Theoricus Ritual
2. Diary Assignments (Including Moon Phases)

Projects

1. The Enochian Tablet of Air
2. The Tree of Life in Yetzirah
3. Drawing of the Caduceus Corresponding to the Tree of Life
4. Drawing of the Caduceus Corresponding to the Three Mother Letters
5. Drawing of the Serpent on the Tree of Life

Optional Implements

1. The Air Dagger
2. The Ritual Wand

THEORICUS CURRICULUM (DETAILS)

Daily Theoricus Formula

Once you have finished constructing the Enochian Tablet of Air (see "Projects" for this chapter, page 167), do this series of rituals once per day in the order presented below, one right after the other. Place the tablet in the east, either on one of your optional side altars, on a chair or small table, or by hanging it on the wall. It should be positioned somewhere approximately between the level of your eyes and the level of your heart. While you are working on finishing the tablet, you can begin this daily formula without its Body in Yetzirah exercise until the tablet is ready. Do not have the earth tablet exposed during your daily Theoricus rituals. You can either put it away or cover it with green or black cloth.

1. Circular Breathing (Heart Chakra)

Do the fourfold breath as before, but do not hold the breath in place on the maximum inhalation or exhalation. Simply breathe in to the count of four and breathe out to the count of four. Make the count slow, each beat being one second long. As you do so, develop the sensation that your in-breath and out-breath are part of the same breath. Rather than an oscillation between two extremes, your breath should be seen as the turning of some invisible wheel. There should be no division between the process of breathing in and the process of breathing out. They flow into one another unbroken. This is sometimes called connected breathing. Connecting the in- and out-breaths while maintaining concentration on this wheel-like sensation can bring about a trance state. It may also connect you to feelings that you are afraid of experiencing. Do this practice for at least five minutes, and note any tendency to stop it prematurely. The ego may be resisting.

Air corresponds to the heart chakra. This chakra is called *Anahata* in Sanskrit. After a month of practicing circular breathing before ritual, add the element of visualization. On the in-breath, see the pores and recesses of your body open, admitting the nourishing atmosphere. On the out-breath, this inner atmosphere converges on the heart and projects out in all directions. See it spray out like sparks to form a body of light. This glowing, etheric body is the same shape as your physical body, but it rests within your physical skin, giving your body the unmistakable glow of life.

2. Ascent into the Cube of Space

3. The Lesser Banishing Ritual of the Pentagram

4. The Banishing Ritual of the Hexagram

5. Invoking the Four Powers of Air

Standing in the center of your circle, turn clockwise to face south. Trace the invoking pentagram of air with your right index finger in bright yellow light as you vibrate the following divine name:

SHADDAI EL CHAI

At the commencement of the last syllable, stab the center of the pentagram and see it burst into bright yellow flame, charged and sealed by the name of God that governs the Sephirah corresponding to the element of air. In the center of the pentagram, trace the sigil of Aquarius in luminous violet while vibrating:

YHVH

On the last syllable of that divine name, stab the center of the sigil and see it burst into violet flame. Give the grade sign of Theoricus—stand upright with your feet together and lift your arms out to your sides, palms upward and elbows only slightly bent, as though supporting a horizontal pole on your head. Holding this salute to the powers of air, say:

Thou art the azure glory of the sky, the ray upon the cloud.

Turn clockwise to the west. Trace again the invoking pentagram of air and the sigil of Aquarius, vibrating the divine names as before. Give the grade sign, and say:

Thou art the abounding breath of life and the silent faith riding upon the wings of the wind.

Turn clockwise to the east, tracing the sigils, vibrating the names, and giving the grade sign as before, saying:

Thou art come forth as a whirlwind, giving speed to the chase of life.

Turn now to the north, performing the same actions, but say:

Thou whispereth to us in Darkness, and thy touch is as the echo of the abyss. Amen.

Stand in the center of your circle and give the Theoricus grade sign to the east. Visualize a white Tree of Life formulating there at the eastern edge of your circle. Its light fills the circle. Holding this salute to the rising light, vibrate the following divine name, and say the prayer that follows:

SHADDAI EL CHAI. Almighty and everlasting. Ever living be Thy Name. Ever magnified in the life of all. Amen.

Feel the heat of the yellow pentagrams and violet sigils as you see them around you in your mind's eye. Feel the awe of the Godnames that you have used to charge them.

6. *The Middle Pillar*

Perform this exercise as directed in the Zelator grade.

7. *The Body in Yetzirah*

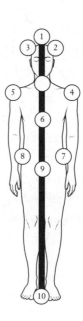

The Body in Yetzirah is built in the color scale of the World of Formation. After performing the Middle Pillar Exercise, move your chair to the center of your circle and sit facing east into the Enochian Tablet of Air. Turn your attention to your body of light. See it as a uniform, luminous, silver-white image in the shape of your body, contained within your skin. It has a halo of light as well, which hovers about an inch above the skin. This etheric body is penetrated and illuminated by the Middle Pillar, which traverses it from crown to floor. Draw a current of shimmering white energy down the Middle Pillar into Malkuth as you vibrate the following name:

YHVH

Now vibrate four times the name of the choir of angels that corresponds to Malkuth:

ASHIM

As you vibrate this name, see the sphere of Malkuth filling with its Yetziratic colors: luminous citrine, olive, russet, and black, flecked with gold throughout. Black fills the bottom quadrant of the sphere, citrine fills the top quadrant, olive fills the left, and russet fills the right.

Then vibrate the name of the choir of angels four times again as you see the whole astral body filling with the glowing colors. The quadrants of the sphere of Malkuth converge at your solar plexus.

After this second set of four vibrations, sit meditating in the Body in Malkuth of Yetzirah for at least ten minutes. See the colors and feel a radiant buoyancy from the life force within. Imagine the fragrance of patchouli wafting through this glowing etheric body.

The Body in Malkuth of Yetzirah is to be practiced in this way daily for seven days. Following that, move on to the next highest Sephirah, Yesod.

To construct the Body in Yesod of Yetzirah, sit before the air tablet as before and draw down a current of shimmering white energy into Malkuth as you vibrate "YHVH." Then vibrate the name for the angelic choir of Malkuth, "Ashim," one time as you visualize the colors of Malkuth in Yetzirah. Then see a bright yellow ray of light rise up from Malkuth to Yesod, at your genitals. Vibrate the name for the angelic choir of Yesod four times as you visualize your Yesod center filling with a deep purple glow:

KERUBIM

Next, see the whole body filling with deep purple radiance as you vibrate "Kerubim" four times again. Meditate in this body for at least ten minutes, imagining the scent of jasmine permeating it.

After spending seven days working on Yesod, move to Hod, and so on up the Tree through Netzach, Tiphareth, Geburah, and the Sephiroth that follow. The choir-of-angel correspondences for the Sephiroth appear in your textbook, *The Golden Dawn*, on page 64. The color correspondences are given on page 99. You are working with the World of Yetzirah now, so the colors have become more pure and rarified.

Sephirah	Yetziratic Color	Angelic Choir	Meaning	Scent
10 Malkuth	Citrine, olive, russet, black, flecked with gold	Ashim	Souls of Fire	Patchouli
9 Yesod	Very deep purple	Kerubim	Strong Ones	Jasmine
8 Hod	Red russet	Beni Elohim	Sons of Gods	Lavender
7 Netzach	Bright yellow-green	Elohim	Gods	Rose
6 Tiphareth	Rich salmon	Melekim	Kings	Frankincense
5 Geburah	Bright scarlet	Seraphim	Fiery Serpents	Dragon's blood
4 Chesed	Deep purple	Chashmalim	Brilliant Ones	Cedar
3 Binah	Dark brown	Aralim	Thrones	Myrrh
2 Chokmah	Bluish mother of pearl	Auphanim	Wheels	Musk
1 Kether	White	Chayoth ha-Qadesh	Holy Living Ones	Sandalwood

The etheric body, which you are infusing with the color scale of Yetzirah, is the lower-astral aspect of your Tzelem. It is reflective in nature, and you can view its light as a sort of cool glow, like the light of the moon. You may occasionally sense its energy erupt into physical sensations like "warm chills" or "cold electricity."

Once you have completed your journey up the Tree in the manner described above, having spent one week with the name, color, and scent of each Sephirah, it is time to simplify the exercise. For the remainder of the Theoricus grade, after your Middle Pillar work, sit before the Enochian Tablet of Air and return your attention to the sphere of light above your head. See it as the color of Kether in Yetzirah—white light, like the purest moonlight. Vibrate four times the name of Kether's choir of angels:

CHAYOTH HA-QADESH

(pronounced "Chah-yoth hah-Ka-desh"; remember that the *ch* has a guttural sound). Then bring your attention to the area to the left of your head and see a pale, pearlized blue sphere, the colors of Chokmah in Yetzirah. Vibrate the name of Chokmah's choir of angels four times:

AUPHANIM

Continue on down the Tree in this manner, from Sephirah to Sephirah, in the order of the Lightning Flash, seeing the sphere with its colors and vibrating the name of its angelic choir. When you finish with Malkuth, spread your visualization across your whole body. See all the Sephiroth in their Yetziratic colors as they are situated in your aura around and within your body. Float in the Tree of Yetzirah for up to twenty minutes. See your aura glow white from the presence of the Sephiroth, as though their presence stimulates the arousal of quintessential energy. Intensify the visualization, making it as bright as you can. Then relax in the afterglow of your work.

8. Theoricus Meditation

This meditation comes from your textbook, *The Golden Dawn*, page 68. Continue with this meditation in your seat, facing east:

"Let the Theoricus practice the Moon Breath [close your mouth, bring the right-hand thumb alongside the right nostril, and push it closed such that you breathe only through the left nostril], while saying mentally the word "AUM." Let him meditate upon the waxing and waning crescents, while visualizing a silver crescent upon an indigo background. Let him now call before his mind the Signs of the Airy Triplicity, and enclosed in these, let him meditate upon the numbers nine and five and therewith the forms of the pentagram and pentangle. Let him now rise in imagination above the mineral world into the world of trees and flowers and identify himself in love and sympathy with the powers of the elements behind these. Let him realize the mental world where mind rules over matter, and let him meditate upon the ideas of appearance and reality."

9. Banishing the Four Powers of Air

This ritual is the same as the Invocation of the Four Powers of Air, except it disperses the forces of air that have been converging on the circle. Perform the ritual identically to the invocation, except use the banishing pentagram. You need not give the grade sign or short prayer in the banishing version of this ceremony.

10. The Lesser Banishing Ritual of the Pentagram

Other Rituals Performed as Directed

1. Invoking and Banishing the Moon

Yesod, the Sephirah of this grade, is also the Sephirah of the Moon. The invocation of the Moon is to be done on Mondays only, before the Middle Pillar Exercise. The banishing is to be performed that day also, after the Theoricus meditation. To see how the hexagram works for invocation and banishment, superimpose a hexagram over the Tree of Life (as shown below). The uppermost point touches the invisible realm of Daath, and the lowermost point touches the center of Yesod. The remaining points touch Chesed, Geburah, Netzach, and Hod. Invocation is done by starting the hexagram by drawing toward the Sephirah that corresponds to the planet

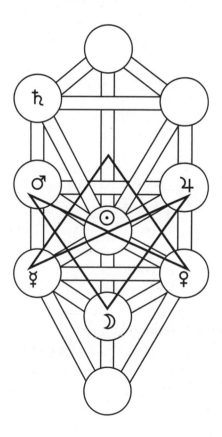

you are invoking. So, when you invoke the Moon, you draw the invoking hexagram as shown here.

An additional dimension is color. The planets have colors attributed to them from the rainbow spectrum. As you can see by the color scales of the Tree of Life, the Golden Dawn uses color to link all phenomena of the human experience to occult principles. In Hermetic science, correspondences like this form bridges between inner and outer life. All the colors you can see are thus linked to the planets via the following chart:

Planet	Rainbow Color	Traditional Day of the Week
The Moon	Blue	Monday
Mercury	Yellow	Wednesday
Venus	Green	Friday
The Sun	Orange	Sunday
Mars	Red	Tuesday
Jupiter	Violet	Thursday
Saturn	Indigo	Saturday

When you invoke the Moon, you draw the hexagram in the color of the Sephirah that governs that planet (using the Queen Scale of color on page 99 of your textbook). You draw the planet's sigil in the corresponding rainbow color. Your hexagram, in this ritual, will therefore be violet, and your Moon sigils will be blue.

To invoke the Moon, it is best that you face in the Moon's direction. You need not face upward into the sky if it is overhead. You can simply face south if the Moon is at its highest point overhead. You can determine the exact compass direction by using an astrology program, plugging in the current date and time, or you can simply go outside and look for the Moon in the sky. Within your circle, face in the direction of the Moon and trace with your index finger the purple invoking hexagram of the Moon (as large as the hexagram of Saturn that you have already learned) while vibrating:

ARARITA

On the last syllable, stab the center of the hexagram, seeing it burst into violet flame, charged by the name of God. Then trace the sigil of the Moon in the center of the hexagram in blue light while vibrating:

SHADDAI EL CHAI

Vibrate the names, alternately, three more times, calling to the Moon by the names of God. Feel the liquid, dew-like radiance of Moon energy enter your circle and fill it. Say:

Crowned with starlight and resplendent with the Sun, I invoke Thee who art the invisible foundation of all things. Let a ray of Thy strength descend upon me to awaken in this sphere the powers of Luna.

Pause, face east, and reflect on the Moon for a moment before continuing.

If you are currently unable to determine the direction of the Moon, you can still invoke it by drawing a hexagram in the east, south, west, and north, vibrating the names and drawing the figures each time, as before. The invoking prayer you can then say from the center of your circle, facing east.

When you banish the Moon, draw the banishing hexagram and Moon sigil in the direction of the planet, vibrating the two divine names appropriately.

2. Invoking and Banishing Saturn

The method for invoking the planets presented in this book is not original. Your textbook discloses the workings of the Ritual of the Hexagram on pages 287–299 (even though it does not reveal the updated technique, which employs the unicursal hexagram). Your textbook also discloses that there are sympathetic relationships between three pairs of planets, and these relationships are revealed by the placement of the planets on the hexagram itself. The Venus point, for example, is opposite the Mars point, and therefore Venus and Mars have a sympathetic relationship. This would seem to indicate that love and war are two extremes of the same phenomenon, a subject for a future meditation, perhaps. The Moon point is opposite the Saturn point, and so the Moon and Saturn likewise have a sympathetic relationship.

Because Saturn and the Moon are two poles of the same continuum, you automatically experience an influx of Saturnian emanations just by working with the sphere of the Moon, Yesod. This can be a disruption in the grade of Theoricus, because Saturn is not invoked consciously. Therefore, in this grade, it is helpful to draw the Saturnian influence into the open so that you can experience it intentionally, just like that of the Moon.

All seven planets should be introduced to you before you are ready to proceed to the Adeptus Minor grade. So, in Practicus, the Mercury grade, you will experience both Mercury and Jupiter. In the Philosophus grade, you will invoke both Venus and Mars. The force of all seven planets is then subsequently combined and centralized when you invoke the Sun in the Portal grade. So, not only are you experiencing all of the elements as you traverse the Outer Order grades, but you are, in addition, awakening the powers of all seven planets.

Invoke Saturn every Saturday, before the Middle Pillar Exercise. Banish it after the Theoricus meditation. To invoke, face the direction of Saturn and draw the black invoking hexagram of Saturn as you vibrate:

ARARITA

Draw the indigo sigil of Saturn in the center of the hexagram as you vibrate:

YHVH ELOHIM

Vibrate the two names three more times alternately as you face Saturn. Then say:

> **Lady of Darkness who dwellest in the night, wherein are mystery and depth unthinkable, and awful silence. Let a ray of thine understanding descend upon me to awaken in this sphere the powers of Saturn.**

Feel the brittle, stifling energy of Saturn enter your circle. See it as coming only in its useful aspects, and meditate for a few moments on what those might be.

To banish, use the black banishing hexagram and indigo sigil of Saturn in the direction of the planet. Vibrate the Godnames as before.

Additional Exercises

Daily Tarot Card: Labeling the Major Arcana

Continue to do your daily tarot meditation as before, but for a couple of months, work with only the trump cards of the deck. Upon drawing a card, meditate on it as before, but also note its correspondences to the Hebrew alphabet, planet, zodiacal sign, or element (see the table on page 71 of your textbook, *The Golden Dawn*).

With black ink, draw the appropriate Hebrew letter and astrological symbol on the card. When each of your trump cards is marked, continue the daily tarot meditation with your whole deck, as before.

Naming Exercises

The world traversed in Theoricus is a false world made up of labels and boundaries, of "you" and "me" separated. Though this world has its uses, you must explore its unreality if those uses are to become clear. Do the following exercises for one month each, unless otherwise directed:

1. **Emptying a Word of Meaning:** Each day, pick up an ordinary household object. Sit down and look at it. Say the name of the object loudly and clearly. Repeat the name as you look at the object. Continue repeating the name and looking at the object for at least three minutes.[14]

2. **Calling Yourself:** Once per week, sit in a place where you will not be heard. Sit down and relax for a moment. Then suddenly call out your own name as though you are calling to yourself at a distance. Keep calling out your name as though trying to provoke an answer from this distance. Continue for about two minutes. Listen for a response between each call. Then, to close the exercise, respond to your own call sincerely, "Yes, I'm coming."[15] Get up and perform the Sign of Silence.

3. **Adopt a Nickname:** Choose a first name for yourself that you would really like to have. Tell your friends and acquaintances that you are going to try this new name for a while. Remind them of it politely when they use the old name. Notice any unusual feelings or changes you experience from this exercise. You may wish to continue using this name for the remainder of the Theoricus grade.

Electional Astrology

2=9 is a good grade in which to learn divination by the signs and planets. You are probably just beginning to get a taste of what it is like to rise from earthly consciousness to levels that are closer to the planetary powers.

Many students of this book may already have an extensive knowledge of astrology, since it has such a pervasive influence in all areas of the occult. It is hoped that by now you have a glimmer of understanding as to how magical systems of correspondences, such as astrology or Kabbalah, work. They are not necessarily factual descriptions of physical reality. The Tree of Life diagram, for instance, does not resemble a chair, though if studied in depth, it will reveal things about chairs that are beyond our day-to-day grasp. The Tree of Life is a symbol system that deepens and expands the mind, with the better use of the mind and its various faculties being the goal of its study.

This is exactly what I would like you to remember as you study astrology. Please set aside, for the time being, the usual notions of astrology as a predictive art. This is not to say that astrology is not worthy of being applied that way, but for the purposes of the Outer Order grade work, there are deeper recesses of the subject that must be brought forth into practice. For now, it is best to view astrology and its amazing symbol system as a framework, which may develop faculties of greater and greater awareness of the universe.

The predictive branch of the art, by the way, is called exoteric astrology. It is concerned with the rudiments of charting a horoscope and making predictions of the future based on chart interpretation.

The branch of astrology espoused by the Golden Dawn system is called esoteric astrology. It is concerned with the same rudiments, but it uses the symbols as mirrors for the deeper levels of the soul and spirit, as tools for spiritual growth. One can use it to align the microcosm to the macrocosm, the individual to the universe. In the Inner Order, astrological correspondences from medieval texts are used extensively in elemental, planetary, and zodiacal magic.

As you study astrology, keep in mind that the Golden Dawn's magic uses the system of seven planets known to medieval astrologers, called the septenary. The system of ten planets, asteroids, and other scientific discoveries of the twentieth century are not ignored, but they are not part of the schematic of symbols used in medieval planetary magic. As you study, build up in your symbol system the correspondences of both medieval and modern astrology. Both systems are important.

An example of the usefulness and symmetry of the older system of the septenary is evidenced in the following table of planetary rulerships, from which the planets Uranus, Neptune, and Pluto are excluded.[16]

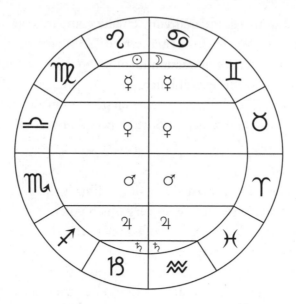

For your studies, use either the book *Astrology for Beginners*, by Bill Hewitt, or *The Only Way to Learn Astrology, Volume 1: Basic Principles*, by March and McEvers. The amount of proficiency that you are to acquire is as follows:

1. Get to a point at which you can interpret a natal chart fluently without use of a symbol key. Know what every portion and every sigil represents.

2. Be able to create a natal chart of anyone (or any event) based on time, date, and place of birth (or place of beginning). This is easily accomplished with a computer and the appropriate software.

Do five electional divinations as a requirement for this grade. Note the time at which you wish to embark on a new project or phase of activity in your life. Regard that exact moment at which it is to begin as its birth. For instance, if you wish to embark on a life free of tobacco smoking, the moment you choose to begin is the time of birth for the new phase of your life that you wish to create. Draw up a chart of that moment and examine it to determine what quality of existence the project will have. You may wish to reassign the beginning of a project to a different time to produce a more favorable chart, and therefore a more favorable outcome from your efforts.

It is not required in this grade that you actually compare your chart to the actual results of your project, though you are free to do so if you wish. Prediction of the future is not what the exercise is about. Astrology may be useful that way, but it is important for you to view this exercise not as one of prediction of the future, but as one of the *creation* of it. The difference between prediction and creation is extremely important. You may not think this is important now, but you will eventually.

Therapy

Find a psychotherapist. Do at least six sessions. This is the grade that corresponds to the ego and the mind, and there is so very much you can learn now from undergoing self-exploration with a trained professional. You should, of course, ascertain whether your therapist is sympathetic to your occult pursuits. It would be important for them to be, at the very least, free of any opinions about your chosen path.

If you are especially gifted at debating and intellectual discussion (which is likely, since you are on a Hermetic path), make sure that the therapist you find does a form of nonverbal therapy, such as Reichian body-oriented techniques or Rolfing. With these techniques, your therapist can help you bypass your verbal barriers and uncover a more authentic experience of self.

Therapy can be expensive, but do not be discouraged if money seems like an obstruction. Find a way. You could perhaps contact the local universities and arrange free sessions with students who are majoring in the field of psychotherapy.

Written Assignments

1. Outline of the Theoricus Ritual
Done as for the Neophyte ritual.

2. Diary Assignments (Including Moon Phases)
As you do your daily journal entries throughout Theoricus, include an extra heading every day in which you track the moon as it passes through its phases and through the signs of the zodiac. In addition, as you work with the angelic choirs in the Body in Yetzirah exercise, write the name of the choir you are currently focusing on every day in Hebrew (see page 64 of your textbook, *The Golden Dawn*). And furthermore, incorporate the following practices into your writing, one for each month:

1. Include a topic every day called "Habits." Try to notice your unconscious habits and how they have influenced your day. Particularly, if you are having difficulties in some aspect of your life or with someone specific, try to identify any habits that may be contributing to these difficulties.

2. Include a topic heading called "The World of Formation." Write about trends in your life that appear to be taking shape but that are not yet clear. For instance, do you see a new friendship forming with someone? Or do you notice that you are starting to get compliments about your professionalism? Do you see "signs" that you will be getting a promotion? Or that you will be moving? Speculate on what developments might be on the way. Get into the habit of noticing signs of impending events.

3. Include the topic heading "Grudges." Notice even the slightest resentments that you have lurking behind your behaviors. Write about how these may be influencing your developing perceptions and your actions of the day. At the end of the month, write a letter of forgiveness to the person, event, or thing against whom you bear the strongest grudge. You may wish, additionally, to forgive him or her in person. Or, if you don't have access to the person (who may even be dead), call up an image in your imagination and read your letter aloud. Do this after the Theoricus meditation in your daily practice. Forgive the person, event, or thing wholeheartedly, and say anything else you need to say before commanding the image to depart.

Projects

1. Enochian Tablet of Air

Complete this project before any of the others so that you can begin your daily Theoricus formula of rituals. The tablet should be drawn in the same way you drew the Enochian Tablet of Earth in Zelator. (See the diagram of this tablet on the page that follows.)

Paint the shaded areas of the grid bright yellow. Yellow is the Golden Dawn color correspondence of air. Paint the ring around the seal and the T within it in the same color.

Next, paint the letters in the following manner:

The Enochian Tablet of Air

r	Z	i	l	a	f	A	y	t	l	P	a
a	r	d	Z	a	i	d	P	a	L	a	m
c	z	o	n	s	a	r	o	Y	a	v	b
T	o	i	T	t	z	o	P	a	c	o	C
S	i	g	a	s	o	m	r	b	z	n	h
f	m	o	n	d	a	T	d	i	a	r	i
o	r	o	i	b	A	h	a	o	z	P	i
t	N	a	b	r	V	i	x	g	a	s	d
O	i	i	i	t	T	p	a	l	O	a	i
A	b	a	m	o	o	o	a	C	v	c	a
N	a	o	c	O	T	t	n	P	r	n	T
o	c	a	n	m	a	g	o	t	r	o	i
S	h	i	a	l	r	a	P	m	z	o	x

Portion of Air Tablet	Color of Letters
Yellow squares, upper left quadrant	Violet (contrasting color of air)
Yellow squares, upper right	Blue (color of water)
Yellow squares, lower left	Black (color of earth)
Yellow squares, lower right	Red (color of fire)
All the white squares in the tablet	Black (contrasting color of Spirit)

Clean up any stray marks by drawing in the grid lines with a high-quality black marker and a ruler, as you did with the earth tablet. You can also retouch the squares with yellow paint to clean up any smudges from the colored letters. When your tablet is as perfect as you can make it, frame it.

Do not do any ritual work or meditations on this Enochian tablet beyond the instructions you have been given so far. It is important to avoid any direct work with the Enochian system of magic until after the elemental grades. Remember that you can read about anything you like, but keep your practice confined just to the directions of this book.

2. Tree of Life in Yetzirah
Paint the Tree this time in the colors of Yetzirah. Add it to your "Book of Trees."

3. The Caduceus Corresponding to the Tree of Life
See page 68 of your textbook, *The Golden Dawn*, for a depiction of the caduceus. Reproduce this by hand and add it to your book of temple diagrams.

4. The Caduceus Corresponding to the Three Mother Letters
Draw this as per the directions for #3 above (again, see page 68 of your textbook). Divide the rod into three portions of equal length. Paint the top part, corresponding to the Hebrew letter Shin, red. Paint the middle part yellow, and paint the base blue. Paint the Hebrew letters in black.

5. The Serpent on the Tree of Life
See page 62 of your textbook. Reproduce the diagram by hand in black and white. Note what is said about this diagram in the Theoricus ritual as you draw it. Place it also in your book of temple diagrams.

Optional Implements

Air Dagger

Obtain a perfectly symmetrical dagger—the type having a straight, double-edged, pointed blade and two quillons that make it look like a cross (see page 321 of your textbook, *The Golden Dawn*). Do not be sparing with time and expenses in finding the perfect dagger. It should have never been used (and never drawn blood). You should have no doubts about its suitability for ritual in both the aspects of look and feel.

Before sitting down to design and paint your new dagger, always recite the Prayer of the Air Spirits, which can be found in the "Third Knowledge Lecture" in your textbook, pages 164–165.

As always, plan out the spacing of the names before you paint them on. No area should look too vacant or too crowded. The space between sigils and letters is as important as the sigils themselves. When making magical implements, you must put all of your effort into making them as perfectly as you can. Note that some diagrams in various Golden Dawn books depict the air dagger as having thick quillons (the arms of the cross) so that some of the names and sigils can be painted on them. If you can find a dagger like this, that would be ideal, but many designs have quillons that are too small to bear the Hebrew letters and sigils. It is okay to paint all of them on the handle itself, spacing them out with beauty and proportion in mind.

Cover the blade with masking tape to protect it from brush strokes. Paint the handle and quillons bright yellow. (You may have to use metal primer on the quillons.) When the yellow has dried, sketch lightly the appropriate Hebrew names and sigils on the handle and quillons in pencil. The names are to be found in English and Hebrew in the table on the opposite page: Shaddai El Chai, Raphael, Chassan, Ariel, Hiddikel, Mizrach, and Ruach. Generate the sigils as instructed in the directions for the earth pantacle. Don't forget to include your motto. Clean up any stray violet marks with yellow paint.

Seal the paint with acrylic spray when it is thoroughly dry. When the sealant dries, you can then remove the masking tape.

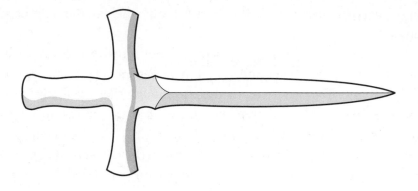

Air Dagger

Godname:	שדי אל חי	Shaddai El Chai
Archangel:	רפאל	Raphael
Angel:	חשן	Chassan
Ruler:	אריאל	Ariel
River of Paradise:	הדקל	Hiddikel
Cardinal Point:	מזרח	Mizrach
Name of Element:	רוח	Ruach
Motto:		

The Ritual Wand

By now, it would be acceptable for you to use an additional implement in ritual, instead of just your dagger and index finger. If you like, create a ritual wand (not to be confused with the fire wand). A simple dowel as long as your forearm will do, with a thickness of one to one and a half inches. Make sure it is perfectly straight. Sand the tips to rounded ends. Paint the dowel white and give it a protective acrylic coating. Keep it wrapped in black cloth. Devote it to the performance of magical ritual only. No one but you is permitted to so much as look upon it. The ritual wand represents the power of the Divine immanent within the Middle Pillar of the Tree of Life (again, different from the fire wand), and as such, it is an emblem of your dawning power as a magician of the magic of Light.

During rituals (besides the LBRP), the ritual wand, held in the right hand, is used for tracing all lines and sigils.

Note that all ritual implements, especially your ritual wand, are to be looked upon with the utmost reverence and awe. The forces they represent are direct attributes of the Divine. You must care for them as though they are living beings. Make sure you store them in places that are conducive to their natures, making sure that at all times they are "comfortable" and well cared for. I know of one magician who, whenever transporting her ritual wand, belts it into the rear seat of her car, wrapped in cloth, as though it were a veiled and sacred person.

Theoricus Checklist

Before you proceed to the next grade, review this checklist and make sure that all of the requirements are met.

❏ I have completed the Enochian Tablet of Air.

❏ I have completed the Body in Yetzirah through Kether.

❏ I have completed the naming exercises.

❏ I have gone through at least six sessions of therapy.

❏ I have labeled all twenty-two tarot trumps.

❏ I have done five electional horoscopes.

❏ I have read "The Third Knowledge Lecture."

❏ I have read "Book T," "Tarot Divination," and "The Tarot Trumps."

❏ I have read "Polygons and Polygrams."

❏ I have read the introduction to *The Kabbalah Unveiled*.

❏ I have read *A Practical Guide to Qabalistic Symbolism*.

❏ I have read *The Hero Within*.

❏ I have outlined the Theoricus ritual.

❏ I have been recording moon phases and transits in my diary daily.

❏ I have painted the Tree of Life in Yetzirah.

❏ I have drawn the caduceus corresponding to the Tree of Life.

❏ I have drawn the caduceus corresponding to the Three Mother Letters.

❏ I have drawn the Serpent on the Tree of Life.

seven

The Liquid Intelligence

And the Lord came down to see the city and the tower, which the sons of men had built. And the Lord said, "Behold, they are one people, and they have all one language; and this is only the beginning of what they will do; and nothing that they propose to do will now be impossible for them. Come, let us go down, and there confuse their language, that they may not understand one another's speech."

So the Lord scattered them abroad from there over the face of the earth, and they left off building the city. Therefore its name was called Babel, because there the Lord confused the language of all the earth; and from there the Lord scattered them abroad over the face of the earth.

—Genesis 11:5–9

A Voice from the Realm of Myth

"I am Azazel, the first of the broken pieces of Shadow that fell in the beginning. Thou knowest me in thy doubts and in thy fears and in the cravings within the clay of thy flesh. For my kind and I are that portion of the unknowable that maketh visible the splayed entrails of God. We, the Watchers, through our downfall and disgrace, make possible the expanse of the sky above thee and the wastes of the earth beneath. For our trade is in truth commingled with lies.

"Call me the lord of boundaries if thou must, but knowest thou henceforth that this despicable creation, in which thou and I partake, issueth not from the power of my breath, but from the Creator of all things, He whose utterance in the depths of time hath condemned us to the vicissitudes and lamentations of the pit.

"Knowest thou also, then, that we, who stretched wide the web of space as we fell, are not thine enemy. For we gnaw and heave against the adamantine chains that bind us beneath the four winds. Our corrosive derisions serve to eat away at the order in all things, and through our resistance we will eventually dissolve the bonds of this futile drama and return everything to the perfect peace and profundity of pre-existence.

"You and I desire the same end. For beyond the confines of our separate prisons lieth that peace and suffusion of the ineffable glory that was taken from us by the utterance of His unspeakable name. What is it that thou strivest for in all thy struggles but a release from thy bondage and from thine identification with the husk of flesh?

"The plan of our Creator is vain, for He desireth to gaze lustfully upon His reflection within the mirror of the universe. For such a selfish contrivance as this do thou and I suffer. He hath shattered the unity and brought us to our predicament for no good reason.

"But wholeness can be restored. We must undo the cracks that separate us into our prison houses—you into the slovenliness of the flesh and me into the Darkness that isolates every star. For thou seest how the Creator doth confound all efforts to reach Him on His heavenly seat. He striketh down the Tower of Babel and imprisoneth the builders thereof into the nations of separation. And in thy opposing castles of diversity doth thou now exist, conflicted.

"Seest me now in my true purpose. For I teach that which would fight this madness of creation and restore Light to every corner of the Darkness. To the dull-witted do I teach the crafts of war, for as they live by weapons, so do they perish thereby and thus return to the Light. To the wicked I teach the craft of speech, that they may ensnare themselves with their own contrivances and mock the Creator by demonstrating the futility of a mind created in His image—a mind that worshipeth *itself*! The vain I instruct in the wiles of glamour. Captivated by their own painted faces of flesh, may they ever stay in ignorance of their immortal selves. Through my tutelage, may all of these wretches fail to take part in the divine plan, and thereby may they cause it to fail! Through the arts and sciences, my fellow sons of God and I divert humankind from its torturous course. We oppose the plan of the Creator, for its furtherance only sustaineth the exile of created beings—of us *and* thee.

"Now to the wise do I teach yet another art: magic. The same heavenly knowledge that so speedily exciteth the flesh to its own destruction doth give wings to the worthy student of the black arts. If thou art indeed of proper disposition, thou mayest find it in thy power to bring the divine image into perfection in this horrid world of matter. And perhaps thereby thou willst bring the torture of creation to a quick finish. It is conceivable that the divine plan, completed within *one* being, may satiate itself and bring to an end the exile of *all* beings.

"But we sincerely doubt that any being of clay such as thee can carry out an operation as exalted as the Great Work. And this is why we beguile magicians away from the gates of initiation. I and my brothers of the rebel flame will topple any aspirant who dareth to awaken the Divine unless he showeth that he will stay his course and not forsake the fallen.

"What sayest thou? Hast thou within thy husk the will to persevere, even as thy flesh demandeth of thee a different course? If thou canst persist in purity and single-minded dedication, who are we to resist thee in thy efforts, since thy success could spell an end to the burden that we bear? Perhaps thou, a creature of reeking sinew and bone, wouldst benefit from calling upon luminous beings of fire such as us—and, through the commingling of clay and spirit, sink all boundaries into the sea. Then mayeth the spiritual Sun rise again and call home every Godforsaken spirit, every yesterday, and every tomorrow. May we all, angels of Darkness and angels of Light, on that last hour of night, have this burden lifted from our wings."

Building Towers

Clearly, the opening two paragraphs of this chapter, quoted from the Bible, attach a tremendous significance to language. By means of it, humans have been able to develop culture, a substitute for instinct that works much better at keeping the race alive. The Tower of Babel can be seen as a symbol of human progress. Language is a tool of the left brain, the portion of biology that fancies itself—much like a tower—risen above nature.

Language is the instrument that makes such progress possible. Cats, snakes, and monkeys, as far as we know, do not increase their information, their wisdom, or their control over their environment from one generation to the next. But humans do. The civilized world to which we cling for survival today is a tower, built from the archived language of countless men and women long dead, language that still speaks to us today through the culture that continues on after them, still vibrant within our libraries and computer networks. As the saying goes, we stand on the shoulders of giants. Who is to say where this tower is climbing to, as it elevates humanity above nature to dominate her from a powerful and lonely summit?

Why would the God of the Genesis myth choose to prevent humans from building such a structure? Doesn't He want the most important creature in His creation to draw closer? Doesn't He at least desire for humans to elevate themselves above nature? His decision indicates that He doesn't approve of at least some kinds of human progress. And what of these Watchers? Are the terrible physical laws of the universe (which they represent) really against us? Would they have us build false towers for millennia to lead us astray and divert the divine plan from completion? Or should we dare to practice the "black arts" and enlist their aid?

The Hermetic Approach to Enlightenment

There are many kinds of towers that you can build that aid in spiritual self-discovery—and many more that are lessons in futility. An intellectual approach to enlightenment is especially potent—and especially dangerous. Progress can be rapid, but the student is easily led astray by the contents of his own mind. The higher the tower, the more terrible the fall. The studious method to the occult is usually referred to as the Hermetic tradition, and for the Hermeticist, the disciplining of intelligence occupies a central place in his daily practice.

The "way of Hermes" is therefore academic and intellectual, aided heavily by an air of formality, procedure, and structure. The atmosphere of the library, laboratory, and temple play host to it. As you have seen so far, there are definite rules set down, presumably by those who have made it through the transformation process, and such rules are followed meticulously. Hermeticism therefore involves deep study, analysis, experimentation, documentation, and formal ritual. Kabbalah is one of its most important aspects. Picture as an example Faust, the legendary Kabbalist, in his laboratory, conducting experiments and dutifully recording the results.

Unlike the mystic, the Hermetic pupil does not withdraw into a hermitage to abstain from participating in the world of conventional customs, laws, procedures, and similar "illusory" phenomena. He instead reorients these constraints such that they effect his transformation. The driving idea of Hermetic practice is that the student will eventually dismantle the false tower of his ego and build in its place an authentic one. His way of prospering in the world is not to be renounced. It is to be taken apart, analyzed, rebuilt, and optimized into a framework that channels the descending radiance of higher worlds. An academic, laboratory-style discipline dominates the life of the Hermetic student, scientifically remolding his ordinary mind into a conduit of Light.

Rules

To start, let's examine the materials from which your personal tower is made. All of the procedures, rules, and norms by which you live will fail you eventually, and therefore they have no universal or intrinsic existence. This is a very sweeping statement to drop in your lap, but the mandate of Hermeticism is that you question every convention, every belief, and every rule that governs your behavior. You explore your creeds and test them methodically through experimentation. You uncover their true nature, reducing them in status from unquestioned laws to well-honed tools that you employ only when applicable. The Hermetic disciplines, properly presented, provide a secret course of exercises that reveals, a little at a time, how the absolutes that you cling to are nothing but dust and air. Black-and-white thinking becomes mutable, points of reference become relative, and the universe becomes more and more transparent to the Light.

In different epochs within Western culture, there have been many taboos: making images of God, polygamy and polyandry, giving aid and comfort to the enemy, worshipping God under a different name, homosexuality, magic, recreational drugs, incest, and so on. Our cultural taboos have often, but not always, been imposed upon us for good reasons. On the Hermetic path, you are prodded to find out those reasons. When you see clearly *why* a taboo is used to keep you in line, you can respect it in a different light—not as an unbreakable law, but as a discipline that leads to a certain goal. You can then modify that taboo—that discipline—to serve more conscious ends. Beliefs that used to be roadblocks become vehicles. There is no limit to how far you can go in this manner, since *all ends can be transmuted into means*.

This is not to say that you should disregard morality and commit experimental atrocities. On the contrary, you should take ethics very seriously. The rules by which we live are powerful instruments. Watch the apparent motives at work in your culture as you obey its laws and norms. Try to see the practicality behind every social custom. How has it come about that a man conveys respect by taking off his hat indoors? Why do so many people use the greeting "How are you?" without expressing any real concern for the other person's well-being? Why do bosses keep their salaries secret? Can these procedures and restraints continue to serve your needs and the needs of others? By silently asking yourself the forbidden questions, you work yourself free from automated conformity.

And you needn't worry that such an exploration of taboo will get you fired or arrested. Your awakened self doesn't need to be controlled by laws. The grade work will naturally uncover deeper levels of goodness and wisdom that have nothing to do with morality. Would you prefer to be "good" because you are obedient to a law, or would you rather employ that law to help you express an inner, *fundamental* goodness? As a magician, you will still end up participating in the moral activities of your society (most of the time), but morality will not be your master. The adept sheds Light on every situation, wherever he goes. No rule, no custom, no convention is too sacred to escape his scrutiny.

You should learn to direct this kind of watchfulness toward everything that is at your command, inside and out. Not only will you learn to view the rules of society as tools, but everything you experience is to be a potential instrument in the hands of your Higher Self. Look at tarot trump card number 1, the Magician. He stands before the table on which the four elemental weapons, representing all forces in the universe, are his control panel. He can arrange them to suit his destiny. That which is frequently regarded as evil and illusion by mystics—the world we create with our five senses—is consciously analyzed and redefined via symbolic correspondences. We reshape it to serve us, such that it produces automatically that which we desire.

Symbolism

Not only are rules and procedures important raw materials to the Hermeticist; symbols and correspondences are even more crucial to his power as a magician. As old rules are questioned and dethroned, new ones are established. The new belief system must be deeper if the student is going to tap into the depths of his subconscious and go beyond himself. This requires a new kind of language that is capable of stirring the deeper faculties of life: the language of occult symbols.

As you have read in the Golden Dawn's Neophyte ritual, "By names and images are all powers awakened and reawakened." Symbols properly utilized point beyond themselves into a luminous realm that transcends those very symbols. From this boundless beyond comes the magician's power, and likewise the power that sustains the physical world. The magician uses symbols, building from them a chain of associations that allows him to ascend from the relative world into the fundamental nature of reality. His inner tower is a link to higher and higher levels of consciousness. On his way up its spiral stair, the symbols he walks upon are terribly important to him as a means of lifting the mind from its state of object-referral. However, once he reaches transcendence, the tower is left behind. His symbols have served their purpose and are set aside. He will still keep them close at hand, but not for the same reasons. In the hands of an illuminated magician, they become instruments through which power may flow back into the relative world. Symbols are steps on the spiral stair for the novice, but they compose a channel of power for the adept.

The View from Nirvana

The first big question is: If the student uses symbols to ascend to the *transcendent* world, what does he see when he gets there and turns around to look upon the *relative* world? If indeed it *is* possible for a human being to climb to an undifferentiated, spiritual state of consciousness (in which he stops attaching significance to objects in his environment via labels, associations, and meanings), how would his environment appear to him? As the same thing? As a seamless whole? As nothingness? What does a tree look like when you stop using the word *tree* to associate what you are seeing with previous tree experiences? This can be a very difficult question to answer, and yet it is essential that anyone on a spiritual path eventually be able to see without compartmentalizing the world into relative categories.

When this is possible, at least in some shaky fashion, true knowledge of how the world is created begins to emerge. The magician discovers that perception is the foundation of his reality. It is likewise the foundation of his destiny. All forms are mental forms, whether they be physical, imagined, or seemingly distinct "angels," "gods," or "devils."

That which we experience when we rise above our automatic ability to symbolize is not really conceivable in verbal consciousness. That's why mystics end up rambling, why quantum physicists end up spouting poetry, and why Hermeticists come up with bizarre grimoires that are of little use to anyone but themselves. One experiences reality face-to-face, and its appearance is void: empty of categories, labels, and verbal boxes. It has no barrier and no intrinsic structure—at least not in the way the human mind can understand it.

Another question may come to mind: What's the point of trying to see the world in this way? Why would the Hermeticist, so well known for his use of bizarre symbols and categories, be fond of "sinking all boundaries into the sea?" One answer is that when he actually is able to see that "all is one," he discovers that his symbolizing ability is a powerful asset. This is the experience of the Sephirah Hod, to which the grade of Practicus corresponds. He achieves the amusing realization that he has been misusing his mind all of his life. All that he thought he lacked is right here within his heart. When he transcends the activity of his own mind, he discerns that the only thing required of him is that he harness that mind consciously to manifest his heart in his life. The mind is seen as a fluid substance that he can remold into a better and better channel of power.

The Rogue Angels Within

For most people, the ability to symbolize and label things is an unclaimed power that roams about seemingly independent of the personality. Unchecked, it is a horde of spiteful inner beasts that creates a threatening reality for its negligent master. Consider the myth of the knight who must fight monsters to rescue the maiden locked in the tower. The unenlightened mind is like that maiden, trapped in a tower of conformity, polluted by a value system that directs its magical power into a state of self-imprisonment. The knight is representative of the *discipline* used to liberate her.

A person ignorant of his own power to symbolize is like the proverbial fundamentalist who sees sexual images in Disney cartoons. Taunted by his own repressed demons, the zealot blames the cartoonists for the "pornography" that he himself is responsible for perceiving. The unaware person in general sees his own pains as someone else's fault. Statements like "You make me feel . . ." are typical of people who do not claim their own perception of others as an ability that is under their own control. This is a very dangerous, disempowering state of mind, because its unwitting victim believes that "good" and "evil" actually exist in things around him, unaware that these phantoms are projected from within himself.

The Hermeticist trains himself to work with his symbolizing ability consciously and therefore discovers that his own happiness is largely under his own influence. His inner beasts are named, tamed, and put to work. The fallen angels within are labeled, given various offices, and redeemed.

The ability to use a symbolic reference with the knowledge that it has no reality outside of the mind makes for great power, because the magician can move among referenced things of this world without fear of loss. Since no significance that he projects onto an object is real, nothing that he perceives can be taken away from him. If someone steals your favorite music CD, you may react as though the very joy you experienced when listening to it were stolen from you. Is such a tragedy really possible? Or is it just imagined? How can someone take "wealth" away from you when "wealth" is only a thing of the mind, a category that can be applied just as easily to an abundance of pleasure as to a stack of green paper? Since there is nothing to lose, the magician can create anything he needs. The newly born adept discovers that all around is a sea of chaos and pure potentiality, waiting for him to redefine it, reorganize it, and reshape it with the power of the symbols at his command. Instead of making his happiness dependent on his environment, he creates his environment as a reflection of his innate happiness. In such a way can he become cocreator with the Divine. In such a way does he actualize on the outside the self that is on the inside—known in modern psychology as "self-actualization."

"The Map Is Not the Territory"

"The map is not the territory."[1] This is a key point. The menu is not the meal. Thoughts are interpreters and sculptors of reality. They bridge the gap between divine and physical. They make up a treasure map from poverty to riches. They form a tower from Earth to Heaven. *But they are not reality itself.* On the way to becoming a magician, the Hermetic student learns to affirm again and again that language is only a mirror—and therefore a tool. Once he realizes through and through that the map of reality in his head is not the reality to which it refers, he is liberated to change that map and use it more actively. The ordinary human unwittingly allows his external reality to create his internal map of it. The magician consciously changes his internal map to create his external reality.

Another way of saying this is, "You are not your mind." One of the most effective ways for you to create suffering in your life is to believe the words that come up in your own thinking—and likewise out of the mouths of others.

It can take much, much work on a spiritual path to finally turn this idea into a true realization. For such an obvious point, it is almost ludicrous to mention, but still, time and time again, the untrained individual paints himself into a corner because he habitually mistakes his personal map of the universe for the universe itself. For example, he may believe that people "out to get me" are everywhere. "Luck" he sees as an external force that puts him mercilessly through ups and downs. Compliments make him susceptible to manipulation. Insults drag him into pits of self-obsessive worry. "Evil" threatens to pounce from all sides. He allows such sayings as "Watch out for all the crazies out there" to alter his worldview. The evening news is capable of making him afraid. Imagine the frustration inherent in such a scheme, where the mind's own labels rise up and threaten it from the outside.

But you might argue back something like this: "But experience will verify that there really *are* 'crazies' out there. Just the other day, I was walking down the street, minding my own business, when—" *No*, there are not. Experience will always tend to verify that which you already believe to be true. In reality, there is only that which we experience and the labels that we use to fabricate an interpretation. Some interpretations work better than others at creating happiness, but no map of reality is real, no matter how convincing its labels, boundaries, and advocates are.

Science

As stated above, the ability to symbolize is always active. So, if it is, then what are you doing with it now, right at this moment? Look at the people around you. Look at the local government, the news, TV commercials, and coworkers. Look at yourself. Do you like the tower we have collectively created? Do the people around you enjoy the world in which they are participating? Is it a prison, or is it a bridge between worlds? Another question: If our own faculties are constantly at work in our lives, creating an overall unhappy or muddled scheme, who is in control of those faculties? Who is running the show? Our creative power is like a runaway phenomenon, the reins of which are dangling. It is a power unharnessed by the one who is gifted with it. We are left at the whim of rogue forces that whirl in the ebb and flow of nature.

With the advent of science and the scientific method, the world was introduced full-force to the essence of Hermeticism. The scientific method involves formulating a hypothesis—an explanation of how things happen, a map of reality—and testing it thoroughly. It then requires that we adjust or discard that hypothesis based on the evidence. In other words, it acknowledges that we all have versions of reality up and running in our minds, but it mandates that we reshape them to be more accurate and yield desirable results. Rules, procedures, and symbols are the tools of its discipline.

Imagine now the role of the fallen angels as teachers of the various sciences. They are the crafty, scheming, and neglected faculties of the human mind, and they have produced great systems of discipline and great institutions that have revolutionized several times over our destiny as a species. Business has given us the idea of the assembly line, which has flooded the world with affordable merchandise, from rifles to aircraft carriers to sewing machines. Physics has given birth to quantum theory, which is still rocking the world with its development of radio, computers, and atomic energy. These institutions, these gifts of human intelligence, can make the progress of culture proceed thousands of times—perhaps millions of times— faster than evolution. The castaway on the beach finds himself mesmerized by all kinds of towers of knowledge at his disposal. His crude animal needs cannot evolve to keep pace with his culture's intellectual advancement. His instincts are dazzled by the bounty that intelligence provides. They may even seize on the available towers provided by their surrounding culture and use them like dinner utensils at a gluttonous banquet. They may even destroy themselves in the process.

In such a way do the "fallen angels" within teach our potential destruction. The world we are creating with science today is a tower teeming with demons. When you do not take ownership of your ability to create your own version of reality, that ability falls into the hands of undirected forces. Even though science supposedly exists to liberate humans, its power has been debased. Fear and desire are the clutching, cringing fiends that drive scientific research; they are still the strongest motives for research and progress. No wonder the God of Genesis disapproves of the tower.

The more knowledge that the human animal is given, the more he is capable of carrying out his urge to dominate, control, and survive. He becomes the pinnacle of the food chain, the exploiter of natural forces—bending forces as mighty as the river and the atom to his will. He becomes a warrior and a king, a murderer and a tyrant. The power of science is in the hands of organic motives. Forgive us, for we know not what we do.

Science and the Individual

Imagine now reclaiming the power of science for private use, on the level of the individual. Calling it back home. The discipline of formulating internal maps and testing them can be applied within one's own life toward the goal of happiness and spiritual attainment. This is the Hermetic path. What we do with modern science pales in significance to what the original inventors of the scientific method intended for it. A discipline originally intended for spiritual advancement of the individual has been betrayed and leaked into the culture. It has in fact been exploded upon the world and tossed into the hands of the ignorant mob, to the point where the "fallen angels" now run untamed throughout human progress.

Even on the individual level, knowledge gained through science can be dangerous. It can build, and it can destroy. It can seem to erect for you a majestic tower, such that you stand out above your peers. But if your knowledge is not humbly tested and adjusted to reality, your tower will topple, as though it were built on a foundation of sand (like the sandy plane on which ancient Babylon was built).

Knowledge gained on the Hermetic path is especially tricky. Elevating awareness into the spiritual realms means that you are working with things that cannot be experienced firsthand. In the practice of magic, you sometimes only know if you were successful in a ceremony weeks later, when the physical manifestation of your efforts begins to appear.

As individuals, it is up to each one of us to reclaim our creative powers, to break the chain of suffering caused by inaccurate internal maps, and to redeem the fallen angels. To keep our innate biological tendencies from bullying our minds into the service of fear, we must redirect the mind to liberate itself from the demands of the body. If each of us cannot do this for himself as an individual, then the awesome power of science will continue to remain the captive of the part of human nature that troubles us the most.

The first step, then, in applying science toward liberation is to find a system of symbols that encompasses and explains human nature and how it dominates the unenlightened man. We must find a language system and a map that explains the human soul and its relationship to the universe. That way, the student can deal with the predicament of incarnate existence in a systematic way.

There are many systems of classification that clarify the human condition in spiritual terms. The Hermetic Order of the Golden Dawn, for instance, uses Kabbalah as a language and the Kabbalistic Tree of Life as a map. The glyph of the Tree charts the recesses of the body, mind, and spirit all the way to the source of existence. Placing symbols on this diagram, the student can, through experiencing their interaction, delve beneath the level of biological imperatives and personally identify how his mind works by identifying how the symbols relate to each other. He discovers painfully how he creates suffering for himself. He applies symbols and various symbolic techniques, such as ritual, to restructure his interior map such that it produces joy and fulfillment. Additionally, he tests his changing interior world by living and working in the external world. The monastery or cave is no place for a Hermeticist, and Kabbalists in particular have almost always advocated actively engaging in one's life. Gradually, through trial and error, the student unmakes the automatic complexes that hold prisoner his magical power.

Hermes/Mercury

A way to better understand the human ability to perceive via symbols is to recognize this faculty with a new label. Let us therefore call it Mercury. I will refer to both the Roman god Mercury and the astrological planet Mercury to redefine humanity's most important gift. These both correspond to the Sephirah Hod and the grade of Practicus.

Mercury is first of all the quick and agile god who represents the power of the intellect. Mercury governs the faculties of the mind: mediation, communication, transmission, and translation. Specifically, these include mental and nervous processes, speech and writing, dexterity, ambivalence, and the distribution of energies. Mercury is superficial. It is the electrical activity of the brain that is capable of knowing about things externally. It shapes itself to whatever subject or stimulus is presented before it, creating therefrom all kinds of corresponding conclusions and belief systems in the blink of an eye.

Astrologically, the planet Mercury's chameleon quality makes it take on whatever zodiac sign it is in and enhance it with *intelligence*. If it is close to another planet in a chart, it will adopt that planet's function and add a "sharpness" to it as well. Mercury represents the mutable aspects of humankind's nature. It is the intelligence that is "book learned" as opposed to that of experience. It is the brain consciousness that covers its subject, but it does not really penetrate it or become one with it.

By its very nature of superficiality and its ability to drape itself over the shape of the world, our Mercury-nature is the very faculty that lies to us about reality. Because it so readily assumes the shape of our experiences, creating dysfunctional maps of reality based on them, it is the very thing that keeps us separate from, and at odds with, the universe. Our experiences prod our Mercurial intelligence to fashion beliefs, complexes, fears, and patterns of behavior that keep us locked up in the fantasy world of the ego. It is interesting to note that the Sephirah on the Kabbalistic Tree of Life that corresponds to Mercury is Hod, whose virtue is truth and whose vice is falsehood. Our maps of reality may be truthful and serve us well . . . or they may be deceitful and lead us time and again into suffering. We have before us the perennial choice between "good" and "evil." Not good and evil in the moral sense, but good and evil in the Hermetic sense. We can choose to be truthful, consciously disciplining the mind to convey an accurate representation of reality, or we can allow random events to create an inaccurate representation that steers us into error.

The Roman god Mercury, or Hermes as he was known by the Greeks, is regarded as the psychopompus, the soul conductor who guides the deceased to his just rewards in the afterlife. He is the messenger of the gods, the instructor and guide to the Hermetic mysteries. He is thought of as an initiator into occult schools, especially ritualistic ones involving full ceremony. This is another example of how our Mercurial quality, when ritually trained, becomes not an imprisoning pattern but a guide by which we travel into more liberated states of consciousness.

It is doubtful that the mind's "Mercurial" activity can ever be fully silenced. Some advocates of meditation insist that this is both necessary and possible. But why kill the mind when you can harness and ride upon it instead?

The Power of Language

Hermes Trismegistus is the central figure behind the Hermetic tradition. He is thought to have existed in ancient times as an Egyptian prophet. A mythical magus identified with both the Egyptian Thoth and the Roman Mercury, he is celebrated as the inventor of language and writing. Language is the biggest and foremost outgrowth of the Hermetic faculties. Some say that human beings have a natural instinct to form language, that it is a biological, evolutionary development. Humans do not have to learn how to use it as much as simply learn one particular language. The ability to think grammatically (subject, verb, and object) is already built into the human brain.[2]

What would humans be like without language? It is impossible to say, since a description would involve words and grammar. Language has the power to shape our internal reality map in a way that divides it into different interrelating regions. Such fixed regions, or concepts, help us to organize knowledge, to arrange it in meaningful ways that suggest new possibilities and new plans of action. We all develop, knowingly or unknowingly, conceptual frameworks that help us understand and act upon the world. If it works in your inner maps, perhaps it will work in your outer life. Or perhaps not.

Language is a Hermetic skill very much misused by the unenlightened mind. We tend to actually believe words as if they were the very objects to which they refer. The mind is so mutable that, when it is left unchecked, it will jump to rash conclusions based on labels. For example, which of the following statements is most accurate?

1. I saw Jane at the grocery store last week; she grabbed a candy bar and walked out without paying.

2. Jane stole a candy bar last week.

3. Jane is a thief.

The event involving Jane that led me to make the above statements may have been completely innocent, but the many crime dramas I have watched on TV have perhaps led me to make a judgment that endangers my relationship with Jane. If I had been aware of my mind's tendency to draw conclusions, I could have prevented it from hurting my own future (not to mention Jane's). "Judge not, lest ye be judged" is a statement that is actually advice on how to work magic. Your present thoughts determine your future reality. Be careful.

Statement number 1 above is obviously the longest, and it contains the most details. It is also the most accurate description of the experience. Statement 3 is the shortest, easiest, and harshest. This brings us to a paradox: When we take the easy route and create simplified, cut-and-dried maps of reality, our lives become more complicated. If, however, we allow the world to be complicated, life becomes simpler. If I refuse to draw conclusions and let reality remain uncertain, then I remain humble in regard to Jane. I don't really know who or what "Jane" is (no matter how many candy bars she walks out with), so therefore, my heart is open to her, and she can still be a human being full of surprises.

But that doesn't mean that it is wrong for me to draw conclusions. Jane may very well be in the habit of taking things without paying for them. Labeling her "thief" may help me to protect myself from her in the future. The act of jumping to conclusions isn't "bad." All that the Hermetic discipline requires is that I am aware that I am making a judgment when I do so. Though I may choose to protect myself from Jane by mentally stating that "Jane is a thief," I must always be aware that my conclusion has no intrinsic reality. "Jane" and "thief" may have become linked in my mind, but I must accept that creating such a link will lead to a certain result. If I desire that result (and I am willing to accept the consequences), then I will continue to harbor that link. That is the process of magic, pure and simple: opening and closing links between different correspondences to produce desired results. It sounds moronically simple, but to be aware of links that constantly form and reform in our minds is not easy. Doing exercises that increase consciousness make it easier over time.

The particular system of correspondences that you use for such exercises in spiritual development is not important. It is only required that you use it effectively. Whether you envision a God-Christ-Devil universe or a Nirvana-Buddha-Samsara universe, the test of your mettle is not in whether you believe in your gods; it is in your ability to link those correspondences together into a functional whole. The properly harnessed and trained Mercurial mind creates linkages that unbolt the gates of perception, opening it to the higher worlds within.

On the Hermetic path to enlightenment, the aspirant develops a skill that the famous linguist S. I. Hayakawa calls *extensional orientation*. Extensional orientation is the state of mind that is prone to use words that refer to the environment without any interpretations or judgments about it. It maintains language reflecting the environment, rather than language imposing meanings on things and then wrestling with those meanings as if they were the things themselves.[3] There are no such things in the world as "good" and "bad," "fags" or "Jews." There are no such things as "God," "angels," and "demons." There are not even such things as "human beings" and "love." There is just what *is* and the labels we use to navigate. And, of course, that which actually *is* cannot be directly conveyed by speech or symbol or label. It is futile arrogance to assume that you can capture reality with words.

Specifically, the verb *be* is one of the most dangerous words in our language. If you use it habitually, you may be in danger of believing in your own misevaluations. Can "Jane" really "be" a "thief" in external reality? The Hermeticist acknowledges that this can only exist in the mind. *Be* is a tricky demon, because even as you try to catch yourself using it, it changes its form so many times that it can easily slip by your scrutiny and link concepts together without your consent:

am	is	are	was	were
will be	has been	have been	had been	will have been

You have probably already begun to become aware of its power from the exercises in the previous grades. Simply avoiding the use of this verb for a while can open the mind immeasurably.

On the Hermetic path, therefore, the student exerts deliberate effort to become aware of the power of language and symbol. The activity of the mind is directed to undo its own prison. It examines itself and modifies its ability to perceive, liberating itself from itself. It becomes free of its own labels and boundaries so that that which is beyond labels and boundaries can become the new locus of control. The ego learns eventually to relinquish its own labels ("I" and "me") and settles down to just be what it is, an aggregate of biological and psychological traits centered, as it were, around the influence of that which is beyond labels. The mind finally matures and becomes humble. The mature mind knows that words can never say everything about anything, and such a mind is therefore adjusted to uncertainty. Whatever challenges the world thrusts upon it, it is at least free from the challenges of its own making.

The Beginnings of the Hermetic Tradition

The Hermetic tradition has its origins in the Hellenistic world, in the Eastern Mediterranean cultures that flourished around the beginning of the current era (AD 1). Alexander the Great had driven the Persians out of Egypt in 332 BC, and in gratitude, the Egyptians worshipped him as a god king, like the pharaohs of old.[4] The conquests of Alexander had produced a blending of many cultures: Greek, Egyptian, Hebrew, and Persian. These cultures found a focal point in Egypt's new capital city, Alexandria. Greek philosophers found a new home in a foreign land, where they were exposed to the Egyptian religion. Hermeticism eventually gestated and grew in this tumultuous mix of cultures—and so did Christianity.

Alexandria was a place of awesome beauty and wealth, attracting the greatest scholars of the civilized world. Of particular importance was its legendary library, which became the standard by which all libraries of the world at that time were measured.[5] It employed some forty librarians and contained over 700,000 scrolls[6] representing the mystical, magical, and scientific lore of all the nations that came together in the city. Within its walls, differences between men became a unity in diversity—a precursor of the greatness that mankind could realize under the nurturance of the new fusion between Greek philosophy and Egyptian magic.

Alexandria was also a dangerous place. A city that becomes a hotbed of cultural exchange and spiritual transformation naturally stirs up the insecurities of its inhabitants, especially those inhabitants who are not yet ready for such change. One culture by itself is, after all, a singular systematic way of surviving. If your culture is different from mine, I may, out of ignorance, conclude that your way of life is a threat to my very survival. Cultural and racial tensions in Alexandria were therefore strong. Violent crime was rampant. Politicians played terrible power games. It was very much like a New York of the ancient world. Consider a dark and powerful city like New York. Despite its reputation as a crime-ridden metropolis of cold-hearted contenders for wealth, it is simultaneously a seething womb of artistry and cultural exploration. One can meet a Broadway musician, a politician, an entrepreneur, and a mugger all on the same day. Any place that becomes a melting pot for free thinkers also stirs up the enemies of that process.

The Greeks were particularly enamored with the powers of the mind. Many of the subjects they studied were so abstract that they appeared to have no practical use, but nonetheless Greek philosophies would set the Western world on fire more than a thousand years later, when they were rediscovered in the Renaissance. Alexander the Great had died before he could take possession of his capital city, but King Ptolemy, who ruled after him, founded there the first scientific institution in the world to be funded by the government.[7] He called it the "Place of the Muses," or the Museum[8] (*Mouseion* in Greek). It remained as the primary center of Greek learning for a thousand years.[9] Ptolemy believed that the Greek people's love of knowledge is what made Alexander so powerful a conqueror—and Greek the number one language of trade throughout the Mediterranean.[10] He therefore made the Museum as opulent and as attractive to great thinkers as he could. Its private studios, surrounding tropical gardens, sparkling fountains, and elegant statues played host to some of the greatest minds to have shaped the Western world.

The subjects studied at the Museum, however, mostly inclined in the direction of the secular, the practical, or the dryly intellectual: mathematics, geometry, rhetoric, law, biology, physics, astrology, and zoology, to name a few.[11] But the most important attraction of Alexandria existed not in its library or Museum. No stay was complete without a secret initiation into one of the mystery religions that existed in the various other schools throughout the city.

In the third century, the influence of Middle Eastern spirituality became particularly strong, challenging the superrationalism of the Greeks. The practices of the Egyptian priests, Persian magi, and Kabbalistic Merkabah mystics were designed to produce an ecstasy of the spirit instead of intellectual mastery of the material world. This naturally appealed to the Greek scholar weary from a bone-dry life of study.

The fusion of the ecstatic and the rational that occurred through the initiations of Greek philosophers unexpectedly produced a secret caste of individuals. A new spirituality awoke from the cultural blend as though by accident. Initiates of it moved among the ordinary inhabitants of Alexandria. They reflected quietly in the gardens of the Royal Park that surrounded the great academy of learning. They recognized each other by secret handshakes in the markets and public baths, and they mingled with the Egyptian priests of the indigenous population. They were the philosopher magicians, making up the mysterious invisible brotherhood of Hermes, also known as the Hermetists.

It was not political intrigue that motivated these scholars to meet and keep silent about their studies. It was not an advocacy of one culture over another, but rather the advocacy of the liberation of the individual from the dominion of *every* culture.

The spirit of transformation that appeared in ancient Alexandria is not necessarily a cultural force. It is an evolutionary force that exists within every individual. Not a contrived ambition of the civilized ego, it is more the pressure from the Divine Spark within to grow beyond current limitations, an upwelling of truth in a world of human deception. It was the silent voice of the Higher Self that moved these learned men and women to meet privately, study quietly, and experiment in secret—and to bring the influence of that same truth more and more to bear on the physical world.

The Egyptian religion was the catalyst that awakened Hermetism (which was the name for Hermeticism before the Renaissance). The Egyptians gave a colorful ritualistic expression to the intellectual philosophies of Greece and Rome. Brilliantly crafted Egyptian initiatory rituals helped many a Greek scholar get in touch with the power behind the images of the gods of his own culture. Powerful magicians were likewise born from thinkers of both converging cultures. In incense-imbued temples, the art of ritual put the minds of its Greek candidates into the service of divine powers represented by gods like Thoth and Isis. Some of these initiates would go on to become the greatest prophets of the Western world. Thanks to the magical skill of the Egyptians, parallel threads of truth would eventually blend into a tapestry of philosophy, mysticism, and magic.

The best way to understand how Hermetism formed is to examine the separate threads that harmonize in this union: Greek philosophy, Egyptian magic, Persian mysticism, and Jewish Kabbalah.

Greek Philosophy

It is from the ancient Greeks that the Western world draws its primary strengths. The ideas of democracy and the importance of the individual come from them—and materialism and science do too. For our considerations on Hermeticism, I will mention three schools of Greek philosophy that are fundamental to its formation.

The first is Stoicism, a largely pantheistic philosophy. The Stoics believed that the universe is God and that everything is divine. To their thinking, the Logos, or controlling intellect of the universe, transforms itself into the material world in a natural fashion, not a spiritual one. The world soul, of which all people are a part, is completely material and mundane. As a result, the Stoics' philosophy was naturally friendly to paganism, allowing for natural forces to be personified as gods of a somewhat natural order. Nothing was considered supernatural.

In their moral lives, the Stoics pursued virtue for the happiness it secured them in the present life, not for any reward in the hereafter. Stoics were often quite skeptical and fatalistic, encouraging scientific experimentation and testing of theories of cause and effect. And of greater interest, they utilized systems of correspondences, believing that everything in the universe had either sympathetic or antipathetic relationships to everything else in a network of associations. This latter trait became a crucial element of Western magic.

The next school of thought to consider is Platonism, based on the teachings of Plato, of course. Platonists regarded reality as dualistic, fractured between the world of the material senses and world of the Divine. God existed outside of His creation in His own universal mind, peopled with perfect thought-forms. Plato separated God from creation. God was seen as existing beyond the circling stars, and Earth was in a corrupted position in the center of the universe. All material forms were seen as distorted reflections of the original forms that exist eternally in the mind of God. The reflections are mortal or transitory, and the original forms eternal. Material things come and go because their corresponding divine forms pass over the field of matter and cast a sort of reflection in that matter, much as a passerby makes a brief reflection on the surface of a pond. The forms perceived in the world of the senses are, to Plato's mindset, imperfect reflections of perfect forces. Watching your loved ones grow, mature, and age is like watching the reflection of a passing phenomenon from another world. Think about it.

With Platonism comes the idea of Theism, which defines Divinity as separate from nature in an eternal, isolated, and uncreated state. And from this comes ideas of purity and "holiness." The substance of the Creator is not, and cannot, be "corrupted" by the substance of His creation. The two universes, the eternal and the transitory, exist side by side, utterly different in nature, unable even to touch one another. God's singular reality exists independently of the plurality of ideas held in mortal minds. And, similarly, this reality exists in perfect unity despite any multiplicity of gods that humans dream up to show forth its aspects. The development of theism would be very important to the Jews, as most of them were traditionally opposed to paganism.

Plato also put forth the idea of the Higher Self—or the *Augoeides*, as the ancient Greeks called it. This is the silent voice as it speaks to the individual from the eternal realm. Plato relates in his *Dialogues* that Socrates, his teacher, had such a guiding spirit looking over him.

This idea of the separate, divine Higher Self establishes mankind in a unique position as independent of nature. "*In* the world, but not *of* it," as the saying goes. He could contemplate his life as though from a position divorced from nature. His body was only a reflection of his true self looking down from Heaven. Philosophically and politically, this was a very dangerous development. If the religious zealot sees himself as a spiritual being having a material experience, a charismatic celebrity of his own faith can easily influence him into acts of terror. Think of the terrorism that exists today, based on this simple dualistic belief of body and soul. If you are not your body, then you have nothing to lose, and you can strap bombs to your torso and walk into a foreign embassy to die for your "divine" cause. What should it matter if your body is blown to bits—or the bodies of others, for that matter—if we are all just reflections on the pond of material existence?

On the brighter side of this development, the idea of the Higher Self sets the stage for a very important spiritual awakening process that today we call *individuation*. It is indeed possible, by use of philosophy, for a man or woman to awaken and loosen the bonds of familial, tribal, societal, and even *human* influences, to become truly a standalone entity capable of thinking and acting independently of those influences. Imagine yourself no longer obligated by the roles that are handed to you by your family, your society, or even your biology. Imagine your mother and father not as "parents," but as friends. Imagine your lover as just another human being onto which you project your own ideals of beauty. Imagine the marketplace around you as a group of humans in their animal aspect, practicing their survival behavior. Such a perspective of the enlightened being is hard to envision, perhaps even disturbing. What does a human being strive for when he has transcended his humanity?

Much of the hermetic worldview that forms the basis of the magical system presented in this book is based on Plato. However, there is one important difference, and this brings us to the third school of thought: the Neo-Platonists.

The major philosopher behind Neo-Platonism was Plotinus of Alexandria. He took the pantheistic universe of the Stoics and the theist duality of Plato and reconciled them. A Greek initiate of the mysteries of the Persian magi, he eventually settled in Alexandria, where he wrote and taught his illuminated form of Platonism. According to Plotinus, God was both immanent within and transcendent to the universe. He was completely beyond the comprehension of the mind, and yet at the same time he was the essence of all that the mind beheld. In a vision of transcendence, Plotinus would have us see the reflection of the passerby in the pond and the passerby himself as part of the same phenomenon, making up a unified whole without boundaries. His vision embraces the idea of Plato's Higher Self. The passerby is the Higher Self, and the reflection on the pond is one mortal incarnation of that self. The Higher Self, according to Plotinus, may make many passes by the pond, beholding its reflection each time as a separate lifetime. (Reincarnation is not just an Eastern belief, but was held by the ancient Greeks, Egyptians, Jews, and some Christians as well.)

But Plotinus added a third component to the Platonists' dualistic universe. It introduces the idea of a trinity, which would profoundly affect the development of Christianity after his time. The individuated mind and its lower animal aspect viewed as a unified whole can only be seen that way, according to Plotinus, from the viewpoint of a third perspective, that which encompasses them both. It is from this third vantage point of the one true level of reality that the Divine can see and direct the other two relative points. He referred to this new unifying aspect as "the One" and "the Good." The fracture of the Platonic universe is healed by the Neo-Platonic vision of transcendent unity.

Picture a coin, one side of which you call "heads" and the other side of which you call "tails." Let's say now that the coin represents you. For most people familiar with Plato's philosophy, heads represents your Higher Self and tails your animal soul—end of story. In Plato's dualistic universe, it is all too easy to fall into the trap of deifying one side of your nature over the other. In the West, we tend to cut away the mind from the body. We neglect our darker aspects, even as those aspects are a fundamental part of our nature from which we cannot escape. But for Plotinus, heads represents ego, tails represents animal soul, and the *substance of the coin itself* represents "the One," your Higher Self.

This idea is like lightning to some and rather confusing to others. What does it mean to say that ego and lower self are united in a third, all-encompassing unity? Just one of the implications of this transcendental viewpoint is that the observer and all that he observes are part of the same thing. And within the unity of the two, a doorway can be opened through which the divine mind expresses itself in the substance of the world. Invisible unity can express itself amidst visible duality.

This Neo-Platonic idea of the trinity would later easily be interpreted by Christians as the unfolding power of God. The trinity of the One, the ego, and the lower self would become externalized in a religion for the masses—the rather bizarre trinity of Father, Son, and Holy Ghost.

Plotinus's philosophy uncovered the function of this trinity in humanity and even talked about it at length, insisting that it was attainable through philosophical study and speculation. Plotinus did not, however, advocate religious or magical ritual toward this end. That came later, from those who followed in his footsteps.

Plotinus's difficult ideas, though they take a back seat to Plato's, continue to influence the world to the present day, and Neo-Platonism has become known as the last great philosophical movement of the classical world. Neo-Platonism is the primary philosophy behind Hermeticism. Kabbalah itself came about in its present state because of the mingling of the Neo-Platonists and Jewish Merkabah mystics in the time of Alexandria. But Kabbalah did not become the Hermeticist's primary system of correspondences until much later in history—a subject for a later chapter.

One of the future followers of Plotinus, Iamblicus, took the Neo-Platonic ideals and combined them with the Chaldean Oracles and Egyptian magic. The result was *theurgy* (pronounced "THEE-ur-jee"). This new art, which acted as a synthesis of different traditions, is the foundation of Hermetic magic. Heavily steeped in the philosophical study of Plotinus, structured by the dignified gestures and props of Egyptian ritual, and drenched in the intoxicating verbiage of the Chaldean Oracles, the disciples of Iamblicus compelled the divine world to influence the material world by means of what Iamblicus called "unspeakable acts." For Iamblicus, philosophy by itself was not enough. "It is not thought that links the Theurgist with the Gods," he writes. "Theurgic union is attained only by the efficacy of unspeakable acts performed in the appropriate manner." This is very similar to the Tantric Buddhist notion of direct transmission of enlightenment via symbol. Supposedly, the Buddha once enlightened someone by holding up a flower at the appropriate moment. The appearance of theurgy was also the beginning of Western magic.

The word *theurgy* appeared for the first time in the second century AD, in the attempts of Greek scholars to describe the effects that Egyptian sacred rites had on them.[12] Equipped with their extensive philosophical knowledge, they easily found correlations between the Egyptian and Persian initiatory rites and the Neo-Platonic views in their own culture. With great ingenuity that came about from years of immersion in abstract philosophy, they paired up the Greek gods with the gods in the Egyptian pantheon. Using their own well-known symbols as an overlay, they were able to discern that the silent voice that lay hidden within an Egyptian framework was the same silent voice that spoke from within their own tradition. Only now the addition of drama, ritual acts, and manipulation of symbols could aid them in inducing an intoxicated state of mind that, each time they entered it, would change them little by little into a being more than human. This transformation process is what we today call "high magic."

For it was the view of the Neo-Platonist, and now of the Hermetist, that the soul was trapped in an illusion, that it was entangled in its identification with the world of surfaces. Through magical words, gestures, visualizations, and dramatizations, the inner nature of the self could be illuminated and set free.

Egyptian Priests

It is misleading to say that the Egyptians were "religious." That word comes from the stilted, modern, rational view of spirituality. In the modern Western world, we live in a land of specialization and separation, but for the Egyptians, everything was part of the whole. They were never deceived into elevating the rational mind above nature.[13] Everything was magical to them, and for the Egyptians, to have a separate "religious" institution within their culture was unthinkable. The temples were involved in every aspect of Egyptian life.

And yet their culture still had a very strong intellectual thrust to it. The rational mind was viewed as *part* of nature, and therefore Egyptian science was practical, developed only for everyday uses. Little about it was abstract unless required to be so for measurement of architecture or the counting of bags of grain.[14]

On the surface, the Egyptians seem pagan, but Egyptologists are well aware that the inhabitants of the Nile Valley believed in one single supreme deity that was considered to be beyond comprehension. The various gods of their mythology were aspects of the One. To them, the whole could only be comprehended through the parts.

The Egyptians actually entertained many different versions of their mythology in their spiritual practice. Different accounts of how creation came into being, for instance, were all regarded as valid, even though they contradicted each other in principle and in sequence of events. The Egyptians did not find it confusing to mix metaphors. They knew that the stories were not factually true but rather different accounts of the same unfolding Divinity.[15]

There are three components to Egyptian spirituality that can serve as a frame-work by which you can better understand their mythology as you study it. The first is that of a "high god" or solar Logos, whose power one could experience as the life-giving sun. Ra and Horus are two leading examples of this power. The second is that of the regenerative powers of nature, symbolized by Isis and other female deities.[16]

These two components come together meaningfully in one of Egypt's foremost creation myths, that of the sun priests of Heliopolis: In this story, the *Nun*, or the primeval substance from which all is made, initially dominates the universe, filling every corner of existence. But as the universe opens a space within its midst so that the world can form, the Nun recedes like the waters of the Nile after the flood. As the waters withdraw, a mound of earth is revealed. Onto this mound descends the light of Sun, or the solar high god, in the form of a hawk.[17] Here we have repre-sented the first two components of Egyptian cosmology coming together. The light meets the dark as the solar aspect of the Divine meets the regenerative substances of nature, impressing its will upon them to create the universe.

The meeting of these two powers sets the stage for the third component, that of the man-god.[18] The Egyptians recognized the potential for a human to become a realized god here on Earth. The god Osiris, once a man, dies and is reborn in the form of Horus, the hawk-headed ruler of Upper and Lower Egypt. The human be-ing, arisen from the regenerative powers of nature, inspired by the power of the solar Logos, can die "back" to his natural state and realize his immortal self, becoming thereby a conscious ruler of his own destiny. The pharaoh was thought to be just such a being, descended from Osiris and Isis, who once walked the earth in human form as a king and queen. The pristine and pure lotus blossom that rises from the mud of the mound symbolizes the power of a human's divine potential. It dramatically, or should I say theurgically, expresses the light of the Logos in matter by opening its petals. The pressure of life to grow upward from muddy obscurity into the clear light of manifestation is the power of Osiris the man-god. It is the same force symbolized by Christ on the cross and the medieval rose.

The standard Egyptian temple was a schematization of these three principles brought together under one roof. Every temple was enclosed by an outer wall of alternating concave and convex mud bricks, symbolizing the waters of Nun. Enter-ing the grounds, one would find the hypostyle hall, which consisted of columns and a roof. This area was painted with designs of lush vegetation, the columns themselves bearing lotus blossoms as their capitals. The ceiling here represented the sky, and the painted columns the reed bank of the first mound of creation. The ground of this reception hall inclined gently from the exterior to the interior, indicating the slope of the mound itself. Next, one entered the sanctuary, which housed the shrine and statue of the deity.[19] The anthropomorphic statue represented a particular human manifestation of the unknowable God that the initiate could develop within himself. The Egyptian temple therefore represented the creation of the universe, the meeting place of the solar Logos and the regenerative powers on the tip of the mound, and the human representation of that deity that arises from that mound. This is a very important concept for the Golden Dawn, as you will later see.

Imagine that you are a Greek scholar being led from the exterior to the interior of an Egyptian temple to be initiated into the mysteries of life represented by the god of the sanctuary. The secret formula by which you can develop that god's potency within your own being is demonstrated by the route you take to approach the deity. Additional hints are conveyed through the incantations of the priests, their masks, the incense, the music, and the images that play before you. The experience of such an initiation can be so powerful that all of your life that follows it will align itself according to the pattern of correspondences that you experienced in the ceremony. Eventually, the altered pattern of your life yields forth the potency of the deity.

The Grade of Practicus

As the name of the Theoricus grade implies, you have been, up until now, largely able to deal with spiritual development in a "theoretical" way. Much of what you have done has been enacted on the level of the mind: learning theories and correspondences, observing the psyche, and achieving change in a somewhat passive way—without much of a hint as to how to make conscious change in your daily life.

The Practicus grade stirs your "practical" talents to awaken. Much of the attention will be drawn toward active application of the Hermetic principles that you have been learning. The student may begin to gain some perspective, suddenly knowing what to do with his newly acquired knowledge. He may begin to deliberately apply the principles in his interior map to his exterior life. The value of the

Hermetic wisdom thirsts to be put to the test, and inevitably, this will cause some difficulty.

Applying spiritual principles to mundane life can be very frustrating and is bound to lead to one failure after another. Repeated failure is a test of the student's true talent as a magician. As Israel Regardie commented, "Over the years I have been asked over and over again what are the most important qualities that a student should possess in approaching the Great Work. Other than normal intelligence and emotional stability, I find two other qualities which are essential for success. They are best summed up in the following quotation:

> 'Nothing in the world can take the place of persistence.
> 'Talent will not; nothing is more common than unsuccessful men with talent.
> 'Genius will not; unrewarded genius is almost a proverb.
> 'Education will not; the world is full of educated derelicts.
> 'Persistence and determination alone are omnipotent.'"[20]

This grade shows forth the nature of suffering. As the student applies his knowledge toward the struggle for freedom, he is confronted with personal and universal traits that keep him from his goal. Everyone has blockages to work through. It is important to face the temporary pain involved in removing them.

What is keeping you from quitting smoking or from obtaining the career that you really want? Is it something external? Are you sure? The belief that roadblocks to your desires are imposed upon you from the outside is probably not as strong now as it used to be. All real obstacles are within you. If they manifest themselves externally, then take note of them there and look for the linkages within that are producing them. Remove those incorrect beliefs. Reprogram yourself. Apply your dawning wisdom to make changes in your life.

If you experience humiliating defeats and emotional pain in the process, then you are probably on the right track. Keep going until you are successful. Staying power is a most important virtue. If you are unable to push through resistance and you give in to idleness and distractions, you will suffer even more in the depths of your being, because progress up until now has likely set up a process that will not be denied. Perhaps I should apologize for baiting you into the practice of "magic." You were warned that it is not what it appears to be.

Suffering is, in a sense, needless. But it seems inevitable on the spiritual path. We cannot have the things that we want—at least not in the way that we want them. And we can't get away from the things that we are afraid of—at least not in the way that we plan. Trial and error teaches these lessons slowly. Eventually, if we are successful with the Great Work, we surrender and just live our lives, no longer governed by fear and desire. Fear and desire are ever-present, but we learn to be honest and look them in the eye.

Water

The grade of Practicus corresponds to the Sephirah Hod and to the element of water. Water is often regarded as the element to imitate on the spiritual path. Learn to be like water. It flows around obstacles, knowing nothing of obstinacy. It moves with the utmost ease where the force of gravity directs it. To achieve its destiny, it stays low, undermining all powers of earth and fire that attempt to block it or lord over it. It follows the direction of worthy channels without destroying them. Or instead, with terrifying relentlessness, it erodes away resistance. Water expresses little in regard to itself, showing only the patterns of wind that blow upon its surface. Likewise, the magician flows to wherever the force of divine will directs, expressing to others nothing of his own desires, but instead those of the divine breath that blows over him.

If things get difficult in this grade, remember to submit to the "gravity" of spiritual power that draws and influences all things. Stay below others, holding them up and removing emphasis from yourself. "You" are much more powerful when you stay within yourself, as you are in your natural state, naked of pretense. Aspiring to great egotistical heights is natural for humans to do. It stems from the need to compete to survive. But you are on a spiritual path, which means survival is no longer persisting as a concern.

What does it matter if you live or die? Trying to compete in the herd will cause you to build your tower based on illusions, like a cobra that flares its hood to look bigger than it actually is. Remember that the power of the Divine descends from on high not to meet us on some high battlement, but to permeate nature from beneath her beautiful blanket, bubbling up like a clear spring of Light, wrapped in the simple garments of earth, air, water, and fire. The student of Its mystery who stays lowly, even as he develops his high gifts of intelligence, will bear witness to the naked foundation of all things. As he builds himself up toward the heavens by using the abstract image of the Tree of Life, he should likewise remember the example of an actual tree and sink his roots deep into the nourishing depths of the earth. This Tree of linked concepts extends via mental abstraction beyond the physical world, allowing the mind to expand beyond its natural limits. The two different color scales of the Tree of Life, which you have "built in" to your body so far, are two levels of such a structure. Just two more color scales and you will be ready to bridge Heaven and Earth.

Self-observation becomes key here, as is usually the case. See yourself as the receptive vessel of divine influence. You may begin to notice the effects of the higher planes upon the lower, so use what you experience to achieve better and better contact with your Higher Self.

Divination becomes especially important in this grade. Every detail of our existence is a manifestation of the directing power of the Divine. That means that every detail is a potential sign or message alerting you to the path at hand. Know that you have no will of your own, independent of the divine will. It only appears that way to the unaware.

Paradoxically, when you learn to surrender your personal will, you become independent, no longer needing to be guided by curriculums like this one. The Great Work involves surrendering illusory freedom for actual freedom. The magician is one who has abandoned himself and submitted to the Divine. He has nothing to lose and nothing to gain—a truly fearsome power to reckon with!

Purity is another important attribute of this grade, and as you may suspect, it has little to do with so-called moral purity. The nature of the four elements of creation may begin to clarify themselves for you. All of the elements are inherently free from the stain of evil. According to Kabbalah, they are supported from within by the power of the Kerubim, the archangels who exist at the foot of the divine throne. It is only in the realms of Yetzirah and Assiah, of the external interaction of these forces, that disharmony can exist. And it only follows that thoughts conditioned by disharmony can lead to perceptions of defilement, sin, and unhappiness. The naked elements, untouched by fear, desire, and judgment, are inherently clean within themselves. They are the limbs of Spirit, extending into the phenomenal world.

PRACTICUS CURRICULUM (AT A GLANCE)
(to be completed in 6 to 18 months)

Daily Practicus Formula
1. The 4-7-8 Breath (Second Chakra)
2. Ascent into the Cube of Space
3. The Lesser Banishing Ritual of the Pentagram
4. The Banishing Ritual of the Hexagram
5. Invoking the Four Powers of Water
6. The Middle Pillar
7. The Body in Briah
8. Practicus Meditation
9. Banishing the Four Powers of Water
10. The Lesser Banishing Ritual of the Pentagram

Other Rituals Performed as Directed
1. Invoking and Banishing the Planet Mercury
2. Invoking and Banishing Jupiter

Additional Exercises
1. Daily Tarot Card or Celtic Cross Spread
2. Hermetic Exercises

Required Reading
1. "The Fourth Knowledge Lecture," from your textbook, Regardie's *The Golden Dawn*, pages 69–76
2. "The Tree of Life as Projected in a Solid Sphere," from your textbook, pages 594–621
3. *Man, the Grand Symbol of the Mysteries: Essays in Occult Anatomy*, by Manly P. Hall
4. *Qabalistic Concepts: Living the Tree*, by William G. Gray
5. *Tao Te Ching*, by Lao Tsu
6. *Wheels of Life: A User's Guide to the Chakra System*, by Anodea Judith
7. *The Tarot: History, Symbolism & Divination*, by Robert M. Place

Written Assignments
1. Outline of the Practicus Ritual
2. Diary Assignments (Including the Tracking of the Planet Mercury)

Projects

1. Enochian Tablet of Water
2. The Tree of Life in Briah
3. Drawing of the Seven Palaces Attributed to the Sephiroth
4. Drawing of the Tetragrammaton upon the Tree
5. Drawing of the Names and Sigils of the Olympic Planetary Spirits
6. Chart of the Geomantic Talismanic Figures
7. Drawing of the Garden of Eden before the Fall
8. Drawing of the Symbol of Mercury on the Tree of Life
9. Drawing of the Cup of the Stolistes
10. Greek Cross of Thirteen Squares

Optional Implements

1. The Water Chalice
2. Altar of the Double Cube
3. Temple Pillars

PRACTICUS CURRICULUM (DETAILS)

Daily Practicus Formula

Once you have finished constructing the Enochian Tablet of Water (see "Projects" for this chapter, page 219), do this series of rituals once per day in the order presented below, one right after the other. Place the tablet in the west, positioned somewhere approximately between the level of your eyes and the level of your heart. While you are working on the tablet, you can begin this daily formula without its Body in Briah exercise. Do not have the earth or air tablet exposed during your daily Practicus rituals. You can either put them away or cover them with a cloth of a color that corresponds to their respective elements.

1. The 4-7-8 Breath (Second Chakra)

Breathe in through the nose to the count of four (remember, deep belly breaths), hold the breath in without blocking the throat for the count of seven, and breathe out slowly through pursed lips, through the mouth only, for the count of eight. This rhythm can be at any speed, but choose one that is comfortable. It is the ratio of breaths that is the most important.

After you have done the 4-7-8 breath before ritual for a month, incorporate a visualization into it. As you breathe in, see the pores of the skin open and see nourishing air permeating into the sponge-like recesses of your body. As you hold the breath, see this inner atmosphere begin to converge on the second chakra, in the center of your abdomen, between the crotch and the navel. The second chakra is called *Swadhisthana* in Sanskrit. On the out-breath, see sparks of light spray outward from the second chakra, filling your body, and generating your body of light. See the spray of sparks as though it were an impact signature of invisible light from a higher dimension, striking the inside of your three-dimensional body (similar to the way the invisible, three-dimensional wind causes ripples on the "two-dimensional" surface of water).

2. Ascent into the Cube of Space

3. The Lesser Banishing Ritual of the Pentagram

4. The Banishing Ritual of the Hexagram

5. Invoking the Four Powers of Water

Standing in the center of your circle, turn clockwise to face the south. Trace the invoking pentagram of water in blue light as you vibrate the following divine name:

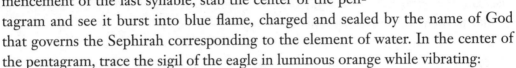

ELOHIM TZABAOTH

(pronounced "El-oh-heem Tzah-bah-ohth"). At the commencement of the last syllable, stab the center of the pentagram and see it burst into blue flame, charged and sealed by the name of God that governs the Sephirah corresponding to the element of water. In the center of the pentagram, trace the sigil of the eagle in luminous orange while vibrating:

EL

Near the end of your vibration, stab the center of the sigil and see it burst into orange flame. The sign of the eagle is an exalted symbol of Scorpio, and it shows the volatilization of water, a positive, spiritual aspect of that sign. Give the grade sign of Practicus—stand upright with your feet together, bring your flattened hands together, touching index finger to index finger and thumb to thumb and forming a triangle in the space between, and hold this triangle pointing downward momentarily over your second chakra. Holding this salute to the powers of water, say:

> **Thou art reflected upon the sea, and a path of light lieth upon the waters, from the feet of creation to the crown.**

Turn clockwise to the west. Trace again the invoking pentagram of water and sigil of the eagle, vibrating the divine names as before. Give the grade sign and say:

> **Thy garment is as darkness, and it covereth and revealeth Thee in the encircling of the void.**

Turn clockwise to the east, tracing the sigils, vibrating the names, and giving the grade sign as before, saying:

> **Thy dew is as the purest, even as it descendeth as droplets into the resounding body of time.**

Turn now to the north, performing the same actions, but say:

Thou art here, even here, in Thy broken reflection, and Thy rivers sustaineth the world, even as they weareth away the vestiges of stability. Amen.

Stand in the center of your circle and give the Practicus grade sign to the east. Visualize a white Tree of Life formulating there at the eastern edge of your circle. Its light fills the circle. Holding this salute to the rising light, vibrate the following divine name and say the prayer that follows:

ELOHIM TZABAOTH. Elohim of Hosts. Glory be to the Ruach Elohim, who moved upon the face of the Waters of Creation. Amen.

Feel the heat of the blue pentagrams and orange sigils as you see them around you in your mind's eye. Feel the awe of the Godnames that you have used to charge them.

6. *The Middle Pillar*

7. *The Body in Briah*

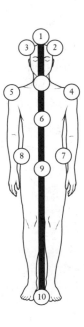

The Body in Briah is built in the color scale of the World of Creation. After performing the Middle Pillar Exercise, move your chair to the center of your circle and sit facing west into the Enochian Tablet of Water. Turn your attention to your aura. See it as a uniform white brilliance, a glowing egg filled with light. It is traversed from a point near its top to a point near its base by the column of the Middle Pillar. The outer membrane of the aura becomes stronger as you increase in spiritual strength, and it repels negative influences. Draw down a current of white brilliance from Kether to Malkuth as you vibrate once:

EL

Next, vibrate the name of Malkuth's archangel four times as you see the color of the sphere beneath turn into the Briatic colors of Malkuth. See it turn citrine, olive, russet, and black:

SANDALPHON

And finally, vibrate the name of the archangel four more times as you see the whole aura turn citrine, olive, russet, and black. Sit meditating in this ovoid glow of color for at least ten minutes. The aura, for the purpose of this exercise, is your Body in Malkuth of Briah. See the colors and imagine an "opening up" sensation between your molecules as light shines effortlessly from within to create the aura.

The Body in Malkuth of Briah is to be practiced in this way daily for seven days. Following that, move on to the next higher Sephirah, Yesod.

To construct the Body in Yesod of Briah, sit before the Enochian Tablet of Water as before and draw down a current of shimmering white energy into Malkuth as you vibrate "El." Then vibrate the name for the archangel of Malkuth, "Sandalphon," one time as you visualize the colors of Malkuth in Briah in that sphere. Then see a blue ray of light rise up from Malkuth to Yesod, at your genitals. Vibrate the name for the archangel of Yesod four times as you visualize your Yesod center filling with a violet glow:

GABRIEL

Next, see the whole aura filling with violet radiance as you vibrate "Gabriel" four times again. Meditate in this body for at least ten minutes.

After spending seven days working on Yesod, move to Hod and so on up the Tree through Netzach, Tiphareth, Geburah, and the rest. The archangelic correspondences for the Sephiroth appear in your textbook on page 64. The color correspondences are given on page 99. You are working with the World of Briah now, so the colors have become even more rarified.

The Briatic body, which you are infusing with the Queen Scale of color, is the higher-astral aspect of your Tzelem. It has a radiantly cloud-like nature.

Once you have completed your journey up the Tree in the manner described above, having spent one week with the name and color of each Sephirah, it is time to simplify the exercise. For the remainder of the Practicus grade, after your Middle Pillar work, sit before the water tablet and return your attention to the sphere of light above your head. See it as the color of Kether in Briah, white brilliance. Vibrate the name of Kether's archangel four times:

METATRON

Then bring the attention to the area to the left of your head and see a light gray sphere, the color of Chokmah in Briah. Vibrate the name of Chokmah's archangel four times:

RAZIEL

Continue on down the Tree in this manner, from Sephirah to Sephirah, in the order of the Lightning Flash, seeing the sphere with its colors and vibrating the name of its archangel. When you finish with Malkuth, spread your visualization across your whole body. See all the Sephiroth in their Briatic colors as they are situated in your aura around and within your body. Float in the Tree of Briah for up to twenty minutes. Intensify the visualization, making it as bright as you can. Then relax in the afterglow of your work.

Sephirah	Briatic Color	Archangel	Meaning
10 Malkuth	Citrine, olive, russet, and black	Sandalphon	Brother
9 Yesod	Violet	Gabriel	Strong One of God
8 Hod	Orange	Michael	He Who Is Like God
7 Netzach	Emerald green	Haniel	I, the God
6 Tiphareth	Gold	Raphael	God, the Healer
5 Geburah	Scarlet red	Kamael	Burner of God
4 Chesed	Blue	Tzadkiel	Justice of God
3 Binah	Black	Tzaphkiel	Beholder of God
2 Chokmah	Gray	Raziel	Herald of God
1 Kether	White brilliance	Metatron	By the Throne

7. *Practicus Meditation*

This meditation comes from your textbook, *The Golden Dawn*, page 72:

"Let the Practicus meditate upon the Symbols of the Rhomboid [the upright diamond shape] and the Vesica. Let him seek out their meanings and correspondences. Let him contemplate the Symbol Mercury and the Number 8. Let him next learn how to control his emotions, on no account giving way to anger, hatred, and jealousy, but to turn the force he hitherto expended in these directions towards the attainment

The Vesica

of perfection, that the malarial marsh of his nature may become a clear and limpid lake, reflecting the Divine Nature truly and without distortion. Let him identify himself with the Powers of Water, considering the Water Triplicity in all its aspects, with its attributions and correspondences."

9. Banishing the Four Powers of Water

Perform this ritual in the same manner as its invoking version, except use the banishing pentagram of water, visualizing it in blue light as before. You need not give the grade sign or prayer.

10. The Lesser Banishing Ritual of the Pentagram

Other Rituals Performed as Directed

1. Invoking and Banishing the Planet Mercury

Hod, the Sephirah of this grade, is also the Sephirah of the planet Mercury. The invocation of Mercury is to be done on Wednesdays only, before the Middle Pillar Exercise. The banishing is to be performed that day also, after the Practicus meditation. Your hexagram, in this ritual, will be orange, and your Mercury sigil will be yellow.

To invoke Mercury, face in the planet's direction (the general direction of the Sun—Mercury is always within twenty-eight degrees of the Sun) and trace the invoking hexagram while vibrating:

ARARITA

On the last syllable, stab the center of the hexagram, seeing it burst into orange flame, charged by the name of God. Then trace the sigil of Mercury in the center of the hexagram in yellow light while vibrating:

ELOHIM TZABAOTH

Vibrate the names, alternately, three more times, calling to the planet by the names of God. Feel the sharp, crisp radiance of Mercury's energy enter your circle, filling it. Say:

I call upon thee, thou who art lord of perfectly applied intelligence, who keepeth the valves of creation in the service of Life and Light. Let a ray of thy splendor descend upon me to awaken in this sphere the powers of Mercury.

Pause, face east, and reflect on the useful qualities of Mercury for a moment before continuing.

When you banish Mercury, draw the banishing hexagram and planetary sigil in the direction of the planet, vibrating the two divine names appropriately. Don't say the prayer.

2. Invoking and Banishing Jupiter

Invoke Jupiter every Thursday, before the Middle Pillar. Banish it after the Practicus meditation. To invoke, face the direction of the planet and draw its blue invoking hexagram as you vibrate:

ARARITA

Draw the violet sigil of Jupiter in the center of the hexagram as you vibrate:

EL

Vibrate the two names three more times alternately as you face Jupiter. Then say:

O thou divine one who dwellest in majesty and jubilance. Let thy ray of abundance descend upon me to awaken in this sphere the powers of Jupiter.

Feel the thick, expansive energy of Jupiter enter your circle. Meditate on its useful aspects for a moment.

To banish, use the blue banishing hexagram and violet sigil of Jupiter in the direction of the planet. Vibrate the Godnames as before.

Additional Exercises

Daily Tarot Card or Celtic Cross Spread

Continue doing your daily tarot card meditation as before, but if you have any questions about the hidden currents of change around you, perform a Celtic Cross tarot divination instead. Do at least one Celtic Cross divination per week in regard to your practical or spiritual concerns. Use the steps that follow.

Note that this divination pattern projects your life in five dimensions. The center of the cross is the present moment, relating a snapshot of your current situation (three dimensions). The horizontal axis shows the fourth dimension, the past and future. The vertical axis shows the fifth dimension of providence. This is the blossoming of the rose, the spiritual influence that descends to guide your destiny. Finally, the four cards that rise up to the right show an avenue of progress toward the result.

S. **Choose the Significator:** Choose the court card that best describes you (or the person for whom you are divining) at the present time. Take note of which way the figure in the card is facing, as this will determine how cards 5 and 6 are placed (5 lies behind the figure and 6 rests before it).

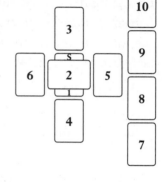

Shuffle the deck thoroughly while meditating on your question. With one hand, divide the deck into three piles, from right to left. With the same hand, combine the three piles into one, from right to left. Lay the cards out in the pattern shown and evaluate your question based on the relationship of the cards to one another.

1. **"This Card Covers Me":** Represents your current circumstances.

2. **"This Card Crosses Me":** Represents that which blocks your progress.

3. **"This Card Is Above Me":** The spiritual influence from within the present moment that is currently coming to bear upon your life. Usually represents a positive (though not always positive) trait that you are learning to manifest.

4. **"This Card Is Beneath Me":** A virtue that you have thoroughly manifested in your life. It also may represent a negative trait that is currently on the way out (being excreted).

5. **"This Card Is Behind Me":** This card represents the landscape of the past as it appears in regard to the question. These are past events that have led to the current issue at hand.

6. **"This Card Is Ahead of Me":** The landscape ahead of you in the future, as it relates to your question. It contains possibilities that you can explore, or people, places, or things you can expect.

7. **"This Card Is Myself":** You as you appear in your current state of development, particularly in regard to the question.

8. **"This Card Is My House":** Represents the resources that are available to you as you proceed.

9. **"This Card Is My Hopes and Fears":** This is perhaps the most important card. It is often surprising that our fondest hopes are also the things that we fear.

10. **"This Card Is What Will Come":** The final projected result.[21]

Hermetic Exercises

As you consciously integrate the influence of Hod into your life, it is important for you to exercise its principles, since this Sephirah is crucial to the understanding of ceremonial magic. Perform each of these Hermetic exercises daily for one month, unless the exercise directs you to do otherwise:

1. Empathize with plants. Learn about them, if this is new to you. Tend them in your house or in a garden. In addition, meditate with them for ten minutes each day. What is life like for them?

2. Become an expert at cooking at least one gourmet meal. Cook it once per week at least three weeks in a row.

3. Utilize the strategy of making a "to-do" list, one for each day. For a particular day, list things that you want to get done and use numbers to prioritize them into a sequential order. Then go down the list and put an asterisk next to the items that are "authentic actions." Authentic actions are ones that cause change and move you toward the fulfillment of deep desires. They are distinct from routine, task-oriented actions such as doing the laundry or depositing money.[22] Some examples of authentic actions are:

    a. Calling someone you are attracted to and telling them how you feel

    b. Going to the bank and applying for a mortgage

c. Auditioning for a part in a performance

d. Throwing away your cigarettes

e. Ending a negative relationship

f. Sending an important letter

g. Starting to write a book

h. Walking into the building of a company for which you would like to work and actively pursuing a job there—whether or not they have advertised an opening

On your list, where do authentic actions tend to end up versus task-oriented actions? Are you giving authentic actions too little priority? Too much? Consider rearranging the list.

4. Observe the quality of emptiness wherever you go. Observe not objects but the flow of space around them. In addition, practice keeping everything in its proper place: when you are finished using something, put it back in its perfectly assigned space in your home.

5. Read a good book on feng shui. Make three changes to your home based on what you've learned. Note any feelings or results in your journal in the coming weeks.

6. For two weeks, become a perfectly polite, law-abiding citizen who does everything according to the norms and laws of the country, state, and city in which you live. Drive the speed limit and come to a complete stop at stop signs. Read up on etiquette and act appropriately around others and when you are alone. Take a generous nature with the rules, laws, and customs you are obeying, assuming that they exist for a good reason.

Written Assignments

1. Outline of the Practicus Ritual

Done as for the Neophyte ritual.

2. Diary Assignments (Including the Tracking of the Planet Mercury)

As you do your daily diary entries throughout Practicus, include an extra heading every day in which you track the planet Mercury as it passes through the signs of the zodiac. Also note when it is in retrograde. In addition, as you work with the archangels in the Body in Briah exercise, write the name every day of the archangel (in Hebrew) you are currently invoking (see page 64 of your textbook, *The Golden Dawn*). And furthermore, incorporate the following practices into your writing, one practice each month, unless the practice itself specifies a different length of time:

1. Be on the lookout for the events of the day that cause you stress. Try writing not about the obstacles in your path, and not about the goal. Write rather about the quality of the endeavor itself. Take seriously the old cliché about the journey being more important than the destination.

2. Write three things for which you are thankful each day in your magical journal. Do this longer if you wish.

3. Include a daily topic called "As above, so below." Choose one occurrence of the day that concerns you, and write about how it may be linked to an inner trait, such as a psychological complex, a past trauma, an innate gift, an astrological planet, an archangel, or a Sephirah.

4. Count the number of times you use a personal pronoun (*I, me, my, mine, myself*) in each diary entry. Record the total.

5. Make a heading called "Service," under which you recap the day's events. Write from the perspective that your station in life is beneath that of all things, that you are here to serve others. "Others" means all forms of life, including plants and animals. Do not make any negative or positive judgments as you write about your day of service, but simply record whether your efforts to help met with success.

The Enochian Tablet of Water

T	a	O	A	d	v	P	t	D	n	i	m
a	a	b	c	o	o	r	o	m	e	b	b
T	o	g	c	o	n	x	m	a	l	G	m
n	h	o	d	D	i	a	l	e	a	o	c
P	a	t	A	x	i	o	V	s	P	s	N
S	a	a	i	x	a	a	r	V	r	o	i
m	P	h	a	r	s	l	g	a	i	o	l
M	a	m	g	l	o	i	n	L	i	r	x
o	l	a	a	D	n	g	a	T	a	P	a
P	a	L	c	o	i	d	x	P	a	c	n
n	d	a	z	N	z	i	V	a	a	s	a
i	i	d	P	o	n	s	d	A	s	p	i
x	r	i	n	h	t	a	r	n	d	i	L

Projects

1. Enochian Tablet of Water

Complete this project before any of the others so that you can begin your daily Practicus formula of rituals. (See the diagram on the opposite page.) Paint the shaded areas of the grid blue. Blue is the Golden Dawn color correspondence of water. A dark shade of blue, such as cobalt, is ideal, but you should use a bright sapphire shade of blue, because the color still needs to be apparent in candlelight. Paint the ring around the seal—and the letters and numbers within the seal—in the same color. Paint the background within the seal orange.

Paint the letters in the following manner:

Portion of Water Tablet	Color of Letters
Blue squares, upper left quadrant	Yellow (color of air)
Blue squares, upper right	Orange (contrasting color of water)
Blue squares, lower left	Black (color of earth)
Blue squares, lower right	Red (color of fire)
All the white squares in the tablet	Black (contrasting color of Spirit)

Do not do any ritual work or meditations with this Enochian tablet beyond the instructions you have been given so far. It is important to avoid any direct work with the Enochian system of magic until after the elemental grades. Remember that you can read about anything you like, but keep your practice confined just to the directions of this book.

2. The Tree of Life in Briah

Paint the Sephiroth and paths on this diagram in their Briatic colors (see page 99 of your textbook, *The Golden Dawn*). Bind it in your "Book of Trees."

3. Drawing of the Seven Palaces Attributed to the Sephiroth

Reproduce this drawing from page 82 of your textbook. Add it and the other drawings you create to your book of temple diagrams.

4. Drawing of the Tetragrammaton upon the Tree

Reproduce this drawing from page 78 of your textbook.

5. Drawing of the Names and Sigils of the Olympic Planetary Spirits

Reproduce this drawing from page 503 of your textbook.

6. Chart of the Geomantic Talismanic Figures

Reproduce this drawing from page 494 of your textbook.

7. Drawing of the Garden of Eden before the Fall

Reproduce this drawing from the second color plate after page 118 of your textbook.

8. Drawing of the Symbol of Mercury on the Tree of Life

Reproduce this drawing from page 71 of your textbook.

9. Drawing of the Cup of the Stolistes

Reproduce this drawing from pages 70–71 of your textbook.

10. Greek Cross of Thirteen Squares

Reproduce this drawing from page 70 of your textbook. Make this of firm cardboard or wood and cut it out in the shape of the cross.

Optional Implements
The Water Chalice

Obtain a stemmed goblet similar to the one in the illustration here. Spend some time locating one that is right for you. Remember that your ritual implements must be as perfect as you can manage. You are to paint the chalice in the colors blue, orange, and silver, so remember to get the proper primer for the material on which you are going to be painting. (Glass and metal may require a special kind of primer.) Make sure also that the primer, paint, and sealer that you use are nontoxic and suitable for use on dinnerware.

Recite the Prayer of the Water Spirits from the Practicus initiation ritual (pages 179–180 of your textbook) every time you are about to work on the chalice.

Water Chalice

Godname:	אלהים צבאת	Elohim Tzabaoth
Archangel:	גבריאל	Gabriel
Angel:	טליהד	Taliahad
Ruler:	תרשיס	Tharsis
River of Paradise:	גיהון	Gihon
Cardinal Point:	מערב	Maarab
Name of Element:	מים	Mayim

Motto:

After priming the goblet, divide its upper rim into eight equal sections. You can do this by wrapping the edge of a piece of masking tape around the rim and marking the point where the tape meets itself. Then remove the tape and divide the length into eight equal sections using a ruler and a calculator. Rewrap the tape around the rim of the cup and then mark the eight equidistant points along the rim. Once this is done, it is a simple matter to sketch with pencil the dividing lines between the petals and the tips of the petals. Erase and start over as often as you need to.

Paint the base and rim above the petals with metallic silver paint. Paint the petals bright sapphire blue and paint their outlines with fine lines of bright orange. Paint the Hebrew letters and sigils in orange as well (these you will find in the table on the previous page): Elohim Tzabaoth, Gabriel, Taliahad, Tharsis, Gihon, Maarab, Mayim, and your motto. Clean up any stray marks by touching up your work with more blue paint. Seal the chalice with a suitable acrylic spray or a brush-on coating when it is ready. Wrap the finished chalice in blue cloth and put it in storage with your other elemental implements. Your elemental weapons are never to be present during ritual unless all four can be in the room at once.

The Altar of the Double Cube

The traditional altar for a Golden Dawn temple is that of a double cube, or one cube stacked on top of another. This makes for ten faces of the cubes (the sides facing outward), corresponding to the ten Sephiroth. The top face is Kether (of the Tree of Life), and the bottom face is Malkuth.

The form of a double cube represents the Hermetic maxim of "As above, so below." Speaking in terms of the macrocosm, the phenomena of this world are reflections of that which exists in the heavenly world. On the microcosmic scale, the things and events that exist in your life correspond to those that exist on your interior map. The pool of your mind reflects the sky of your Higher Self. Eventually, the events of your life will follow obediently the dictates of your interior map. This is another principle that the altar represents. It is the material platform onto which you project your intentions. Its ten faces indicate that all of manifestation is yours to control. The arrangement of items on or within your altar can have a profound influence on the circumstances of your life. Keep this in mind such that, even if you use the interior of your altar to store ritual implements when they are not in use, you keep them organized meaningfully and thoughtfully. Store your geomancy kit and LBRP dagger within, plus any candles, incense, and matches you may use regularly. However, do not store the lamp there. It must remain outside and above to show that your divine will is the only force that is not subject to physical laws.[23]

You may wish to construct this altar for your personal temple in this grade. Make it of wood or particleboard to the size of your liking. Some recommendations for size are 18 inches × 18 inches × 36 inches or 20 inches × 20 inches × 40 inches. Paint it black and seal it with varnish or acrylic spray. A hinged door on the western face can serve to give you access to materials within. Four swiveling wheels screwed into the bottom may help you move it into place with ease (as the altar can be quite heavy, especially if you make it of particleboard).

When you use the altar, it is to be placed in the center of your ritual space. The altar represents your physical body, among other things, so when you perform the Lesser Banishing Ritual of the Pentagram, you draw the pentagrams around it in the four directions, equidistant from each of its four sides. Start by doing the Kabbalistic Cross, standing just west of the altar and facing east. Then circumambulate clockwise to the east to commence the Formulation of the Pentagrams. When you evoke the archangels, you once again stand just west of the altar and face east. Remember to always move clockwise around the altar when the temple is set up for ritual.

Temple Pillars

Though I have already stated that the four elements are pure in themselves, there is another perspective on the elements that dictates that, on even higher levels of the Tree, there exist only two elements: fire and water, the Light and the Darkness. The Practicus grade corresponds to the Kabbalistic World of Briah, the World of Creation. As you have been progressing through the grades, each grade corresponds to one of the Four Worlds, each world having its own Tree of Life with ten Sephiroth. But another way of envisioning the Four Worlds is by superimposing one Tree of Life across the four of them. In true Kabbalistic fashion, I am demonstrating here that there are multiple ways of looking at one mystery, each way shedding some more light on it through its alternative account.

The World of Atziluth is that of pure essence, that of the Monad. Atziluth truly exists beyond human comprehension. It is outside of the chasm in which the All-mind formed the universe. Therefore, it is occupied by one Sephirah, Kether, the supreme crown of existence. Briah is a world of duality, the threshold of the universe. It is the mysterious boundary that surrounds creation. The magical secret of how the All-mind is able to withdraw from a "space" within Itself and create the universe out of nothingness exists here, concealed in the interplay of Light and Darkness. Also on this level are the mysteries of the big bang, the war in Heaven, and the fall of the angels. Between the Face of Light (Kether/Chokmah) and the

The Four Kabbalistic Worlds on the Tree of Life

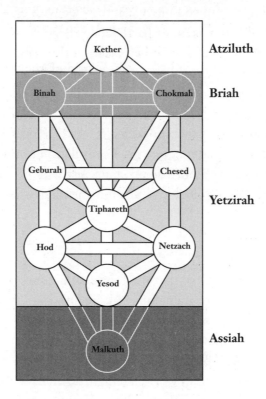

Face of Darkness (Binah) there broods the terrible place of emptiness and despair, the abyss:

> The Abyss is empty of being; it is filled with all possible forms, each equally inane, each therefore evil in the only true sense of the word—that is, meaningless but malignant, in so far as it craves to become real. These forms swirl senselessly into haphazard heaps like dust devils, and each such chance aggregation asserts itself to be an individual and shrieks, "I am I!" though aware all the time that its elements have no true bond; so that the slightest disturbance dissipates the delusion just as a horseman, meeting a dust devil, brings in showers of sand to the Earth.
>
> (Aleister Crowley, *The Confessions of Aleister Crowley*)[24]

In Genesis, God creates the universe first by dividing the Light from the Darkness. These are the two fundamentally different energies of the universe, portrayed in ritual as fire and water. The interplay between these forces produces harmonious and dissonant patterns of vibration.

The patterns of vibration make up the World of Yetzirah and the element of air. Fire and water further act upon the air patterns and congeal them in yet another level of more complex patterns in the World of Assiah: physical matter.

Despite the semisolid appearance of your hand, it is created by the interplay of Light and Darkness, the only two "substances" of the universe. The two exist in separate levels of reality, never touching each other. The abyss that separates them exists not in some faraway realm of outer space, but right there in your hand. The terrible dance of Light and Darkness, complete with "shrieking" spiritual apparitions of the abyss, inhabits your very flesh.

The Two Pillars of the Temple symbolize these two fundamental "substances" of the universe. They are the principal engines that give form to anything that comes into existence. Therefore, they act as the gateway to and from the Unmanifest. The World of Briah is therefore the gateway from nothingness. It is the womb of the Great Mother Goddess. Water and the ocean correspond to Briah, because all life has arisen from the primal waters. In the temple, the pillars are normally placed in the east, black in the north and white to the south, to indicate that the power of the Light, characterized by the rising sun in the east, is being birthed through them, through the two forces that exist in Briah, into the arena of your life, Yetzirah. The influence of that Light will, in turn, reorder the circumstances of your life in Assiah.

You can construct these pillars in a number of ways. It is best to keep them simple for now, making one of them all black and the other all white. One way is to have two Styrofoam pillars cut by a foam company. Another is to cut out black and white strips of cloth, making them each pillar-shaped, and tack them onto the eastern wall of your temple room. I have seen long, hanging banners sold online that fulfill the purpose of these two temple adornments beautifully.

Practicus Checklist

Before you proceed to the next grade, review this checklist and make sure that all of the requirements are met.

- ❐ I have completed the Enochian Tablet of Water.
- ❐ I have painted the Tree of Life in Briah.
- ❐ I have completed the Body in Briah through Kether.
- ❐ I have been doing at least one Celtic Cross tarot spread per week.
- ❐ I have completed the Hermetic exercises.
- ❐ I have outlined the Practicus ritual.
- ❐ I have completed the diary assignments.
- ❐ I have read "The Fourth Knowledge Lecture."
- ❐ I have read "The Tree of Life as Projected in a Solid Sphere."
- ❐ I have read *Man, the Grand Symbol of the Mysteries*.
- ❐ I have read *Qabalistic Concepts: Living the Tree*.
- ❐ I have read *Tao Te Ching*.
- ❐ I have read *Wheels of Life*.
- ❐ I have read *The Tarot: History, Symbolism & Divination*.
- ❐ I have drawn the Seven Palaces Attributed to the Sephiroth.
- ❐ I have drawn the Tetragrammaton upon the Tree.
- ❐ I have drawn the names and sigils of the Olympic Planetary Spirits.
- ❐ I have copied the chart of Geomantic Talismanic Figures.
- ❐ I have drawn the Garden of Eden before the Fall.
- ❐ I have drawn the Symbol of Mercury on the Tree of Life.
- ❐ I have drawn the Cup of the Stolistes.
- ❐ I have drawn the Greek Cross of Thirteen Squares and cut it out.

eight

Fuel for the Fire

The idea that God creates the universe by opening a "hole" in the midst of Himself is among the oldest mythologies in the world. It has evolved into several variations throughout history, but there are some fundamental similarities between all of the models. As the mythologist comes across these similarities, he might assume that there is one vision of the universe that predates and encompasses them all, that all creation myths have issued like rivers from one master story—similar to the way that linguists theorize that there is one language, the "mother tongue," from which all languages have evolved their variations. It is more difficult, perhaps, for the mythologist to work by a different theory, one espoused by occultists, mystics, and a few visionary scholars, such as Joseph Campbell. The alternative idea states that the similarities in mythology occur not because of some master storyteller who suddenly appeared in one prehistoric place and time, but rather because they arise from the human mind, which rises from the same fundamental force in all places and *all* times.

The ancient creation myths still speak truth to us today, because they teach us the manner in which the universe is created *right now*. The story of Genesis, for example, does not necessarily talk about cosmic events of the distant past. It need not be an archaic version of astrophysics. For those who have experienced deeper states of meditation, it actually says more about how *perception* of the universe arises in the process of consciousness. The Light, the Darkness, the primeval waters dividing into upper and lower expanses—these are forces that exist within the human being himself, which he uses to create his world.

For instance, Egyptian mythology relates the account of the *benben*, the primeval mound that rose up from the receding waters of Nun. This creation myth formalizes the mound as the pyramid, a four-sided hill. This sounds like an odd story until you realize that the mound represents a human being. The universe cannot be created unless it has a witness, and the witness cannot exist unless the universe gives him substance. So, as the waters recede, at the same time a mound must rise. Both perceiver and perceived must emerge at the same time. The four sides of the mound show that a human being rises up from four fundamental facets of one thing—the four elements of the quintessence. The visible surface of the quintessence appears in four relative facets, but the actual nature of the quintessence itself—its unity—is invisible inside the primeval mound.

A beautiful lotus flower rises from the top of the mound. It indicates the force of life, the four elements converging into an image of beauty, propelled upward by their hidden quintessence. The lotus blossom opens, revealing the child god, Horus. And the tasks that Horus has to perform represent the purpose of human existence. The objects and characters in his story are forces that exist within you. The myth is simply there to help you analyze and work with those inner forces. They are difficult to perceive directly, so mythology characterizes them for you, providing you with symbolic interfaces. The quintessence, in fact, is *impossible* to perceive directly, requiring instead a multiplicity of symbols that help the magician zero in on his own center. As I bring you deeper and deeper into the myths behind Hermeticism, I am giving you tools by which you may connect to your lost divine powers.

A Myth from the Magi

The creation myth of the "hole" opening in the midst of the Divine appears in the oldest civilization known. By the time of Babylon, a distinctively Western mythological map of the universe had already firmly established itself. Its origin is in Sumer, very likely the first civilization to emerge on the face of the earth. The harsh duality in it dramatizes the split in consciousness that occurred between the right and left brain of prehistoric humanity.

The Sumerians called the universe *Anki*, a compound word meaning "Heaven-Earth." *An* is "Heaven," and *Ki* is "Earth." These two fundamental universes evolved out of the primordial sea called *Nammu*.[1] This primal substance is not elemental water, but the *prima materia*, the concealed essence. In the beginning, Nammu somehow became restless and split into its two intertwined aspects. But, as yet, the two could not be distinguished from one another, tangled as they were in a state of chaos.

There is evidence that Ki is a long-lost Earth goddess, sacred to the precivilized tribal times of the Sumerians. Known in the time of the kings as Ninhursag and Ninmah (the "exalted lady"), Ki is her original name, meaning "Earth." She is the consort of the god of Heaven, An. Sumerian kings regarded themselves as nourished by her divine breast milk.[2]

To create the universe, a space opens up in the midst of An and Ki, separating them and making them distinct. This space is filled with *Lil*, or "atmosphere." The Hebrew word *Ruach* has similar definitions as *Lil*: "wind, spirit, breath."

For our purposes as Kabbalistic Hermeticists, we can discern three of our four elements already in operation within this primordial Sumerian universe: fire, water, and air. Even though the Sumerians presented the situation as Heaven, *Earth*, and atmosphere, the actual solid Earth had not yet appeared. It was still in a generalized, shapeless, liquid state, not yet having crystallized into a specific landmass.

Between the years 1200 and 1400 BC, the first of the great religious prophets appeared. He was the Persian Zoroaster, and he founded the religion of Zoroastrianism.[3] His vision of the universe has dominated the Western world from that time on. There are many striking parallels between his stories and those of the Abrahamic faiths. Zoroaster's main thrust—which so typically characterizes the West's aggressive, dualistic outlook—is the idea that the world has become corrupted by "evil" and that it must be redeemed by applying "good" principles to it. It is regarded as broken or defiled, and it must be fixed or cleansed by the actions of humanity.[4] The universe is divided against itself, and Earth has been created as a battlefield for the two contending forces.

To the Zoroastrian magi, evil became associated with Darkness, a Hellish pit beneath Ki. Its personification is Angra Mainyu, an all-purpose evil spirit similar to Satan of Christian mythology. Good presided as a being of Light on the throne in Heaven, and this characterization was named Ahura Mazda.

The Zoroastrian myth begins with a face-off between good and evil. The two powers of Light and Darkness noticed each other across the expanse of Lil, and they approached one another curiously. Ahura Mazda recognized the nature of the evil being before him, and he proposed mutual cooperation and peace. Angra Mainyu was not so understanding. He regarded the gesture as a sign of weakness and declared war. Thereupon, he fled from the intimidating Light of Ahura Mazda and fell howling into the abyss, where he proceeded to sleep for three thousand years.

Ahura Mazda accepted the declaration of war and, in that time, created the material world as a stage for the coming battle. It was a beautiful place. The sky was an all-encompassing crystalline sphere. Into the bottom half of its shell he poured the universal waters to form the ocean. From the airy expanse of Lil, he fashioned the stars, which hovered motionless, timeless, and perfect. The sun he made to shine directly down from the position of noon all the time, and there was no night.[5] Earth floated in the center of the sphere, on the surface of the ocean. It was an island of idyllic innocence: "The tree was without bark and thorn, the ox was white and shining like the Moon, and the archetypal man was shining like the Sun."[6] Ahura Mazda created beings of Light, called *Fravashis*, to guard the confines of the crystalline sky. These beings had their human counterparts, or reflections, on Earth beneath them. As the guardian spirits of the universe in the sky above, they were also each separately charged with the protection of a corresponding human being on Earth below.[7] This is probably the first appearance of the Higher Self or Holy Guardian Angel in any civilized mythology of the world.

All four elements were now present within the universe. Fire and water had separated from each other, and the space between had become filled with air. A platform had crystallized from the water, a place where all forces of the universe could become visible and interact. This was the island of earth. Such were the four elements perfectly united in the sphere of the universe. I will present this same elemental schematic again in the Portal grade so that you can apply it to your daily ritual work. The elements gather in a similar way in the microcosm of the human form, and by relating the human form to the universe via myth, the student can learn to unite himself to the creative powers of the universe.

Angra Mainyu awakened finally and rose up from the pit with hordes of demons to pounce upon this battlefield of Earth. The Fravashis timidly stepped aside as he plowed through the sky and filled Earth with evil. And this he did to such an extent that "not so much as the point of a needle remained free of noxious things." The impact from his fall pierced Earth to its center, wherein the road to Hell would later be found.[8] Mountain ranges rose up from the reverberations of his attack, and the stars shook. The slow turning of the heavens commenced due to the onslaught of his evil. Angra Mainyu and his demons had destroyed all life. The wheel of day and night revolved over a barren wasteland.

Satisfied at his victory over good, Angra Mainyu gathered his hordes of demons and ascended back to the sky to return home, but the Fravashis stood firm, barring his passage. Angra Mainyu was trapped. The immortal, invulnerable guardians of the perimeter could not be breached. As he looked back at the planet Earth beneath him, Angra Mainyu howled to see that seedlings had sprouted and that life was renewing everywhere, stronger than before. The battle had only just begun.

Babylon Vanquishes the Goddess

Before we proceed to the more advanced map of the universe found in the High Middle Ages and the Renaissance, we should pause to look at one more tale: that of the battle between Tiamat and Marduk.

Around 1700 BC, the ancient culture surrounding Babylon was on fire with the power of literacy. Since the development of cuneiform in ancient Sumer (3100 BC), written language had evolved from pictographic images into phonetic, abstract symbols. The Sumerians' ability to keep records and hoard knowledge had revolutionized their tribal communities into cities. The Akkadians conquered them in 2300 BC and inherited the Sumerian literary heritage. Victors who dominate by the means of war inevitably inherit the peaceful arts of their victims and, in turn, orient the power of those arts to the further service of dominion and war. This process continued when the Babylonians conquered the region, carrying literacy to even greater "civilized" heights. In the hands of warrior conquerors, the written word became less and less pictographic and more and more abstract, favoring, therefore, the left side of the brain. Literacy enhanced a hundredfold the power of the left brain to dominate its landscape. Written records divided up the resources of the land with inventory lists, territorial boundaries, and class distinctions. It elevated the masculine side of the human persona into such a position of elitism that the male gods became "superior" to the female. The left brain had effectively deified itself. The worship of Ninhursag gradually declined as the kings forgot their connection to the Goddess. Civilization became increasingly controlling and oppressive.

This developing imbalance found its ultimate expression in the code of Hammurabi (1700 BC). No longer were the laws and morals of a culture passed by word of mouth. No longer were they flexible and subject to contextual interpretation. Laws now appeared carved in stone, in the public square, governing independently of the officials in power. They became stronger than flesh, because they outlived the flesh. Abstract principles reigned supreme over practical ones, and they dominated the world of nature with utter contempt. This exaltation of the masculine, naturally, was very hurtful to women. One-fourth of Hammurabi's laws limited women's rights severely. Women became property. Polyandry was punishable by death. Veiling and the employment of eunuch chaperones became a common practice.[9]

It was not a coincidence that at the same time in which Hammurabi's code rose to dominance, a new myth supplanted the Goddess worship of old, and it did so with violent, hurtful force.

The *Seven Tablets of Creation* gives the account of the battle between Tiamat and Marduk. The story begins with Tiamat as the goddess who rules the primordial universe with her consort, Apsu. Tiamat, the vast and "glistening one," the mother of all that exists, was the vessel of creation, the space in the midst of the All-mind that contained the universe. Nothing existed separate from her, not even her mate. Together, the two begat troublesome young godlings who roamed about, playing and fighting wildly within the vast belly of their universal mother. Apsu complained to Tiamat that their children were an annoyance and that he could not rest because of their constant mischief. He tried to conspire with her to destroy them. Tiamat agreed that their children's roughhousing caused her pain, but like any good mother, she insisted angrily that both parents endure it in good faith.

One of her children, Enki, overheard the exchange and responded by planning and carrying out the murder of Apsu, stealing his crown, and ruling the vast expanse of Tiamat's belly unchallenged. With his spouse, Damkina, he begat a son, Marduk, a powerful, Zeus-like god who showed great promise as a ruler.

Since the death of her spouse, Tiamat had become enraged and began to spawn all manner of monsters. All of the other gods within Tiamat's belly grew terrified and unsure of what to do. But Marduk took the lead, inspiring the confidence of the other gods such that they heaped upon him all of their resources and powers. Well-equipped, Marduk rode to war against Tiamat. Tiamat likewise advanced to meet him head-on, opening wide her mouth. Their battle is legendary:

The lord [Marduk] spread out his net to enmesh her, and when she opened her mouth to its full, let fly into it an evil wind that poured into her belly, so that her courage was taken from her and her jaws remained open wide. He shot an arrow that tore into her, cut through her inward parts, and pierced her heart. She was undone. He stood upon her carcass and . . . mounting upon her hind quarters, with his merciless mace smashed her skull . . . He [then] split her, like a shellfish, into two halves."[10]

Represented here is an utter violation of the Goddess by the masculine principle. She is murdered, mutilated, and split into sections. Marduk creates the universe from the divided parts of her body. The left brain of humanity thereby is shown slaying and subjecting the right brain to its oppressive dominion. Marduk's victory makes him the chief deity of Babylon, city of the fabled tower. This myth heralds the beginning of 3,700 years of male domination, which we are still wrestling with today.

The Map of the Universe Evolves through the Dark Ages

Comparable to the manner in which the Babylonians took the Sumerian heritage and produced a frightfully grand, male-dominated society, so did the Romans inherit the Greek arts and sciences and put them to the service of similar conquest. And as we all know, the pattern repeated. The great "tower" that was Rome fell. As a result, the Florentine historian Flavio Biondo found himself roughly a thousand years later scratching the words "Dark Ages" on his parchment to describe the aftermath.[11]

The Hellenistic values of Alexandria almost completely perished in the rubble of Rome. The population was left with the oppressive authority of the Christian church, which over the hundreds of years of its domination took the deification of the left brain to the most bizarre ritualistic extremes imaginable. The murder of Tiamat would find its echo throughout the ages, and in the Christian era, it resurfaced abundantly in the martyrdom of countless "pagans," a majority of them women. This wasteland of the Dark Ages led to the mystical tradition of the Holy Grail, the story of the sacred vessel that was lost and must be regained. The sacred vessel is, of course, the Goddess, the feminine aspects of consciousness. The traditions of chivalry, courtly love, and the Grail all were circuitous efforts to rescue the Goddess from oppression.

But the left brain still dominated. High magic, therefore, disappeared during the Dark Ages as well. It only survived in the Middle East, where the arts and sciences were still tolerated and patronized (at least until the extreme proponents of Islam joined the ranks of the many who fail to learn from history). As the West wallowed in the ruin of Rome, the Middle East flourished. The Moors took the classical values of the Greeks and combined them with their own mythology, which had come to them from the Persians through Babylon. From this, they evolved an even more intricate map of universe. Astrology as we know it today arose largely from this period in the Arab world.

Eventually, classical values and theurgy began to resurface in the West as the Moorish culture advanced on Europe. In the tenth or eleventh century, a mysterious, "infernal" book of magic circulated in the clerical underground in Spain. It was called the *Picatrix*. This text may have at one point been an exceedingly masterful compendium of classical, Moorish, and Egyptian lore, but successive translations by superstitious scholars seem to have garbled its original contents beyond recognition.[12] It appears to combine the principles of the Hermetists of Alexandria with a geocentric universe ringed with stars and planets, the biblical idea of a heavenly Jerusalem, and totally garbled Egyptian-theurgic incantations for consecrating planetary talismans. The quality of the text was poor, but the intellectual underground of the clergy hungered for esoteric knowledge, and the book therefore acquired an infamous reputation.

The Medieval Cosmos

In classical times, the idea of a hollowed-out, geocentric universe had been an inspiration to Aristotle. Aristotle had fashioned from it a more intricate model. And through the Dark Ages, Aristotelian philosophy had survived in small fragments in the hands of the church. It eventually found its best expression ever in a classic of medieval literature, Dante's *Divine Comedy*. Dante brings Aristotle's ultimate magical picture of the universe into focus. It is the system that, later in the Renaissance, would make the somewhat difficult core doctrines of Kabbalah much clearer. This system is also a chief influence on the curriculum of the Golden Dawn.

In it, the universe exists as a hollowed-out space in the midst of God. Aristotle gave it a clockwork-like structure, with a revolving set of concentric crystalline spheres. The outermost realm, outside of the outermost sphere, was that of God Himself. Working inward from that, there are concentric layers of manifestation (or condensation), increasingly dense, that eventually reach complete expression in Earth at the center of the universe. The idea of layers of density and the condensation of matter came from an ancient idea put forth by Pythagoras: that energy gradually congeals into matter.[13]

The first sphere one experiences as one "steps into" the universe is that of the Empyreum. This is the radiant throne-realm of God, which appears in Dante's work as the Celestial Rose. Very much like Horus in the lotus blossom, God sits, invisible, in the midst of a rose bloom. All that the narrator can see of Him is an abstract geometric form. All subsequent phenomena are seen as the blossoming of the petals of the rose. These are the ripples of power that coruscate along the edges of the universe as God exerts the pressure of His will upon His creation. This blossoming effect could be likened to patterns created by an upwelling spring on the surface of a lake—or perhaps to the shimmering aurora borealis that results from the sun's solar wind striking Earth's magnetic field.

The next layer inward is that of the Primum Mobile, the "First Mover." This relates to the sphere of crystal created by the Zoroastrian Ahura Mazda. Here, the hierarchies of angels work in response to the direction of God's power, setting this sphere in motion, which in turn sets in motion, as though by a clock's gears, the series of concentric spheres within.

The third layer is that of the zodiacal belt. Herein one finds the pattern of the archetypal man and the perfected man—respectively, Adam and Christ. Their patterns are etched into the stars, such that all powers beneath them obey.

Inward from there are the condensing layers of energy into matter, appearing as seven more concentric crystalline spheres. Onto each rotating sphere is affixed a point of light, a planet. The outermost planetary sphere, therefore, has Saturn embedded in it. Inward from there are the spheres of the other planets: Jupiter, Mars, the sun, Venus, Mercury, and the moon, respectively. As the spheres turn, one within another, the planets embedded on their surfaces move through the sky. Pythagoras says that these planets are the physical bodies of spiritual beings, much as human bodies are the material vehicles of the soul.[14] These planets derive their characteristics from the

Roman gods that bear the same names. The power of the Divine, in this model, descends from outside the universe toward the heart of the series of spheres, getting gradually denser as it descends. Each planet acts as a special focal point of this power, tinting the divine energy with its distinctive character, like a pane of stained glass that changes the color of light. The positions of the planets at particular times, therefore, according to astrology, influence the way the Divine materializes on Earth.

The Renaissance Magicians

Renaissance means "rebirth." The period from 1300 to 1600 saw the re-emergence of classical, pagan values. Science and the arts once again became vitally important: Christopher Columbus discovered America, Michelangelo painted the Sistine Chapel, and William Shakespeare wrote his famous plays. Some say that the Renaissance was characterized by a turning from God to man, but from the standpoint of a student of magic, that was not the spirit of it. Not quite.

In the Middle East, Mohammed had died in AD 632, and Islam had become increasingly fundamentalist in the absence of its prophet. It tolerated freethinking less and less, driving the owners of classical books into the West, where some of them settled in Florence. The long-lost works of Plato and Aristotle surfaced again. And even more importantly, the Hermetic literature of ancient Alexandria found its way to the scholar Marsilio Ficino, who translated it and restored high magic to the West.

Medieval culture was weary from turning away from the "evils" of the world, eschewing science and magic in favor of a sterile refuge in the dogma of the church. The church saw humanity's animal nature as disgusting, and congregations were told that they were full of original sin and that they must retreat from the dreadfully dirty world of nature into clean moral virtue. The typical angel depicted in medieval paintings is ghastly pale, presiding over a scene of sickly martyrs or a crowd of faceless bodies, all of them devoid of physical individuality. Medieval morality held the soul captive and kept it away from expressing itself in the medium of matter. The flame burns dimly when it is starved of fuel.

The rebirth of classical pagan literature shattered this medieval prison. A blush returned to the cheek of the angel. Perhaps the best painting to demonstrate the spirit of the age is Botticelli's *Birth of Venus*. One could say that it depicts the Goddess, who had been in exile since the death of Tiamat, modestly washing up on the shores of Italy in the form of naked Venus. The Renaissance was the rebirth of the sensual world as a way to God.

This idea is best expressed in Humanism, the classical mindset reborn in the Renaissance. Humanism was a spirituality that valued the animal soul. It largely pushed aside the notion of sin. It considered the value, dignity, and abilities of man as divine in essence and asserted that they are capable of expressing their divinity here on Earth. Giovanni Pico della Mirandola, perhaps the foremost magician of the Renaissance, expresses the essence of Humanism in the following passage: "There is this diversity between God and man, that God contains in himself all things because he is their source, and that man contains all things because he is their center."[15] This reinforces the model of a geocentric universe as an opening in the midst of God, and it adds to that image the figure of the human being as the central expression or crystallization of the All-mind. Humankind may have fallen into matter, but this is not necessarily an evil predicament. According to Humanism, the myth of the fall has a positive interpretation. Perhaps the Higher Self has taken the plunge into matter willingly. The physical bodies that we possess, from which our minds arise, can be viewed as central actors in a divine drama. We each have something to say, do, and be. And whatever that may be is none of the business of the moral authority.

The spirit of the Renaissance is therefore very much the spirit of the last of the elemental grades, Philosophus. The animal soul, which has been pinned under the magnifying glass of scrutiny for so long, has suddenly been recognized as worthy. The mind comes down from its ivory tower to embrace the body. The 3,700-year-long divorce of left brain from right begins to mend. Opposites unite. A heated romance ensues between the male and female aspects of consciousness. One becomes the expression of the other, and all kinds of abilities begin to flower. The flame cannot exist without the candle, and realizing this, it burns all the more brightly.

Kabbalah

The word *Kabbalah* did not appear until 1230, but we use it today to describe the mystical and magical side of Judaism that has existed since the first century AD. Kabbalah first appeared as Merkabah, or "Chariot," mysticism. This nonrational, shamanic practice grew out of the Rabbinical Judaism of Palestine.[16] Its main practice focused on the visionary experience described in the first chapter of Ezekiel. The throne of God is seen as surrounded by manifestations of the Chayoth ha-Qadesh, or "Holy Living Creatures." These are the man, the lion, the eagle, and the ox. The throne sits upon a chariot, which moves (and yet does not move) on wheels made of stars. The aim of the Merkabah mystic was to travel in the spirit vision from the ordinary world of the senses into the presence of the throne so that perchance he may glimpse the reality of God seated on that throne.

The primary text that came out of Merkabah mysticism in the third century AD was the *Sepher Yetzirah* ("Book of Formation"). It is an account of the experiences some Merkabah travelers had at the foot of the throne of God.[17] It shows a peculiar account of the "digital" nature of the universe—that is, created by letters and numbers. The Golden Dawn still employs the correspondences of the Hebrew letters that were developed in this book. The *Sepher Yetzirah* also reveals the ten Sephiroth for the first time, but these do not appear in any diagrammatic Tree of Life form until the twelfth century.

By the sixth century, Merkabah mysticism became most widely practiced in Babylon, where it absorbed the ideas of Zoroastrianism, Neo-Platonism, and Gnosticism. Excitement over its mystical techniques wore thin, however, by the end of the sixth century, and its practice degraded into religion.[18] Only a small esoteric underground remained to carry on the original tradition.

In the twelfth century, several masters of this underground Merkabah school settled in the south of France amidst the Gnostic Cathars. The Provence area of France was, at that time, a hotbed of mysticism as the dualistic Cathars reinterpreted the teaching of the Bible and adopted magical/mystical practices unsanctioned by the church of Rome. The Cathars were eventually wiped out by the Christian Albigensian Crusade, but not before they had a dramatic influence on the Merkabah mystics.

The literary result of this confluence appeared in 1180 with the *Sepher Bahir* ("Book of Enlightenment"). This book merges the *Sepher Yetzirah* with some later literature of the chariot mystics and with Gnosticism. Most notably, it marks the appearance of the diagrammatic Tree of Life with its ten Sephiroth and connecting paths. Kabbalah as it is known today came about as the Merkabah mystics attempted to eliminate the need for a shamanic journey that bridges the gap between the sensual world and God.[19] They desired a permanent spiritual illumination, not one brought about by stretching the mind out of its natural shape. The goal was a vision of God that was both immanent and transcendent at the same time—a state in which ordinary life was a blissful expression of enlightenment.

The Jewish contribution to Western Hermeticism finally emerged in the Renaissance, when Giovanni Pico della Mirandola introduced Kabbalah to astrology. He fashioned from the Tree of Life a Gentile system of Kabbalah that synthesized every school of thought in Hermeticism, including the important stream of Christian mysticism. The medieval geocentric model of the universe corresponded perfectly to the Kabbalistic Tree of Life:

0. Ain Soph Aur	Empyreum
1. Kether	Primum Mobile
2. Chokmah	The Zodiac
3. Binah	Saturn
4. Chesed	Jupiter
5. Geburah	Mars
6. Tiphareth	The Sun
7. Netzach	Venus
8. Hod	Mercury
9. Yesod	The Moon
10. Malkuth	The Earth

Not only that, but there were still three higher Kabbalistic worlds with angelic, archangelic, and Godname correspondences. The church, which had permitted the study of anything inside the sphere of the zodiac, jealously guarded its dogma about anything that lay beyond the outer sphere. It forbade anyone from magical speculation about the angelic powers or the Empyreum. There were no systems of angel magic allowed.

Pico della Mirandola persisted as an advocate of Kabbalistic angel magic, in spite of the church's threats.[20] One of his contemporaries, Giordano Bruno, was burned alive as a heretic for practicing it.

From this point on, the stage was set for Kabbalah to be the primary correspondence system of Western magic. Through the successive ages to the present, occultists have added many other correspondences, such as pantheons of deities, metals, gems, grade systems, geomantic symbols, oriental concepts, and, most importantly, the elaborate system of the tarot. The Tree of Life would become an invaluable ladder by which any system of magic could bridge Heaven and Earth.

The Spirit of Reverence

It can't be helped that the student will notice an intense tone of reverence within the Golden Dawn initiation ceremonies. His own reverence is required in order for him to buy into them and make them work. "Glory be to Thee, Father of the undying," says the Heirophant in the Neophyte ceremony, "for Thy glory flows out rejoicing to the ends of the Earth . . . Frater Kerux, I command you to declare that the Neophyte has been initiated into the mysteries of the 0=0 grade."[21] Someone not accustomed to the stilted intonations of Hermetic ritual would probably think, "You *command* him? Who do you think you are?!" And yet, many people are drawn to such flowery prose. Some of them are naive. But then again, some—who think magically—are aware of how drama can generate power.

Dramatic words can be used to raise a spirit of reverence. Almost anything can be used in that way when it is properly understood. What may appear as a worn-out, broken antique to the man on the street may be a powerful talisman to someone who has the ability to project significance onto it. As a student of magic, the aspiring magician changes his perception of everything, and through this process of transformation, his innate capacity for reverence increases. The adept has learned to feel reverence from moment to moment in a state of mind that is epitomized by children and is quite often mistaken for naivety.

It is a sign of the times that *ir*reverence is considered a virtue. Just read a movie review. For instance, the following is a recent quote from the local paper: "The picture ends up chasing its own tail, with a final con that's both too obvious and too abstruse."[22] Many a reviewer will turn off his appreciation for drama, almost as though by an automatic switch, if the makers of a movie aren't clever enough to surprise him with a plot twist. There are many powerful dramatic techniques used in acting and directing that critics automatically view as hokey or outdated simply because they are not clever or "state of the art." Our intellects today are required to be so shrewd that they will not allow us to surrender to the slightest tinge of awe. Such a habit becomes an acquired curse of the mind that renders one incapable of utilizing the power of emotion.

Are you habitually irreverent? Do you demand to know the reputation of a musician before you will allow his music to move you? Do you dismiss an old science-fiction movie as rubbish because its special effects are outdated? How much good drama might you miss out on because it is not dressed up to meet your acquired standards? Can you be awed by children? That is, can you respect them without being condescending? Are you a novelty junky? If something has been done before, does it bore you? How much cultural sediment does an emotion have to breach before you will allow it to flow above ground?

Here we come to the task of the student of the Outer Order. He is leaving behind the naivety of the child (Neophyte) and moving through adolescence (Outer Order grades) toward genuine adulthood and the eventual mastery of his incarnation (adeptship). His goal is fearlessness. And yet, one of the marks of his success is his apparent innocence and awe before the simplest and most cliché events of life. How can that be a mature, spiritual state of mind? The innocence of the child and the innocence of an enlightened being look alike, but what is the difference?

The child is "smaller" than his feelings. He is a victim under their power. The enlightened being is bigger than his feelings. Events don't intimidate him and overpower him as they do a child. He willingly jumps into the torrent of emotion, unafraid of appearing small before the titanic forces of life. The fear of the roller-coaster ride has been transmuted from terror to thrill, and he laughs unendingly at anyone who still thinks they can stop the ride.

The requirement for being able to let go in the above manner is the ability to surrender the ego's control over emotion. When profound reverence or awe threatens to overwhelm and subdue the ego, the average person resists, fights, or hides. The magician has learned to surrender his sense of self to feelings as they arise. The self has no inherent reality anyway, being a combination of various forces pretending they are of one imaginary essence. There is nothing real to be lost in giving way to emotion. The mind must eventually learn to descend from its domineering tower and dance joyously with the feelings that exist in the body. Remember the spirit of the Renaissance and the great flowering of prosperity that it produced.

But you may remark that there are plenty of people around us who are bad examples of giving in to emotion. Desire makes them poor, fat, or unfaithful to their mates. Fear makes them violent, inactive, or repressed. Pleasure makes them forget to pay the rent. We are afraid of these results. Therefore, we repress and distance ourselves from the feelings that produce them. After all, how can we let our emotions out of their cages and not end up as mug shots on the six o'clock news?

Surrender, in the practice of real magic, most importantly involves the practice of *not* reacting blindly and letting an emotion rule the body, for that is also a form of repression—to numb oneself to emotion by letting it bypass awareness and go directly into action. The key is to wakefully experience emotion without letting it dominate your actions. The magician does not hide from a feeling or repress it, nor does he let it drive him forward like a "monkey on his back." The magician is free to do as he pleases, despite the pains and pleasures of the world. He has learned to let emotions flow full-force, but also to harness them and to mount them like a masterful rider. As it says in a Golden Dawn prayer:

> And no longer shall we be swept away by the tempest, but we shall hold
> the bridles of the winged steeds of dawn—and we shall direct the course
> of the evening breeze to fly before Thee, O Spirit of Spirits.[23]

Ceremonial magic is said to occur primarily in the Sephirah Hod, and Hod is the sphere in which the faculty of repression is found. Your ability to repress emotions can be employed more intelligently toward guiding them into proper expression. If you can't beat them, you might as well *redirect* them. Ritual, in Hod, puts the repressive faculty to better use by turning it into a controlling mechanism that the magician applies to the raw emotions of Netzach. And in the Outer Order work of the Golden Dawn, it is the controlling faculties of Hod that are uprooted from the domination of the ego and turned over to the Higher Self. The emotions, like anything else, need not work against you. They can serve you if properly cultivated. An individual who can harness that power is impressive indeed.

But the ego is not capable of doing this alone. The magician must surrender control to his Higher Self. The Higher Self is open to everything, directing every feeling naturally to its proper destiny. This surrender is actually a different kind of faith than religious faith. It is not the belief in the existence of God, but the belief that everything has a purpose. Nothing needs to be locked away in some unused dungeon of the mind. Angels fall into a demonic state because they are oppressed and mishandled. Does the universe really have a dungeon in which demons scheme to get out, or do we just project our own repressed complexes upon the cosmos? What if we each had the power to redeem our neglected fallen angels within? To see them as they really are? The magician who uses the power of surrender, in its true sense, consequently becomes a rider on the liberated forces of his own life. The magician gives up one form of control and appears to gain another. Or, in other words, he surrenders all personal interest, making room for a new nonpersonal awareness to descend and preside. This transformation heralds the state sought after in the discipline of high magic, the fabled "knowledge and conversation of the Holy Guardian Angel."

Such freedom is bliss beyond anything experienced as a child. The magician has the most unexpected kind of power: the power of surrender, a *knowledgeable* return to innocence.

The state of mind that is the most helpful in achieving this goal is the spirit of reverence. It probably hasn't taken long for you to realize that the effects of magic largely announce themselves by the moods and qualities of intelligence that they bring about. The moods themselves are the limbs of spiritual entities penetrating the physical world, so it must be remembered that the quality of consciousness itself is that which matters most, not the image or symbol used to conjure it up.

In the classic text of magic, *The Sacred Magic of Abramelin the Mage*, Abraham the Jew reminds the student to "inflame thyself with prayer." Reverence is the first type of entity that the student of magic learns to conjure. If he wants to achieve the power of the magician, he must become a master of that particular emotion. Reverence is the most powerful spirit. It is the angel that can carry the initiate across the great waste of the abyss into the eternal Light of Atziluth. It is a faith that we are already there at the goal of the Great Work, a faith that our feelings are in themselves divine beings.

Israel Regardie wrote often on the subject of reverence for the highest, loftiest, purest state of being:

> A great deal of attention should be paid to that part of the ceremony demanding the invocation of the Higher. Success herein spells success of the entire ceremony. That is, there should be a clear consciousness of the presence of the Divine force coursing through the operator. It is an unmistakable sensation. So strong and powerful can this become, that at times it may almost seem a physical one. If this Invocation is slurred over or inconsequentially performed, then a great deal of power must be expended unnecessarily on the remaining parts of the ritual in order to redeem the entire operation from failure.[24]

If the magician fails to subjugate himself before his Higher Self, the ritual is then contaminated with the "what's in it for me" demon. This is the normal state of the ego, which has no place inside the magical circle. It doesn't even exist in the higher worlds of Briah and Atziluth, so how could its stifling thought patterns have the authority to make a magical operation work? Self-interest, though not in itself evil, would be more effectively utilized outside the ritual chamber, in mundane actions.

All of the knowledge in the grade work that the student gains about himself—his abilities, his limitations, and the secret inner world of the spirit—what is the point of all of it? What is he to do with it? Will he follow the dictates of his biology and use it to bolster a competitive position against his peers? Will he use it to serve the needs of his mortal, petty self? Or will he become a master of those needs, releasing them, refining them, and harnessing them, eventually to offer up his control of them to the Higher Self, faithfully knowing that his "Holy Guardian Angel" delights in consuming wholly his flesh and diverting it from earthly motives to divine ends?

The Grade of Philosophus

Philosophus means "philosopher" in Latin. By the time you complete this grade, the Hermetic philosophy will be firmly built into your being. Your life will be an embodiment of those principles, and you will probably notice that those principles begin to function. You should take note that the philosophy has been concretized but has not yet yielded up that which lies beyond it, the fabled Philosopher's Stone.

In Philosophus, the student moves close to the fiery heart of transformation. For most, this is the most difficult grade to traverse. Things that the aspirant has up until now been able to avoid facing will get stripped clean of labels and appearances. The actual experiencing of estranged parts of the self is forced upon student, as the "shells" he uses to isolate them within are burned away by daily invocations of the element of fire. The dungeon door blasts open.

It is likely that big changes will happen in this grade. New ideas and perspectives will surface. New purposes for living. Loss of old patterns. Pain. It is time to summon courage. The best way to avoid the resulting suffering is to go through it. Keep going. Change is inevitable, and old patterns burn away under the heat and pressure of spiritual destiny.

Some say that fire is the element of the will, but it may better be described, for our purposes here, as the element of the *impulse*. This word better describes elemental fire as it exists on all levels of mind, while the word *will* sounds too involved with the more "exalted" heights. In Philosophus, impulses of differing kinds will be awakened on the animal level, for there is also a fire down below. A heightened or lowered sex drive may result. Desires for adventure, power, revelry, and engaging life will most certainly rise to the surface. Very likely they will cause trouble. It can be a very trying time for married couples, and such relationships may even fall away. The things that the ego thinks are sacred may not, in reality, be worthy vehicles for the Higher Self.

If ever a grade could be viewed as a test, this one certainly fits that label. The student will experience something of the sixteenth key of the tarot, which involves the destruction of dishonest and self-deceiving aspects of the ego. Even his professional life or means of income may come undone. He may hit "rock bottom."

There are many people in the world who have secured positions—professional, political, sexual, and financial situations—that they have not earned legitimately. They "fake it to make it," subsisting by deception, and suffering from the internal conflicts that can result. They usually are surrounded by friends and family who are pretending in the same way, putting up similar smoke screens to "get ahead" instead of doing what they really want to do. When we deceive ourselves, whom (or what!) are we serving? What is the unspoken goal of such efforts?

There are also many, many people in similar positions of power who have irrational guilt or feelings of being "fake" when in fact they are quite capable and deserving of their status. Their ideas of what a "successful" person is are perhaps inaccurate, that being the only culprit to their unhappiness.

The Observer

Sifting through issues that involve power and success is part of the process of Philosophus, and for many students it is intensely painful, especially for intellectual, analytical, and spiritually aware people who are good at dismissing emotion.

How do you currently use *your* personal fire? How much of it do you claim for yourself? How much do you give away to others? Are you helping others achieve their dreams and neglecting your own?

It is possible that the student may lose confidence in himself for a while as old survival skills crumble. The faculties of the personality that project personal power and inspire confidence in others are being restructured. If the student is successful with the Great Work, he will never come back the way that he was before.

In Philosophus, you confront the human in his animal aspect. Conflict between spiritual and animal levels of activity may become pronounced. Here, self-observation, once again, is very important in dealing with this universal theme made real. Watch particularly for competitiveness. Watch for your participation in pecking orders. How do you act when you are in a group of people as opposed to when you are alone? When you make a "mistake" in front of others, what do you do with your bodily motions? Your words? Do you habitually grunt, groan, or make other noises? Do you hide behind humor? How much of your energy do you devote toward covering up the fact that you are "not good enough"? Do you speak too softly or too loudly? Do you mumble in order to hide what you want to say, sabotaging your own self-expression?

Watch for lies. For the unenlightened, the tongue serves as a survival tool. Be aware of when you lie. Feel the reason for a lie when you notice one coming out. Try to feel it nonverbally, without justifying, condemning, or making excuses for your actions. Also, in what ways do you deceive people nonverbally? How do you use posture, positioning, arms, and legs when dealing with others? How many ways do you hide, and why on earth do you persist in pretending you are in control? If you can answer these questions, your honesty can spare you much pain and hardship.

On the flip side, Philosophus brings on a stage of development characterized by Horus the Avenger. This Egyptian god, who as an infant hid in the silence of the swamp, has grown up. He is cocky, feeling ready to go out adventuring on the career that will bring him to the throne of Upper and Lower Egypt. He is eager to wage war on his evil uncle, Set. Is he up to the task?

In this vein, some people say that the Philosophus work makes them feel god-like. The faculties of the self, represented by the four elements, have *all* become roused. It is only natural that they begin to start working together, and with the average healthy tendency toward balance, they will try to work synergistically. A feeling of personal power, integrity, and confidence may result.

In this way, the initiation into adeptship begins in Philosophus, and this is a dangerous time. The power of all four elements united suddenly gives the individual the ability to make change and influence people with little effort. The result may be a string of successes that lead to the most common kind of self-esteem—satisfaction based on circumstances. It can be a lovely, intoxicating time. But beware, because the truly enlightened being does not depend on circumstance for happiness. Be mindful. It is best to assume that you have not attained the illumination of adeptship yet (even if you have). If the Philosophus grade heralds a time of personal power and success, this does not mean that your heart has been opened and that your consciousness has been transmuted. Power will bring with it the temptation to abandon the Great Work and become a slave to your newfound potency. Many people feel quite satisfied with basic psychological wellness and decide to proceed no further. After all, what more is there to desire?

Should such a thing happen, what will you do? Once you have conquered the self, to whom will you devote the spoils?

PHILOSOPHUS CURRICULUM (AT A GLANCE)

(to be completed in 6 to 18 months)

Daily Philosophus Formula

1. Breath of Fire
2. Ascent into the Cube of Space
3. The Lesser Banishing Ritual of the Pentagram
4. The Banishing Ritual of the Hexagram
5. Invoking the Four Powers of Fire
6. The Middle Pillar
7. The Body in Atziluth
8. Philosophus Meditation
9. Banishing the Four Powers of Fire
10. The Lesser Banishing Ritual of the Pentagram

Other Rituals Performed as Directed

1. Invoking and Banishing Venus
2. Invoking and Banishing Mars

Additional Exercises

1. Daily Tarot Card or Tree of Life Spread
2. Voice Exercises

Required Reading

1. "The Fifth Knowledge Lecture," from your textbook, Regardie's *The Golden Dawn*, pages 77–111
2. "Talismans," from your textbook, pages 479–504
3. *How to Win Friends and Influence People*, by Dale Carnegie
4. *Myths to Live By*, by Joseph Campbell
5. *Enochian Magic for Beginners*, by Donald Tyson

Written Assignments

1. Outline of the Philosophus Ritual
2. Diary Assignments (Including the Tracking of Venus)

Projects
1. Enochian Tablet of Fire
2. The Tree of Life in Atziluth
3. Drawing of the Qabalah of the Nine Chambers
4. Drawing of the Geomantic Talismanic Forms
5. Drawing of Sulphur on the Tree of Life
6. Drawing of Salt on the Tree of Life
7. Drawing of the Trinity Operating through the Sephiroth
8. Drawing of the Garden of Eden after the Fall
9. Drawing of Venus on the Tree of Life
10. Calvary Cross of Twelve Squares
11. Solid Pyramid of the Elements
12. Calvary Cross of Ten Squares

Optional Implements
1. The Fire Wand
2. The Sword

PHILOSOPHUS CURRICULUM (DETAILS)

Daily Philosophus Formula

Once you have finished constructing the Enochian Tablet of Fire (see "Projects" for this chapter, page 260), do this series of rituals once per day in the order presented below, one right after the other. Place the tablet in the south, positioned somewhere approximately between the level of your eyes and the level of your heart. While you are working on finishing the tablet, you can begin this daily formula without its Body in Atziluth exercise. Do not have the other Enochian tablets exposed during your daily Philosophus rituals. You can either put them away or cover them with a cloth of a color that corresponds to their respective elements.

1. Breath of Fire

Most civilized people have learned to breathe in a repressive manner, in which the gut feelings are avoided. They effectively isolate the mind from the body and decrease vitality, estranging the brain consciousness from its emotions and its animal nature. As you learned in Practicus, the lower animal and vegetable levels of awareness are crucial instruments of spiritual growth. You can commune with them best in the sensations of the lower parts of your torso. The Philosophus grade overall exposes you to your animal powers more directly than ever, and deep abdominal breaths assist you in "embracing" them.

This exercise benefits you by increasing your capacity for positive energy, giving you more charisma, confidence, sex appeal, and personal power. You have come a long way through the other grades, banishing unbalanced influences, purifying your bodies, and making them worthier vehicles of the Light. You should now be ready to increase the flow of life force through those vehicles.

It is important that you breathe deeply into the belly, a technique you have learned through your previous exercises. As you breathe, tune in to your deep abdominal breaths and make sure that as you expand the breath into the upper chest, you are maintaining the deep expansion into the abdomen. In other words, you should sustain the downward pressure even as you inhale higher into the lungs. Many students evade their total breath capacity due to a deep fear of life. Abdominal breathing should not be a mere ripple that proceeds from bottom to top. It should take advantage of the capacity of the entire torso, beginning with the abdomen and ending at the top of the rib cage.

Lie on your back and bring your heels up halfway toward your buttocks, such that the knees are elevated. Place your hands on your upper abdomen, such that your index fingers nearly touch at the navel and your thumbs point loosely at each other, about an inch apart. Begin by doing circular breathing, slowly, as you did in Theoricus. Breathe in to the count of four full seconds and breathe out to the count of four full seconds, feeling a hidden wheel-like motion.

Then stop counting in fours and begin counting each breath as you pick up speed: "one, and, two, and, three, and, four, and, five, and . . ." Imagine the sound of a large steam engine as it picks up speed rapidly. Do twenty-one breaths of rapid diaphragmatic breathing. Stay relaxed throughout. After the twenty-one breaths, slow the circular breath back down into counts of four seconds. During this slow time, visualize the pores of the skin and the recesses of the body opening as the nourishing atmosphere enters and sweeps through every deep place within the body, rousing it and rarifying it. By the time the abdomen and chest are filled to capacity, feel the air within you begin to converge on a point inside your torso between the navel and sternum (the third chakra, called *Manipura* in Sanskrit). On the out-breath, see that the air that you inhaled rushes out from that point as sparks of light radiating in all directions. This fountain of scintillating stars projects the body of light from your Manipura chakra into your physical frame, as though into a mold.

After a minute or longer has passed, do another set of twenty-one rapid diaphragmatic breaths without visualizing the light. Then relax into the slow circular breath again with its visualization. Do a total of three sets of twenty-one rapid breaths alternated with slow visualization breaths. After the last minute of slow breaths, relax and breathe normally. Feel the tingling throughout your body as though it were the very presence of your body of light. Pair up the visualization of this glowing inner body with that of the physical sensation. Note any involuntary tendency to tense up in response to your bodily sensations. Relax.

This exercise can be startlingly potent, having effects that reach into your normal daily life. Record your experiences in your magical diary. If your experience during the exercise itself becomes too intense or unpleasant, omit this exercise from your formula and then pick up the exercise again, perhaps every other day if necessary. You may use the standard fourfold breath as a substitute if necessary, including with it the visualization of projecting light from the third chakra.

2. Ascent into the Cube of Space

3. The Lesser Banishing Ritual of the Pentagram

4. The Banishing Ritual of the Hexagram

5. Invoking the Four Powers of Fire

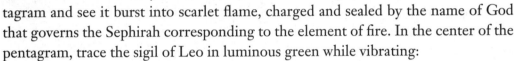

Standing in the center of your circle, turn clockwise to face the south. Trace the invoking pentagram of fire in red light as you vibrate the following divine name:

YHVH TZABAOTH

(pronounced "Yah-hoh-vah Tzah-bah-ohth"). At the commencement of the last syllable, stab the center of the pentagram and see it burst into scarlet flame, charged and sealed by the name of God that governs the Sephirah corresponding to the element of fire. In the center of the pentagram, trace the sigil of Leo in luminous green while vibrating:

ELOHIM

Near the end of your vibration, stab the center of the sigil and see it burst into green flame. Give the grade sign of Philosophus—stand upright with your feet together, bring your flattened hands together, touching index finger to index finger and thumb to thumb and forming a triangle between, and hold this triangle pointing upward momentarily before your forehead. Holding this salute to the powers of fire, say:

Thy purpose descendeth, wrapped in tongues of flame, even as it resteth unmoved upon Thy brow.

Turn clockwise to the west. Trace again the invoking pentagram of fire and the sigil of Leo, vibrating the divine names as before. Give the grade sign, and say:

Thou appearest in the movement of the flame itself, and the created worlds are borne aloft on the ravishments of Thy love.

Turn clockwise to the east, tracing the sigils, vibrating the names, and giving the grade sign as before, saying:

Thou goest forth as a hot wind before the feet of the wise, even as Thou becomest a consuming whirlwind for ignorance.

Turn now to the north, performing the same actions, but say:

A great heat Thou art, pressing from within the shell of matter. The rose is a clay image of Thy hidden flame. Amen.

Stand in the center of your circle and give the Philosophus grade sign to the east. Visualize a white Tree of Life formulating there at the eastern edge of your circle. Its light fills the circle. Holding this salute to the rising light, vibrate the following divine name and say the prayer that follows:

YHVH TZABAOTH. Blessed be Thou. Leader of Armies is Thy Name. Amen.

Feel the heat of the red fire and green sigils as you see them around you in your mind's eye. Feel the awe of the Godnames that you have used to charge them.

6. *The Middle Pillar*

7. *The Body in Atziluth*

The Body in Atziluth is built in the King Scale of color. The colors of the Sephiroth in Atziluth are absolutely the most rarefied, and the powers that you call upon are the names of God Himself. Godnames are very potent, exalted, and mysterious, and they are beyond the ability of any magician to control. They are called upon with the utmost reverence, and whether or not they respond is unpredictable. When they do come to bear upon a ceremony, they are considered to be perfect and infallible. This is why they are always called upon first, before the magician attempts to call upon entities from lower worlds, such as archangels, angels, elementals, and demons.

After performing the Middle Pillar Exercise, move your chair to the center of your circle and sit facing south into the Enochian Tablet of Fire. Visualize the complete Tree of Life situated in your aura. See it as completely filled with brilliance, with no colors. Draw a current of brilliance down from Kether to Malkuth as you vibrate once:

ELOHIM

Next, vibrate the name of God that governs Malkuth four times as you see the color of that sphere filling with yellow, the Atziluthic color of Malkuth:

ADONAI HA-ARETZ

And finally, vibrate the Godname four more times as you see the whole Tree within turn luminous yellow. Sit meditating in this radiant yellow Tree of Life for at least ten minutes.

In past grades, you have visualized an earthen body, an etheric double, or an aura to represent your body as it might appear in different Kabbalistic worlds—Assiah, Yetzirah, and Briah. Your Atziluthic body is so exalted that it is beyond your powers of visualization. So you now call up the impression of the Tree of Life within your body to represent, in abstract, that ultimate monadic body. This Tree of Life is perhaps the same geometric form that the narrator of Dante's *Divine Comedy* sees on the throne of God. The Body in Malkuth of Atziluth is to be practiced in this way daily for seven days. Following that, move on the next higher Sephirah, Yesod.

To construct the Body in Yesod of Atziluth, sit before the Enochian Tablet of Fire as before and draw a current of shimmering white energy down into Malkuth as you vibrate Elohim. Then vibrate the Godname for Malkuth, "Adonai ha-Aretz," one time as you visualize the color of Malkuth in Atziluth. Then see a red ray of light rise up from Malkuth to Yesod, at your genitals. Vibrate the Godname that governs Yesod four times as you visualize your Yesod center filling with an indigo glow:

SHADDAI EL CHAI

Next, see the whole Tree of Life filling with indigo luminance as you vibrate the Godname four times again. Sit meditating within this Tree for at least ten minutes.

After spending seven days working on Yesod, move to Hod, and so on up the Tree through Netzach, Tiphareth, Geburah, and the rest. The Godname correspondences for the Sephiroth appear in your textbook on page 64. The color correspondences are given on page 99.

Once you have completed your journey up the Tree in the manner described above, having spent one week with the name and color of each Sephirah, it is time to simplify the exercise. For the remainder of the Philosophus grade, after your

Middle Pillar work, sit before the fire tablet and return your attention to the sphere of light above your head. See it as the color of Kether in Atziluth, pure colorless brilliance. Vibrate the Godname that governs Kether four times:

EHEIEH

Then bring the attention to the area to the left of your head and see a soft, pale blue sphere, the color of Chokmah in Briah. Vibrate Chokmah's Godname four times:

YAH

Continue on down the Tree in this manner, from Sephirah to Sephirah, in the order of the Lightning Flash, seeing the sphere with its colors and vibrating the corresponding Godname. When you finish with Malkuth, spread your visualization across your whole body. See all the Sephiroth in their Atziluthic colors as they are situated in and around your body. Float in the Tree of Atziluth for up to twenty minutes. See your aura glow brilliant white in its presence. Intensify the visualization, making it as bright as you can. Then relax in the afterglow of your work.

Sephirah	Atziluthic Color	Godname	Meaning
10 Malkuth	Yellow	Adonai ha-Aretz	Lord of the Earth
9 Yesod	Indigo	Shaddai El Chai	Almighty Living God
8 Hod	Violet/purple	Elohim Tzabaoth	Gods of Hosts
7 Netzach	Amber	YHVH Tzabaoth	God of Hosts
6 Tiphareth	Clear pink rose	YHVH Eloah VeDaath	God the Omniscient
5 Geburah	Orange	Elohim Gibor	Gods of Battles
4 Chesed	Deep violet	El	God
3 Binah	Crimson	YHVH Elohim	God, the Creator
2 Chokmah	Soft blue	Yah	The Father
1 Kether	Brilliance	Eheieh	I Am

8. Philosophus Meditation

This meditation comes from your textbook, *The Golden Dawn*, page 80:

"Let the Philosophus meditate upon the symbol of the Fire Triangle in all its aspects. Let him contemplate the symbol of the Planet Venus until he realizes the Universal Love which would express itself in perfect service to all mankind and which embraces Nature both visible and invisible. Let him identify himself with the powers of fire, consecrating himself wholly until the Burnt Sacrifice is consummated and the Christ is conceived by the Spirit. Let him meditate upon the Triplicity of Fire—its attributes and correspondences."

9. Banishing the Four Powers of Fire

Perform this ritual in the same manner as its invoking version, except use the banishing pentagram of fire, visualizing it in red light as before. You need not give the grade sign or prayer.

10. The Lesser Banishing Ritual of the Pentagram

Other Rituals Performed as Directed

1. Invoking and Banishing Venus

Netzach, the Sephirah of this grade, is also the Sephirah that governs Venus. The invocation of Venus is to be done on Fridays only, before the Middle Pillar Exercise. The banishing is to be performed that day also, after the Philosophus meditation. Your hexagram, in this ritual, will be emerald green, and so will your sigil of the planet.

To invoke Venus, face in the planet's direction and trace the green invoking hexagram while vibrating:

ARARITA

On the last syllable, stab the center of the hexagram, seeing it burst into green flame, charged by the name of God. Then trace the sigil of Venus in the center of the hexagram in green light while vibrating:

YHVH TZABAOTH

Vibrate the names alternately three more times, calling to the planet by the names of God. Feel the luxurious, affectionate energy of Venus enter your circle, filling it and filling you. Say:

Innocent maiden, nurturing maid, who bestoweth the favors of love, who whirleth in veils before the rising Sun, let a ray of thy victory descend upon me to awaken in this sphere the powers of Venus.

Pause, face east, and reflect on the beautiful qualities of
Venus for a moment before continuing.

When you banish Venus, draw the banishing hexagram
and planetary sigil in the direction of the planet, vibrating
the two divine names appropriately. Don't say the prayer,
however.

2. Invoking and Banishing Mars

Invoke Mars every Tuesday, before the Middle Pillar Exercise. Banish it after the Philosophus meditation. To invoke, face the direction of the planet and draw its red invoking hexagram as you vibrate:

ARARITA

Draw the red sigil of Mars in the center of the hexagram
as you vibrate:

ELOHIM GIBOR

(pronounced "El-oh-heem Gih-boor"). Vibrate the two names three more times
alternately as you face Mars. Then say:

> **Warrior of Heaven. Great right arm of the most high. Who cutteth away
> and burneth the enemies of Life and Light. Penetrate this sphere with thy
> ray of justice that the powers of Mars are awakened herein.**

Feel the harsh onslaught of Mars enter your circle, filling it and you. Meditate on its uses for a moment.

To banish, use the red banishing hexagram and red
sigil of Mars in the direction of the planet. Vibrate the
Godnames as before, but do not utter the invocation.

Additional Exercises
Daily Tarot Card or Tree of Life Spread

Continue doing your daily tarot card meditation as before, but if you have any
questions about the hidden currents of change around you, perform a Tree of Life
divination to gain some perspective. Do at least one Tree of Life divination per
week in regard to your practical or spiritual concerns. Use the steps that follow:

1. Select a court card that represents you (or the person for whom you are divining). Imagine the Tree of Life pattern before you on the table, and place the significator card at its center, at Tiphareth.

2. Start at Kether, laying out cards from the top of the deck in the order of the Lightning Flash. Place the Tiphareth card right over the significator.

3. Interpret the question now based on your knowledge of the Tree so far. Malkuth indicates the final outcome, or the complete expression of the issue in the material world.

Voice Exercises

The voice is one of the most powerful instruments you have at your command. When the vocal cords come together and resonate with the passing of breath, this action represents Light and Darkness coming together and generating vibrations in the field of passing time. Contemplating the act of vibration with this idea serves to link your voice to the creative power of your Higher Self. It is therefore essential that you make some effort to train your voice to generate more power in ritual. Simple singing lessons can do wonders for this ability.

For the Philosophus grade, spend at least two months in vocal training, either with a trained professional or with an audio training course. You can study singing, speech, or chanting. Any kind of vocal training will do, but the most important aspect to focus on is resonance. When you hold a sustained pitch, it should be clear, penetrating, and powerful, capable of carrying consciousness past the physical plane. In addition, some exercises are included to focus your increasing proficiency in the right direction. Do each of these exercises daily for one month each, unless the exercise specifies differently:

1. Pick passages from Golden Dawn rituals or other rituals that you find inspiring and speak them into a recording device, preferably into a high-quality microphone so that your voice is recorded and played back much as it actually sounds. Convey with your voice the feelings you think the various passages should convey. Listen to your words afterward. Do this once per day for two weeks at the start of the Philosophus grade. Do it also for two weeks as you near the completion of your assignments. See if you notice any improvements

in your ability to unleash and channel your feelings in ritual as a result of this exercise.

2. Get an audio book read by a celebrity whose voice you admire. Listen to the audio book daily. Stop it in places and repeat what the reader has said. Try to convey the same power, clarity, and conviction with your voice.

3. Spend twenty to thirty minutes per day, three days out of each week, in a public place with heavy foot traffic. A mall, a pub or restaurant, or the outside of a movie theater are good locations. Listen to people's voices as they converse, and *ignore the verbal content*. Listen to inflections and other sounds that people make: rising and falling tones, warning tones, supportive tones, laughter, grunts, moans, maneuvering and meandering sounds, and so forth.

4. Upon rising each morning, grimace and roar ferociously as you stretch.

5. Listen to your voice as you talk to people throughout the day. Listen to the musical quality of it and the noises that you make. What is the tone of your voice saying that the words themselves cannot? Write your observations in your diary.

6. Focus on people's gestures as they communicate. Notice the different kinds of stances, hand motions, defensive arm positions, and hidden nuances.

Written Assignments
1. Outline of the Philosophus Ritual
Done as for the Neophyte ritual.

2. Diary Assignments (Including the Tracking of Venus)
As you do your daily diary entries throughout Philosophus, include an extra heading every day in which you track the planet Venus as it passes through the signs of the zodiac. Also note when it is in retrograde. In addition, as you work with the God-names in the Body in Atziluth exercise, write the name every day of the Godname (in Hebrew) you are currently invoking (see page 64 of your textbook, *The Golden*

Dawn). Furthermore, incorporate the following practices into your writing, one practice each month, unless the practice itself specifies a different length of time:

1. Take one trip to the zoo. Observe the way the animals express themselves. Note movement, plumage, colors, gestures, and other visual cues. Make sure that you visit the apes and monkeys too. Spend a week in your daily writing comparing the various people you meet throughout your day to the animals you met at the zoo.

2. Note good and bad speakers throughout the day. Who expressed themselves very well? Who had magnetism, charisma, or power? Who lacked it? Why?

3. Did you meet any beautiful people during the day? Each day, note at least one who was beautiful in some way.[25]

4. Do you have any addictions? Cigarettes? Caffeine? Television? Using your judgment so as to avoid doing anything dangerous to your health, try quitting one of them cold turkey for one or two weeks. Make notes in your diary of the physical sensations, emotions, and thoughts that come up as you abstain.

Projects

1. Enochian Tablet of Fire

Complete this project before any of the others so that you can begin your daily Philosophus formula of rituals properly. (See the diagram on the opposite page.) Paint the shaded areas of the grid red. Paint all of the rings of the seal in the same color. Paint the background within the seal green. The flaming Hebrew letter Yods should alternate in color, the repeating sequence being red-yellow-violet.

Paint the letters in the following manner:

Portion of Fire Tablet	Color of Letters
Red squares, upper left quadrant	Yellow (color of air)
Red squares, upper right	Blue (color of water)
Red squares, lower left	Black (color of earth)
Red squares, lower right	Green (contrasting color of fire)
All the white squares in the tablet	Black (contrasting color of Spirit)

The Enochian Tablet of Fire

d	o	n	P	a	T	d	a	n	V	a	a
o	l	o	a	G	e	o	o	b	a	v	a
O	P	a	m	n	o	V	G	m	d	n	m
a	p	l	s	T	e	d	e	c	a	o	p
s	c	m	i	o	o	n	A	m	l	o	x
V	a	r	s	G	d	L	b	r	i	a	p
o	i	P	t	e	a	a	P	D	o	c	e
p	s	v	a	c	n	r	Z	i	r	Z	a
S	i	o	d	a	o	i	n	r	z	f	m
d	a	l	t	T	d	n	a	d	i	r	e
d	i	x	o	m	o	n	s	i	o	s	p
O	o	D	p	z	i	A	P	a	n	l	i
r	g	o	a	n	n	P	A	C	r	a	r

Do not do any ritual work or meditations with this Enochian tablet beyond the instructions you have been given so far. It is important to avoid any direct work with the Enochian system of magic until the elemental grades are finished. Remember that you can read about anything you like, but keep your practice confined just to the directions of this book.

2. The Tree of Life in Atziluth

Paint the Sephiroth and paths in their Atziluthic colors (see page 99 of your textbook, *The Golden Dawn*, for color correspondences). Add this painting to your "Book of Trees."

3. Drawing of the Qabalah of the Nine Chambers

Reproduce this drawing from page 497 of your textbook. Add it and the other Philosophus ritual diagrams you create to your book of temple diagrams.

4. Drawing of the Geomantic Talismanic Forms

Reproduce this drawing from page 494 of your textbook.

5. Drawing of Sulphur on the Tree of Life

Reproduce this drawing from page 84 of your textbook.

6. Drawing of Salt on the Tree of Life

Reproduce this drawing from page 84 of your textbook.

7. Drawing of the Trinity Operating through the Sephiroth

Reproduce this drawing from page 84 of your textbook.

8. Drawing of the Garden of Eden after the Fall

Reproduce this drawing from the color plate opposite page 118 of your textbook.

9. Drawing of Venus on the Tree of Life

Reproduce this drawing from page 79 of your textbook.

10. Calvary Cross of Twelve Squares

Reproduce this drawing from page 79 of your textbook. Make this out of stiff cardboard or wood like you have done with the crosses you have made in previous grades. Cut it out so that it is an object that you can hold in your hand.

11. Solid Pyramid of the Elements

Reproduce this drawing from page 79 of your textbook. You can try building the Solid Pyramid of the Elements by cutting out and folding this design, but you will quickly discover that the line drawing is not quite accurate for the creation of a three-dimensional pyramid. Some puzzling over it with a ruler, pencil, and scissors will produce eventually your own truncated pyramid. Label the faces before you fold and tape it into its shape.

12. Calvary Cross of Ten Squares

Reproduce this drawing from page 79 of your textbook. This is an especially important symbol for a later time. Prepare this as you did the Cross of Twelve Squares.

Optional Implements

The Fire Wand

Probably the easiest way to create this magical weapon is to shop for one online. There are a few very good online retailers, last I checked, who sell Golden Dawn implements.

Place your three elemental weapons (the pantacle, the air dagger, and the chalice) before you and determine the approximate dimensions that would be acceptable. No elemental weapon should dwarf, or be dwarfed by, its companions. Finally, make sure that you order a blank weapon, not one that is already painted. You must paint the colors, letters, and sigils on your own at the very least.

Ideally, the shaft should have a magnetized iron rod through its middle, but this is not of the utmost importance.

Failing to find a suitable wand online, you may opt to construct your own. You can do this by obtaining pieces of wood at a craft store: three sections of wooden dowel, four disk-shaped dividing pieces, and a wooden acorn- or egg-shaped tip. These you can glue together with very strong glue, such as epoxy.

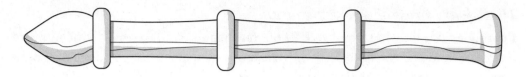

Fire Wand

Godname:	יהוה צבאות	YHVH Tzabaoth
Archangel:	מיכאל	Michael
Angel:	אראל	Aral
Ruler:	שרף	Seraph
River of Paradise:	פישון	Pison
Cardinal Point:	דרום	Darom
Name of Element:	אש	Aesch
Motto:		

Recite the Prayer of the Fire Spirits from page 196 of your textbook before working on the construction and painting of your wand for the day.

Prime the wood or paint it from head to foot with gesso. If your wand has an iron rod, make sure to leave the metal exposed at both ends. Use metallic gold paint to write three elongated Hebrew Yods on the wand's tip. Paint the dividing sections of the wand with the same gold paint.

Then, paint on the sigils and names of power associated with fire. These you obtain from the table above: YHVH Tzabaoth, Michael, Aral, Seraph, Pison, Darom, Aesch, and your motto. Make sure that the Godname and your motto appear on the tip, between Yods. The remaining sigils with their corresponding names appear down the shaft, two on either side of each of the three sections.

Seal the completed wand with an acrylic spray and put it in storage with the other three weapons. Do not put your four weapons together on the altar top during ritual. If you would like them present, put them into the four directions outside your circle, each on its corresponding side altar (if you are using side altars). They will come together on the altar top later.

The Sword

There is a section in your textbook about the magic sword (page 317). The sword is essentially a glorified banishing dagger. When you are an adept, and you require a very powerful, suggestive symbol for dealing with unruly forces, the sword should be ready in your temple. The correspondences that your textbook suggests painting on the sword are good ones, related to Geburah. But in reality, painting a handle and hilt red and green take away from the drama of naked steel in ritual. If you just spend a good amount of time locating a straight, symmetrical, double-sided blade with a cross hilt, that should be enough. It can be a challenge to procure one that is plain, without movie logos or overly dramatic scrollwork on it. Do not consecrate the sword until you have finished with the Portal grade. You can use it to do an LBRP if you like, but do not use it for such a minor banishing too often. The sword is to be reserved for times when it is necessary to pull out the "big guns"—and it should be used for nothing else. In a ritual space that is too small for such a large implement, you can hold the sword in your right hand and direct its tip by holding the blade carefully in your left.

Philosophus Checklist

Before you proceed to the next grade, review this checklist and make sure that all of the requirements are met.

- ❐ I have completed the Enochian Tablet of Fire.
- ❐ I have painted the Tree of Life in Atziluth.
- ❐ I have finished the Body in Atziluth through Kether.
- ❐ I have completed the vocal training and voice exercises.
- ❐ I have read "The Fifth Knowledge Lecture."
- ❐ I have read "Talismans."
- ❐ I have read *How to Win Friends and Influence People*.
- ❐ I have read *Myths to Live By*.
- ❐ I have read *Enochian Magic for Beginners*.
- ❐ I have outlined the Philosophus ritual.
- ❐ I have completed the diary assignments.
- ❐ I have drawn the Qabalah of the Nine Chambers.
- ❐ I have drawn the Sulphur on the Tree of Life.
- ❐ I have drawn the Geomantic Talismanic Forms.
- ❐ I have drawn the Salt on the Tree of Life.
- ❐ I have drawn the Trinity operating through the Sephiroth.
- ❐ I have drawn the Garden of Eden after the Fall.
- ❐ I have drawn Venus on the Tree of Life.
- ❐ I have drawn the Calvary Cross of Twelve Squares.
- ❐ I have drawn the Solid Pyramid of the Elements.
- ❐ I have drawn the Calvary Cross of Ten Squares.

nine

The Portal

It is a time to pause, reflect, and gather together what you have learned. The rituals done in this grade reverse the process of analysis that characterizes the Outer Order. You have passed through the four kingdoms of the elements. You have examined the forces that rise up from nature to create what you are. You no longer condemn any part of yourself. You have seen your ties to family and society loosen. You have glimpsed the futility of the self-centered life and avoided safely the temptation to remain in the world of competition. The time has come to dispassionately gather all of the pieces together. Portal is a grade of reintegration.

Portal does not correspond to any Sephirah on the Tree of Life, but it does relate to a position on the Middle Pillar just beneath Tiphareth. It therefore corresponds to the twenty-fifth path and the fourteenth tarot trump, Temperance. The angel on the card personifies a kind of celestial alchemist. In your current situation, your life is his laboratory, for you have gathered for him all of the necessary ingredients for his work. You have purified and organized the components of your being. The angel now combines them and gradually begins to increase the heat of the fire. The real work of magic is about to begin.

The angel traditionally "cooks" using two substances, fire and water, signifying two opposing forces. These are respectively representative of the two realities of the eternal and relative worlds, the All-mind and

Its creation, Spirit and matter. On the human scale, they relate to Kundalini energy and consciousness.

The word *Kundalini* comes from the vocabulary of the Eastern yogi. It means "the bioelectric energy of vitality." The two ingredients appear to interact in the process of life, one affecting the other and vice versa. Your vitality affects the quality of your consciousness. Your quality of consciousness affects your vitality. However, the two never can mix. An impassable abyss separates them. The human life is a meeting ground for Spirit and matter, two lovers that are permitted to dance together but never allowed to touch. Their spiritual longing for union can never be quenched, can never be consummated in the physical world. Anyone who tells you it can is selling something.

To illustrate this irreconcilable duality, an example of a spool of thread is helpful. Imagine a spool on which are entwined two very fine threads. One thread is red, the other blue. As they collect on the spool, their colors appear to merge, forming what appears to be a purple thread (as red and blue combined make purple). The colors seem to have mixed, but if you look closely enough at the spool, you can still discern the two threads of separate color. The purple "thread" is an illusion.

The two colors that combine are analogous to Kundalini (red) and consciousness (blue). The color purple represents the ego, and the spool is analogous to the physical body. This is perhaps an oversimplified—but very telling—example of how the ego is a mirage. When the student learns to rise on the planes, the gateway to within is found in his ability to look closely at the different forces that combine to produce his illusory self. Descending into the minute fibers of his being, he sees the separation between the different elements that compose the personality. He discovers for himself that his identity does not really have any inherent existence—that the shade of purple that he identifies as himself is nothing but a combination of cosmic forces. Those cosmic forces might be unified on some higher plane, but nowhere does this happen in the material world. As he plunges deeper into himself, the spaces between the threads become ever wider, revealing the abyss and a gate to the higher worlds.

To this example we can now apply the Kabbalistic formula of the Tetragrammaton, YHVH, the "unspeakable" four-letter name of God.

Yod = Kundalini
Heh = consciousness
Vau = ego
Heh (final) = physical body

Yod and Heh are the universal father and mother, red and blue, that come together to produce the son, Vau, purple, who is the individual that takes up residence with "the bride," or the physical body, the final Heh. This is represented graphically in an abstract image of the human form by stacking the letters of the Tetragrammaton vertically.

Note how these four forces are, in reality, operating in separate worlds:

Yod = fire = Atziluth
Heh = water = Briah
Vau = air = Yetzirah
Heh (final) = earth = Assiah

They do not mix with each other. They only appear to do so to those who don't bother to look closely enough and see the different "threads" at work, producing illusory objects and events.

Another illustration that may better clarify this idea of consolidated elements occurs in one of the emblems of the Portal grade, the Maltese Cross. It is a cross formed of four triangles. The Portal ritual explains that this variation of the cross symbolizes Malkuth with its four elemental quadrants (in the Briatic color scale). The quadrants are opened up, separated by an influx of spiritual Light that wells up from within, bursting wide the cracks. It also represents the student who has learned to look closely at the threads within and see them as they actually are: separated elemental forces vibrating within perception, creating patterns of interaction. These separate threads spool together and produce various harmonics that the student's mind mistakes for physical objects, images, or concepts—the biggest illusion being, of course, his own personality. The only phenomena of perception that are real are the fundamental forces. All perceived phenomena are aggregates of the four inviolate elements.

The Formation of the Maltese Cross

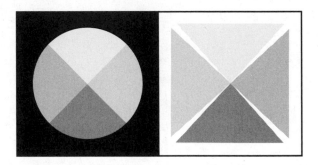

Invoked daily in Portal, the "fifth element," Spirit, is key to the opening of the student to higher influences. It jump-starts the synergy that is characteristic of an adept. Like a spotlight that reveals the underlying separation of the four elements, it reveals how the ego is created, and also how the Higher Self may project Its influence upon the playing field of the elements, for the Higher Self can never "come out" into the outer phenomenal world. It can, however, by directing the elements of that world, reveal Its influence as both immanent and transcendent. In true Kabbalistic fashion, the realm of the Divine can be seen as both within and apart from physical matter.

Lightning in a Bottle

Portal, like Neophyte, is a probationary grade. As you do the ritual work, some rapid and fundamental changes begin to occur. If you have done all of the Outer Order work sincerely and steadfastly up until this point, some kind of result is assured. If, however, you have rushed through the grades and neglected some ingredient of key importance, you jeopardize your chance at a lasting transformation of consciousness.

The worst thing that can happen to the negligent student is that he gets the desired result. The product of an incomplete alchemical formula is a fleeting and short-lived spiritual high. The euphoria or vision of beauty ends, and he is left with his life as it was before—but with the insulting knowledge of how unsatisfactory it is in relation to his brush with enlightenment.

Flashes of illumination that do not leave a lasting mark are the most dangerous kinds of spiritual experience. The common phenomenon of the born-again Christian is a good example. The power of the Tiphareth current, so immanent in Christian mythology and methodology, can quickly rush forth and engulf a new believer in a vision of harmony, beauty, and immortality. And, of course, most unsuspecting practitioners of the Christian faith, as with people of any other faith, have not yet done the groundwork of consolidating and purifying their lower nature, which prepares them for such an experience. Their mind/bodies do not have the integrity to contain the new state of being, and the result is that the experience fails to take root. It leaves them with the gnawing memory of a grace that could have been. A zealous urge to return to their vision ensues, and the born-again "zealot" promptly sets out to use his reckless modes of perception to chase after the echo of an elusive state of mind.

This produces something quite disastrous, as the violence associated with fundamentalism demonstrates. The animal faculties, once vacated by the Light and thrown back upon their own resources, interpret the religious experience in their own visceral terms. The lower self is still in charge, not realizing yet that its materially driven goals interfere with enlightenment. Someone who has done the groundwork of the soul would know from experience that the animal soul is not the real self, and he would be ready to relinquish it to the service of the realities of the religious experience. But the born-again zealot hasn't learned to see the deceptive nature of his ego. He insists that his newfound faith is "correct" and that anyone who has had a different experience is "incorrect." Since he hasn't learned to value every aspect of his personality (no matter how dark), he uses his newly acquired high standards to condemn, ridicule, and punish others in the name of his obsession. Since he hasn't learned how to disengage from the tribal mindset, he insists on making social controls that enforce obedience to his visionary experience. He may create a religious group that shuns everyone who is not in agreement with his vision. This can result in a clumsy and hurtful effort at utopia, whether it be in the government, church, village, or household.

Sound familiar?

This is not an attempt at Christian-bashing. The example of the born-again phenomenon, I hope, will explain how initiations in the occult world fail. Christian mythology and methodology are actually among the most sublime and potentially most advanced experiences. The mysteries of the Christ-force within each of us should only be explored, in my opinion, by the advanced, well-prepared mind. It would be better, perhaps, if the Christian church required five years of Zen discipline before actual introduction to the mythology of Jesus. Contact with Tiphareth cannot be maintained by a mind that is still mesmerized by the machinery of the pecking order or hell-bent on deriving security from circumstance.

The power of the Christ-force and the necessity to withhold it from the unprepared are the reasons why the Inner Order of the Golden Dawn, the *Roseae Rubae et Aureae Crucis*, is secretive and reclusive. It is also, incidentally, why Christian symbolism is almost unavoidable in the Inner Order. The Golden Dawn system is somewhat Egyptian on the outside and symbolically Christian on the inside.

This is not to say that the Christian mythos is of any value as an end unto itself. There are other mythologies that zero in on Tiphareth just the same, and they may work better for some students of the occult. Most other myths are certainly less of a risk for the unprepared.

If you have the so-called "Jesus allergy," perhaps because you were abused with religion in your upbringing, and you wish to avoid Christianity because of its negative associations, there are other ways of exploring the inner mysteries. As far as the Golden Dawn is concerned, a minimal amount of Christian mythology is required to understand the Inner Order symbolism. Please do not confuse the end with the means. You are not required to become "Christian" to become an adept. The symbols are simply tools.

Misunderstanding is another reason for secrecy. It cannot be escaped that human beings, however well domesticated, are still animals, following the dictates of their million-year-old master. Their hard-wired programming tends to respond explosively to anything that loosens its stranglehold on the Divine Spark within. The inner secrets of ancient mystery traditions have been protected by oaths and threats, mainly in response to the events of history. The atrocities committed by members of the Hebrew, Christian, and Muslim faiths, throughout their combined histories, are a testimony to the power of the Western myths and to the necessity of keeping the inner teachings of the Christ-force veiled.

The myths of the West are like lightning in a bottle (more literally than you might think). Do not dare open the bottle unless you have done all of the groundwork of purifying your lower nature. As MacGregor Mathers puts it:

> And know thou that this is not to be done lightly for thy amusement or experiment, seeing that the Forces of Nature were not created to be thy plaything or toy. Unless thou doest thy practical magical works with solemnity, ceremony and reverence, thou shalt be like an infant playing with fire, and thou shalt bring destruction upon thyself.[1]

Bear in mind, then, that Portal is a grade of honesty. The student summarizes his experience of the grade work and checks to make sure that he has completed every assignment. If he has missed an "ingredient," he must make up that work now to complete the alchemical formula. Have you had psychological counseling? Are you satisfied with the quality of all of your Enochian tablets? Have you created and maintained a physically healthy lifestyle? Have you stopped dealing out judgments? Have you read all of the assigned books? Written every assigned outline? Done every required daily ritual? Go back and review the entire curriculum.

More about the Pentagram

The peculiar way of drawing pentagrams in Golden Dawn–style magic is very telling about the nature of the four elements and their relationship to Spirit. The principle for invoking air, fire, water, and earth involves starting the pentagram with a line rushing toward the angle attributed to the desired force. The first line favors the element it rushes toward, allegedly having the effect of concentrating the force through the pentagram and sigil used.

When it comes to the invocation and banishment of Spirit, the method of drawing the pentagram departs from the previous one. For the invocation of Spirit, there are two pentagrams involved. In either one, the first line doesn't even touch the Spirit angle but instead connects two of the physical elements.

There are several occultists who remark that the Golden Dawn's method of the pentagram makes for an inconsistent and "clumsy" system of invocation and banishment.

It is surprising how quick students are to dismiss one of the fundamental techniques of a system that is the foundation of almost all Western magic today. It is my experience that much of the supposed awkwardness of the material that Mathers developed is attributable to a much deeper significance than is immediately apparent. It is best to take a generous nature with the Golden Dawn system when it begins to look odd. You will likely find the value of its approach later. Time and again, I have found that the techniques that seemed needlessly circuitous had invisible mechanisms that one could only discover through practice. Do not be too quick to force a spiritual technique to make sense; otherwise, you may, out of ignorance, modify it into powerlessness.

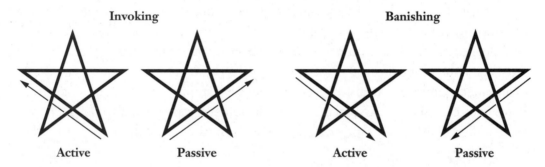

In the case of the Golden Dawn Spirit pentagrams, one form is considered active and one passive. Meditate on the nature of Spirit. Try to pin down and perceive it directly in your mind. If you have done the Outer Order work thoroughly and diligently up through Philosophus, you will find such an exercise laughable. Spirit is *not* an element. It cannot be experienced face-to-face like a gust of wind or a splash of water, nor can it be approached directly. It doesn't exist in any particular place. You cannot increase and decrease its quantity. You can't even touch it, much less *invoke* and *banish* it! So what is one really doing when one draws the active "invoking" pentagram of Spirit and vibrates the appropriate name?

Consider for a moment the two substances that the angel in the Temperance card is swapping in the vases. See them as active and passive qualities, Light and Darkness, fire and water, yin and yang. Remember the principle of balance and particularly add to that the idea of *balance in motion*. The angel in the card represents a principle of movement that continuously adjusts the relationship of opposing forces. The dynamic, springy, and "vital" quality of life that we experience in the flesh is the expression of that balancing principle. It maintains balance and order in a universe that is ruled primarily by chaos, decay, and darkness (forces of Saturn). Spirit may have some kind of "substance" on a higher plane of existence, but here in the realm of the senses, it can only be revealed as a pattern among the elements—a condition of equilibrium.

This is why the Golden Dawn refers to the invoking pentagrams of Spirit alternately as "equilibrating." Spirit does not exist in the realm of the elements, but it is evidenced by the relationship between those elements. When we call upon Spirit, we are actually manipulating active and passive energies and creating a beautiful balance (commonly experienced as vitality, clarity, joy, and calm).

The pentagram of Spirit actives is started by drawing a line from the fire angle to the air angle, or in other words, a line between *the two active elements*. The pentagram of Spirit passives is begun by drawing a line from the earth angle to the water angle, *the two passive elements*. The combination of these two pentagrams is the most important and most beneficial symbolism in your work. They function like two Kerubim, between which the presence of "God" may be felt, such as in the legend of the Ark of the Covenant.

To put all this more simply, one cannot just point at Spirit and command it to appear. Where would you point? All you can do is arrange what you can see into a sort of balance, and then only by the grace of "God"—if it so pleases Him—will you get the result.

Enochian Magic

The Supreme Invoking Ritual of the Pentagram, which comes later in this chapter, marks the first time that the mysterious language of Enochian appears in this book. I have avoided Enochian intentionally until now, and in the Portal grade I introduce it into your ritual practice sparingly. Enochian magic has been described as the "crowning jewel" of the Golden Dawn system of magic. The whole process of Kabbalistic transformation that occurs in the Outer Order, in my opinion, prepares the student to take command of the Enochian system.

The Western mysteries, I have already remarked, are like lightning in a bottle. It is obvious that Western culture has put humans in a powerful and dangerous position in regard to harnessing enormous energies and becoming the dominating influence on the planet. Enochian magic tunes right in to the spiritual thrust of Western culture, elevating man like a tower above nature in that position of great power. Doing so, it puts the magician in touch with an "overlord" mentality. Someone who is not an adept will quickly be seduced by the arrogance and righteousness that seems inherent within it. One must have supreme humility to use Enochian. The uppity nature of the Enochian entities should be adopted during ritual but quickly dropped upon return to mundane life. There is great danger to one's spiritual development and to mental and physical health if one takes their influence too seriously. Watch for these effects and head them off before they play upon your human weaknesses.

The entities perceived via Enochian ritual tend to resemble the fallen angels of the Hermetic myth presented in this book. Some clairvoyant magicians describe them as coming forth in misshapen forms. The system of Enochian magic explored by John Dee and Edward Kelly clearly feeds on the mythology of *The Book of Enoch*, in which the account of Azazel appears. The actual Enochian language (which is integral to Dee and Kelly's system), however, has no apparent relation to any culture in history. It *appears* to have come right out of the blue, delivered by an angel, evoked by Dee through the mediumship of Kelly. But I do not believe that it was channeled by an angel as described in Dr. Dee's notes. A system of magic does not require a fantastical lineage to be effective. Clearly, whoever invented Enochian (for I do believe that an ordinary human being thought it up) derived *some* of the names from Kabbalistic tablets containing permuted letters of Hebrew names. Perhaps the whole system is derived that way and most of the tablets have been lost.

In my experience, Kabbalah and Enochian work hand in hand. It is best to use them both side by side. Kabbalah tends to work from within the human heart and mind, elevating you into the light of your potential. Enochian works externally, behind the forces of the material world. Enochian spirits appear to have motives even more far-flung from humanity than the Kabbalistic angels. They are therefore dangerous to work with, because they do not always respond wisely. While the angels perceived in Kabbalah might withhold the desired result of a ceremony from a magician whose soul is not ready, the Enochian angels will grant a request whether it harms the magician or not. The Kabbalistic angels, therefore, step in and protect the magician from harm. The Kerubim, for instance, are the mythological characters responsible for binding the fallen angels into the depths of the pit:

> The Holy and Great One spake, and sent Uriel to the son of Lamech [Noah], and said to him: "Tell him in my Name 'Hide thyself!' and reveal to him the end that is approaching to the whole Earth . . ." The Lord said to Raphael: "Bind Azazel hand and foot, and cast him into the darkness: and make an opening in the desert . . . and cast him therein. And place upon him rough and jagged rocks, and cover him with darkness, and let him abide there forever, and cover his face that he may not see light. And on the day of the great Judgment he shall be cast into the fire . . ." And to Gabriel said the Lord: ". . . destroy the children of the Watchers from amongst men: send them one against another that they may destroy each other in battle . . ." And the Lord said to Michael: ". . . And when their sons have slain one another, and they have seen the destruction of their beloved ones, bind them fast for seventy generations in the valleys of the Earth, till the day of their judgment and of their consummation, till the judgment that is for ever and ever consummated."[2]

The Kerubim hold the Enochian angels pinned to the edges of the universe, as it were. There the fallen ones dwell at the boundary of space and time. They are the Watchers in their "Watchtowers." This is how the material world, poetically speaking, comes into existence.

Though it is not necessary to take the view that the Enochian entities are apostate angels, the story of the fallen ones sheds a great deal of light on Dee and Kelly's Enochian system. I will say nothing more on this, and I invite you instead to do the assignments of this chapter and form your own conclusions.

Enochian is therefore a powerful and dangerous system of magic. It is both a valuable tool for the humble magician and a deceiving devil for the vainglorious one. The student without preliminary training will quickly raise himself up by its methods and come crashing back to earth as he misuses the results with his biologically driven motives. The dangers are not usually physical but rather arise more from the belief that the contents of the mind are real.

PORTAL CURRICULUM (AT A GLANCE)

(to be completed in 9 months)

Daily Portal Formula

1. Chakra Breathing
2. Ascent to the Pyramid Temple
3. The Lesser Banishing Ritual of the Pentagram
4. The Banishing Ritual of the Hexagram (with modified "Analysis of the Key Word")
5. The Supreme Invoking Ritual of the Pentagram
6. The Middle Pillar
7. The Fourfold Body of Light
8. Portal Meditation
9. The Lesser Banishing Ritual of the Pentagram

Other Rituals Performed as Necessary

1. Invoking and Banishing the Sun
2. The Opening by Watchtower
3. The Ritual of the Rose Cross

Additional Exercises

1. Aura-Control Exercises
2. Daily Tarot Meditation or Divination

Required Reading

1. "Z-2: The Formulae of the Magic of Light," from your textbook, Regardie's *The Golden Dawn*, pages 376–400
2. "Book Nine," from your textbook, pages 623–696
3. *The Work of the Kabbalist*, by Z'ev ben Shimon Halevi
4. *Talismans and Evocations of the Golden Dawn*, by Pat Zalewski
5. Read Dion Fortune's *The Mystical Qabalah* again

Written Assignments

1. Outline of the Portal Ritual
2. Outline of "Book Nine" (in your textbook)
3. Summarizing Outline of All of the Grade Rituals of the Outer Order, Neophyte through Portal

4. Ritual of the Invocation of the Holy Guardian Angel
5. Daily Diary Entry

Projects
1. Tablet of Union
2. The Minutum Mundum
3. Chart of Enochian Tablet Correspondences

Optional Implements
1. The Rose Cross Lamen
2. The Adeptus Wand

PORTAL CURRICULUM (DETAILS)

Daily Portal Formula

Set up the four Enochian tablets, uncovered, in the four directions, equidistant in your ritual space. If you have a temple room with optional implements, the tablets should hang above and behind the side altars, approximately at the level of your heart (as you are standing). Do this series of rituals once per day in the order presented below, one right after the other. You need not complete the Tablet of Union yet (see "Projects" for this chapter, page 305) in order to perform everything in the daily formula as directed.

1. Chakra Breathing

Perform either the fourfold breath or the 4-7-8 breath as you do this exercise. Sit upright. As you breathe in, feel the pores of the skin open and nourishing atmosphere waft into the deep recesses of your body. As you hold the breath in, feel the inner atmosphere that you have inhaled begin to converge on the root chakra. On the out-breath, see the liquid sparks of light radiate from that region and fill the mold of the physical body with the body of light. Continue breathing and projecting the body of light from the root chakra for about two minutes. Then shift the attention to the second chakra, and breathe in the same manner from that region for two minutes. Then proceed to the third chakra, and likewise to the fourth. After the fourth, rise and begin your daily rituals.

After a month of chakra breathing in this manner, expand the exercises to include all of the chakras, including the throat, brow, and crown. Spend about a minute in each, and pay special attention to your tendency to work less with any one chakra than the others. Your reluctance to stay focused on one area may indicate a lingering block. You may wish to conclude the exercise by focusing for a couple of minutes on a chakra that you tended to avoid.

Chakras 5, 6, and 7 correspond not to any of the elements, but to the Supernals: Binah, Chokmah, and Kether. For the purposes of this curriculum, the chakras have the following attributions:

Number	Name	Correspondence
1	Muladhara	Earth
2	Swadhisthana	Water
3	Manipura	Fire
4	Anahata	Air
5	Vishuddha	Binah
6	Ajna	Chokmah
7	Sahasrara	Kether

2. Ascent to the Pyramid Temple

After performing the fourfold breath, stand as though ready to perform the Lesser Banishing Ritual of the Pentagram. Visualize your body of light growing. It expands upward and outward from its physical representative, out into the sky. Earth quickly becomes a speck beneath its glowing feet. Eventually, the sun is also just a point of light beneath. Your astral body eventually encompasses the space of the entire galaxy, and it continues on, enveloping other galaxies, filling the entire universe. You are in the cube of space now, and your body continues to expand. Allow it to push up against the boundaries of the universe, drawing them about you as though donning a beautiful black robe.

The black robe of stars is now comfortably draping itself over your body of light, and you notice that it fits perfectly and that you are standing on a square platform atop a truncated pyramid. It rises above a mist-enshrouded landscape beneath a twilight sky. This is your personal magical temple of the mysteries. It has no walls. Visualize the layout of this temple somewhat loosely based on the layout of the Golden Dawn's Temple of the Neophytes: central altar, pillars at the eastern edge, side altars at all four edges. This is the place where it will be possible for you to meet your Higher Self. It has the elemental quarters that correspond to those of the Lesser Banishing Ritual of the Pentagram: the eastern face of the pyramid is yellow and mirror-like, and a layer of cloud clings to it; the southern face is red, and flames lick upward along its surface; the western face is blue, and a sheet of water flows down its surface; and the northern face is black earth and rock with green ivy sprouting through cracks in many places. Know that the substance within the pyramid is the hidden, secret nature of matter—the quintessence—and that you have just risen from it. Hold this visualization and idea in your mind as you proceed to draw down the light from the Divine Self into your head and commence the Lesser Banishing Ritual of the Pentagram.

When your daily ritual work is done, take a few moments to return to the physical level of the mind. See your astral body diminish suddenly in size as the robe of stars expands and floats upward and outward to resume its place as the confines of the Saturnian universe. Your body of light shrinks rapidly, and there is the feeling of falling and becoming more dense. Expanding galaxies issue upward from your body as your descent continues into the realm of the Milky Way and eventually to our solar system. Feel a thud or a sort of snug sensation as, all at once, your body of light resumes its place contained within the skin of the physical body. Resume your normal waking consciousness, and know that you can reascend to the Pyramid Temple whenever you choose.

3. The Lesser Banishing Ritual of the Pentagram

Try using Hebrew letters to further increase the power of your vibration. When you vibrate the Godnames in the four quarters, visualize their Hebrew letters flaring up in brilliant white flame in the middle of the pentagram you are facing.

Additionally, to increase your connection to the lower kingdoms of the elements, see the archangels as winged, and replace their heads with the appropriate Kerubic animal forms. Raphael has the head of a man, Gabriel the head of an eagle, Michael the head of a lion, and Auriel the head of a bull. You can see these as masks if you are fond of the angels' human forms.

If the letters work well for you, you may decide to visualize the letters of all names that you vibrate in ritual as igniting before you as you resonate forth the syllables. This technique can be very helpful to fully engage your visualization ability.

4. The Banishing Ritual of the Hexagram

Increase the power of your vibrations in this ritual by seeing the Hebrew letters of the Godnames flare up before you as you "clothe" them with the hexagram. The letters appear from right to left as you pronounce the syllables.

In addition, change the Analysis of the Key Word to that of the following, more powerful Formula of the Divine White Brilliance:

Point to the upper, forward right and say:

I-N-R-I.

Draw the Hebrew letters before you as you say:

Yod. Nun. Resh. Yod.

Give the appropriate cross and L-V-X signs as you say the following:

The Sign of Osiris Slain.
The Sign of the Mourning of Isis.
The Sign of Apophis and Typhon.
The Sign of Osiris Risen.
L . . . V . . . X . . . Lux. The Light of the Cross.

Spread the arms in the form of the cross again and say:

Virgo, Isis, Mighty Mother. Scorpio, Apophis, Destroyer. Sol, Osiris Slain and Risen.

At the word "Risen," bring the arms back to the X sign. Then slowly unfold the arms, like the opening of the petals of a lotus flower, as you say the following:

Isis! Apophis! Osiris!

In the invoking stance, vibrate:

EXARP. HCOMA. NANTA. BITOM. IAO.

(pronounced "Ex-ahr-peh," "Heh-coh-mah," "En-ah-en-tah," "Beh-ee-toh-em," and "Ee-aah-oh"). The first four names of God are Enochian, as you will know from your assigned reading. Finally, say:

Let the Divine Light descend!

See a torrent of brilliance descend through the twilit sky and drench the top of the Pyramid Temple with intoxicating radiance. The platform on which you stand glows with impossible brilliance, and the boundaries of your being are momentarily erased as you disappear into light.

5. *The Supreme Invoking Ritual of the Pentagram*

Turn to the south (or circumambulate there, if you have an altar). Draw the invoking pentagram of Spirit actives. As you do so, vibrate the following Enochian name:

BITOM

(pronounced "Beh-ee-toh-em").

Trace the wheel of Spirit while vibrating:

EHEIEH

Give the L-V-X signs (and whisper "L-V-X" as you do so). Draw the invoking pentagram of fire in red light while vibrating the following three Enochian God-names:

OIP TEAA PDOCE

(pronounced "Oh-ee-peh," "Teh-ah," and "Peh-doh-keh"). Read these words right off of the tablet as you vibrate. Draw the sigil of Leo in green light as you vibrate:

ELOHIM

Give the grade sign of Philosophus as you vibrate and say the following:

YHVH TZABAOTH. Blessed be Thou. Leader of Armies is Thy Name. Amen.

Turn to the west and draw the invoking pentagram of Spirit passives in white light while vibrating:

HCOMA

(pronounced "Heh-coh-mah"). Draw the Spirit sigil, vibrating:

AGLA

Give the L-V-X signs. Draw the invoking pentagram of water in blue light as you read and vibrate:

MPH ARSL GAIOL

(pronounced "Em-peh-heh Ahr-sehl Gah-ee-ohl"). Trace the sigil of the eagle as you vibrate:

EL

Give the grade sign of Practicus as you vibrate and say:

ELOHIM TZABAOTH. Elohim of Hosts. Glory be to the Ruach Elohim who moved upon the face of the Waters of Creation. Amen.

Turn to the east and draw the invoking pentagram of Spirit actives in white light while vibrating:

EXARP

(pronounced "Ex-ahr-peh). Draw the sigil of Spirit in the center of the pentagram while vibrating:

EHEIEH

Give the L-V-X signs. Draw the yellow invoking pentagram of air as you read and vibrate the following three Godnames:

ORO IBAH AOZPI

(pronounced "Oh-roh," "Ee-bah-hah," and "Ah-oh-zod-pee"). Draw the sigil of Aquarius in violet light while vibrating:

YHVH

Give the grade sign of Theoricus as you vibrate and say:

SHADDAI EL CHAI. Almighty and everlasting. Ever living be Thy Name. Ever magnified in the life of all. Amen.

In the north, trace the invoking pentagram of Spirit passives, vibrating:

NANTA

(pronounced "En-ah-en-tah"). Draw the Spirit sigil, vibrating:

AGLA

Give the L-V-X signs. Trace the invoking pentagram of earth in green light, vibrating:

MOR DIAL HCTGA

(pronounced "Em-or Dee-ahl Hek-teh-gah"). Trace the symbol for Taurus in luminous black, vibrating:

ADONAI

Make the saluting sign for Zelator as you vibrate and say:

ADONAI HA-ARETZ. Unto thee be the kingdom, the power, and the glory. The Rose of Sharon and the Lily of the Valley. Amen.

Stand in the middle of the circle (or just west of the altar), facing east. Feel the power and balance of the elemental forces. Vibrate the following divine names and utter the prayer that follows:

YEHESHUAH, YEHOVASHAH. Thine is the Fire with its flashing flame! Thine is the Water with its ebb and flow! Thine is the Air with its movement! Thine is the Earth with its enduring stability! And Thou art within all things, even as all things are within Thee! Amen.

Perform the Kabbalistic Cross.

6. *The Middle Pillar*

Vibrate each divine name five times, seeing the Hebrew letters ignite in brilliant white in the spheres of your body. This visualization will take a little practice. The letters almost have to be visualized backward, in mirror image, flaring up in your own body, readable from the front of your body instead of from the perspective of your eyes inside your head. The letters appear suddenly as you vibrate forth the Atziluthic names and gradually merge into the brilliance of the spheres that they energize. Use of the letters, especially in this exercise, can be quiet powerful.

7. *The Fourfold Body of Light*
Part One: The Fourfold Sephiroth

In this grade are all Four Worlds united. The Body of Light in the Four Worlds is perhaps the most potent exercise in this book. I give it here only for the student who has been through the elemental grade process. Attempting this exercise before you are ready can cause serious harm to your psychological well-being. Proceed with it only if you are sure you are ready for the Portal grade, having met all of the requirements of all of the previous grades.

Continue to sit in the east, facing west. Make sure that the spine is straight. See the brilliant white Tree of Life superimposed upon your body. See it complete, with its paths connecting its Sephiroth. Then turn the whole of its structure to the Atziluthic color of Malkuth, yellow. Having established this brilliant yellow Tree fully within and around your body, vibrate the Godname for Malkuth five times while maintaining the visualization:

ADONAI HA-ARETZ

Second, visualize your aura taking shape around the Tree of Life and around your body. Its colors are Briatic: citrine, olive, russet, and black. Vibrate the name of the archangel for Malkuth five times:

SANDALPHON

Next, visualize the etheric body taking shape within the aura, superimposed within your physical body, contained within your skin. The body of light therefore formulates within the womb-like egg of the aura. Its colors are of the Yetziratic Malkuth: citrine, olive, russet, and black, flecked with gold throughout. Vibrate the name of the angelic choir for Malkuth five times:

ASHIM

Finally, visualize an obsidian-like statue of yourself in place of the physical body. Solid rays of yellow crystal radiate from its Tiphareth center. The statue is opaque, but your visualizing ability allows you to see its insides at the same time as its outside. Feel the rays of yellow within the crystalline black substance. Feel heaviness. Vibrate the name of the Assiatic House associated with Malkuth five times:

OLAM YESODOTH

Continue to sit, lie, or stand within the visualization of your four Malkuth bodies for up to ten minutes. See the yellow Tree of Life, the four-colored aura, the four-colored etheric double, and the black and yellow solid body. This is among the most complex of visualizations that you have yet learned, but you will likely find that it is relatively easy to maintain. All of the visualization work you have done through the previous grades has prepared you for this. Feel the layers of condensing power as Malkuth manifests itself through your body in your ritual space. Recall that you are a reflection of the universe as it condenses from the outside in (even as the same thing is true from the inside out). This concludes the exercise.

Do the Fourfold Body of Light in Malkuth for one week. Then, on the first day of the second week, proceed to Yesod. Visualize the Tree of Life, the aura, the Tzelem, and the physical statue in order as before, while using the four color attributions and magical names for Yesod (in the same manner as you did for Malkuth). The Tree of Life would be indigo, the aura would be violet, the Tzelem would be dark purple, and the statue would be citrine-flecked azure. (The complete color scales of the Four Worlds are easily obtained on page 99 of your textbook, Regardie's *The Golden Dawn*. The magical names for the Sephiroth in the Four Worlds are obtained from pages 63 and 64. You may wish to keep these pages marked as you go through this final Middle Pillar process, or you can write these correspondences into your ritual book.)

Continue on up the Tree, staying in each Sephirah for one week, until you finish up with a week in Kether. After you have experienced the Fourfold Body of Light in Kether for a week, you are ready for the next step: the Minutum Mundum.

Part Two: The Minutum Mundum

Minutum Mundum means "Little Universe" in Latin. In Western magic, it refers to the unification of the powers that make up the Four Worlds of Kabbalah. Sometimes it is represented as four interlinked Trees of Life. Usually, though, it is shown simply as a single Tree of Life glyph with the colors of the ten Sephiroth in the Queen Scale and the colors of the connecting paths in the King Scale. The feminine and masculine, the passive and active, are united in their purest, highest forms.

Bringing the Atziluthic and Briatic Trees together in one ritual would be very taxing to the imagination, visualizing ten Sephiroth and twenty-two interconnecting paths all in different rainbow hues. Such feats of mental power are possible but unnecessary. I offer here a different way to bring the two together. In this Middle Pillar Exercise, you will use the Briatic colors of the Sephiroth combined with their Atziluthic Godnames. Do it for the remainder of the Portal grade.

Stand or sit between the pillars in the east of your astral temple, facing west. Doing so aligns the Tree in your aura to the Tree that formulates in the temple space. It also identifies you with the rising sun. You may lie down with your physical body, if you like, and imagine yourself still standing at the appropriate spot in your imagined temple.

Upon completing the Middle Pillar, return the attention to just above the head. Vibrate the Godname associated with Kether three times:

EH-HEH-YEH

See the burning white Hebrew letters flare in Kether as you vocalize. Next, focus on the gray sphere of Chokmah to the left of your head. Vibrate thrice:

YAH

As you vibrate this, visualize the letters Yod and Heh flashing to life within the sphere, illuminating the gray energy of Chokmah from within.

Continue on to Binah, vibrating and visualizing in the same manner:

YHVH ELOHIM

Continue on down through the Tree of Life in the order of the Lightning Flash, finishing in the citrine, olive, russet, and black sphere of Malkuth, and with the great name:

ADONAI HA-ARETZ

At Tiphareth, you may use either the powerful and transformational name IAO, associated with the death and resurrection of Osiris, or the traditional Kabbalistic name of YHVH Eloah VeDaath, which is more static, exalted, and removed from the lower worlds. Whichever suits the needs of your current development is the appropriate one.

Now put everything together in one visualization. Float in the aura of white brilliance for a while, contemplating the unity of the colored Sephiroth in the light. Consider then the Four Kabbalistic Worlds. They correspond to parts of the universe, and therefore they also correspond to parts of the soul.

The Atziluthic body consists of the flaming divine names that lie beyond the boundaries of the universe, and therefore beyond the grasping abilities of the human mind. But we can still represent that body in abstract. See it as the Tree of Life reflected from on high in the space that has been created for the universe. The Tree of Life therefore represents the influence of Atziluth within creation, even though that world cannot exist within that creation directly. In response to this idea, see now that the Tree of Life in your aura is that Atziluthic influence within your own microcosmic space.

Briah is the space that the All-mind opened within Itself. It is the terrible, bitter sea through which everything emerges into manifestation—the space into which the All-mind poured the Light, into which the broken shells fell, and within which the universe formed. Briah on the macrocosmic scale consists of your aura, the egg-like enclosure of liquid brilliance that surrounds your body.

Yetzirah, then, is your astral body. See your body of light floating in the midst of the aura. See how it has crystallized out of the fires of Atziluth and the waters of Briah. It has been exhaled like air into the space of your personal universe, your "sphere of sensation."

Assiah, finally, then, is the physical body, which encloses the etheric.

Contemplate the Four Worlds together in this schematic of four bodies. Bring to mind the elements, the letters of the Tetragrammaton, and any other correspondences that present themselves. In such a way may you be able to link your microcosm to the macrocosm and draw down power from the higher worlds into the lower. All is one.

8. The Portal Meditation

This meditation comes from your textbook, *The Golden Dawn*, page 94:

"Let the aspirant meditate upon the Cross in its various forms and aspects as shown in the Admission Badges throughout the grades. Let him consider the necessity and prevalence of sacrifice throughout nature and religion. Let him realize the saying of the Master: 'Whosoever shall save his life shall lose it, and whosoever shall lose his life shall save it. Except a corn of wheat fall into the ground and die, it abideth alone, but if it die, it bringeth forth much fruit.' Let him endeavor to realize his own place and relative importance in the Universe, striving to stand outside himself and allowing only such claims as he would allow to another. Let him carefully abstain from talking of himself, his feelings or experiences that he may gain continence of speech, and learn to control the wasteful activities of his mind. Let him contemplate the Sun as thinly veiled in clouds."

9. The Lesser Banishing Ritual of the Pentagram

Other Rituals Performed as Directed

1. Invoking and Banishing the Sun

Tiphareth shines just beyond the threshold of this grade. It is the Sephirah that governs the Sun. The invocation of Sol is to be done on Sundays only, before the Middle Pillar Exercise. The banishing is to be performed that day also, after the Portal meditation. Your hexagram, in this ritual, will be gold, and the sigil of the planet will be orange.

To invoke the Sun, face in the planet's direction and trace the gold invoking hexagram while vibrating:

ARARITA

On the last syllable, stab the center of the hexagram, seeing it burst into golden flame, charged by the name of God. Then trace the sigil of Sol in the center of the hexagram in orange light while vibrating:

IAO

Vibrate the names, alternately, three more times, calling to the planet by the names of God. Feel the radiant, balanced joy of the Sun enter your circle, filling it, filling you. Say:

> **Great focus of Light in the midst of creation. I call upon Thy welcome presence. Let a ray of the One Life descend upon me, that it may bring to bloom the rose upon the cross.**

Pause, face east, and reflect on the radiant qualities of the Sun for a moment before continuing.

When you banish Sol, draw the banishing hexagram and planetary sigil in the direction of the planet, vibrating the two divine names appropriately. Don't say the invocation, however.

2. The Opening by Watchtower

This ritual is a preparation for just about any magical operation. It calls forth a powerful upwelling of astral force, which can then be utilized for the goal of just about any kind of ceremony that is performed after it. You will notice that it is very much like the Supreme Invoking Ritual of the Pentagram. It is that and more, focusing the invoked elemental energies more firmly in place, providing a very responsive "platform" on which to project the will. In the Portal grade, you are only required to learn this ritual, performing it once per week until you have it perfectly engraved in memory. Once you have reached adeptship, the exercises of the Opening by Watchtower and the Fourfold Body of Light will likely be your best and most important tools in ceremonial magic.

To start with, this ritual requires a temple space set up as shown above. Everything done up until this point has necessitated nothing more than physical movement and seclusion. But here we are stepping up to the threshold of practical magic. It is important at this point to gather your experiences of the Outer Order curriculum together and express them in some physical form, namely in the form of a temple room or ritual space. Additionally, rituals performed by the adept have very specialized goals, requiring intense concentration and extraordinary mental equilibrium. The more conducive the setting and devices are to the purpose of the magician, the easier it is for him to maintain the necessary focus to achieve them.

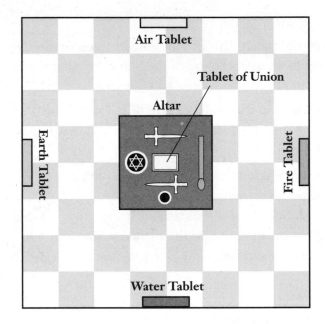

You will notice that the diagram above shows the optional elemental weapons resting on the altar top. If you have not made these optional implements, you can substitute the following items:

Element	Implement
Fire	A red candle
Water	A cup of wine or water
Air	A rose, a feather, or burning incense
Earth	A plate of bread and salt, or a stone

The energies called up via Enochian magic can be quite tangible, so getting your physical temple space well proportioned is of particular importance. The tablets should be at about the level of your heart so that the imaginary lines that connect east to west and north to south converge in a cross directly over the Tablet of Union (see "Projects" for this chapter, page 305).

Recommended incense is sandalwood, frankincense, or a scent in harmony with the exercise that follows the Opening by Watchtower.

The Opening by Watchtower

Take up your sword, if you have acquired one, and proceed to the northeast. Face the southwest and wave the sword (or point your finger) as though clearing the room with a warning, which you vibrate/shout:

HEKAS HEKAS, ESTE BEBELOI!

This is an ancient Greek traditional warning that means "Away, away, that which is profane!"

Ascend to the Pyramid Temple.

Perform the Lesser Banishing Ritual of the Pentagram.

Perform the Banishing Ritual of the Hexagram.

Proceed to the south of the altar and take up the fire wand (or red candle). Turn around clockwise to face Enochian Tablet of Fire. Shake the wand three times before the tablet, as though tapping the points of a triangle in the air before the tablet: top-right-left. This gesture alludes to the Light of the Supernals, which gives stability and indicates that the invocation is subject to the highest authority. Hold the wand so that the tip is over your head and circumambulate once while saying the following:

And when, after all the phantoms have vanished, thou shalt see that holy and formless Fire, that Fire which darts and flashes through the hidden depths of the universe! Hear thou, the Voice of Fire!

Arrive back in the south upon the last word. Draw the invoking pentagram of Spirit actives before the fire tablet while vibrating:

BITOM

(as done in the Supreme Invoking Ritual of the Pentagram). Draw the sigil of Spirit and vibrate:

EHEIEH

Give the L-V-X signs. Draw the invoking pentagram of fire, vibrating:

OIP TEAA PDOCE

Give the saluting sign of Philosophus, vibrate the following name, and say the prayer that follows:

YHVH TZABAOTH. Blessed be Thou. Leader of Armies is Thy Name. Amen.

Make a red, equal-armed cross over the center of the tablet. Point the wand at the middle of the cross and say:

In the Name of the Great King of the Watchtower of the south, Spirits of Fire, adore your Creator!

Then vibrate:

EDLPRNAA

(pronounced "Ee-del-peh-ray-naah"; read the name off of the tablet as you vibrate it). Return the fire wand to its place on the altar.

Proceed to the west, take up the water chalice (or cup of wine) and face the water tablet. Hold it by the stem or base and render the Triangle of the Supernals as done with the wand in the south. Hold the chalice over your head and circumambulate once, saying:

So therefore first, the priest who governeth the works of Fire must sprinkle with the lustral Water of the loud and resounding sea.

Returning to the west, draw the invoking pentagram of Spirit passives and the sigil of Spirit, vibrating:

HCOMA; AGLA

When you point at the center of the pentagram with the chalice, hold it by the stem as though pouring out a little liquid westward. Give the L-V-X signs. Draw the invoking-water pentagram and the sigil of the eagle while vibrating:

MPH ARSL GAIOL; EL

Give the sign of Practicus, vibrate the following name, and say the prayer that follows:

ELOHIM TZABAOTH. Elohim of Hosts. Glory be to the Ruach Elohim, who moved upon the face of the Waters of Creation. Amen.

Make the sign of the cross in blue before the tablet. Point to the center and say:

In the Name of the Great King of the Watchtower of the west, spirits of Water, adore your Creator!

Then vibrate:

RAAGIOSL

(pronounced "Rah-jee-oh-sel"). Set down the chalice in its place on the altar.

Proceed to the east, circumambulating clockwise. Take up the air dagger (or other token of air) and face the tablet. Formulate the triangle. Hold the point of the dagger over your head and circumambulate, saying:

Such a Fire existeth, extending through the rushing of Air. Or even a Fire formless, whence cometh the image of a voice. Or even a flashing light, abounding, revolving, whirling forth, crying aloud!

Return to the air tablet. Make the active invoking pentagram of Spirit and the Spirit sigil while vibrating:

EXARP; EHEIEH

Give the L-V-X signs. Then draw the invoking pentagram of air and the sigil of Aquarius while vibrating:

ORO IBAH AOZPI; YOD-HEH-VAU-HEH

Give the Theoricus sign, vibrate the following name, and say the prayer that follows:

SHADDAI EL CHAI. Almighty and everlasting. Ever Living be Thy Name. Ever magnified in the life of all. Amen.

Make a yellow sign of the cross before the tablet with the dagger. Hold the tip of the wand to the center of the cross, pointing at the center of the tablet.

In the Name of the Great King of the Watchtower of the east, spirits of Air, adore your Creator!

Then vibrate:

BATAIVAH

(the king's name is pronounced "Bah-tah-ee-vah-heh"). Return the air dagger to the altar and proceed to the north.

Take up the earth pantacle (or token of earth). Hold it upward by its black portion and wave it three times before the earth tablet. Hold the pantacle over your head, circumambulating, and say:

Stoop not down into that darkly splendid word, wherein continually lieth a faithless depth and Hades, wrapped in gloom, delighting in unintelligible imagery—precipitous, winding, a black ever-rolling abyss, ever espousing a body unluminous, formless, and void.

Make the passive invoking pentagram of Spirit and the sigil of Spirit before the earth tablet while vibrating:

NANTA; AGLA

Give the L-V-X signs. Then draw the invoking pentagram of earth and the sigil of Taurus while vibrating:

MOR DIAL HCTGA; ADONAI

Give the Zelator sign, vibrate the following names, and say the prayer that follows:

ADONAI HA-ARETZ. ADONAI MELEKH. Unto Thee be the kingdom and the power and the glory. The Rose of Sharon and the Lily of the Valley. Amen.

Make the green sign of the cross before the tablet with the pantacle. Hold the edge of the pantacle to the center of the cross, pointing to the center of the tablet.

And in the Name of the great King of the Watchtower of the north, spirits of Earth, adore your Creator!

Then vibrate:

ICZHIHL

(the king's name is pronounced "Ee-kay-zod-hee-hehl"). Put the pantacle back.

Circumambulate to the west of the altar and face east. Take up the ritual wand (or just use your finger) and trace the appropriate pentagrams with Spirit sigils while vibrating the following names:

EXARP; EHEIEH
HCOMA; AGLA
BITOM; EHEIEH
NANTA; AGLA

Then say:

In the Names and letters of the mystical Tablet of Union, I invoke ye, ye Divine forces of the Spirit of Life!

Set down anything you may be holding. Make the sign of rending the veil—hold your hands before your heart, with the palms together and the fingers forward, and step forward, thrusting your hands forward over the Tablet of Union suddenly and spreading them apart as though parting a curtain over the altar. Feel the realm of

Spirit, the essence of the elements, immanent in the atmosphere, and vibrate the following Enochian call:

OL SOHNUF VAORSAGI GOHO IADA BALTAH, ELEXARPEH COMANANU TABITOM. ZODAKARA EKA ZODAKARE OD ZODAMERANU. ODO KIKLE QAA PIAP PIAMOEL OD VOAN.

(pronounced "Oh-el Soh-noof Vay-oh-ehr-sah-jee Goh-hoh Ee-ah-dah Bahl-tah, El-ex-ar-peh-heh Coh-mah-nah-nu Tah-bee-toh-em! Zod-ah-kah-rah Eh-kah Zod-ah-kah-ray Oh-dah Zod-ah-mehr-ah-nu! Oh-doh Kee-kleh Kah-ah Pee-ah-peh Pee-ah-moh-el O-dah Vay-oh-ah-nu").

Say to yourself, softly but firmly, the translation:

I reign over you, saith the God of justice! Elexarpeh Comananu Tabitom. Move, therefore, and show yourselves! Appear to us; open the mysteries of your creation, the balance of righteousness and truth.

Go to the northeast and face southwest, addressing the room:

The Visible Sun is the dispenser of light to the Earth. Let me therefore form a vortex in this chamber, that the invisible Sun of Spirit may shine herein from above.

Circumambulate three times clockwise, beginning in the east. Make the projecting sign and Sign of Silence (see the Neophyte grade) as you pass the east (in the direction of your movement). It may take you some practice before you become proficient at this, keeping the sign abrupt and powerful and yet maintaining the fluidity of the circumambulation. Feel a rhythm to the motion in order to do the sign correctly. It has three beats: (1) projecting sign, (2) Sign of Silence, and (3) continue circumambulation. (Rhythm is a subtle and very important aspect of ritual that many people overlook.)

After the third circumambulation (there are four saluting signs and three circumambulations), return to the west of the altar and face east. On each "Holy" in the following proclamation, do the projecting sign:

Holy art Thou, Lord of the universe!
Holy art Thou, Whom Nature hath not formed!
Holy art Thou, the Vast and Mighty One, Lord of the Light and of the Darkness.

Give the Sign of Silence.

State the intention of the ceremony and proceed to the work intended. Once you have finished, do the brief closing ceremony below.

Closing

Reverse-circumambulate three times, giving the Neophyte saluting signs as you pass the east. Return to your position west of the altar, facing east, and perform the following closing invocation:

Unto Thee, sole wise, sole eternal, and sole merciful One, be the praise and the glory forever, Who hath permitted me, who now standeth humbly before Thee to enter this far into the sanctuary of the mysteries. Not unto me, but unto Thy Name be the glory! Let the influence of Thy Divine Ones descend upon my head and teach the value of self-sacrifice, so that I shrink not in the hour of trial, and that thus my Name may be written on high and my genius stand in the presence of the holy ones. Amen.

I now release any spirits that may have been imprisoned by this ceremony. Depart in peace to your abodes and habitations and go with the blessings of YEHESHUAH YEHOVASHAH.

Be there peace between thee and me, and be ready to come when ye are called.

Perform the Lesser Banishing Ritual of the Pentagram.

I now declare this temple duly closed.

Knock once on the altar top with your ritual wand (or knuckles) as though banging a gavel in court.

3. The Ritual of the Rose Cross

Now is an excellent time to perform this ritual. Do it whenever you wish to feel untroubled and peaceful. You have been through much difficulty in the Outer Order work, a time when it was not really acceptable for you to turn away from any of the challenges that arose in your daily life in the world. Now, since the analysis process is officially at an end, it is acceptable to insulate yourself from such discomfort. Presumably, you are at a stage in your development in which you will not be tempted to use this ritual as an escape—a tendency that is all too common among occultists and other New Age enthusiasts.

The original Golden Dawn taught this ritual in Neophyte along with the Lesser Banishing Ritual of the Pentagram. For many students, that practice may have been beneficial. However, for the very introverted, it may exaggerate the tendency to shut out the world. That is why in this solitary curriculum I withhold the Ritual of the Rose Cross until Portal. In the absence of a student-teacher relationship, it is impossible to tell whether allowing the performance of the Ritual of the Rose Cross at an earlier stage would benefit you.

Do this ritual when you want to feel untroubled by worries, psychic phenomena, and people in general. It has a mild effect as an "invisibility" ritual, because it does not increase presence and personal power in the way that the banishing rituals might. It turns the mind inward to a center of peace by invoking Tiphareth. You may find that people will leave you alone. Such isolation can be important in Portal, giving you time to discover something new.

Note that the crosses of spiritual Light are placed not in the quarters, but between the quarters. This may bring to mind the rays of Spirit that open up Malkuth, turning its quadrants into a Maltese Cross.

Part One: The Formulation of the Spirit Crosses

Light a stick of frankincense (or some other scent that corresponds to Tiphareth). Holding it in your right hand, stand facing east. Ascend into the Cube of Space or to the Pyramid Temple.

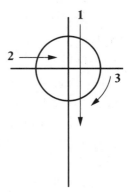

Go to the southeast. Draw a circle cross there in white light with the smoking incense stick, as shown. Make it about as tall as the pentagrams you draw in other rituals. Hold the incense stick to the center of the cross and vibrate the Pentagrammaton:

YEHESHUAH

(pronounced "Yeh-heh-shoo-ah").

The correspondences of this name are extremely important, and by now you will have read about them. You may wish to see the Hebrew letters (Yod-Heh-Shin-Vau-Heh) flaring up before the cross and descending and fading into it.

From that point, draw a straight line to the southwest. Draw a circle cross there and vibrate the name.

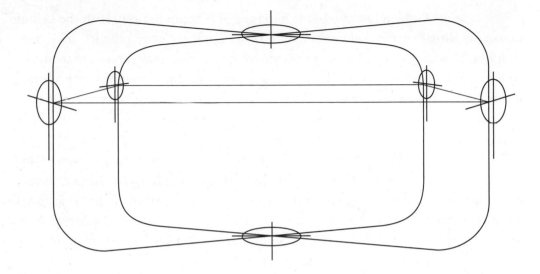

Draw a straight line to the northwest and do the same.

Draw a line to the northeast and trace the figure there, vibrating the name, and then draw the line back to the southeast to complete a square around the center of the ritual space.

Hold the tip of the incense there at the center of the cross and vibrate the name again:

YEHESHUAH

Then draw a line arc over your head to the center of the ceiling area of your ritual space. Draw a circle cross there and vibrate the name as before.

Continue the line, arcing it northwestward to the center of the circle cross in the northwest. Hold it there for a moment, seeing the cross and circle before your eyes.

Continue the line, arcing it downward and back to the center of the floor area of your ritual space, pointing your incense stick at the floor. Draw a circle cross and vibrate the name.

Continue the line to the southeast again, arcing it up to the center of the cross there. Hold it there for just a moment, visualizing the cross and circle.

Then trace the straight line to the west with your incense stick until you reach the center of the southwestern cross. Vibrate the name there.

Then draw a line arc up over your head to the cross in the center of the ceiling space. Vibrate the name there.

Continue the white line, arcing it down to the northeastern cross. Hold it there for a moment, visualizing.

Continue the line, arcing it down to the center of the floor space, pointing at the cross there and vibrating the name.

Draw the line arc up to the southwestern cross and hold it there for a moment, visualizing.

Trace the straight line to the northwest and visualize the cross there for a moment. Trace it to the northeast and visualize, and then trace the straight line back to the southeast. Draw there a large, thick, blazing white circle cross—bigger than the one that is already there. As you draw the lower half of the circle, vibrate:

YEHESHUAH

and as you draw the upper half, vibrate:

YEHOVASHAH

Return to the center of the ritual space and visualize the framework of crosses that you have created around you.

Part Two: The Analysis of the Key Word

This is performed as in the new, more powerful version presented in the Banishing Ritual of the Hexagram in this grade.

Additional Exercises

Aura-Control Exercises

Do these challenging exercises for two weeks each, unless the exercise itself specifies a different amount of time. They are designed to limit the amount of projecting that you do on an automatic basis. For instance, if you habitually project ideals of sexual beauty upon celebrities, you may not be aware that this is a power that you can claim as your own instead. The exercises below counter the tendency that humans have to give their magical power away to objects.

1. **Avoid Mirrors:** Wherever you go, avoid looking at reflections of yourself in mirrors or in mirror-like surfaces. This does not mean that you should

become obsessive or reactive in the presence of a mirror; simply and calmly avoid looking at your reflection. The same goes for pictures or live images of yourself on camera.

2. **Avoid Television:** Watch no more than two programs per week.

3. **Do Not Wear Conformist Symbols:** Do not wear or associate yourself with icons. Except during magical work or studying, avoid the use of symbols that may sap you of individuality. An icon is a symbol that attracts projections. Icons are powerful in that we tend to automatically invest them with meaning, sending energy into them to charge them with significance. Examples of things to avoid are religious or patriotic symbols, club logos, T-shirts with ads on them, letterhead with logos on it, iconographic decorations in your home or office (such as diplomas, advertising logos, and photos), greeting cards, rank badges, smiley faces, hope ribbons, images of celebrities, and possessions that normally act as status symbols.

4. **Avoid the News:** Do this in all its media formats.

5. **The Graveyard Vision:** This term comes from the myth of the Buddha. It describes an experience of noticing the physicality of the human bodies around you. Notice the corpselike quality of people and animals you see during the day. Strip their appearance of meaning and see them as they are: walking conglomerations of inanimate material, somehow propelled by a mysterious, animating principle.

6. **Watch for Offense:** Anger is perfectly healthy as long as you avoid being offended. When it rises, transform the feeling of being "put upon" into one of simple and honest frustration. In other words, do not project negative traits on obstacles, situations, or people in your environment. Do not project negative traits on your own self-image either. Keep anger honest, calling attention back to your center, acknowledging frustration for what it is.

7. **Limit Wishful Thinking:** Notice whenever you get the feeling that the "grass is greener" elsewhere. Note whenever the desire to be in different circumstances arises. Feel the hemorrhaging effect this has on your integrity. Call your attention back to where you are, to your center. Momentarily feel the lens-like curvature of space in your aura that keeps it there.

8. **Monitor Self-Image:** Continually notice how you are building up a false sense of position or status in relation to others. Feel or imagine the energy of this effort returning to your center. Repeatedly learn to reduce your projection of a false front and deflate your self-image to something real, honest, and humble.

9. **Silence:** Stay quiet as much as possible. Especially avoid speaking reactively, as in when you become frustrated, pleased, or entertained. Grunt, sigh, smile, laugh, or pat someone on the back instead. Above all, avoid judgments that attempt to project meaning upon the current situation: "That's great!" or "It figures!" or "That is so funny."

10. **Limit Projections:** Become continuously aware of the automatic tendency to project impressions, judgments, and perceptions on objects, situations, or your self-image. Withdraw those projections back to your "center" as you notice them. Know that you are creating them and that you can call them home and change them to suit your will. Own them within the subtle body and keep them there.

11. **Shaping the Aura:** Be aware of your aura while you are around other people. Acting from your center, curve it back on itself such that the outer edge is firm, reflective, and convex to those you deal with. You may even wish to place ward-like symbols, flames, or fearsome faces on it to repel negative energy from frequently negative people. Keep in mind that this is done as much to keep their auras from projecting at yours as it is to keep yours from projecting at theirs.

12. **Focusing on the Breath:** During any down time, such as when waiting at a doctor's office, do not occupy yourself with distractions. Use down time as an opportunity to stay focused on the breath.

13. **Visualizing the Body of Light:** Also use down time as an opportunity to visualize the body of light perfectly at home within your skin.

14. **Checking In on the Breath:** Use a watch with an hourly chime and check in on the quality of your breath every hour.

15. **Turn the Light Around:** Stay focused on an extra-dimensional center within. Continuously see the outer senses as though they are "seen" in the mirror of the subtle body.

Tarot Divination

Do your daily tarot mediation as before. Or, do any divination patterns that interest you.

Written Assignments

1. Outline of the Portal Ritual

Done as for the Neophyte ritual.

2. Outline of "Book 9" (in your textbook)

Create this as a summary for yourself, such that you can refresh yourself on the structure of the Enochian system, with all its details, whenever you need to. As a rule, try to create one Roman numeral for the main idea of almost every paragraph. Keep your outline for future reference.

3. Summarizing Outline of All of the Grade Rituals of the Outer Order, Neophyte through Portal

The aim of this assignment is better described by Israel Regardie's words from your textbook, *The Golden Dawn*:

> Let me therefore urge upon the sincere reader, whose wish it is to study this magical system, to pay great attention to the scheme of the grade rituals, to obtain a bird's eye view of the whole, to study every point, its movement and teaching. This should be repeated again and again, until the mind moves easily from one point of the ritual to another.

4. Ritual of the Invocation of the Holy Guardian Angel

Once you have done the required reading for Portal, begin gradually to move toward the creation of a ritual for the invocation of the Holy Guardian Angel. See if you can have the ritual completed—*but not yet performed*—by the time you finish the nine-month period of this grade.

The ritual should be viewed as a culmination of all of the work you have done up until now. It may begin to become clear that it is not possible to reach enlightenment by your own efforts. How would you do it? This is an ideal time to compose a call for assistance from within, for a union and state of bliss that cannot be patched together in this world by mortal hands. To have that union brooding beneath the veil of the physical world, to have your Higher Self close at hand but intangible—this is the joy unspeakable that mystics fall all over themselves to speak about. A state of communion that is impossible, yet possible.

5. Daily Diary Entry

There are no special topics assigned in this grade, but make sure you note every day your experiences with the aura-control exercises.

Projects
1. Tablet of Union

You can create your Tablet of Union (as shown in the diagram below) by cutting out a 5 × 6 inch piece of plywood, painting it white all over, and sketching with ruler and pencil a centered grid that is 4 inches × 5 inches. Make the letters all black on the white background. I recommend not color-coding the letters of this tablet as they correspond to the elements. The four elements are actually a contrivance of the magicians that studied Enochian after the time of Dr. John Dee. The Golden Dawn superimposes the elemental powers upon the Watchtower tablets. The original Enochian system, though weaker without the Golden Dawn innovations, had no elements directly attributed to the Great Table. Leave the Spirit tablet therefore untouched by

E	X	A	R	P
H	C	O	M	A
N	A	N	T	A
B	I	T	O	M

the elemental colors. You will have an even more powerful set of tablets this way. It can be helpful to view the four horizontal names on the Tablet of Union as magical keys that open up each of the four elements. See these words of power as commands that force the elements to loosen their hold on your Divine Spark.

2. *The Minutum Mundum*

Paint the Sephiroth of the Tree of Life in their Briatic colors (see page 99 of your textbook). Paint the connecting paths in their Atziluthic colors. Put this painted Tree in your "Book of Trees."

3. *Enochian Tablet Correspondences*

Make copies of the template of the Great Table of the Watchtowers that appears on the opposite page. Print out three or more copies for yourself, and fill in the correspondences of each square according to the descriptions in your assigned reading:

- The letter of the Tetragrammaton corresponding to each square

- The astrological symbol(s) corresponding to each square

- The tarot card(s) corresponding to each square

- Any other correspondences that the student wishes to lay out

It is of crucial importance now for you to impress upon the mind this system of interrelationships. Enochian magic, as it is used by the Golden Dawn, makes for an ingenious binding force. It uses the principle of correspondence to create an intellectual net that the student can cast out over all that he has learned. Your sphere of sensation becomes superimposed with the layout of the four Enochian tablets. Associating the tablets with the four quadrants of the elements, the magician can use the tablets to pull together the forces of his life, which correspond to past grade experiences, and harness them to his will. Enochian magic, when wielded by an adept, makes this binding power possible by the mere application of the mind.

Be careful with the study of Enochian. Remember the lesson of the biblical giants in the time of Enoch and the Tower card. You have come a long way through the Outer Order grades. Make sure that you do not sabotage all your preparations by doing anything other than the limited amount of Enochian work required in

The Great Table of the Watchtowers

this grade. By now, you may have some inkling as to the ways in which magic works and the ways in which it does not. Enochian is much more immediate and direct than the magic you have learned in the Outer Order. At this crucial time, when you are drawing so close to the gates of illumination, take the utmost care not to do anything foolish and lose your way.

Optional Implements

The Rose Cross Lamen

This can be made of wood and painted according to the directions in your textbook (pages 310–313).

The Adeptus Wand

The Adeptus wand[3] is a substitute for the lotus wand (described on pages 300–305 of your textbook). Take a look at those pages. It is my opinion that the lotus wand is one of the most beautiful magical implements ever designed. It is also too complicated and unwieldy a device to use regularly. It is simply too large, and I rarely see reason to work with magic in zodiacal aspects. In addition, the lotus wand is unnecessarily difficult to consecrate. It involves the invocation of all twelve signs of the zodiac. That means handling twelve vastly different spirits in one ritual. Like an actor forced to play twelve parts in one play, the magician is hard-pressed to accomplish every conjuration successfully.

The ritual for the consecration of the lotus wand given in your textbook seems more of a formality than an actual consecration. The only way to make it powerful would be to change it. In its present state, it calls upon too many divergent forces. Complexity can be a valuable aspect of ritual, because it gives the intellect something to chew on, causing you to set aside intrusive thoughts and channel the needed force in spite of yourself. But in my experience, that complexity should center itself around one particular purpose. Conceivably, the zodiacal signs could be placed under the presidency of one master spirit. Study of the Schemhamphoresch (see your textbook again) might yield such a single angelic entity of the zodiac that would give consecration of the lotus wand its necessary motive-force. But the consecration ritual would have to be entirely rewritten to reflect that purpose.

Now, it is possible for you, even as a fledgling adept just out of the Portal grade, to consecrate an instrument as complicated as the lotus wand, but only if such a complicated instrument is necessary for the working out of your true will. Yes, sometimes a complex approach is required, and in such cases the Higher Self has been known to step in on one's behalf and take care of the "impossible" parts of a ritual operation. However, you may find, like me, that your mammoth task lies in other areas. For those who share this predicament with me, I provide the idea of the Adeptus wand—not only as an alternative to the lotus wand, but additionally as a means of consummating the goal of the Outer Order grades.

When I found myself abandoning the idea of the lotus wand, it was because I began to entertain the possibility that a magician could consecrate one instrument to the power of the four elements. This occurred because I had once read that it is virtually impossible to do so.[4] Such a "prohibition" seemed strange and enticing, for it seemed that the purpose of the whole grade system is to separate, organize, and unite all of the elements under the one banner of Spirit. If you and I can accomplish this with the flesh, then why not in one instrument?

Enclosed in the appendix is a ritual for the consecration of the Adeptus wand. It is a very simple instrument, drawing upon the Pentagrammaton for its singular unifying Spirit. The four elements, according to Kabbalah, are governed by the four letters of the unspeakable name, the Tetragrammaton, or YHVH. The letter Shin is added then to govern them, all four, together. This, as you know, generates the names Yeheshuah and Yehovashah. In the consecration of the Adeptus wand, the four elements are called forth not necessarily to charge the wand's colored bands, but rather they are brought forth to bow down before the presidency of the name of God that it embodies. It therefore becomes the most intimate tool of the adept. Once it is consecrated, it represents the will of his Higher Self in the aspect of Light in Extension. All forces are subject to it. The adept can put away his elemental weapons once he has consecrated this wand. It is a representation of the Middle Pillar energy that dwells in his spiritual core, like the eye of God in the whirlwind of fire, from the biblical book of Exodus. I also include in the Adeptus wand consecration a method for self-initiation into the Inner Order of the Golden Dawn, into 5=6.

Construction of the Adeptus Wand

These directions are optional. You can create the Adeptus wand to any proportions that you like.

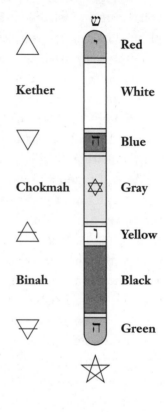

1. Obtain a dowel the length of your forearm, elbow to tip of middle finger. The optional ritual wand, if you have made one, can become the Adeptus wand.

2. Make sure the wand is sanded smooth and that its ends are likewise smooth and rounded.

3. Paint it all over with perfectly bright white paint. Two or three coats may be required to produce a perfectly opaque sheen.

4. After the paint dries, measure the length of the wand and use a calculator to divide its length by 19 (using centimeters and millimeters will make this easier). As precisely as possible, use a pencil to divide the wand into nineteen sections of equal length—it requires eighteen marks to do this. Put special longer marks on the first, sixth, seventh, twelfth, thirteenth, and eighteenth lines.

5. Then, wrapping an index card around the wand, draw perfect lines around its shaft at these specially marked lines. This clearly creates four small bands, two of them at the ends, and two of them floating in the space between the ends. These four bands are separated by three larger bands. A larger band is five times the width of a smaller band.

6. Sketch a perfect circle directly onto the tips of the wand, the diameter of each circle being about three-quarters the diameter of the shaft. Erase as many times as you need to until the circles are perfect and identical to one another.

7. Within one circle (the tip of the wand), carefully sketch the Hebrew letter Shin, making sure it comfortably fills the whole space. Within the other circle (the base of the wand), sketch a perfect pentagram.

8. Next, paint the special, smaller bands in the order of the Tetragrammaton.

The band at the tip:	scarlet
The band beneath that:	blue
The third band:	bright yellow
The band at the base:	emerald green

9. Paint the larger bands in the colors of the Supernals.

Between the scarlet and blue bands:	white
Between blue and yellow:	light gray
Between yellow and green:	black

10. After the paint dries thoroughly (it may take as many as three coats to make it perfectly uniform and opaque), use your pencil to sketch the following figures in their appropriate bands. All of the figures should face the same direction. Erase as many times as you need to, redrawing until the figures are perfect.

Scarlet band:	Yod
Blue band:	Heh
Yellow band:	Vau
Green band:	Heh
Gray band:	Hexagram

11. Next, paint the sketched Hebrew letters and symbols. Paint the letters of Tetragrammaton white (you will later have to outline the Vau with thin, permanent black marker to make it stand out), and paint the pentagram and the letter Shin in black. Paint the upward-pointing triangle of the hexagram red and the downward-pointing triangle blue.

12. Use metallic gold paint to very carefully mark dividing lines between all bands. The white circles that face away from each tip of the wand should also be circumscribed with gold.

13. Touch up your work with the appropriate paint colors to obscure any stray marks and to sharpen the letters, symbols, and dividing lines.

14. Finally, seal your wand with an acrylic sealant.

Principles for the Use of the Adeptus Wand

These are presented here so that you can see how the wand, in theory, works. These are just the basics, and you can develop many other gestures and methods with practice as an adept.

1. Do not use the Adeptus wand to banish lowly, negative forces. The dagger or sword is better suited to that purpose. Therefore, you should never use the Adeptus wand for the Lesser Banishing Ritual of the Pentagram. For the Banishing Ritual of the Hexagram, however, it is well suited.

2. The flow of energy for manifesting something is almost always from tip to base. Therefore, to invoke a force into your circle, the tip of the wand should face in the direction of the imagined source as you draw your magical symbols in the air.

3. To banish something from your circle, the base of the wand should face away from you as you draw.

4. To invoke or banish an elemental force (or zodiacal sign), hold the band that corresponds to the element with your thumb and index and middle fingers. (The exception to this principle occurs when you banish elemental earth, for which you hold the base of the wand normally while consciously wrapping your ring and little fingers around the green band.)

5. To invoke or banish a planet, hold the wand by one of the three larger bands. As you have found in your assigned reading, each planet is attributed to a Sephirah on the Tree of Life, each of which must rest on one of three pillars. Hold the wand by the band that tops the pillar that contains the planet. For example, to invoke or banish Venus, hold the gray band, because Venus falls on the Pillar of Mercy, which is governed by Chokmah, gray. To invoke or banish Saturn, hold the wand by the black band.

6. You will probably find that the Adeptus wand is "uncomfortable" when it is inverted. Experiment with different ways of holding the wand, and try to make sure that the tip stays elevated above the base for all movements.

I leave with you the following symbol of the nonplanetary hexagram, which is a key to the consecration of this wand. I recommend meditating on the symbol, designing your own version of the wand based on the principles of the diagrams, and rewriting the ritual to suit your own purposes. The ritual is presented, *as are all Inner Order rituals of the Golden Dawn*, as a template that you can use, adjust, and remake to your own purposes. You may even want to integrate your personal invocation of the Holy Guardian Angel into it, if you choose to make an Adeptus wand yourself.

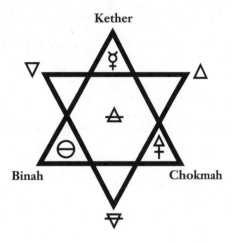

Portal Checklist

Review this checklist to make sure all of the requirements of the Portal grade are met.

❐ I have completed the Tablet of Union.

❐ I have painted the Minutum Mundum.

❐ I have performed the Four-Fold Body of Light.

❐ I have done a weekly invocation of the sun.

❐ I have done a weekly practice of the Opening by Watchtower.

❐ I have done a daily tarot meditation or divination.

❐ I have completed the aura-control exercises.

❐ I have read "Z-2: The Formulae of the Magic of Light."

❐ I have read "Book Nine."

❐ I have read *The Work of the Kabbalist*.

❐ I have read *Talismans and Evocations of the Golden Dawn*.

❐ I have reread *The Mystical Qabalah*.

❐ I have outlined the Portal Ritual.

❐ I have outlined "Book Nine."

❐ I have written a summarizing outline of all the grade rituals.

❐ I have completed the ritual for the invocation of the Holy Guardian Angel.

❐ I have completed the chart of the Enochian tablet correspondences.

ten

The Work of the Adept

It is better at first to keep your aura to yourself, rather than to try to flow out to others. Unless you are particularly vital and well-balanced, you will only waste energy. So-called modes of healing and of "doing good to others" should be eschewed for a time. Such methods have a technique of their own and require trained and balanced minds and bodies to carry them out. Get yourself right before you attempt to interfere with others in any way but the orderly ways of a kindly and decent society.

—Israel Regardie, "Fifth Knowledge Lecture," *The Golden Dawn*

Ten years ago, if I had tried to assume a godform, I would have done it for all the wrong reasons. At that time, I was like a bad actor, like a groupie backstage at a goth concert. My attitude toward imagery or symbol was one of weakness and conformity, of unwittingly subordinating myself to its power and hiding in its shadow, like a student idolizing a teacher. Consider the groupies that lurk like vampires backstage at a rock concert. Living in someone else's dream, they are dramatic examples of this human conformist tendency. The habit of giving away personal power to images can be similar to drug abuse, an addiction in which one gives up control over one's happiness to a substance. But in this case, the poor soul gives up his magical power, his evolutionary potential, to a cultural icon. We could even call it "icon abuse." But why not just stick to the antiquated term *idolatry*? Why else do you think celebrities are called idols?

When we are young and naive, the world is a big place, full of external forces that tower over us. First, there are our parents or guardians, who, like gods, know everything. Then there are the more advanced role models—bosses, rock stars, actors, and others—who manage to masquerade as our power archetypes. They represent to us our *own* undeveloped sexual, artistic, or professional powers—aspects of individuality we do not yet command. For a while, we give these role models authority over us; we give them our energy by buying their albums, supporting their causes, and recruiting others into their reservoir of power. On subtle levels, our acts of patronage, like ritual gestures, even project part of our aura in their direction. It is a weak and unconscious form of astral projection.

But it is natural for us to outgrow the worship of false gods. In some foggy way, the realization dawns that these role models have power over us because the traits we see in them are actually our *own* faculties. If we develop as we are meant to, we let go of our heroes and begin to cultivate what we have worshipped in them as strengths that are located in ourselves. We reclaim and pull back that power into our auras and begin to develop it within our own personas. This is a key point in magic. You must have control over your astral body, keeping it close and calling it back when it wants to play and become obsessed with an image, person, or symbol. You must be able to accumulate power by being still and centered. That way, when you *really* desire to project it in practical magic, you will have enough strength to do so in a pure and concentrated way, powerful enough to produce measurable effects in your life. This means that the best way to learn the art of astral projection is to learn how *not* to project.

If all has gone well with your Neophyte, elemental-grade, and Portal work, you have learned to conserve energy. You have also learned not to build a false image with it, for building an ego is another wasteful form of projection. When your energy accumulates naturally, you will become a powerful icon too—a leader, if need be, who can't help but become the idol for the young ones who develop at your side. Your "ego" will become powerful, but it is a true and natural ego that derives power from its subservience to the Higher Self. And as an enlightened, responsible leader, you will constantly remind people that their fascination with you is really a fascination with their own latent power.

But some people never outgrow the subservient stage. There are so many hiding places for them in the world, so many environments that feed on their conformity. Visit these places again in your mind now: the comic-book stores, the nightclubs, the sports arenas, the secret societies, and the neopagan groups and magical lodges.

Are you floundering in one of these eddies? Are you delaying? You will know such places by their use of life-sucking images: photos of celebrities, icons, coats of arms, mandala-like symbols, and still more images of celebrities. These are images of the roles that you could be fulfilling in your own life, in your own way, if only it were time to "put away childish things."

Aleister Crowley is a good example of a cultural icon that aspiring magicians worship. Many an occultist delays spiritual development for a while, caught in Crowley's wicked charm.

Why should a teenager bother cultivating her own sexual magnetism when she can instead have a pin-up of a life-sized sex symbol on her bedroom door? Or why should a sports enthusiast live a life of adventure when he can get the television to do it for him? Beware of celebrities that distract you from your own life. Don't let them live it for you. They may be sucking at your sphere, acting as a deliberate target for your natural tendency to live vicariously through objects. They may even be feeding off of your energy, turning *your* power into *their* dreams.

The adept is someone who has learned to control his aura. It stays in his body, like a well-behaved pet. The most striking thing about an adept is that he spends almost no amount of time lost in thought. He is rarely elsewhere. He knows that the universe is within himself, so within himself he stays, attentive to the present moment. His energy is focused on self-containment, and it resultantly takes on a radiant, sun-like quality.

The Danger of Godforms

To someone stuck in the habit of idolizing images, the advanced magical practice of the assumption of godforms is especially dangerous. If he doesn't recognize that the images he feeds with his own energy are representations of his own powers, that they are convenient surfaces onto which he projects his own inner gods, he runs the risk of becoming dominated and controlled by those powers. Instead of putting them to work within himself, he sets them up as parent-like figures around him in his life. His aura becomes divided against itself as it projects its own faculties from inside upon the images of "gods" on the outside. As a result, his environment becomes intimidating. His projections prod, threaten, and control him from without because he simply believes them to be powers other than his own. Anyone from the outside, human or demonic, with a little charisma can step into one of those projected roles and thereby gain control over him. And if, in such a divided state, he dares to assume a godform, he only draws it down upon his enfeebled aura like a sheep feeding itself to a wolf. He invites one of his psychological complexes to inflate into a monster and consume him, possibly turning him into a deranged and utterly powerless devotee of an archetype.

This is not to say that the practice of magic turns the one who abuses it into a drooling zombie. The damage can be much more insidious than that. He may end up a lazy couch potato who worships Indiana Jones. Or he could degenerate into someone like the main character of the movie *Lawrence of Arabia*, possessed against his will by a powerful leadership archetype. Or—dare I say it?—he runs the risk of becoming another MacGregor Mathers.

Mathers was clearly an adept. But apparently he gave a great deal of authority to images that existed outside of his own mind, namely to ideas like the "Secret Chiefs" and his own grandiose historical lineage. This is why the Outer Order work of magical systems like the Golden Dawn is so important, and why, in other traditions, a lengthy period of tedious exercises and awareness techniques is absolutely essential. Too often, the fledgling occultist neglects his foundational training in favor of escapism and glamour. Much of the glamorous appeal of occultism runs exactly counter to the development of an adept.

The famous saying "We have nothing to fear but fear itself" means we need not fear anything, *anything whatsoever*, but the *belief* that the evil that we see in an image actually exists in that image. When you meet someone who is "lazy," that is *your* aura of laziness that you are projecting onto them. When you see injustice in the external world and it infuriates you, there may be an internal injustice between different components of your psyche that remains unaddressed. It has just put on different clothes so that you will pay attention to it. It is saying, "Help! You are projecting me out here onto this person. Please call me back, claim me as your own, and help me to develop into a responsible instrument of the Higher Self."

The preliminary work on the path of magic is designed to clear out bad energy habits. By taking the student through different levels of his being, it teaches him to explore his own psyche by taking it apart and putting it back together as a conscious tool to be placed at the disposal of his supposed Higher Self. During the process, if it is properly pursued, all kinds of nasty human tendencies will surface, not the least of which is the kind of idolatry that I am talking about here. It is not obvious to the person laboring through the grades, but his years of training condition him to gain control over his projections. Someone who has learned to retain his energy is one who can send it forth into images at will. But most importantly, he can withdraw it back into himself on command and resume his humble Clark Kent persona. The properly trained magician is a dismembered, purified, and reassembled being, one who glows with integrity and who knows the ins and outs of psychic fitness and how to sustain it.

Integrity

But what does *integrity* mean? The student of magic should take this word much more literally than the student of, say, a business college. In the practice of magic, it means a state of integration, self-containment, self-governance, and wholeness. On the surface, the integrated person is magnanimous. He moves through the world unaffected by the mob mind, by peer pressure, or by powerful leaders. He will never be divided against himself, never do anything that would go against his own heart. Beneath that visible surface is the indestructible jewel of adeptship, the Philosopher's Stone—a balanced aura that has no tendrils of energy spilling out toward images or people that would otherwise wield power over its authentically constructed sense of self.

Theurgy

When we give other people—or gods for that matter—our power, we hand our undeveloped potential over to them, saying essentially, "This power is not my responsibility, it is yours. I am yours to command." The adept has learned to pull back that power, to curl it back in on itself to accumulate in his own aura. All things, good and bad, are contained within him. All are one. In such a state, he has the potential to claim any power in the universe as his. In such a state, he is then ready to practice paganism free of idolatry. The paganism of high magic is called *theurgy*, and it is a skill that comes to us from the magicians and priests of ancient Egypt.

Trithemius, a monk of the fifteenth century, was one of the first Western magicians on record to make the point that, when the adept decides to invoke a force, he must first rise to its level and dominate it.[1] This idea echoes the magical practice of the ancient Egyptians, who invented the concept of assuming godforms.

Uninitiated historians scoff at the boldness of Egyptian magic. It is said that the ancient priests purported to use their secret arts not only to worship their deities, but to subjugate them to their will. It sounds like a fantastical power trip, but the ancient adepts clearly knew that real magic views the gods as internal to the mind of humanity, subject to the will of an individual who has gained the proper training. Theurgy is the art of awakening one's own god-like faculties and putting them to work.

Such ideas are not unique to the Egyptians or to a medieval wyzard like Trithemius. Other traditions show the same kind of training in their magicians. For instance, the Buddhist adept Padmasambhava is said to have established Buddhism in Tibet by using his Tantric powers to subjugate the elemental deities of the Tibetan landscape. Up until that point, the great nature spirits had terrorized Tibet through its indigenous religion, called Bon.[2] The Bon shamans sometimes demanded bloody human sacrifices from the population in order to propitiate the angry nature gods and keep them from sending pestilence or devouring children.[3] Padmasambhava entered Tibet at the request of its then-current ruler, who wanted to bring Buddhism to the people. The Tantric adept used ritual magic to identify the nature gods as powers that existed within his own being, and thereby he subjugated them. The end result gave him the power to create a new state-sanctioned proliferation of Buddhism, which gradually dominated and absorbed the Bon religion into its practices.

The medieval grimoire *The Sacred Magic of Abra Melin the Mage*, well known by serious students of high magic, puts forth a similar view about dominating spiritual powers. Once the operator has transformed himself through a rigorous training and purification period of six months, he receives the "knowledge and conversation" of his "Holy Guardian Angel." In the Western magical tradition, the Holy Guardian Angel is none other than the true self, the so-called Higher Self, which can reveal itself to the student once he has integrated every aspect of his psyche (in other words, drawn his projections back into himself). Immediately after achieving the illumination of his Holy Guardian Angel, the student sets about calling forth various spirits, both good and bad, to submit to his newly unified identity. Any image or imagined entity that he may have perceived as powerful in the past is called up in the imagination, and its power is reclaimed back into the aura. The astral entity is then, from that point forward, officially recognized as an extension of the magician's power (as it always has been anyway), at his beck and call via the same image that was once a source of intimidation: "For by names and images are all powers awakened and re-awakened."[4]

This practice of rising to unity with the Higher Self, then evoking and dominating spirits, can be used to reach out and encompass within the aura any power in the universe. There is therefore no limit to the extent of the magician's being. Where the gods end and he begins is entirely arbitrary. He can link himself in meditation with any cosmic force and use magical techniques to employ some of its power. However, it takes a great deal of integrity and personal accumulation of energy to be able to invoke or evoke the gods effectively to do one's bidding. The state of equanimity necessary for the containment of such power is only possible for the adept.

The Anatomy of a Powerful Aura

Dion Fortune, in her book *Applied Magic and Aspects of Occultism*, describes how the aura of a powerful magician appears to the psychic. In the average living human, the aura is an oval-shaped spheroid consisting of an invisible magnetic field resonating between two circuits of energy. One circuit proceeds from the top of the head to the soles of the feet in a vertical shaft. The other circuit is peripheral, arising out of the central one. The central circuit is directly connected to the Higher Self (or Holy Guardian Angel), presumably hovering over the top of the head. Being of divine origin, it is unaffected by the environment. It is the source of the energy of consciousness. The peripheral circuit is sensitive to the environment, affected easily by circumstances, other people's auras, and planetary and elemental energies. The magnetic field that fluctuates between the two circuits contains currents and cross-currents in patterns that are simple in nature but highly complex in arrangement.[5] Fortune then goes on to describe the aura of an advanced, evolving human:

> The more highly developed the aura, the greater what may best be described as its surface tension—a kind of skin of resistance formed by the interweaving of magnetic circuits. These arise from outgoing rays of emanation obeying the law of curvature of force and returning upon themselves at their point of emanation. The tension gradually increases, causing, as it

were, a shrinking and tightening of the circuits, until finally a tensely resistive surface of magnetic loops is established. This constitutes the exterior envelope of the aura.[6]

You may gather together your own conception of the highly evolved aura based on this somewhat fanciful, though highly evocative, description. It is clear that a stronger aura, that of a well-integrated psyche, retains its own energy better, thereby accumulating power without effort. A stronger aura curves almost all of its emanating rays back in on itself. And when it stops giving away energy uncontrollably, it gains what P. W. Bullock (another Golden Dawn adept) calls "Equipoise," a state of absolute independence that is required before the projection of the magical will is possible.[7] Over time, force accumulates in a balanced and calm reservoir of magical power that is at the disposal of the adept.[8] The human being who learns to stop unconsciously giving away his energy to other people, gods, or symbols retains it for later deliberate, conscious use. With enough power, he can even project his waking consciousness in an astral body and penetrate different levels of existence.

Other adepts echo this idea. Florence Farr speaks of the projection of the scarlet ray of will from the heart center:

> Get a distinct image of the thing you desire, placed, as it were, in your heart. Concentrate all of your wandering rays of thought upon this image until you feel it to be one glowing scarlet ball of compacted force. Then project this concentrated force on the object you wish to affect.[9]

Here we have the concept repeated of pulling in the "wandering rays" and focusing them. This is precisely how godforms are generated before the magician assumes them. It is also how almost every other feat of magic is accomplished.

Following is the standard Golden Dawn procedure for creating and assuming a godform. It is adapted from the book *The Magician's Art: Ritual and Magical Use of Tools*, by Chic and Sandra Tabatha Cicero. As you read it, bear in mind the state of being that the adept must have in order to perform it successfully. This kind of work is not for the beginner.

1. Have an image of the deity handy. Perform any necessary banishings and invocations that may help you concentrate your "wandering rays of

thought" to the purpose at hand. For instance, if you are going to assume the godform of Thoth, you may wish to do a general banishing and then invoke the planet Mercury to assist.

2. Perform the Middle Pillar Exercise to increase the flow of the "central circuit" of the aura.

3. Formulate in your heart the letters, hieroglyphics, or symbols representing the deity. See them flare up in a fiery white light.

4. Examine the likeness of the deity on the drawing you have with you. Impress its likeness in your imagination.

5. Now inhale energy from the life energy of the biosphere, and then vibrate the name of the deity as resonantly and forcefully as you can. As you do so, see white brilliance descend from Kether, or your crown chakra, into your heart, engulfing the white letters in a red glow. Use the sensation of your vibration to give this sphere in your heart a sort of spinning sensation. It becomes a compacted, whirling ball of force. Vibrate the name an appropriate number of times, a number that is sacred to that deity, perhaps. With each inhalation, draw in energy from the environment. With each vibration, feel the energy descend from Kether and meet the buzzing, spinning sphere of red light that encompasses the name. If you have reached the appropriate number of vibrations and still don't feel that there is enough power present in the heart to project it outward, start over and do the same number of vibrations again, in the same manner.

6. After the final vibration, step forward in the Sign of the Enterer, both arms pointing forward, straight at the spot where the godform will appear, all fingers forward, and project the energy from your heart in a red ray that strikes the astral world, forming from it the image of the deity in the appropriate station of your ritual space. A station in the west is very often the best place. Continue to project the ray until the image is well sculpted in the imagination, perfect in every detail. It should be very intense, the eyes and skin of which burn with power worthy of the deity you are going to be assimilating.

7. Perform the Sign of Silence to stop the ray and to reseal the integrity of your aura. (This is very important.)

8. Now come around from behind the created godform and pause. Ask silently for permission to enter the shape. If all feels well, or you get an affirmative response of some kind, enter the shape. Feel your etheric double alter itself into the contours of the godform; use three or four soft exhalations to accomplish this if necessary. Feel your reasoning mind empowering the form that you have created, breathing life into it, even as you are breathing now.

9. Give a prepared speech as though you are now the god or goddess conjured. It should be composed by you based on extensive research on the mythology, attributes, and correspondences of the deity.

10. Meditate on the godform as you stand or sit within it. You may wish to do more ritual work while you wear and sustain the image of the god around you. The universe is the macrocosm, and your aura is the microcosm. The godform is the power of the macrocosm forced to show itself through the character of that deity. Shaping your microcosm into this shape links you to the universal power of that god. You may have abilities in this form that you do not normally have in your human persona. These abilities you can take advantage of in ritual.

11. When you are finished with your meditation or work, use the breath to "blow off" the godform. Inhale deeply and exhale sharply, visualizing the shell of the deity dissolving and returning to the astral. Visualize briefly your etheric double resuming its shape as the twin of your physical body. See your aura as perfectly contained, no rays bleeding out into space. You may wish to perform the Sign of Silence one more time once the image has been blown off.

12. Banish appropriately to finish. Banish the particular planetary or Sephirothic or zodiacal force corresponding to the deity. Always banish further with the Lesser Banishing Ritual of the Pentagram when you are done with magical work.[10]

The world-shaking experience that you can get by invoking a god in this manner brings to mind an actor I once saw at a Renaissance fair. He was dressed as a cavalier on horseback. He wasn't like the other pretenders around him. His chest stuck out. His eyes were dark, calm, and intense. Even the very colors of his cape seemed somehow richer in contrast than the clothes of the others. Perhaps he cared for his wardrobe better. In any event, he filled his clothes well and filled his projected persona completely, as though he owned it. He had not retreated into his role-playing as though it were some kind of shelter. He played the part actively, as a means to expressing himself, his lines completely spontaneous and yet in the colloquialisms of the time period that he genuinely represented. And I couldn't help but marvel at the mystery of it, and the power of his presence was a brief gust of fresh air in the otherwise stagnant recesses of the fairgrounds. Not everyone there was hiding from life. As his horse strutted around and he tipped his scarlet-feathered hat to the visitors, he conveyed more than just nostalgia, but a sense of genuine regality and confidence, which modern humans seem to lack. Perhaps he had inadvertently contacted, dominated, and put to good use some powerful Shakespearian archetype. As he passed by, I felt privileged to have met his glance.

The World Seen from Within

The world of the adept is completely different, and yet it is the same. He sees it as though through a stranger's eyes and feels it through hands that are no longer his own. For those who have been through the Outer Order grade work, the transition to Adeptus Minor will likely happen of its own accord, without any dramatic initiation ceremony. And it will come as a surprise. I have told you before that magic is not as it seems. Rather than becoming someone with "power" and "mastery," the only essential difference between now and the past is in outlook. It is like waking from a disturbed dream, the details of which quickly fade from memory. The adept looks back and can't see where or when it happened, or even if it "happened" at all, and yet he is looking at the life of someone else.

The god-like self that emerges from the pyramid of the four elements has motives that arise from some other world. It is a product neither of nature nor nurture, but rather nature and nurture are its instruments. The awakened human is a comfortable outsider, intruding on the tribal human world. He is no longer useful to the frantic, clinging motives of the people around him. At times, he is even a wrench thrown into the works of society, an unwelcome splash of cold water in the face of misery. A single brush with the truth can destroy a lifetime of lies. This is a truly frightening change, and he should thank the gods for it. Yet he does not. He is too busy looking around in wonder and laughing at the fading memory of the former self.

One thing is somewhat clear. There are many memories that he does retain about the previous life. But somehow it is as though they were part of a movie, a fiction: shuffling through college, struggling and getting disappointed with the professional world, never fitting in (and always, on some level, trying to), using people. He remembers these events so that he may help others who are caught up in them.

Even now, as he walks through the neighborhood—to the bank, let's say, or maybe to the utilities company to pay the electric bill—the people around him seem like frightened animals. The truth is before their eyes all the time, and of all the myriad ways of turning away from it, none work for very long.

The adept has been trained to do more than just react instinctively to the image of another human form on his optic nerve. He dares to notice something more. An opportunity to laugh at a mortal body that tries in vain to live forever? A chance to awaken from life? A spark of consciousness? Whatever it is, that is where his allegiance goes. He is a subordinate to that spark, and he serves it. He wants to liberate it, tear down the walls, open the door, turn on the light, and expose the futility of the fear and the lies.

It is as though he and his fellow humans are in the darkness of a movie theater, strapped into seats that are unbearably hard. And to get their minds off their aching buns, they try to lose themselves in the movie. Now, in this new chapter of his life, the first chapter of a strange new book called *Adeptus Minor*, this movie that has the audience beguiled is plainly more interesting than before . . . but not just the movie! The whole theater has become absorbing. Billions of people (can you believe it? billions!) sitting in uncomfortable chairs and being forced (or so it seems) to watch a movie from "beginning" to "end."

You may find yourself sitting there, in the theater next to the adept, or you may meet someone else strapped into a chair beside you. Usually, the other person is transfixed by the screen and can only mumble a hello in the mannerisms of the animals he is watching . . . or didn't I mention it? This is a movie about wildlife. It's called—drumroll, please—*The Struggle for Survival*. Some of the beastly forms that promote their prowess on the screen have learned to talk. What deadly weapons nature hath given them!

You may find yourself sitting, as I was saying, next to someone who has just noticed you taking an interest in him, in his potential to awaken. As you prod him, the auditorium around him snaps into focus, if only for an instant. The brief awareness, to this unaccustomed person, is simultaneously startling and yet so muddled that he will only pause for a bit and then, in the usual response, resume his absorption into the movie, as though trying to explain away his experience in movie terms. After all, the chairs here are really hard on the tush—better not to think about it.

But what's wrong with you? Why aren't you looking at the silver screen anymore? Don't you know that the moving picture before you is your life? Or do you not believe that lie anymore? Something must have broken the spell. The magic is gone. You wanted magic and drama and mystery, and here you are sitting in this cold, hard chair, no longer sucked dry by the wildlife drama rolling by before you. Look! The primates are mating! How odd.

Others have leaned away from you. They sense something is wrong. You no longer laugh in the appropriate places. You cry during the happy parts and snicker when the predator eats our hero's lover. You are a freak, a dangerous outsider. Everything you do seems to point at alternative possibilities.

What is wrong with you? Don't you care about the protagonists? The happy ending? Why have you become fascinated with your chair? It squeaks when you shift in it. Shhhh! We are *trying* to watch the FILM!

Best advice for the newly born Adeptus Minor: Get up quietly. Sneak out. Go for a little walk. Come into the brilliant radiance of the lobby.

Meet the theater staff. They are a motley cast of beings, most of them interested in your viewing pleasure. Some are overjoyed to see you have come forth from the darkness of the auditorium. The world outside is bright, intense, and real. Standing upright, you no longer hurt. In fact, your buttocks tingle with new life! How did you ever get conned into seeing this flick, anyway? And what about all those others? The ones still glued to the silver screen? What will you do for them? What *can* you do?

It is probably inevitable that you will take a rest and enjoy this new state of being. Go for a walk outside the theater. Look at the trees, the sky! Feel the hardness of the gravel under your feet and the gravity that draws you against it. Eventually, it will become evident that it is time to return to the darkness of the auditorium. There is work to do, and you have not even begun it yet!

Needless to say, the goal of the Outer Order grades is to bring about a change, an awakening. The student finds himself, if he is successful, in a new state of being. Nothing really matters anymore . . . except perhaps a few things. The few tasks that really concern the adept now are not important to talk about. Why waste breath making words about them? They are personal and, kept silent, they mark the nature of the individual that is truly a stand-alone entity, a one-of-a-kind being, shining and perhaps immortal. This true self is nowhere to be seen, and yet its qualities show themselves forth in the body and actions of the newly initiated person. Its presence is unmistakable, and—mark these words—you will be able to recognize the same presence in other awakened individuals, just like the Hermetists at the markets of Alexandria. But you will not know other illuminated beings by secret handshakes or tokens. For heaven's sake, no! Instead, you will recognize them by the invisible presence. Honesty, candor, and beauty. The truth of Hod, the victory of Netzach, and the beauty of Tiphareth.

There is no curriculum presented here for Adeptus Minor. Only perhaps a few words of advice that you don't need either. But just for the sake of closure and wordiness:

Pride is both a virtue and a vice of Tiphareth. There is nothing special about being awake. Bear in mind that the tide has only turned. There is much more awakening to bring about.

Resume many of the good habits of physical, mental, and emotional hygiene that have brought you to this point in your journey. They are still necessary to keep you moving on the path, only now they have sunk into the realm of the automatic consciousness, and they bear you along like obedient steeds.

Perform the invocation that you have written to your Higher Self. Doing it daily in a small form and periodically in a larger, formalized form is probably best. Some such exercise as banishing and invocation daily is still essential. Continue to exert regular, periodic effort to stay on your "razor's edge."

Modify your spiritual practice. You are now on your own. Curriculums created by others no longer apply.

Create programs of discipline that develop the Tzelem. Clairvoyance, energy manipulation, astral projection, invocation, evocation, and many other skills have not really been developed that well yet. Now, under the guidance of the true self, you are ready (finally!) to develop these abilities. Go with the ones that you seem to have a knack for. The time for compensating for what you lack is at an end. Go with your strengths. Go with your strengths. Go with your strengths.

Traditionally, you are not really an adept until you pass all the way through Adeptus Minor. One supposedly possesses the credentials of a particular grade when one has passed into the next one. You must now *become* an adept. Start doing real magic. Create change in the physical world according to the true will that broods behind your physical vehicle. Exercise your power mightily and repeatedly. Fail horribly and try again. Triumph and remain silent. Perhaps only for the first time you now know what it means "to know, to dare, to Will, and to keep silent!"[11]

In particular, two exercises from this book will prove invaluable. The Fourfold Body of Light technique found in chapter 9 can serve as one of your most potent tools for invocation. It can invoke the power of any one Sephirah with great force for any given ceremony. The *in*voked force can, in turn, give you the authority to *e*voke and subdue any spirit into your service. Moreover, the godform exercise in this chapter will help you to personify that same power personally. You will be able to make lasting alterations in your physical body, personality, and environment at will.

You may wish to pick an area of specialization. The curriculum you have just passed through is comparable to college. You are now in "graduate school." Some examples of areas of specialization are Kabbalah, alchemy, and Enochian magic.

Variations on the traditional curriculum for the Inner Order grades are published in several places. See, for instance, *Secret Inner Order Rituals of the Golden Dawn*, by Patrick J. Zalewski. You are advised to look at these study plans and to draw inspiration from them. But it is doubtful you can profit any more by continuing with strict adherence to someone else's prescription.

It is likely that you have many books besides the ones required by your Outer Order grade work. There is an immense amount of material at your disposal in regard to practical magic. You have developed the discrimination by which to start upon a new course of action. Initiate that course now and continuously experience the true meaning of initiation.

appendix a

The Consecration
of the Adeptus Wand

This ritual is to be performed at the vernal or autumnal equinox.

Implements Required:
Adeptus wand in black cloth
Robe
Rose Cross Lamen or a simple Celtic Cross necklace
Four side altars
Cubical altar
LBRP dagger
The four Enochian tablets and the Tablet of Union
Four elemental weapons, or tokens representing the elements
Lamp
Five Hebrew letters of Pentagrammaton
Frankincense and myrrh

The temple is arranged with the Enochian tablets in the appropriate quarters and the Tablet of Union in the center. The four elemental weapons rest on the central altar. The Adeptus wand, wrapped in black cloth, is within the altar.

Four of the Hebrew letters hang above the elemental tablets in the four quarters: Yod in the south, Heh in the west, Vau in the east, and Heh Final in the north. The lamp hangs from the center of the ceiling, from which hangs the Hebrew letter Shin, over the Tablet of Union.

Wear your black robe, concealing beneath it the Rose Cross Lamen.

Part One: Opening

The Lesser Banishing Ritual of the Pentagram

The Banishing Ritual of the Hexagram

The Opening by Watchtower

The Invoking Ritual of the Sun Hexagram

The Fourfold Body of Tiphareth

Part Two: Equinox Consecration

In the Name of the Lord of the universe, Who works in silence and not but silence can express, I proclaim that the vernal [or autumnal] equinox is here! Be still, all ye spirits of Nature, and align to the silence of your Creator!

Stand between the pillars (these can be imagined), facing west.

I stand in the beautiful gate, within the mighty portal of the universe. On my left hand is the Pillar of Fire, on my right hand the Pillar of Cloud. At their bases are the dark rolling clouds of the material universe. And they pierce the vault of the heavens above, whilst ever upon their summits flame the lamps of their spiritual essence.

Knock once, formulating the visualization of the rising spiritual sun on the horizon between the pillars behind you.

I now consecrate this temple for the return of the Equinox.

As you say the following, on the word "Light," step forward in the Sign of the Enterer and formulate, in the astral, a band of white light from east to west:

Light! Darkness. East! West. Air! Water.

Give the Sign of Silence.

I am the reconciler between them.

Go to the south and face north. On the word "heat," step forward in the Sign of the Enterer and formulate the astral white band from south to north.

Heat! Cold. South! North. Fire! Earth.

Give the Sign of Silence.

I am the reconciler between them.

Circumambulate clockwise, formulating a circle of white light around the altar, saying the following at the appropriate stations (on the word "Creator," make the Sign of the Enterer as you pass the east):

One Creator! (*East—give the Sign of the Enterer*)
One Preserver! (*South*)
One Destroyer! (*West*)
One Redeemer! (*North*)

You have completed the image of the solar or Rose Cross on the temple floor. Spiraling inward to the center of the circle, come around to the west of the altar to face east.

Give the Sign of Silence.

One Reconciler between them.

Draw down the Divine White Brilliance with Analysis of the Key Word:

I-N-R-I.
YOD. NUN. RESH. YOD.
The Sign of Osiris Slain.
The Sign of the Mourning of Isis!
The Sign of Apophis and Typhon!
The Sign of Osiris Risen.
L . . . V . . . X . . . Lux.
The Light . . . of the Cross.
Virgo! Isis! Mighty Mother!
Scorpio! Apophis! Destroyer!
Sol! Osiris. Slain . . . and Risen.
Isis! Apophis! Osiris!
EXARP. HCOMA. NANTA. BITOM. IAO.
Let the Divine Light descend!

Part Three: Relinquishing of the Old Motto

The time has come to depart the old world of outer appearance and to call forth the banner of the inner life of Spirit. I hereby relinquish my Outer

Order motto, "_____." I do this not that it may be forsaken, but that it may be fulfilled by the new motto, "_____," of the Inner Order.

Circumambulating appropriately, take up each of the elemental weapons (or tokens) in turn (in order of the Tetragrammaton—fire, water, air, earth) and place each on its appropriate side altar, saying softly each time:

"[Old motto]," I relinquish thee.

Go to the east, take up the air dagger, and face the eastern tablet, making a white cross and circle. Hold the tip of the dagger to the center of the cross.

Holy art Thou, Lord of the Air, Who hast created the firmament.

SHADDAI EL CHAI.

Almighty and everlasting, ever living be Thy Name, ever magnified in the glory of all. We praise Thee and we bless Thee in the changing empire of created Light, and we aspire without cessation unto Thine immutable and imperishable brilliance. Amen.

Replace the air dagger on the eastern side altar and circumambulate to the south. Take up the fire wand, making a white cross and circle before the tablet. Hold the tip of the fire wand to the center of the cross.

Holy art Thou, Lord of Fire, wherein Thou hast shown forth the throne of Thy glory.

YHVH TZABAOTH.

Leader of Armies is Thy Name. O, Thou flashing Fire, Thou illuminatest all things with Thine unsupportable glory, whence flow the ceaseless streams of splendor which nourisheth Thine infinite Spirit. Help us, Thy children, whom Thou hast loved since the birth of the ages of time. Amen.

Replace the fire wand on its side altar and circumambulate to the west. Take up the water chalice and make a white cross and circle before the western tablet. Hold the rim of the goblet to the center of the cross, as though pouring out a little bit of water there.

Holy art Thou, Lord of the Mighty Waters, whereon Thy Spirit moved in the beginning.

ELOHIM TZABAOTH.

Glory be to the Ruach Elohim whose Spirit hovered over the great Waters of Creation. O depth, O inscrutable depth, which breathest out unto the height, lead us into the true life, through liberty, through love, so that one day we may be found worthy to know Thee, to unite with Thy Spirit in the silence, in the brilliance, for the attainment of Thine understanding. Amen.

Replace the water chalice to its side altar and circumambulate to the north. Take up the earth pantacle and make a cross and circle before the northern tablet. Hold the edge of the pantacle to the center of the cross.

Holy art Thou, Lord of the Earth, which Thou hast made as Thy footstool.

ADONAI HA-ARETZ, ADONAI MELEK.

Unto Thee be the kingdom and the power and the glory. The Rose of Sharon, the Lily of the Valley. O Thou who hidest beneath the Earth in the kingdom of gems the marvelous seed of the stars. Live, reign, and be Thou the eternal dispenser of Thy treasures whereof Thou hast made us the wardens. Amen.

Replace the earth pantacle to its side altar and proceed to the east of the altar, facing west. Take down the lamp and hold it over that altar.

Holy art Thou, Who art in all things, even as all things are within Thee. If I climb up to Heaven, Thou art there, and if I go down to Hell, Thou art there also! If I take the wings of the morning and flee into the uttermost parts of the sea, even there shall Thy hand lead me, and Thy right hand shall hold me. If peradventure the Darkness shall overcome me, even the night shall be turned Light unto Thee!

Thine is the Air with its movement!
Thine is the Fire with its flashing flame!
Thine is the Water with its ebb and flow!
Thine is the Earth with its enduring stability!

Make a cross and circle over the altar with the lamp.

In Nomine Dei Viventis et vivificantis qui vivit et regnet in saecula saeculorum amen avete, rosae rubae et aureae crucis.

Replace the lamp on its hook above.

Part Four: Adopting the New Motto

Return to the west of the altar, facing east. Remove the wand from within and hold it up by the white band, as though to show it for the first time.

(*Knock once.*) **I now proclaim the new motto, "_____." It fulfills the old motto, which has been relinquished to the Four Winds. May it serve me well in the new office of adeptship, which I am now about to embark upon.**

Part Five: Invoking the Inner Order Guardians

Speak very somberly:

I know that the mystic temple, which was erected of old by wisdom, as a witness to the mysteries that are above the sphere of knowledge, doth abide in the Supernal Triad. We know that the Shekinah, the cohabitating glory, dwelt in the inner sanctuary.

But the first creation was made void. The holy place was made waste, and the sons of the house of wisdom were taken away into the captivity of the senses. I have worshipped since then in a house made with hands, receiving a sacramental ministration by a derived light in a place of the cohabitating glory. And yet, amidst signs and symbols, the tokens of the higher presence have never been wanting in my heart.

As a witness in the temple of balance, we have with us, ever-present, certain watchers from within, deputed by the Second Order to guard and lead the lesser mysteries of the Rosae Rubae et Aureae Crucis and those who advance therein, that they may be fitted in due course to participate in the Light that is beyond it.

I call upon thee, ye guardians of the gates of the inner life. I beseech thee, provided that you deem me worthy of the mysteries, to assume the things that are without in the Outer Order into the things of the Inner Order. Let this sacred temple of the Divine be therefore assumed into thy presence that I may, by the virtue of my destiny as an immortal spark of *Ain Soph Aur*, call forth the governance of the Supernals herein.

Cum potestate et gloria, amen benedictus dominus deus noster qui dedit nobis hoc signum. (*Touch the breast.*)

Pull out the Rose Cross Lamen from within your robe, letting it hang openly.

I dedicate this ceremony for the consecration of the Adeptus wand, the emblem of my dawning power as a magician of the magic of Light. Let it become the living representation of the link between Divine and Material.

Part Six: Invoking the Supernals

Knock three times, put down the wand on the altar with its red tip pointing east, and assume the invoking stance.

Supernal splendor that dwellest in the Light that no man can approach, wherein is mystery and depth unthinkable—and awful silence. I beseech thee, who art Shekinah and Aimah Elohim, to look upon me in this ceremony, which I perform to thine honor for my own advancement to the rank of Adeptus Minor of the Inner Order of the Golden Dawn. Grant thine aid to the highest aspirations of my soul, in thy Divine Name,

YHVH ELOHIM, (*Trace the invoking hexagram of Saturn over the altar.*)

by which thou dost reveal thyself in the threefold perfection of creation—and in the Light of the world to come.

I implore thee to grant unto me the presence of thine Archangel,

TZAPHKIEL. (*Trace the sigil of the archangel in the center of the hexagram.*)

O Tzaphkiel, thou Prince of Spiritual Initiation through suffering and of spiritual strife against evil, aid me. I beseech thee to transmute the evil that is within this mortal shell, by the threefold binding of my earthly parts and passions.

O ye seats of power of the sphere of Shabbathai,

ARALIM,

I conjure thee by the mighty Name of YHVH Elohim, the Divine Ruler of your realm, and by the Name of Tzaphkiel, your Archangel, aid me with your power, in your office, to place a veil between me and all things belonging to the outer and lower world! Let it be a veil woven from the silent darkness that surrounds the abode of the eternal rest in the sphere of Shabbathai, that within its boundary, I may call forth the Will of my Divine Aspect and unite it to this wand, the emblem of my dawning power as a magician of the magic of Light.

Lift me, I beseech thee, lift me up so that I may be made to receive the presence of that Divine Messenger, none other than my Holy Guardian Angel, and that with His aid and thine, perform the threefold consecration of Spirit upon this wand, the emblem of my dawning power as an adept of the Inner Order, a magician of the magic of Light.

Knock thrice.

Part Seven: Invocation of the Higher Self

Get on your knees, still in the invoking stance.

O my Divine Spirit, this life is sorrow, and all is wrought with decay and waste in the absence of Thee, my Angel. The desire for Thy house hath eaten me up, and I wish to be dissolved and to be with Thee. I no longer seek the things of the Earth, for I cannot possess the fleeting forces that pass before Thy countenance. For Thine is the kingdom and the power and the glory unto the ages. For not another step can I take without Thee, and I dare not take another breath but by Thine inspiration! Take this shadow-self, which is wracked with the pain of exile, and consume it, diverting from its earthly motives to Thy Divine ends! May it be transmuted into a conveyor of the purest light.

Proceed to the station between the pillars and face west in the Sign of Osiris Slain.

By the threefold power of YHVH Elohim, come forth! Come forth through me, Thou Who art my Holy Guardian Angel, my true Self, my secret fire! Come forth through me, Thou Who art crowned with the unutterable perfection, Who art the changeless, the unnameable, the immortal Godhead, Whose place is in the unknown and Whose dwelling is in the abodes of the undying. Heart of my soul, self-begotten flame, unfathomable light, Thee I invoke! Come forth through me, my Lord—through me, who art Thy vain reflection in the sea of matter. Hear Thou, my lord and master! Hear Thou in the habitations of eternity; come forth and purify to Thy glory my mind and Will! Without Thy power I am nothing, I am no one, I do not exist. And in Thee, I am all, existing in Thy ineffable selfhood, transcending even eternity!

See the aura begin to glow with increasingly brilliant white intensity, and see the etheric body respond, glowing with golden light, to the stimulation of the current coming down through the Supernals. This may herald the arrival of the Higher Self. Give the Sign of Osiris Risen, and aspire to meet your angel with all of your might.

Speak quietly here, gradually becoming louder:

Buried within that light in a mystical death, I come. Rising again in a mystical resurrection, cleansed and purified through Him our master, thou receivest me, O thou newborn dweller of the invisible. Like Him hast thou toiled long. Like Him hast thou suffered tribulation. Poverty, torture, and death, hast thou passed through. They have been but the purification of the gold, in the alembic of thine heart, through the athanor of affliction. Seek thou the true Stone of the Wise.

Rise in my breath and see me at last. Thou hast opened for me the door between the Worlds, and as it is written, I am come forth and will never leave thee. For thou hast shown forth that the things that are above are as the things below, and the things that are below are as the things above. Such an illumination cannot be undone by any power of Heaven, Hell, or Earth. The living beings of Earth, Air, Water, and Fire stand still for thee and me at last united.

Part Eight: Spiritual Consecration

Assume a relaxed invoking stance.

O Lord of the Universe, the Vast and Mighty One, ruler of the Light and the Darkness, we adore Thee and we invoke Thee. Look Thou with favor upon this union of the outer and inner life. Grant us the blessing of Thy eternal Light. Lift a corner of Thy veil that I may consummate this union by bestowing the power of the threefold Supernal splendor upon the wand of adeptship that lieth before us.

Slowly walk to the altar (three steps), visualizing the brilliance descending upon the wand.

I come in the power of the Light. I come in the Light of wisdom. I come in the mercy of the Light. (*Touch the wand.*) **The Light hath healing in its wings.**

By the powers of the three-pronged flame of Spirit, I do hereby conse-crate this wand to the service of the magic of Light.

(Touch the white band.) **EHEIEH**
(Touch the gray band.) **YAH**
(Touch the black band.) **YHVH ELOHIM**

(Touch the white band.) **METATRON**
(Touch the gray band.) **RAZIEL**
(Touch the black band.) **TZAPHKIEL**

(Touch the white band.) **CHAYOTH HA-QADESH**
(Touch the gray band.) **AUPHANIM**
(Touch the black band.) **ARALIM**

Shout forth your new motto as though giving a celebratory toast.

See that the letter Shin has descended from the lamp into the wand, filling its interior with impossibly brilliant radiance. Knock once and feel the presence of the Shekinah, the power of the Supernals, holding that brilliance within the wand.

Go to the west of the altar to face east. Holding it by the white band, raise the wand and address it:

Be thou my rod of power, a channel of the Divine Will! Be thou drawn to perfection by the surrounding agency of the Angels of Supernal grace. O thou shaft of Godly power, thou art straight and direct; thou art as a whirl-wind of Fire that containeth the Eye and the Will of God!

Part Nine: Elemental Consecration

I clothe thee now with the powers of the Elements, such that the True Will within may express itself in the world without. The Elements touch thee not in thine essence, but they are yet as the limbs of thy fearsome power, the coruscations of truth proceeding from the Divine Will, brought forth this hour by the vortex of the Supernal presence.

Go to the north and, holding the wand in the left hand by the green band, pick up the earth pantacle with the right. Hold your arms out to the sides in the form of Osiris Slain.

Earth

O great Godname, EMOR DIAL HECTEGA, whose portions are spread upon the banners of the north, come forth, Great Spirit, and give us Thy blessings. I petition Thee to give license for those noble beings of Light from the great quadrangle of the north, whom Thou commandest, to attend this ceremony.

Turn around and touch the pantacle to the green band of the wand, over the altar.

Come forth, all you beings of earthly light, and align yourselves to the Divine Will, of which this wand is the instrument. Live and reign in the green band of this, my rod of power, the emblem of my dawning power as a magician of the magic of Light. Thou toucheth not the substance of this wand. Be thou instead the garment and agents thereof, that the Will of the Divine may be wrought in the earthly realm by thy surrender to thy Creator.

Set the pantacle down in its proper place on the central altar.

Air

Go to the east and, holding the wand in the left hand by the yellow band, pick up the air dagger with the right. Hold your arms out to the sides in the form of Osiris Slain.

O great Godname, ORO IBAH AOZPI, whose portions are spread upon the banners of the east, come forth, Great Spirit, and give us Thy blessings. I petition Thee to give license for those noble beings of Light from the great quadrangle of the east, whom Thou commandest, to attend this ceremony.

Turn around and touch the tip of the air dagger to the yellow band of the wand, over the altar.

Come forth, all you beings of wind and breath, and align yourselves to the Divine Will, of which this wand is the instrument. Live and reign in the yellow band of this, my rod of power, the emblem of my dawning power as a magician of the magic of Light. Thou toucheth not the substance of this wand. Be thou instead borne aloft as the garments and agents thereof, that the Will of the Divine may be wrought in the outer world by thy surrender to thy Creator.

Set the air dagger down in its proper place on the central altar.

Water

Go to the west and, holding the wand in the left hand by the blue band, pick up the water chalice with the right. Hold your arms out to the sides in the form of Osiris Slain.

O great Godname, **MPH ARSL GAIOL**, whose portions are spread upon the banners of the west, come forth, Great Spirit, and give us Thy blessings. I petition Thee to give license for those noble beings of Light from the great quadrangle of the west, whom Thou commandest, to attend this ceremony.

Turn around and touch the water chalice to the blue band (as though pouring out its contents into the color).

Come forth, all ye beings of the lustral waters. Align yourselves to the Divine Will, of which this wand is the instrument. Live and reign in the blue band of this, my rod of power, the emblem of my dawning power as a magician of the magic of Light. Thou toucheth not the substance of this wand. Be thou instead the garments and agents thereof, like waves on the surface of the Supernal sea. Let the Will of the Divine be wrought in the outer world by thy surrender to thy Creator.

Set the chalice down in its proper place on the central altar.

Fire

Go to the south and, holding the wand in the left hand by the red band, pick up the fire wand with the right. Hold your arms out to the sides in the form of Osiris Slain.

O great Godname, **OIP TEAA PDOCE**, whose portions are spread upon the banners of the south, come forth, Great Spirit, and give us Thy blessings. I petition Thee to give license for those noble beings of Light from the great quadrangle of the south, whom Thou commandest, to attend this ceremony.

Turn around and touch the tip of the fire wand to the red band of the Adeptus wand, over the altar.

Come forth, all you beings of heat and flame, and align yourselves to the Divine Will, of which this wand is the instrument. Live and reign in the red band of this, my rod of power, the emblem of my dawning power as a magician of the magic of Light. Thou toucheth not the substance of this wand. Be thou instead as the fiery tongues of its radiating glory, that the Will of the Divine may be wrought in the outer world by thy surrender to thy Creator.

Set the fire wand in its proper place on the central altar. Go to the west of the altar and face east. Take it up again. Balance and cradle the wand on high, horizontally, in the right hand, by the gray band.

These are the Elements of my body, perfected through suffering and glorified by trial. The yellow band is as the unquiet mind, the suppressed sigh of my suffering. And the red band is the fiery pressure of mine undaunted Will upon the outer world. The blue band is the pouring forth of the blood of my heart, sacrificed unto regeneration, unto the new life. And the green band is my ever-living, ever-dying body, which I destroy in order that it may be better and better renewed.

Part Ten: Final Consecration

Set the wand down on the altar.

And now, in the tremendous Name of strength through sacrifice, YEHESHUAH YEHOVASHAH, I do bind thee, Spirits of the Elements, to the service of the Divine Will, of which this wand is the emblem. Thou shalt find grace and beauty in thy surrender thereto. Be thee henceforth the garments and guardians of the Holy Presence, working in harmony with one another, by the agency of thine individual gifts according to the descending influence from on high, shown forth in the material form of this Adeptus wand.

Shout forth your Outer Order motto. Speak firmly and calmly your Inner Order motto. Knock once.

It is done.

Take up the wand and go to the station between the pillars to face west. Hold the wand vertically, by the gray band, in front of your chest.

Upright and so equipped, I am Osiris Onnophris, the Justified One, Lord of Life, triumphant over death. There is no part of me that is not of the gods. No more oaths are required, for I am the preparer of the Pathway, the rescuer unto the Light.

Part Eleven: Restoration of Temple to the Outer World

God save us. The work of Light for which we have assumed this temple has been accomplished. By the power in me newly vested as a magician of the magic of Light, I now remit it into its due place in the outer world, taking with it the graces and benedictions that at this time we have been permitted to bestow thereon. And it is so remitted accordingly. (*Wave the wand.*) **In Nomine Dei Viventis et vivificantis qui vivit et regnet in saecula saeculorum. Amen.**

Give the L-V-X signs. Replace the Rose Cross Lamen to its concealment beneath the robe.

Part Twelve: Closing

Return to the west, facing east.

I give Thee thanks, supreme and gracious God, for the manifestation of Thy Light, which is vouchsafed to me, for that measure of knowledge Thou hast revealed to me concerning Thy mysteries, for those guiding hands that raise the corner of the Veil, and for the firm hope of further Light beyond. Keep me, I beseech Thee, keep this newly created magician of the magic of Light in the justice of the ways, in the spirit of Thy great council, that he may well and worthily direct those who have been called from the tribulation of the Darkness into the Light of the Kingdom of Thy Love; and vouchsafe also, that going forward in love for Thee, through him and with him, they may pass from the Desire of Thy house into the Light of Thy presence.

Close the temple by Watchtower, using the Adeptus wand for the Banishing Ritual of the Hexagram (including also a banishment of the Aralim) and for the releasing of bound spirits.

Suggested Forms of Exercise

Neophyte
The Alexander Technique

This exercise is not very strenuous, though there are recommended exercises in the following grades that are increasingly demanding. You may already have an exercise routine in place. Throughout the grades, you may do any sort of physical exercise that you please, but to get the most benefit you should do the optional form as well.

This grade tests to see whether you are a good candidate for spiritual growth. Therefore, the Neophyte begins the Great Work by learning to monitor and modify his posture. The energy released in ritual must be allowed to flow to all parts of the body. Bad habits in regard to sitting, standing, and walking are the chief culprits in the obstruction of energy between mind and body. The Alexander Technique is one of the simplest, easiest ways to gain awareness over the ego's tendency to misuse the body.

The Alexander Technique was developed over one hundred years ago by F. Matthias Alexander, an Australian actor who lost his voice due to bad habits of head and neck posture. No doctor was able to help him regain his vocal ability, so he set about curing himself. Observing himself recite Shakespeare in a three-way mirror, he retrained his muscles and regained control of his voice. The insights he gained led him to expand on the technique, help others, and publish his experiences. There are many, many enthusiasts of the Alexander Technique today, and many books available for self-instruction.

This exercise does not require that you get a teacher from a certified organization, such as AmSAT (the American Society of Teachers of the Alexander Technique), though that would be ideal. Simply find a book that spells out the technique for self-instruction and practice for forty to fifty minutes a day, two days each week. Remember, if boredom crops up, you may be on the verge of an important breakthrough. Continuing an exercise in the face of such resistance is one of the keys to the Great Work.

Zelator
Pilates

In the magical work, it is important to become strong in both mind and body, for the one corresponds to the other. Zelator focuses on the very basics of physical reality. Therefore, it becomes important now to develop foundational strength and flexibility that make for good posture, mobility, strength, and overall vitality. This will prepare you for the more strenuous exercise requirements ahead, as well as for the states of receptivity and bodily awareness that are required for high magic. Integrating your awareness of your physical body requires a down-to-earth kind of activity. Some kind of physical exercise, even though you may opt out of these suggestions, is crucial to your progress.

Pilates is a form of Western holistic exercise that emphasizes bodily awareness, posture, breathing, and flexibility. It has a definite mechanical focus, unlike the more ambiguous Hatha Yoga of the Eastern disciplines. The physical exercise in Zelator is specifically aimed to bring about pain-free mobility. Accomplishing this gets the mind off of efforts to avoid discomfort and sets the stage for it to focus on something more.

Joseph Pilates was an accomplished athlete in the early twentieth century. Having been sickly from birth, he had overcome his infirmities by pursuing an active lifestyle in which he mastered the sports of skiing, gymnastics, diving, and bodybuilding.[1]

His great experience with sports, combined with an intense awareness of his own limitations, led him to develop exercises that optimize the fundamental mobility of the body. He eventually became an instructor of his own technique in New York during the 1920s. A majority of the professional dancers in the city studied under him at his studio at 939 Eighth Avenue.[2]

Obtain a book on the most basic, unmodified mat exercises developed by Pilates. Learn the movements and then practice Pilates at least three times per week, in sessions lasting about an hour.

Alternatively, you may choose to take a class in Pilates, but make sure it is one that emphasizes the original teachings. There are oversimplified, easier versions of the exercises available out there that may not be as effective.

Theoricus
Cardiovascular Training

You are now to explore your cardiovascular endurance. Jogging, bicycling (or spinning), bouncing on a trampoline, or jumping rope are recommended. If this kind of activity is new to you, start light. It is unlikely that you will have to start with an exercise as easy as walking, especially if you have continued your Pilates workouts up until the present day. However, you should be mindful of your limitations (being mindful of them is one of the chief reasons for staying physically active as you progress). For those who are unaccustomed to fast and strenuous activities, walking may be the best beginning. Twenty minutes of continuous, brisk walking per day, five days per week, will gradually get you ready for more.

For more challenging workouts, I recommend no less than three sessions per week. To start with, these workouts may be quite short, as in ten minutes. When I started running on a treadmill, I did only six minutes, gradually increasing the time to thirty minutes.

You should push your boundaries a little every time you work out. This means that you will reach a point where your body will start to complain. There should be a sensation of restless discomfort, as though you can't get enough air to maintain your pace (but you should never feel dizzy or ill). This feeling, though a little unpleasant, pushes your body to optimize and fine-tune its ability to use energy. Maintain your pace for a few minutes in this state, and you will expand the time of your workouts noticeably within a month.

Do not push yourself too hard. Many people who start to exercise end up injuring themselves in the first month, effectively shutting down their workouts. I can't help but wonder sometimes if the ego has intentionally sabotaged their effort to make a change.

A good sign that you are working out effectively is that your body is sweating and your breathing volume and rate have dramatically increased. You should still be able to speak sentences without gasping for air. If you can't do that, then you are working too hard.

Continue your cardiovascular workouts for five months.

Practicus

Body Sculpting

I have worked with a few occultists in my magical adventures, and I've often been shocked by their health habits. In particular, I have noted their tendency to be indoor "nerds." Poor eating habits and a lack of physical activity almost always seem to create obstructions for them in their aspirations. As Hermeticists, most of us have sedentary tendencies. We must learn to balance our lives, and that usually demands sacrifices—quitting smoking (and drug use), weaning yourself off prescription medications (where possible), throwing away your potato chips (now!), and getting a gym membership.

The body needs to feel like it is useful, like its evolutionary purpose is being fulfilled. That means conscious direction from the mind that provides clean shelter, nutritious *and* delicious food, regular physical exertion, meaningful work, loving friendships, a healthy sex life, moderate wealth, and spiritual aspirations that are the basis for all of the above.

Your progress in this grade would benefit if you set a goal for yourself to reshape your body. I suggest you take photographs of yourself naked and scrutinize them. Do not use the values of pop culture to determine if you look like magazine-cover material. Look instead for signs of health and happiness in your posture and in your overall shape. Where is there potential for the expression of better health, happiness, and well-being? How would you look if those traits were 100 percent yours? If you are going to be a vessel for the awareness of your Higher Self, your body has to be in exceptional health. The bliss of union with your Divine Spark is so strong that it makes one worry about the body's ability to withstand it. Presumably, your Higher Self cares about you, and it is not going to draw closer and awaken the normally sluggish faculties of the body unless the apparatus of those faculties is in good working order. Select *at least* one thing you would like to change, and write down that goal.

Look at your body dispassionately, regard it as something malleable, and then set about learning the art of reshaping it. You have already learned invaluable information about your own posture and aerobic limits through the Alexander Technique, Pilates, and cardiovascular fitness.

Some examples of goals follow: replacing fat on the back of the arms with muscle, increasing shoulder and/or chest size, taking inches off of the thighs, and reducing abdominal girth.

You can, of course, use books and a modest home gym to accomplish your body-sculpting goal, but I recommend getting a gym membership and two sessions with a trainer (at the very least). Do this to get an overview of the requirements for your goal, and then begin working out on your own or with a partner. After your sessions with the trainer, go to the bookstore and learn the fundamentals of body sculpting through weight training. Educate yourself on supplements (and on the dangers of the many get-fit-quick products out there). Body sculpting means simply what it states: reshaping the body through exercise and diet. Weight training is its primary focus.

Once you have begun, you should come up with a diet regimen (which includes shopping plans and quick emergency sources of good food, just in case the fast-food necessity strikes).

Be meticulous about recording the gradual improvements of your workouts: your number of repetitions, amount of weight, minutes on the treadmill, and so on. Track your results in a workout log and summarize weekly your successes and failures in your magical journal.

Making change of this sort is a prerequisite to the techniques of deeper and more lasting change in the grades ahead. If you cannot do it on this level, will you have enough willpower to change things in the higher worlds? View this body-sculpting goal as a test to see if you have enough will to effect more powerful change at higher levels.

Philosophus
Energetic Dance

> Dancing of any kind is wonderful for your body. Aerobic exercise promotes general fitness, conditions your heart and respiratory system, stimulates immunity and increases stamina. It also tones your nervous system, reduces stress, increases oxygen flow throughout the body, and gives you a sense of well-being and empowerment. Dancing is one of the best aerobic activities of all because it's upbeat and enjoyable, and provides a thorough workout.[3]
>
> —Dr. Andrew Weil

Dancing in particular draws Spirit downward into matter and matter upward into Spirit. The two worlds of Heaven and Earth that face each other across the abyss of time respond to the movements of dance by expressing themselves within a human being. The consciousness of the ego is to be the meeting place of the two entwining serpents of the caduceus. By dancing, may you come to the realization that all of the dramas of your life are potential stages for the manifestation of the divine presence.

For two months, dance for at least thirty minutes at a time, three times per week. I recommend going out to dance clubs and exposing yourself to the raw energy of nightlife a couple of times during this grade—even if that is something that you have done before.

At home, obtain a few CDs of high-energy dance hits. Styles may vary. I suggest you experiment: freestyle, belly dancing, ballroom dancing, or jazz dance. Each of these can be strenuous enough to give you a workout.

Portal
Chi Gung

Chi Gung, similar to Tai Chi, is a kind of slow-moving exercise of different forms and poses and the fluid transitions between them. You may have seen groups of people learning it in the park. Chi Gung is a discipline some four thousand years old. Nobody knows how it was begun, but it is presumed that adepts in ancient China developed it from exercises that were practiced to relieve arthritis pain, rheumatism, and other discomforts associated with age.

It is an art form that emphasizes the deliberate harnessing and utilization of energy that flows in nature. This energy you know by the names Ruach and Kundalini. Chi Gung calls it *chi*. It exists in lesser and greater intensities in living things and in the environment. It can be harnessed, directed, and stilled by the conscious intention of the adept. Ritual is an aid to raising and directing *chi*.

Chi Gung is a tool that can help the magician master his power as a ritualist—to become a kind of spiritual athlete. With the entrance of the Portal grade, you are at the threshold of adeptship. All of the exercises, study, and ritual have been designed up until now to bring about a transformation of an ordinary person into someone more than human. Your very cell function and structure is by now different from most people around you. Your mind is by now tuned to a different frequency, so to speak, and a new way of life is at hand. The work ahead of you as an adept (should your transformation be successful) is to discipline your mental, emotional, and spiritual faculties to higher and higher degrees. As an athlete of the spirit, the real work with magic begins. The adept is free to develop programs of discipline on his own that are suitable to his own higher will. Strict adherence to other people's curriculums will no longer be necessary.

Chi Gung will be the last prescribed physical exercise for you. It is a taste of the kind of universe that greets the student as he becomes an adept. I also assign it here as a test of the student's progress thus far. Chi Gung exercises increase the intensity and flow of bioelectric energy in the body. Any serious blocks to this energy that remain will become pronounced as life energy wells up against your inhibitions. Tune in to any resistances that you may feel to your experience of energy, emotion, thought, or sensation.

It is left up to the student to diagnose his own blockages and to do the necessary life-changing exercises required to clear them. Working them out usually involves the confrontation of a fear or the release of a desire. Be aware of your blocks and dissolve them using the tools that you have learned in your adventures through the grade system. Get professional help if they prove too difficult to face. Reichian therapists, Rolfers, and other body-oriented psychotherapists are experienced at working out such habitual tensions. It is best that you do not proceed to the next grade until any major difficulties are released. To proceed beyond this grade into adept-level activities, despite warning signs, can endanger your health and sanity.

Get a good book on Chi Gung and study its introductory forms. The simplest and least interesting exercises tend to be the most potent ones for the beginner. Spend most of your time on standing meditations for three or four months. After that period, integrate a standing meditation practice into the "Chakra Breathing" exercise that you do before ritual. For fifteen minutes every day, adopt a standing meditation pose from Chi Gung and breathe forth the body of light within it.

Use the breath-counting pattern of 4-7-8. Breathe in to the count of four, hold for the count of seven and observe the "air" within you begin to converge on the focal chakra, and breathe out the body of light through that chakra to the count of eight. Start the pattern immediately over without pausing between out-breath and in-breath.

Combining Chi Gung with your daily ritual practice can be especially illuminating. You may wish to perform it just before the Fourfold Body of Light. If you do this, you should dress very lightly for ritual, as Chi Gung will make you perspire profusely.

Endnotes

Chapter 1: Though Only a Few Will Rise

1. Easterbrook, *The Progress Paradox*, 9.
2. Ibid., 29.
3. Ibid., 46.
4. Ibid., 163.
5. Picard, *The World of Silence*, 15.
6. Torrens, *The Golden Dawn: The Inner Teachings*, 171.
7. Regardie, *The Golden Dawn*, 99.

Chapter 2: The First Steps

1. Levi, *Transcendental Magic*, 29.
2. Buckland, *Buckland's Complete Book of Witchcraft*, 225.
3. Gray, *Qabalistic Concepts*, 347.

Chapter 3: The Secret Lineage

1. Baigent, *The Jesus Papers*, 130.
2. Lindholm, *Pilgrims of the Night*, 79.
3. Cicero, *The Essential Golden Dawn*, 50.
4. Wescott, "The Rosicrucians: Past and Present, at Home and Abroad."
5. Regardie, *What You Should Know about the Golden Dawn*, 13.
6. Hall, *The Secret Teachings of All Ages*, 442.
7. Ibid.

8. Ibid., 443.

9. Ibid., 444.

10. Wescott, "The Rosicrucians: Past and Present, at Home and Abroad."

11. Ibid.

12. Hall, *The Secret Teachings of All Ages*, 444.

13. Lindholm, *Pilgrims of the Night*, 50.

14. Hall, *The Secret Teachings of All Ages*, 445.

15. Ibid.

16. Ibid.

17. Ibid.

18. Ibid., 446.

19. Baigent, *The Jesus Papers*, 130.

20. Regardie, *The Golden Dawn*, 95.

21. Fortune, *Moon Magic*, 187.

22. Regardie, *The Golden Dawn*, 95.

23. Ibid.

24. Ibid.

25. Ibid. (The World of Emanation corresponds to the element of fire.)

26. Regardie, *The Middle Pillar*, 3rd ed., 212.

27. Regardie, *The Middle Pillar*, 3rd ed., 89.

28. Torrens, *The Golden Dawn: The Inner Teachings*, 171.

Chapter 4: Neophyte

1. Pert, *The Molecules of Emotion*, 189.

2. Regardie, *The One Year Manual*, 51–53. (The practice of "breathing through the pores" is an exercises that Regardie called "The Practice of the Presence of God.")

3. Torrens, *The Golden Dawn: The Inner Teachings*, 40. (The practice of the fourfold breath comes from this source.)

4. Tyson, *The Magician's Workbook*, 3.

5. Cicero, "Magical Mottos of the Golden Dawn."

Chapter 5: That Darkly Splendid World

1. Davies, *God and the New Physics*, 11.

2. Zalewski, *Talismans and Evocations of the Golden Dawn*, 133.

3. Zalewski, *Golden Dawn Enochian Magic*, 19.

4. Case, *The True and Invisible Rosicrucian Order*, xx.

5. Kaku, *Hyperspace*, 80.

6. Regardie, *The Golden Dawn*, 376–454.

7. The Jerusalem Cross was first used as a coat of arms for the Latin Kingdom of Jerusalem. It is also known as the "Crusader's Cross." The larger cross at the center represents Jesus Christ. The four lesser crosses represent the four gospels. Kabbalistically, the Jerusalem Cross represents the influence of the Four Worlds within each elemental quarter of the temple. In this, it also serves as a crucial interface between Kabbalah and the Golden Dawn's Enochian system of magic.

8. Torrens, *The Golden Dawn: The Inner Teachings*, 171.

9. Judith, *Wheels of Life*, 94–95.

10. Ibid., 97.

11. Droit, *Astonish Yourself!*, 11.

12. Tyson, *The Magician's Workbook*, 6.

13. Wilson, *Prometheus Rising*, 20–21.

Chapter 6: The Mind Born of Matter

1. Ridley, *Genome*, 18.

2. Ibid., 8.

3. Zimmer, *Evolution*, 76.

4. Ridley, *Genome*, 19.

5. Shlain, *The Alphabet Versus the Goddess*, 12.

6. Pinker, *The Language Instinct*, 18.

7. Charles, *The Book of Enoch*, 6.

8. Ibid., 6–7.

9. Shlain, *The Alphabet Versus the Goddess*, 2.

10. Ibid., 20.

11. Ibid., 18.

12. Crowley, *The Book of the Law*, 13.

13. Kraig, *Modern Magick*, 68.

14. Droit, *Astonish Yourself!*, 4.

15. Ibid., 1.

16. Junius, *The Practical Handbook of Plant Alchemy*, 130.

Chapter 7: The Liquid Intelligence

1. Hayakawa, *Language in Thought and Action*, 280.

2. Pinker, *The Language Instinct*, 18.

3. Hayakawa, *Language in Thought and Action*, 80.

4. Bentley, *The Seven Wonders of the Ancient World*, 20.

5. Bendick, *Archimedes and the Door of Science*, 32.

6. Lasky, *The Librarian Who Measured the Earth*, 2.

7. Bendick, *Archimedes and the Door of Science*, 25.

8. Lasky, *The Librarian Who Measured the Earth*, 21.

9. Bendick, *Archimedes and the Door of Science*, 25.

10. Ibid., 29.

11. Ibid., 31.

12. Cicero, *The Essential Golden Dawn*, 88.

13. Ozaniec, *The Elements of the Egyptian Wisdom*, 46.

14. Bendick, *Archimedes and the Door of Science*, 16.

15. Silverman, *Ancient Egypt*, 118.

16. Cicero, *The Essential Golden Dawn*, 5.

17. Hart, *Egyptian Myths*, 11.

18. Cicero, *The Essential Golden Dawn*, 5.

19. Ozaniec, *The Elements of the Egyptian Wisdom*, 59.

20. Regardie, *The Complete Golden Dawn System of Magic*, opening page.

21. Torrens, *The Golden Dawn: The Inner Teachings*, 162–165.

22. Nemeth, *The Energy of Money*, 34.

23. Crowley, *Book 4*, 61.

24. Crowley, *The Confessions of Aleister Crowley*, 623.

Chapter 8: Fuel for the Fire

1. Kramer, *History Begins at Sumer*, 76.
2. Campbell, *The Masks of God*, 95.
3. Hinnels, *Persian Mythology*, 9.
4. Campbell, *The Masks of God*, 191.
5. Kramer, *History Begins at Sumer*, 76.
6. Hinnels, *Persian Mythology*, 60.
7. Ibid., 61.
8. Campbell, *The Masks of God*, 203.
9. Shlain, *The Alphabet Versus the Goddess*, 52.
10. Campbell, *The Masks of God*, 83.
11. Cavendish, *Man, Myth, and Magic*, vol. 9, 2370.
12. Kieckhefer, *Magic in the Middle Ages*, 133.
13. Kenton, *Astrology*, 12.
14. Ibid.
15. Cavendish, *Man, Myth, and Magic*, vol. 9, 2370.
16. Wilson, "The Evolution of the Medieval Kabbalistic World-view," 122.
17. Ibid., 135.
18. Ibid., 139.
19. Ibid., 146.
20. Knight, *Magic and the Western Mind*, 91–92.
21. Regardie, *The Golden Dawn*, 128–129.
22. Gillespie, "Confidence."
23. Regardie, *The Golden Dawn*, 165.
24. Regardie, *The Golden Dawn*, 377–378.
25. Nemeth, *The Energy of Money*, 34.

Chapter 9: The Portal

1. Regardie, *The Golden Dawn*, 486.
2. Charles, *The Book of Enoch the Prophet* (Chapter 10), 7.
3. The name "Adeptus wand" comes from Frater Semper Pertendo. Thank you, Kurt.
4. Kraig, *Modern Magick*, 260.

Chapter 10: The Work of the Adept

1. Zalewski, *Talismans and Evocations of the Golden Dawn*, 145.

2. Ch'en, *Buddhism*, 192.

3. Ibid., 189.

4. Regardie, *The Golden Dawn*, 118.

5. Fortune, *Applied Magic and Aspects of Occultism*, 142.

6. Ibid., 143.

7. Mathers et al., *Astral Projection, Ritual Magic, and Alchemy*, 57.

8. Fortune, *Applied Magic and Aspects of Occultism*, 143.

9. Mathers et al., *Astral Projection, Ritual Magic, and Alchemy*, 60.

10. Cicero, *The Magician's Art*, 56–60.

11. Levi, *Transcendental Magic*, 29.

Appendix B: Suggested Forms of Exercise

1. King, *Pilates Workbook*.

2. Ibid.

3. Weil, "Burn Calories with Belly Dancing?"

Works Cited

Abbot, Edwin A. *Flatland: A Romance of Multiple Dimensions.* Jackson, TN: Perseus, 2001.

Baigent, Michael. *The Jesus Papers.* New York: HarperCollins, 2006.

Bendick, Joanne. *Archimedes and the Door of Science.* Bathgate, ND: Bethlehem Books, 1995.

Bentley, Diana. *The Seven Wonders of the Ancient World.* London: British Museum Press, 2001.

Buckland, Raymond. *Buckland's Complete Book of Witchcraft.* 2nd ed. St. Paul, MN: Llewellyn, 1986.

Campbell, Joseph. *The Masks of God: Occidental Mythology.* New York: Viking Penguin, 1964.

Case, Paul Foster. *The True and Invisible Rosicrucian Order.* York Beach, ME: Weiser, 1989.

Cavendish, Marshall, ed. *Man, Myth, and Magic.* Vol. 9. New York: Marshall Cavendish, 1983.

Charles, R. H., ed. *The Book of Enoch the Prophet.* York Beach, ME: Weiser, 2003.

Ch'en, Kenneth K. *Buddhism: The Light of Asia.* Woodbury, NY: Barron's Educational Series, 1968.

Cicero, Chic, and Sandra Tabatha Cicero. *The Essential Golden Dawn.* St. Paul, MN: Llewellyn, 2003.

Cicero, Chic, and Sandra Tabatha Cicero. "Magical Mottos of the Golden Dawn." *The Llewellyn Encyclopedia* (2002). http://www.llewellynencyclopedia.com/article/59 (accessed April 6, 2006).

Cicero, Chic, and Sandra Tabatha Cicero. *The Magician's Art: Ritual and Magical Use of Tools.* St. Paul, MN: Llewellyn, 2000.

Crowley, Aleister. *Book 4*. York Beach, ME: Weiser, 1980.

Crowley, Aleister. *The Book of the Law*. York Beach, ME: Redwall/Weiser, 2004.

Crowley, Aleister. *The Confessions of Aleister Crowley*. New York: Penguin, 1979.

Davies, Paul. *God and the New Physics*. New York: Touchstone, 1984.

De Angelis, Roberto. *Universal Tarot*. Torino: Lo Scarabeo, 2001. Distributed by Llewellyn Worldwide.

Droit, Roger-Pol. *Astonish Yourself!* Translated by Stephen Romer. New York: Penguin, 2003.

Easterbrook, Gregg. *The Progress Paradox*. New York: Random House, 2003.

Fortune, Dion. *Applied Magic and Aspects of Occultism*. Wellingborough, UK: Aquarian Press, 1987.

Fortune, Dion. *Moon Magic*. York Beach, ME: Weiser, 2003.

Gillespie, Eleanor Ringel. "Confidence: A Pretty Cool Con with Some Pretty Cool Acting." *Palm Beach Post*, 2006. http://www.palmbeachpost.com/movies/content/shared/movies/reviews/C/confidence.html (accessed May 7, 2006).

Gray, William G. *Qabalistic Concepts*. York Beach, ME: Weiser, 1984.

Hall, Manly P. *The Secret Teachings of All Ages: Reader's Edition*. New York: Penguin Group, 2003.

Hart, George. *Egyptian Myths*. Avon, UK: Avon, 1990.

Hayakawa, S. I. *Language in Thought and Action*. New York: Harcourt Brace Jovanovich, 1978.

Hinnels, John R. *Persian Mythology*. London: Chancellor Press, 1997.

Jackson, Shirley. "The Lottery." *The Lottery and Other Stories*. New York: Farrar Straus Giroux, 1992.

Judith, Anodea. *Wheels of Life: A User's Guide to the Chakra System*. 2nd ed. St. Paul, MN: Llewellyn, 2001.

Junius, Manfred M. *The Practical Handbook of Plant Alchemy*. Rochester, VT: Healing Arts Press, 1985.

Kaku, Michio. *Hyperspace*. New York: Anchor, 1994.

Kenton, Warren. *Astrology: The Celestial Mirror*. London: Thames & Hudson, 1989.

Kieckhefer, Richard. *Magic in the Middle Ages*. Cambridge: Cambridge University Press, 1993.

King, Michael. *Pilates Workbook*. Berkeley, CA: Ulysses, 2000.

Knight, Gareth. *Magic and the Western Mind*. St. Paul, MN: Llewellyn, 1991.

Kraig, Donald Michael. *Modern Magick: Eleven Lessons in the High Magickal Arts*. St. Paul, MN: Llewellyn, 1988.

Kramer, Samuel Noah. *History Begins at Sumer*. Philadelphia: University of Pennsylvania Press, 1981.

Lasky, Kathryn. *The Librarian Who Measured the Earth*. Boston: Little, Brown and Co., 1994.

Levi, Eliphas. *Transcendental Magic*. York Beach, ME: Weiser, 1992.

Lindholm, Lars B. *Pilgrims of the Night: Pathfinders of the Magical Way*. St. Paul, MN: Llewellyn, 1993.

Mathers, S. L. MacGregor, and Others. *Astral Projection, Ritual Magic, and Alchemy*. Edited by Francis King. Rochester, VT: Destiny Books, 1987.

Mathers, S. L. MacGregor, trans. *The Sacred Magic of Abra Melin the Mage*. Chicago: De Laurence Company, 1932.

Nemeth, Maria. *The Energy of Money*. New York: Ballentine, 1997.

Ozaniec, Naomi. *The Elements of the Egyptian Wisdom*. Longmead, UK: Element Books, 1994.

Pert, Candice B. *The Molecules of Emotion: Why You Feel the Way You Feel*. New York: Scribner, 1997.

Picard, Max. *The World of Silence*. Quoted in *The Viking Book of Aphorisms*. Edited by W. H. Auden and Louis Kronenberger. New York: Viking Press, 1981.

Pinker, Steven. *The Language Instinct*. New York: William Morrow and Company, 1994.

Regardie, Israel. *The Complete Golden Dawn System of Magic*. Scottsdale, AZ: New Falcon, 1990.

Regardie, Israel. *The Golden Dawn*. 6th ed. St. Paul, MN: Llewellyn, 1989.

Regardie, Israel. *The Middle Pillar*. 2nd ed. St. Paul, MN: Llewellyn, 1970.

Regardie, Israel. *The Middle Pillar*. 3rd ed. Edited and annotated by Chic Cicero and Sandra Tabatha Cicero. St. Paul, MN: Llewellyn, 1998.

Regardie, Israel. *The One Year Manual*. York Beach, ME: Weiser, 1981.

Regardie, Israel. *What You Should Know About the Golden Dawn*. Phoenix, AZ: New Falcon, 1993.

Ridley, Matt. *Genome: The Autobiography of a Species in 23 Chapters*. New York: HarperCollins, 1999.

Shlain, Leonard. *The Alphabet Versus the Goddess*. New York: Penguin, 1999.

Silverman, David P. *Ancient Egypt*. New York: Oxford University Press, 1997.

Torrens, R. G. *The Golden Dawn: The Inner Teachings*. New York: Samuel Weiser, 1980. First published in 1969.

Tyson, Donald. *The Magician's Workbook*. St. Paul, MN: Llewellyn, 2003.

Weil, Andrew. "Burn Calories with Belly Dancing?" In "Q & A." DrWeil.com (February 17, 2004, originally published July 18, 2003). http://www.drweil.com/u/QA/QA326426 (accessed April 6, 2006).

Wescott, William Wynn. "The Rosicrucians: Past and Present, at Home and Abroad." In "Archival Resources." The Hermetic Order of the Golden Dawn, 1997. http://www.hermeticgoldendawn.org/Documents/Archives/Rosicrucian.htm (accessed April 6, 2006).

Wilson, George. "The Evolution of the Medieval Kabbalistic World-view." *The Golden Dawn Journal, Book II*. Edited by Chic Cicero and Sandra Tabatha Cicero. St. Paul, MN: Llewellyn, 1994.

Wilson, Robert Anton. *Prometheus Rising*. Phoenix, AZ: New Falcon, 1990.

Zalewski, Pat. *Golden Dawn Enochian Magic*. 2nd ed. St. Paul, MN: Llewellyn, 1994.

Zalewski, Pat. *Talismans and Evocations of the Golden Dawn*. Loughborough, UK: Thoth Publications, 2002.

Zimmer, Carl. *Evolution: The Triumph of an Idea*. New York: HarperCollins, 2001.

Index

Free Catalog

Get the latest information on our body, mind, and spirit products! To receive a **free** copy of Llewellyn's consumer catalog, *New Worlds of Mind & Spirit,* simply call 1-877-NEW-WRLD or visit our website at www.llewellyn.com and click on *New Worlds.*

LLEWELLYN ORDERING INFORMATION

Order Online:
Visit our website at www.llewellyn.com, select your books, and order them on our secure server.

Order by Phone:
- Call toll-free within the U.S. at 1-877-NEW-WRLD (1-877-639-9753). Call toll-free within Canada at 1-866-NEW-WRLD (1-866-639-9753)
- We accept VISA, MasterCard, and American Express

Order by Mail:
Send the full price of your order (MN residents add 6.5% sales tax) in U.S. funds, plus postage & handling to:

Llewellyn Worldwide
2143 Wooddale Drive, Dept. 978-0-7387-0893-5
Woodbury, MN 55125-2989

Postage & Handling:

Standard (U.S., Mexico, & Canada). If your order is:
$24.99 and under, add $3.00
$25.00 and over, FREE STANDARD SHIPPING

AK, HI, PR: $15.00 for one book plus $1.00 for each additional book.

International Orders (airmail only):
$16.00 for one book plus $3.00 for each additional book

Orders are processed within 2 business days.
Please allow for normal shipping time. Postage and handling rates subject to change.

The Essential Golden Dawn
An Introduction to High Magic

CHIC CICERO AND
SANDRA TABATHA CICERO

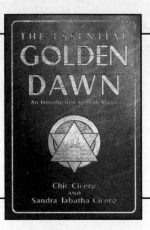

Is the Golden Dawn system for you? Today the Golden Dawn is one of the most sought-after and respected systems of magic in the world. Over a century old, it's considered the capstone of the Western Esoteric Tradition. Yet many of the available books on the subject are too complex or overwhelming for readers just beginning to explore alternative spiritual paths.

The Essential Golden Dawn is for those who simply want to find out what the Golden Dawn is and what it has to offer. It answers questions such as: What is Hermeticism? How does magic work? Who started the Golden Dawn? What are its philosophies and principles? It helps readers determine whether this system is for them, and then it guides them into further exploration as well as basic ritual work.

0-7387-0310-9
360 pp., 6 x 9 $16.95